Residential Housing

by

Clois E. Kicklighter
Dean, School of Technology and
Professor of Construction Technology
Indiana State University
Terre Haute, Indiana

Joan C. Kicklighter, C.H.E.
Author of Home Economics Instructional Materials
Terre Haute, Indiana

South Holland, Illinois
THE GOODHEART-WILLCOX COMPANY, INC.
Publishers

Copyright 1986

by

THE GOODHEART-WILLCOX COMPANY, INC.

Library of Congress Catalog Card Number 86-4686
International Standard Book Number 0-87006-590-4

23456789-86-0987

Library of Congress Cataloging in Publication Data

Kicklighter, Clois E.
  Residential housing.

  Includes index.
    1. Architecture, Domestic—Planning. 2. Room
  layout (Dwellings) I. Kicklighter, Joan C. II. Title.
  NA7115.K463 1986   728   028 86-4686
  ISBN 0-87006-590-4

Introduction

Residential Housing gives you practical information about planning, building, and decorating a home. It explains how and why the intended functions of a home should serve as bases for the home's construction and decoration decisions. Information in the text is applied to individual rooms, the structure as a whole, and the overall landscape.

The text introduces you to today's various housing options. It explains how different options can be used to meet the tastes and lifestyle needs of individuals and families.

Residential Housing helps you choose the appropriate materials for the structure, its furnishings, and its decoration. Wood, masonry, concrete, metals, glass, ceramics, plastics, finishes, and textiles are discussed. The text helps you evaluate a material in terms of appropriateness, strength, versatility, maintenance requirements, and cost. With the help of charts and illustrations, you will learn to identify the style and judge the quality of home furnishings.

Residential Housing shows you how housing needs affect electrical, plumbing, and climate control systems. It shows you how certain structural features, appliances, and alternative energy sources can be used to improve the energy efficiency of a home.

The text introduces you to techniques for presenting your housing ideas. Renderings, presentation boards, models, and other presentation techniques are described. Information is also provided on exterior design, landscaping, remodeling, lighting, and careers.

Contents

1-1 Homes may be categorized according to location such as urban, suburban, or rural; seashore, mountain, or desert.

1 Fundamentals of Housing

After studying this chapter, you will be able to:
- Describe physical factors outside the house which affect housing choices.
- Explain the relationship between lifestyle and housing choices.
- Describe the seven main types of housing.
- Compare the strengths and weaknessess of the different types of housing.

The term *housing* refers to more than just a dwelling. It also includes all that is within the dwelling and all that surrounds the dwelling. Housing is the creation of a special environment in which people live and grow. Housing affects the way people feel and act, just as values and personality affect people's housing choices. People and housing are inseparable, and for that reason the term "lifespace" is sometimes used to describe housing. Lifespace (housing) provides shelter, security, privacy, prestige, and a means of self-expression. Housing is an important part of people's lives.

FACTORS AFFECTING HOUSING CHOICES

Housing choices are affected by several factors such as location, climate, availability, cost, taste, and lifestyle. Each of these factors must be considered if a functional solution to the housing challenge is to be found. A brief examination of these factors will show the effect they exert on housing choices.

Location

Location refers to the specific placement of a home. On a large scale, location choices range from urban to suburban to rural. Location choices also may be categorized as seashore, mountain, desert, and so on. Homes in various locations are shown in 1-1.

A home that takes advantage of its surroundings reflects the character of the area. For example, a home in Florida should be different in its design and materials from a home in Minnesota, 1-2. A home located in the city should show an awareness of the characteristics resulting from its location. Since most city lots are small, most city homes are designed as compact, multilevel structures. A home

designed for a mountain view should be oriented to take maximum advantage of its location.

Location, on a large scale, is thus an important consideration in the design and construction of a home. The materials used to build the structure as well as the fur-

1-2 Homes should fit their surroundings. The top home has a light-colored exterior that is well-suited to its Florida location. The bottom home looks sturdy and warm enough for its Minnesota location.

nishings used to decorate the interior can be affected by the location.

Location, on a smaller scale, also affects housing choices. A home is part of a neighborhood and should be viewed in the community setting. Each occupant has needs which must be met by the larger community. Facilities for education, transportation, worship, health care, shopping, and recreation are factors to be considered when making housing choices.

Selecting the right neighborhood may be a bigger task than determining the basic requirements of the house or apartment. A tour of the area and visits with neighbors may reveal important characteristics about the community.

While looking for features that add to or detract from the quality of life in the area, ask the following questions: Has the community's growth followed a logical plan, or has its growth been uncontrolled? Is the home under consideration in the same price range as surrounding homes? Are the neighbors in about the same socioeconomic group as the prospective resident? Does the community have a high rate of turnover due to the resale of homes? Have property values increased as they have in similar neighborhoods elsewhere? Do the residents of the community take pride in the upkeep of their homes, or do the homes look run-down? Does the community have modern schools, several places of worship, quality shopping areas, and a variety of recreational facilities? Are there adequate services for health care, police and fire protection, utilities, and garbage collection? Is the home near the prospective resident's place of work? Is public transportation available?

These and other factors are important considerations in the selection of a neighborhood. When making housing choices, remember that a home cannot be separated from its location in a neighborhood.

Climate

Climate has always been a major consideration in housing choices. Climates vary from warm to cool and from dry to humid. Some areas receive more sunshine than others. Some climates are mild all year, while others have four distinct seasons.

The choice of a climate in which to live automatically affects the choice of housing design. A house built in northern Michigan should be designed for comfort during cold winters with lots of snow, 1-3. It needs ample insulation and a tight shell to keep cold air out. The roof slope is important so that snow will not build up to damage the structure. The amount of glass in a cold-climate home is also a concern since heat loss is greater through glass than through walls. The interior of such a structure should promote a feeling of warmth and friendliness to help its occupants endure the long winters.

Homes designed for desert climates would be expected to have thick masonry walls. Such walls would shield the occupants from the high daytime temperatures and would release heat during the cool nights, 1-4. Homes in warm

1-3 This Michigan home was built for cold winters with lots of snow. The walls have several inches of insulation, and the windows have insulated glass.

climates also should have wide overhanging roofs to shade the walls and thus reduce heat buildup.

Climates that receive excessive amounts of rain, have high winds, or have an abundance of insects also affect the way a functional structure is designed. Adverse conditions must be considered when solving the housing problem.

Availability

Availability of desirable housing in a given area is often limited. Because of our growing, shifting population, housing is sometimes in short supply. Many apartments, condominiums, and houses have been built in recent years to accommodate the rising demand for housing, but shifts in population do not always coincide with construction patterns. Therefore, availability is often the determining factor in acquiring housing.

RED CEDAR SHINGLE AND HANDSPLIT SHAKE BUREAU

1-4 Thick masonry walls and a wide overhanging roof make this home suitable for the hot, arid climate of the Southwest.

1-5 Mobility is the hallmark of this residence. The owners' values and individuality are reflected in their choice of a home.

Some people do not have to worry much about the availability of housing. They take their homes with them. Each year more people buy trailers, motor homes, mobile homes, and houseboats. These dwellings offer personalized comfort for their occupants while providing the ultimate in mobility, 1-5.

Cost

Cost is a crucial factor in housing choices for almost everyone. Cost becomes increasingly important as construction expenses continue to rise. Not only is the initial cost of housing critical, but repairs, taxes, and insurance costs must also be considered. The total cost severely reduces the variety of choices open to the average person seeking housing.

Taste

Taste is the sense of what is fitting, harmonious, or beautiful. In other words, "good" taste is that which seems agreeable or pleasing. Taste reveals much about the personality of an individual. A person's taste is probably acquired through the sum of experiences and cultural influences.

Some people prefer to be surrounded with a myriad of colors or objects. Others choose just the opposite. Taste preferences vary not only from person to person but also from time to time throughout a person's life. Taste changes as a person matures, meets new friends, and has new experiences. Group taste also affects individual taste. The "in" fashions in clothing, home furnishings, color, and art set trends which influence individuals' taste preferences.

Another aspect of good taste in design is function. A reading area should be designed not only for beauty. In addition, the chair should be comfortable and adequate light should be provided. A tasteful kitchen design is not only pleasant. It is also efficient, with the frequently used dishes and appliances within easy reach.

Personal taste must be considered when designing a lifespace if that lifespace is to be functional, comfortable, and pleasing for its occupants. All of us have certain objects, colors, and shapes that make us feel that we are in familiar surroundings — in our own territory. In such a setting, we can relax and feel good. Thus, design that follows personal taste is likely to be pleasing, 1-6.

Lifestyle

A household's lifestyle is related to the values, social status, and activities of the household members. Their lifestyle influences their housing choices and dictates how their home is used. For some people, a home is merely a place to sleep and get ready for the next day. For others, it is a bustling center of activity. Some use their home as a peaceful retreat, while others use it mainly for social gatherings. However the home is used, it should be designed to complement the lifestyle of those who live in it.

A truly functional lifespace is a logical extension of a household's lifestyle. This is true of both the overall design of the structure and the use of the inside space. Space inside a home may be described as individual space, group space, and support space. All homes need all three types of space, but the amount needed of each type varies according to lifestyle.

NIELSEN

1-6 The pleasing design of this home reflects the personal taste of its occupants.

9

Individual space is needed for sleeping, dressing, studying, and relaxing in privacy, 1-7. The amount needed varies depending on how many household members there are and how highly they value privacy.

Group space is needed for family recreation, conversation, dining, and entertaining, 1-8. The amount needed varies with the household's lifestyle and social values.

The amount of support space needed in a home varies widely from household to household. Preparing food and doing laundry are two common support activities, 1-9. Many other types of work also may be done in the home, thus requiring more support space.

Space for individual, group, and support activities does not necessarily have to be divided into separate rooms.

It's true that some activities are restricted to specific areas, but others may be performed in several locations throughout the home. And in some cases, the spaces for different activities may overlap. The main concern is to provide space for the activities of each member as well as of the group. A home should be designed to achieve this goal.

TYPES OF HOUSING AVAILABLE

Several types of housing are available. These include: tract houses, custom houses, manufactured houses, mobile homes, and multifamily dwellings such as cooperatives, condominiums, and rental apartments.

1-7 Each individual in a household needs private space in which to work, think, relax, and sleep.

1-8 Group space is necessary for activities involving the interaction of two or more persons.

Tract Houses

A tract house is built by a developer who subdivides a large piece of land into lots. The developer then builds several houses using just a few basic plans. The number of different designs is limited to reduce the cost of each house and speed the work. The developer often provides financing or assistance in obtaining financing. An example of each house design is generally completed and displayed to entice prospective buyers.

Tract houses have several advantages. The buyer can see what he or she is buying, and a firm price can generally be negotiated even before construction begins. The fact that the subdivision has been planned as a whole may be another advantage—if it has been planned well. A tract house usually costs less than a custom house, and it usually increases in value as the development grows. Therefore, those who buy early may realize a handsome profit on their investment.

Disadvantages are also associated with tract houses. They may be monotonous and have little individuality. They often look bare and unfinished for a few years until trees and shrubs grow. The lots are generally of minimum size so the developer can sell as many houses as possible. Also, a buyer takes the risk of not knowing how successful the development will eventually be.

1-9 The kitchen is a good example of support space in the home.

The advantages and disadvantages of tract houses must be weighed on an individual basis. Some tract houses are well-designed and built with quality materials. Others are poorly designed and poorly constructed. The buyer must evaluate the variables to determine if a tract house is the answer to his or her housing needs.

Custom Houses

A custom house is one designed and built to meet the needs of a specific household. It may be designed by an architect, a home designer, or the prospective homeowner. A special designer or builder is not what makes a house a custom house. Rather, the fact that it is designed and built to meet the needs of a specific household distinguishes it as a custom house. It is different from all other houses, 1-10.

A custom house costs more per square foot than other types of housing, but it is the most functional for the people for whom it is designed. Not only is the structure designed for specific individuals, but it is also tailored to

AMERICAN PLYWOOD ASSN.

1-10 An architect designed this custom house. It is compatible with the site and climate conditions as well as the lifestyle of the occupants.

a certain building site. This type of house is the dream of most people.

Those who want a custom house, but cannot afford to hire an architect, may purchase a stock plan from a magazine or other source and have it modified to fit their needs. This is usually done by the builder in consultation with the prospective homeowner. A house built from a stock plan will not be truly unique, but it should be functional if care is taken in choosing a good design. Thousands of plans are available which have been well-designed by professionals, and many include provisions for modification. An example is shown in 1-11.

Many people desire the rewarding experience of designing and building their own homes. However, some people find that it requires skills that they do not have. Design is probably the most important step in home building. Even good quality construction, beautiful decoration, and creative use of materials will not be satisfactory if the basic design is poor. A truly functional living space must complement the lifestyle of those who occupy it. A household

The Bentley

Model: B90-2
From 912 sq. ft. to 1062 sq. ft.

Sliding glass doors flood room with light—lead directly to outdoor living area. Compact "L" shaped kitchen combines efficient work area with family dining room. Gracious living room has unbroken walls for easy furniture arrangement. Privacy of a quiet bedroom wing away from living-work area. Convenient closet and storage rooms for easy access.

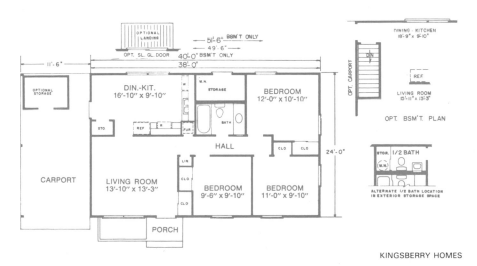

KINGSBERRY HOMES

1-11 A stock plan can be modified to meet the needs of the prospective homeowner.

1-12 This striking custom house is well-suited to its unique site as well as the lifestyle of its occupants.

should not have to alter their activities to fit their home. Rather, their home should be designed to accommodate their activities. A dwelling should also be designed to make the most of the site where it is located. The site is an integral part of the whole and will add to or detract from the appearance of the finished structure, 1-12. Those who are considering designing and building their own homes should look objectively at their skills. They should make honest decisions about what they can and cannot do and then get help if and when they need it.

Advantages of designing one's own home include the great experience that is gained from completing such an endeavor, the savings in labor charges, and the satisfaction of having everything built to personal specifications. As with any other approach, there are some disadvantages. Designing and building a home is complicated and requires a lot of patience and hard work. It is sometimes difficult to get a loan to cover the expenses of an owner-built house. Codes in some areas require a licensed contractor to perform certain tasks. This approach to housing will be ideal for some but not for others.

1-13 Standard modular components were used to assemble this dome house.

VINNELL STEEL CO.

1-14 These large modules are ready for delivery to the site. Interior walls will be constructed once the basic structure is fastened together on the foundation.

Manufactured Houses

Manufactured houses are available in several forms and degrees of completion. Modular components, prefabs, kit houses, and precuts are marketed by scores of companies throughout the country.

Most manufactured houses consist of modular components or building parts which have been preassembled. Parts such as roof panels, floor panels, wall sections, kitchens, and baths are all produced as modules. A completed house may then be built from these modules, 1-13.

Some houses are virtually complete when they leave the plant as large, finished modules ranging in size from 12 ft. by 20 ft. to 12 ft. by 40 ft. and larger. See 1-14. Others are delivered as large panels ready for erection on the site. This option is generally referred to as *prefab* housing. *Kit houses* are also available. They are similar to prefab houses except that only factory models are available as kits, whereas many companies will make prefab houses of any design. *Precuts* are packaged materials already cut to size for a customer's plan, 1-15.

BOYNE FALLS LOG HOMES

1-15 The logs for this custom house were precut according to the customer's own plans. They were made from 5 1/2 in. Northern White Cedar logs.

Manufactured housing has come a long way in recent years. In the past, manufactured houses were thought to be cheap, poorly constructed, and void of design. Today, this simply is not true. Many companies are producing houses that are well-designed, well-constructed, and beautiful. In most instances, it is impossible to recognize a factory-built structure once it is in place on the site, 1-16.

Advantages of choosing manufactured houses include lower costs and reduced time in building. Quality is frequently better, and various components can be selected much as you would choose options for a new car. However, there are some disadvantages. The selection is limited, and special equipment is necessary in some cases to install large modules. Shipping large modules can be expensive if the house is to be located far from the factory. The field of manufactured housing is growing and provides a viable solution to housing needs of many people. This type of housing is likely to continue growing in the future.

Mobile Homes

A mobile home is designed to be movable. It is constructed on a frame that has wheels attached for towing. One unit is sometimes joined to another to form a larger home. A mobile home may be placed on a temporary or permanent foundation. See 1-17.

Mobile homes are fully equipped with major appliances, furniture, carpeting, and even draperies included in the purchase price. Modern mobile homes are much larger, more convenient, and more adaptable than the "house trailer" of twenty or thirty years ago.

Mobile homes may be moved by professionals who know the problems involved and have the necessary equipment, but moving is expensive. States have different laws relating to mobile homes, and it is important to know these laws before attempting a move.

The main advantage of a mobile home is economy. The purchase price is comparatively low, and very little upkeep is required. Monthly license fees are generally much lower than property taxes on a typical house. Another advantage is that some mobile home parks offer exceptional recreational facilities and services. A mobile home has the additional advantage of being movable. A permanent site is not required.

There are some disadvantages, however, to mobile homes. They depreciate rapidly and may lose half their resale value in five years. Mobile homes are sometimes considered to be "second class" housing. Many cities limit their location to a specific area. Further, they are not really very mobile once they reach their initial location. The cost of moving a mobile home, the need for professional movers, and highway restrictions all reduce the mobility.

SCHOLZ HOMES, INC.

1-16 *Who would ever guess that this house is a manufactured house? It has the beautiful, detailed look of a custom house.*

1-17 Mobile homes make efficient use of space and are generally more economical than many other types of housing.

1-18 Cooperatives are dwellings whose management is run as a corporation.

The would-be purchaser should be aware of the moving, zoning, and taxing regulations as well as the facts about financing before choosing this type of housing.

Cooperatives

The term cooperative refers to a type of ownership, not a type of building. See 1-18. Cooperative ownership is most common in multifamily dwellings, and each family's living space is usually called an apartment.

Cooperative ownership combines the advantages of home ownership with the convenience of apartment living. Under the cooperative form of ownership, an apartment building is managed and run as a corporation. The buyer purchases stock in the corporation that runs the building and, thereby, receives an apartment. The value of the apartment determines the amount of stock purchased. The buyer receives a lease which grants him or her exclusive right to possession of the apartment.

1-19 Condominiums look no different than cooperatives or rental apartments, but the owner may sell his or her unit without the consent of other owners.

Since the buyer owns the apartment, he or she does not pay rent. The buyer does, however, pay a monthly fee which is used to pay the property taxes and maintenance costs of the building. The corporation takes care of maintenance and repairs with the money collected from the stockholders.

Owners have a voice in how the "co-op" is run which is an advantage over a rental apartment. Owners also have a say in who their neighbors are to be. Residents generally vote on whether or not a family should be allowed to purchase an apartment in the building.

The major disadvantage of a co-op is that each member must abide by the wishes of the total group. If the group makes a bad decision, then all suffer.

Condominiums

Unlike the owner of a cooperative, who buys stock, the owner of a condominium buys the apartment and a share of the common ground. The owner receives a deed to the apartment and pays taxes on it just as though it were a separate house. It is his or her apartment, 1-19. Owners of units in a condominium building have joint interest in all the shared property and facilities. These may include hallways, laundry areas, parking lots, sidewalks, lawns, tennis courts, and swimming pools. Common property is maintained with money collected from monthly assessments (as it is under cooperative ownership).

An owner of a condominium unit may sell the unit without consent or approval of other owners. In matters relating to common property, each owner has a vote in proportion to the original value of the unit he or she owns.

A condominium complex may consist of a single building or a group of buildings and surrounding property. It may even include a mixture of apartments, townhouses, and duplexes. The special feature of a condominium is that each unit is owned individually with a joint interest in common property.

Rentals

Any type of dwelling may be rented, but apartments are by far the most common rentals, 1-20. Apartments are especially popular among the young, poor, newly married, and elderly. This probably stems from the fact that rental apartments usually require less expense and effort in upkeep than other types of housing.

In many cases, several apartment buildings are planned and built at the same time in a group. This makes good use of the land and helps provide greater security.

AMERICAN PLYWOOD ASSN.

1-20 Rental apartments are a viable choice for many Americans. They are available in many locations and in a wide range of prices.

Rental apartments have definite advantages for large segments of the population. They offer a variety of lifestyles, and they are readily available. In recent years, many new apartments have been built in attractive settings with conveniences to meet almost any need. Choices are unlimited in terms of style, size, price range, and facilities. Apartments are often conveniently located near public transportation, shopping centers, and recreation areas. Another advantage is that they require little time or effort from the renter for upkeep and maintenance.

Disadvantages relate mostly to loss of control over the living space. Renters have little or no voice in how the apartment building is managed or maintained — although this has improved in recent years. Neighbors may move in and out so often that no true neighborhood spirit is developed. Also, money spent on rent is not applied toward ownership. After paying rent for years, renters have no property to show for their payments. In spite of the disadvantages, the rental apartment is the best answer to the housing needs of many people.

REVIEW QUESTIONS

1. What are the six main factors to consider when choosing a house?
2. What features in a community might keep a person from buying homes that they like?
3. How might a home in North Dakota be different from a home in Arizona?
4. What activities take place in each of the three types of space in the home?
5. How does a tract house differ from a custom house?
6. What factors need to be considered in designing a custom-built house?
7. What are some advantages and disadvantages of a manufactured house?
8. What problems may be involved in moving a mobile home?
9. How does a cooperative differ from a condominium?
10. What features might persuade a person to rent rather than buy a house?

WESTERN WOOD PRODUCTS ASSN.

A housing choice should reflect the tastes and lifestyles of its owners.

2 Evaluating Floor Plans

After studying this chapter, you will be able to:
- Map a circulation pattern and evaluate its quality.
- Identify the specific activities and areas involved in family circulation, work circulation, service circulation, and guest circulation.
- Determine the utility of a floor plan in relationship to a family's needs.
- Identify the seven types of drawings included in a set of house plans and explain their purposes.
- Interpret the symbols on a plot plan, foundation/basement plan, floor plan, exterior elevation, electrical plan, and construction detail drawing.

The starting point of evaluating a floor plan is to make a list of your needs and wants related to housing. This list can help you decide which type of housing is most desirable for a specific situation. It can help you determine how much space is needed and how the space should be divided for most effective use.

The first items on your list should meet absolute needs. These would include bedrooms, baths, storage closets, and room for all necessary furniture and appliances. After listing all these needs, begin listing other features that are wanted in the home. Housing wants might include a fireplace, a patio, or room for a ping pong table. Try to be farsighted when making this list so that changing needs can be met in the future.

Once you know what is needed and wanted in a home, begin examining floor plans. In each floor plan, identify the three main areas of the home: living, sleeping, and service. The living area includes the living room, dining room, and family or recreation room. It also includes special rooms such as a study, den, library, music room, or hobby room as well as entryways, patios, and porches. The sleeping area includes the bedrooms, bathrooms, and dressing rooms. Other rooms such as the kitchen, clothes care center, utility room, basement, and garage comprise the service area. (Chapters 3, 4, and 5 provide in-depth analyses of these areas.)

As you study a floor plan, you may want to shade each of the three areas with a different colored pencil. This may help you visualize the location and contents of each area more easily. In most good plans, the rooms in each area are grouped to form a compact unit since they share similar functions. Compare the plans in 2-1 and 2-2 to see how the grouping of areas is different.

CIRCULATION

If you have identified the three areas of the home on the floor plan and you like how they are grouped, the next step is to map the circulation. *Circulation* is the route that people follow as they move from one place to another in the home. Circulation is not limited to hall space; it may pass through a room. Generally 3 to 4 feet of space should be allowed for circulation paths. When reviewing the circulation of a floor plan, it is important to check not only what routes are followed but also how often they are followed. *Circulation frequency* refers to the number of times a route is repeated in any given period of time. Generally, routes with high circulation frequency are short and direct in a good floor plan. The habits, needs, and special considerations also affect the quality of circulation. Therefore, a given plan may be good for one household but not for another.

Types of Circulation

The four basic types of circulation patterns are family, work, service, and guest. Each type of circulation should be mapped and identified as you evaluate the floor plan. See 2-3. Use different colored pencils for the different patterns. This procedure should help you evaluate the efficiency of the floor plan.

Family circulation. Family circulation is the most complex and difficult pattern to identify. Members of each household have different living habits which produce different circulation patterns. Try to map movements on a room-to-room and activity-to-activity basis. A good family circulation pattern usually follows these principles:

A bath is located close to the bedrooms.

The indoor living area is readily accessible to the outdoor living area such as a patio or deck.

Related rooms are close together.

High frequency circulation routes are short and simple.

Excessive hall space is avoided.

Rooms are not cut in half by circulation routes.

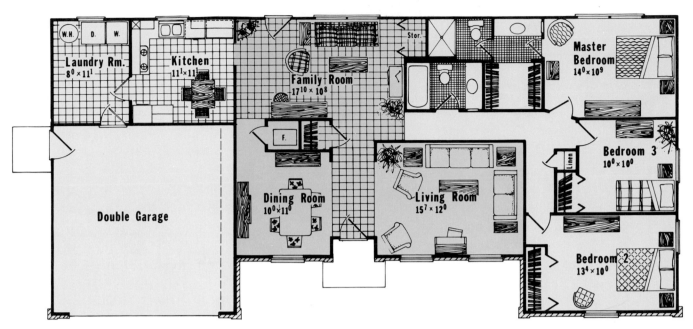

2-1 *In this plan, the rooms in each area—living, sleeping, and service—are grouped together. This is usually a sign of a convenient, well-designed floor plan.*

2-2 *The sleeping and service areas are divided in this floor plan. Although some efficiency is lost as a result, many households would find the plan satisfactory.*

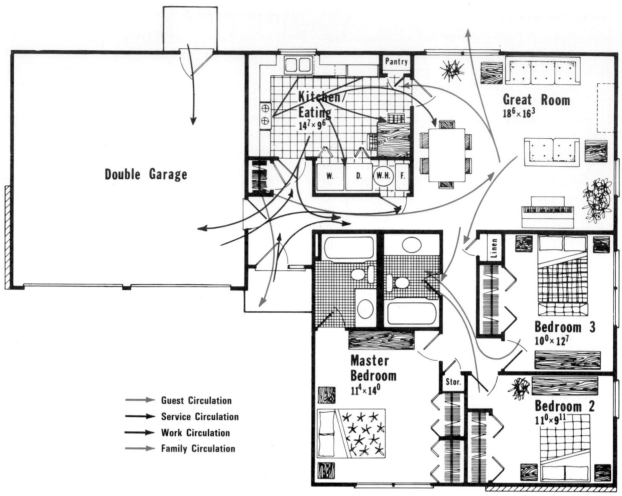

2-3 To evaluate the circulation aspect of a floor plan, draw the family, work, service, and guest circulation patterns on the plan.

A floor plan that follows these principles is likely to be convenient for household members.

Work circulation. The kitchen is generally the hub of the work circulation pattern. Circulation should move easily from the sink to the refrigerator to the cooking units and to the eating areas. The route between the sink, refrigerator, and range is called the *work triangle* and should not exceed 22 feet in total length. Small work triangles save steps, allowing kitchen tasks to be done quickly and easily.

The kitchen should be located adjacent to the dining area. No cross traffic should be allowed to interfere with the circulation moving back and forth between the cooking and eating areas. This rule is intended to help prevent spills and broken dishes. The kitchen also should be located near the service entrance for convenience in many tasks. Good accessibility to other parts of the home such as bedrooms and baths is also desirable. Consider the number of trips that must be made from the kitchen to other rooms while cooking and cleaning.

Another aspect of a good work circulation pattern is that it provides easy access to the basement, garage, and storage areas throughout the home. The clothes care center also needs a convenient location since many trips are made to

this work area. Any area of the home in which work is performed should be easily accessible to those who use it.

Service circulation. Service circulation relates to the movement of people in and out of the home as they make service calls, deliver goods, read meters, take garbage out, and so on. It makes no difference whether or not these tasks are done by household members. The result is the same as it relates to the floor plan. In a good floor plan, no one should have to cross the kitchen to get to the basement or cross the dining room with groceries.

Good service circulation may be provided by locating a service entrance near the kitchen and basement stairs. A good floor plan provides easy access to and from the kitchen, basement, garage, and other service areas.

Guest circulation. This circulation pattern is the easiest to define. It simply involves movement from the entry to the coat closet and to the living room with access to powder room facilities. Guests should be able to move from the entry to the living area without passing through other rooms. A small house or apartment may not have a separate foyer. In this case, guests may enter directly into the living room. They still should have access to a coat closet and powder room without having to pass through the main part of the living room.

Circulation Frequency

After the various circulation patterns have been identified and analyzed, they should be evaluated in terms of circulation frequency. For example, how often does a family member travel from the recreation room to the kitchen as compared to a guest coming to visit? If the answer is about 20 family trips for every guest's visit, logic would indicate that the route from the recreation room to the kitchen should receive a higher priority. It should be shorter and more direct than the guest's circulation route. This example shows that even though a floor plan may have a good circulation pattern, it may not meet the needs of a household because of their particular circulation frequency patterns.

Realistically, all floor plans are compromises. One plan may have a perfect service circulation pattern, while another has excellent family circulation. Still others may be average on all counts. The main consideration is if the floor plan and circulation patterns are compatible with the lifestyle of the household.

Room Relationships

The satisfaction household members receive from their living space is determined largely by the floor plan of their home. Other factors influencing satisfaction are the sizes and shapes of the rooms and the relationship of each room to the others.

The size of a room is not always an accurate indication of its usable space, 2-4. Poorly located doors, windows, and closets or too many architectural features interrupting wall space can greatly reduce usable space. See 2-5. When evaluating floor plans, study the potential for furniture arrangement and circulation within each room.

The relationship of one room to another dictates how functional the space will be. For example, the dining area should be located adjacent to the living room for convenience in entertaining. The dining area also should be located next to the kitchen for ease in serving food. If the plan has more than one dining area, then the one that will be used most often should receive priority. It should be closest to the kitchen. If food is often prepared or served

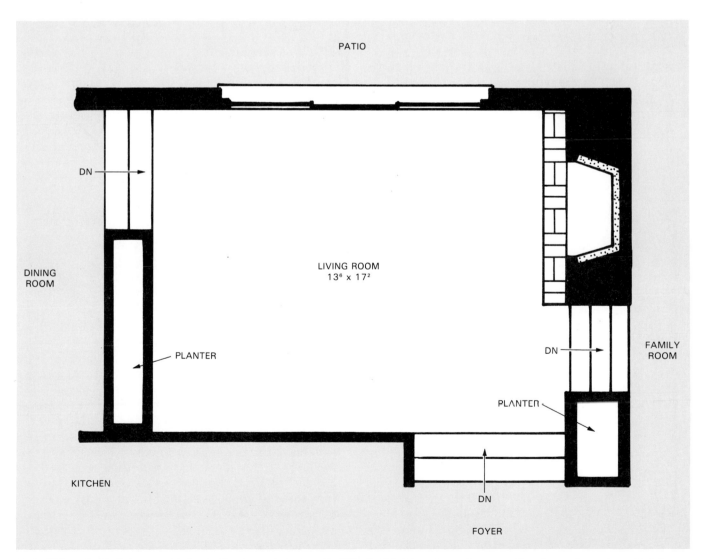

2-4 Although this living room is large, furniture placement is difficult. The room has only one wall surface of any size which is not interrupted by an architectural feature. The design severely limits space utilization.

on a patio or porch, then that area should also be located near the kitchen.

The relationship between bedrooms and bathrooms deserves attention. These rooms should be close together for convenience. Two other major concerns are privacy and accessibility. Privacy should be considered in terms of both sight and sound. For good accessibility, at least one bathroom should be located where people can reach it without having to go through another room.

The floor plan in 2-6 shows logical and functional room relationships. The dining room is adjacent to both the living room and the kitchen. Another, smaller eating area is located in the kitchen itself. For added convenience, the kitchen has an access to the garage. The living room is large enough to accommodate several people. The walkway along one side promotes good circulation and adds space to the room. A coat closet and powder room are easily accessible to guests. All the bedrooms are near the bath and linen closet. The bath is centrally located which is important since the plan includes only one bath. A second bath (for the master bedroom) could replace the current exterior storage.

2-5. This bedroom has a desirable location, shape, and size, but it presents a problem for furniture placement. The two exterior walls are dominated by the large windows, while the wall next to the bath is used for the closet. Only one wall (the one most visible from the doorway) remains for taller pieces of furniture.

READING HOUSE PLANS

A typical set of "house plans" or construction drawings generally includes the following specific drawings:

Plot plan
Foundation/basement plan
Floor plan
Exterior elevations
Electrical plan
Construction details
Pictorial presentations

These drawings, together with a set of specifications, form the basis for a legal contract between the owner and

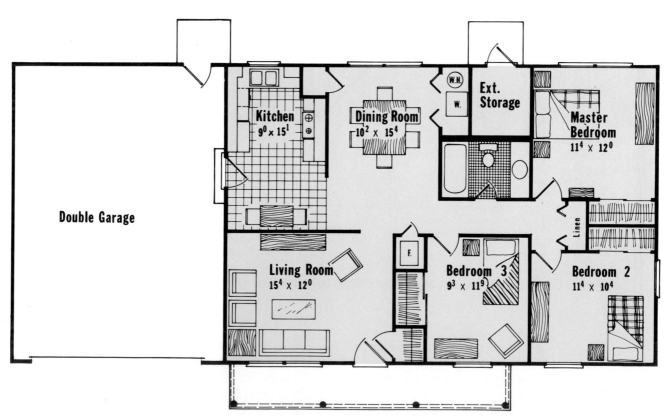

2-6 This 28 by 40 ft., three-bedroom home packs a lot of convenience into the 1120 square feet of living space.

builder. The specifications describe the quality of materials and construction techniques to be used. The specifications take precedence over the drawings in the event of a disagreement.

Description of Drawings

The following descriptions of the drawings generally found in a set of construction plans are intended to communicate the role that each drawing plays in the total plan.

The *plot plan,* 2-7, shows the location of the structure (house, apartment, mobile home, etc.) on the site. Its scale is generally 1 in. equals 20 or 30 ft. A plot plan shows the following items:

Location, outline, and size of buildings on the site.
Streets, driveways, sidewalks, and patios.
Location of utilities.
Easements for utilities and drainage (if any).
Fences and retaining walls.
Length and bearing of each property line.
Contour of the land.
Trees, shrubs, streams, and gardens.
Elevation of property corners.
Meridian arrow (north symbol).
Well and septic tank and field (if any).
Lot number or address of the site.
Scale of the drawing.

The plot plan is drawn using information provided by a surveyor and recorded on a site plan. The plot plan shows both the property and the proposed construction. Lending agencies, building inspectors, and excavators all need this drawing.

The *foundation/basement plan,* 2-8, shows the location and size of footings, piers, columns, foundation walls, and supporting beams of the structure. A foundation and/or basement plan ordinarily includes the following items:

Footings for foundation walls, piers, and columns.
Foundation walls.
Piers and columns.
Dwarf walls (low walls).
Partition walls, doors, and bath fixtures.
Furnace, water storage tank, water softener, hot
  water heater, etc.
Openings in foundation walls such as windows, doors,
  and vents.
Beams and pilasters.
Direction, size, and spacing of floor joists.
Drains and sump (in basement).
Details of foundation and footing construction.
Grade elevation.
Complete dimensions and notes.
Scale of the drawing.

The foundation plan is prepared mainly for the excavator, masons, and cement workers who build the foundation. Generally, a scale of 1/4 in. equals 1 ft. is used.

The *floor plan,* 2-9, is the heart of a set of construction drawings and is used by all tradespeople. The floor plan is actually a section drawing taken about four feet above the floor. A floor plan is drawn for each floor level

of the structure. A scale of 1/4 in. equals 1 in. is used for the drawings. It generally includes the following items:

Exterior and interior walls.
Size and location of windows and doors.
Built-in cabinets and appliances.
Permanent fixtures.
Stairs and fireplaces.
Porches, patios, and decks.
Room names and approximate sizes.
Material symbols.
Location and size dimensions.
Scale of the drawing.

Exterior elevations, 2-10, show the outside of the building. Each side of the building requires one elevation. The purposes of an elevation are to show the finished appearance of a given side of the building and to show height dimensions. The scale for these drawings is usually 1/4 in. equals 1 ft. Most elevations include the following items:

Identification of the specific side of the building which
  it represents.
Grade lines (level of the soil against the building).
Depth of foundation (in hidden lines).
Finished floor and ceiling levels.
Location of exterior wall corners.
Windows and doors.
Roof features and materials.
Roof pitch.
Chimneys.
Deck railings and outside steps.
Patios, decks, and porches.
Exterior materials.
Vertical dimensions of features.
Scale of the drawing.

The *electrical plan,* 2-11, is similar to the floor plan in appearance, but its purpose is to show the locations and types of electrical equipment to be used. The plan is generally in a scale of 1/4 in. equals 1 ft. Most electrical plans include the following items:

Meter and distribution panel.
Electrical outlets.
Light fixtures.
Switches.
Telephone.
Door bell and chimes.
Circuit data (optional).
Lighting fixture schedule (optional).
Appliances which use electricity.
Home security system.
Scale of drawing.

Construction details, 2-12, are usually drawn for those features which require more information to fully describe the construction. Typical details include:

Foundation and footing details.
Typical wall sections.
Truss details.
Fireplace and chimney details.
Stair details.
Kitchen and bathroom details.

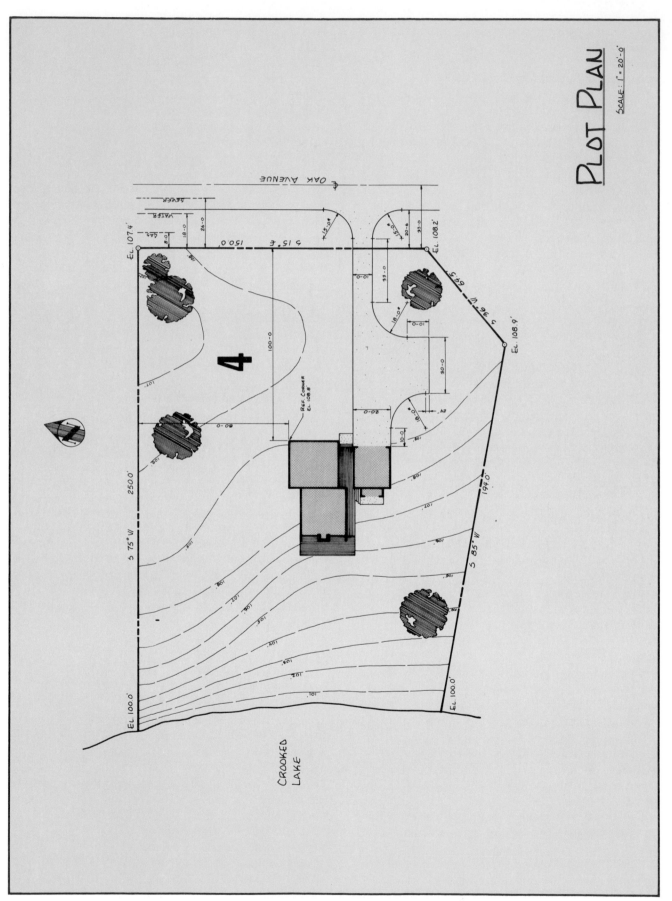

PLOT PLAN

SCALE: 1" = 20'-0"

2-7 A typical plot plan shows the location of the structure on the site and other pertinent features.

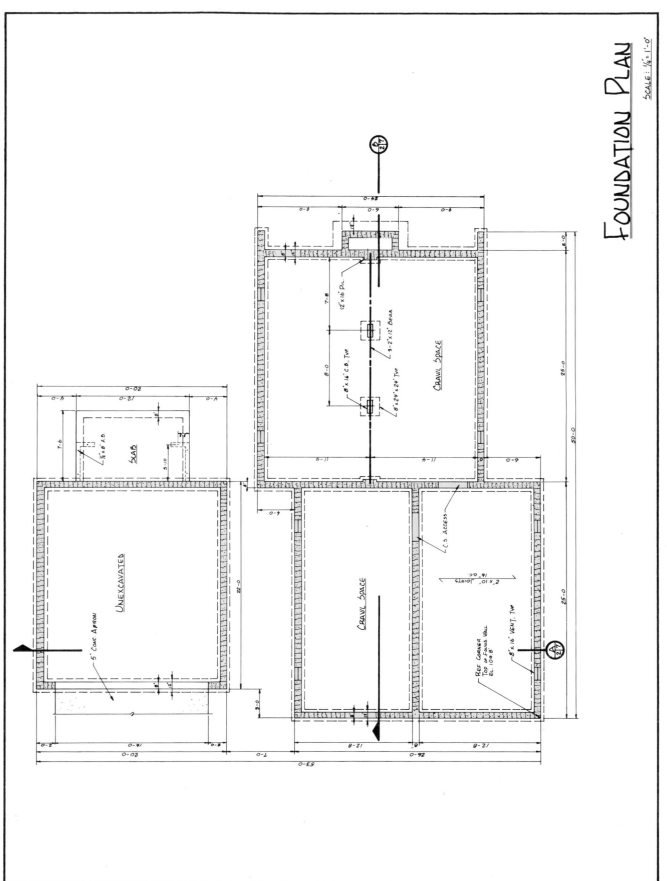

FOUNDATION PLAN
SCALE: 1/4" = 1'-0"

2-8 The foundation/basement plan is used for excavation and construction of the footings and foundation walls.

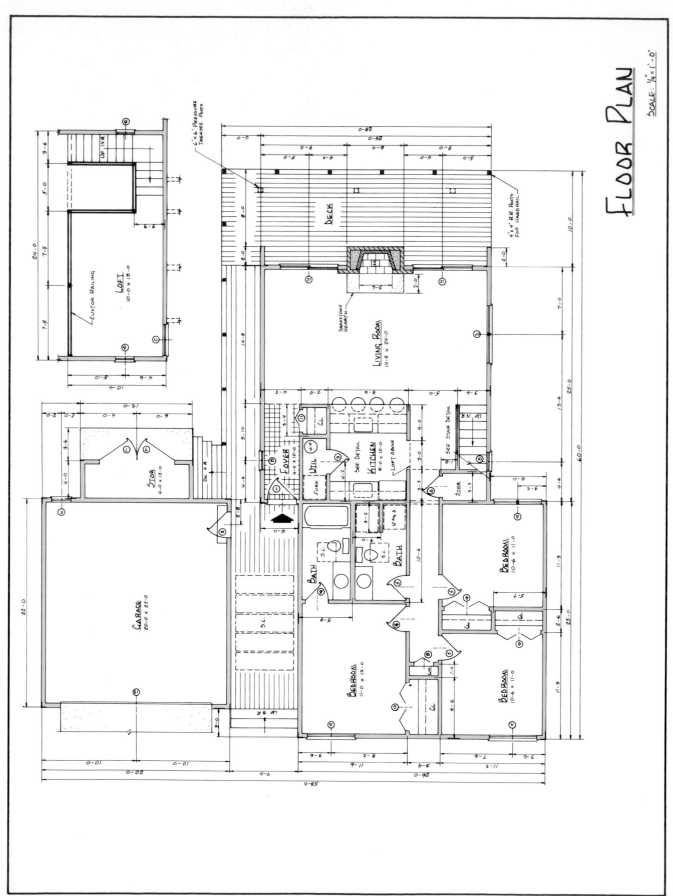

FLOOR PLAN

SCALE: 1/4" = 1'-0"

2-9 A floor plan is drawn for each above-grade level of the structure. The floor plan forms the heart of a set of construction drawings.

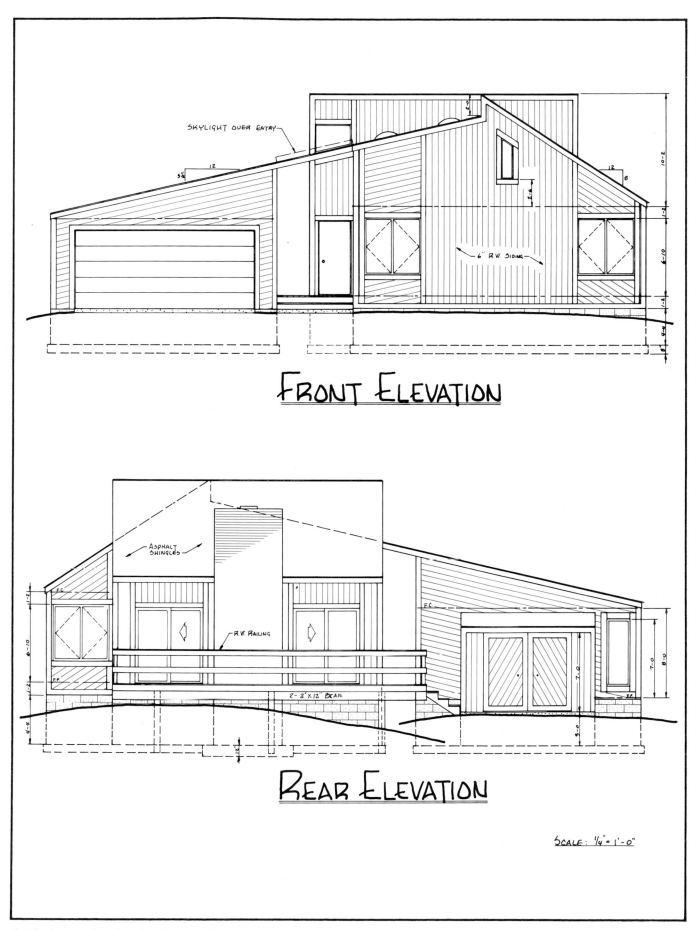

FRONT ELEVATION

REAR ELEVATION

SCALE: 1/4" = 1'-0"

2-10 An exterior elevation is drawn for each side of the building to show the finished appearance.

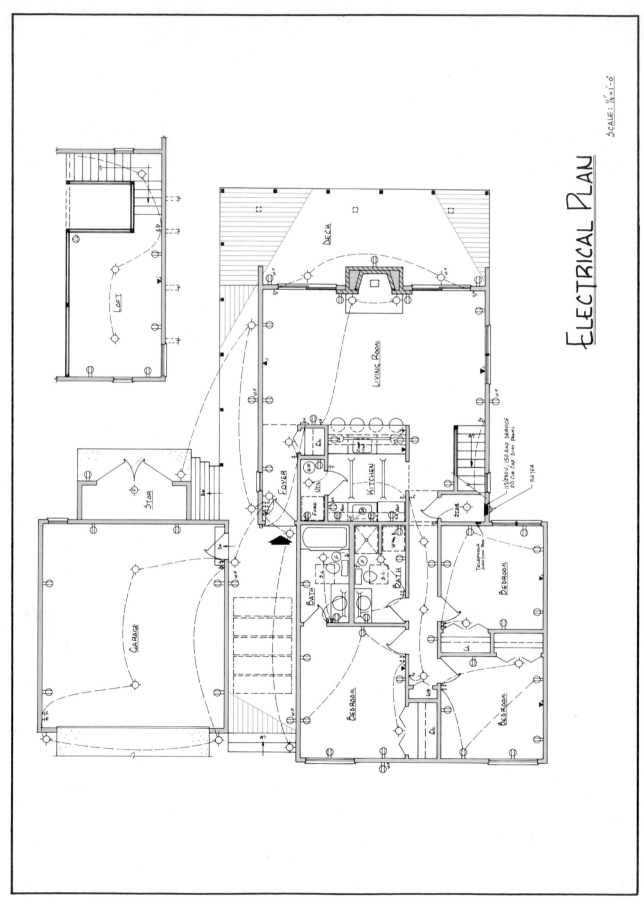

ELECTRICAL PLAN

SCALE: ¼" = 1'-0"

2-11 An electrical plan for each floor of the building is prepared to show the locations and types of electrical equipment to be used.

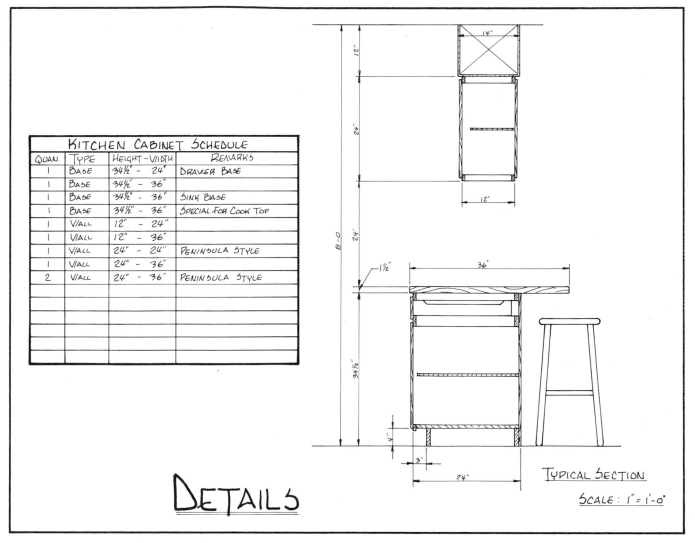

KITCHEN CABINET SCHEDULE			
QUAN.	TYPE	HEIGHT - WIDTH	REMARKS
1	BASE	34½" - 24"	DRAWER BASE
1	BASE	34½" - 36"	
1	BASE	34½" - 36"	SINK BASE
1	BASE	34½" - 36"	SPECIAL FOR COOK TOP
1	WALL	12" - 24"	
1	WALL	12" - 36"	
1	WALL	24" - 24"	PENINSULA STYLE
1	WALL	24" - 36"	
2	WALL	24" - 36"	PENINSULA STYLE

DETAILS

TYPICAL SECTION

SCALE: 1" = 1'-0"

2-12 *Several pages of construction details are often required for a typical structure. These details help to fully describe the intent of the designer.*

Window and door details.
Flower planters.
Decorative screens.
Soffit details.
Unique construction.
Built-in cabinets, bookcases, etc.
The scale of these drawings is almost always larger than 1/4 in. equals 1 ft. Typically, 1/2, 3/4, 1, or 3 in. are used to represent 1 ft.

Pictorial presentations are often included in the package of drawings to better communicate how certain features of the entire structure will appear. The pictorial method often used is the perspective. Presentation drawings sometimes are rendered in color to make the drawing more lifelike. They are intended primarily for those who cannot visualize the completed product from the construction drawings or simply as a communication device.

Other Drawings

In rare cases, a set of residential construction drawings may include a climate control plan and a plumbing plan.

These, however, are more likely to be included in the construction drawings for a larger building such as an apartment or condominium complex.

A *climate control plan* shows the loction of the heating, cooling, humidification, dehumidification, and air cleaning equipment. It also shows distribution routes and means of transmitting the conditioned air to the various rooms.

A *plumbing plan* shows the fresh water supply lines to the water storage tank or house main as well as waste water lines and water conditioning equipment. Plumbing fixtures such as sinks, water closets, showers, and tubs are also shown.

Construction drawings are very useful. Often, problems during the building process are avoided because they were solved on paper before the building began.

REVIEW QUESTIONS

1. How does circulation frequency affect the type of path allowed for circulation?
2. What are the four basic types of circulation?

3. What principles should a good family circulation pattern follow?

4. What is a work triangle? Why is it important that this triangle be small and that no cross traffic should interfere with it?

5. Where would you locate a service entrance for the most efficient service circulation pattern?

6. What parts of the house are involved in guest circulation?

7. What features may cause a large room to have a greatly reduced amount of usable space?

8. What rooms would you place adjacent to a kitchen? What rooms would you place away from the kitchen?

9. What specific drawings are included in a typical set of house plans?

10. If the information on a floor plan conflicted with the information in the specifications for a house, which information would be considered correct?

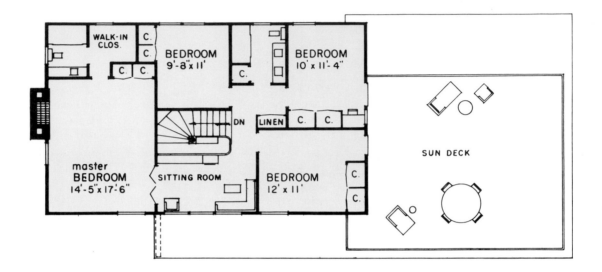

SECOND FLOOR

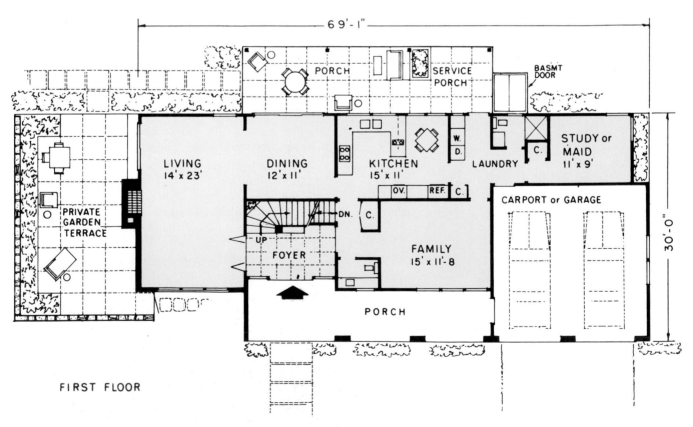

FIRST FLOOR

Seeing a floor plan of a house can help a family better determine whether the house will meet their family's needs.

3 Living Areas

After studying this chapter, you will be able to:
- List the rooms and activities involved in the living areas of a house.
- Judge the appropriateness of a living room for a family according to its location, size, and arrangement.
- Identify a dining room that meets the size and location needs of a specific family.
- Recognize various types of entryways according to purpose and location.
- List possible uses and styles of patios, porches, and courts.

The living areas of a home serve two groups of people: household members and guests. Living areas serve as places for conversation, recreation, dining, entertaining, enjoying hobbies, and relaxing. Several rooms constitute the living areas of a home. Included are the living room, dining room, family room, entryway and foyer, and patio or porch. Other rooms, used for specialized activities, may be included in the living area. Such special rooms might include a study or den, a library, a music room, or a special hobby room. The number and types of rooms in the living area are determined by household size, special activities and hobbies, and budget.

GORDON'S, INC.

3-1 The circular window in this living room provides a spectacular view and serves as a focal point for the room.

LIVING ROOMS

The midst of activity, for many households, is the living room. It may be used as a conversation area, a TV room, or a place to entertain guests, depending on the specific occasion. The living room may also "host" music, reading, indoor games, and hobbies. The lifestyle of the household helps to determine the living room's location, size, arrangement, and functions.

Location

The living room in a newly built home may be located in the front or back of the home, depending on individual preference and the building site. If one part of the building site has a pleasing view, you may want to locate the living room so that it overlooks the view, 3-1.

Location not only refers to the location of the living room on the building site. It also refers to the living room's location in relation to the main entry and the other rooms in the home. Location of the living room should not require members of the household to use it as a main circulation route. To avoid circulation directly into the living room, have the main entry open into a foyer or hallway, 3-2. A change in floor level also can help set the living room apart and eliminate major circulation through it.

Since entertaining and dining are two activities often done together, the living room should be located adjacent to or near the dining room. A combination living room and dining room is sometimes planned to serve both entertaining and dining purposes. A screen, flower planter, dwarf wall, furniture arrangement, or fireplace can be used to separate the two areas. A change in floor levels can also set apart the two rooms.

Another factor to consider in the location of the living room is noise. The living room should be located so that noise from the kitchen does not interfere with quiet activities in the living room. On the other hand, the living room should be located away from the sleeping area so that living room activities will not interrupt the quiet of the sleeping area.

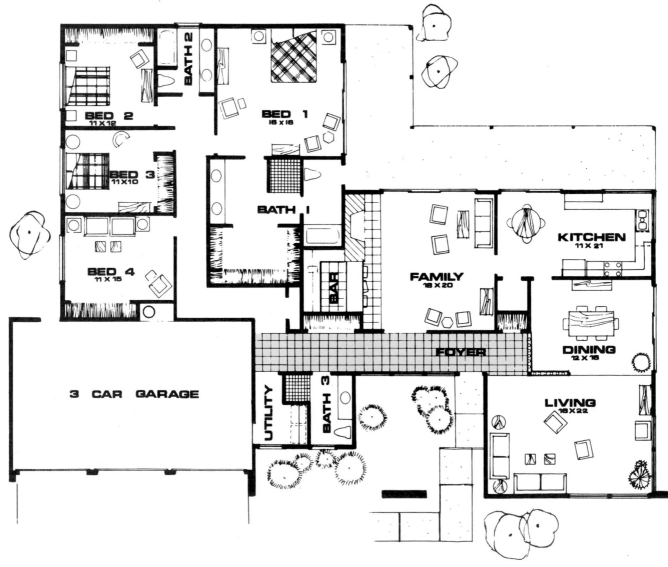

3-2 A foyer at the main entry prevents major circulation through the living room.

ALUMINUM GREENHOUSES, INC.

3-3 An adjacent porch can help to extend the size of the living room.

Size and Arrangement

Living rooms are designed in a variety of sizes and shapes. The ideal size of a living room is determined by the number of people who will use it, how and when it will be used, the furniture intended, and the size of the other rooms in the home. Another factor that may influence the ideal size of a living room is the presence of a patio, porch, deck, or balcony adjacent to the living room, 3-3. This added space can make a room appear more open and extend the use of the room.

Every living room requires an area for conversation. The dominant furniture grouping in the living room is called the primary conversation area. The ideal primary conversation area is circular in shape and about 8 to 10 feet in diameter.

To accommodate an 8 to 10-foot conversation circle, a living room needs to be 10 to 14 feet wide. Living room widths greater than 14 feet are generally not recommended. Exceptions occur when the extra space is used for circulation along one side of the room or for a secondary furniture grouping, 3-4. A secondary furniture grouping may be a small conversation area that seats two or three

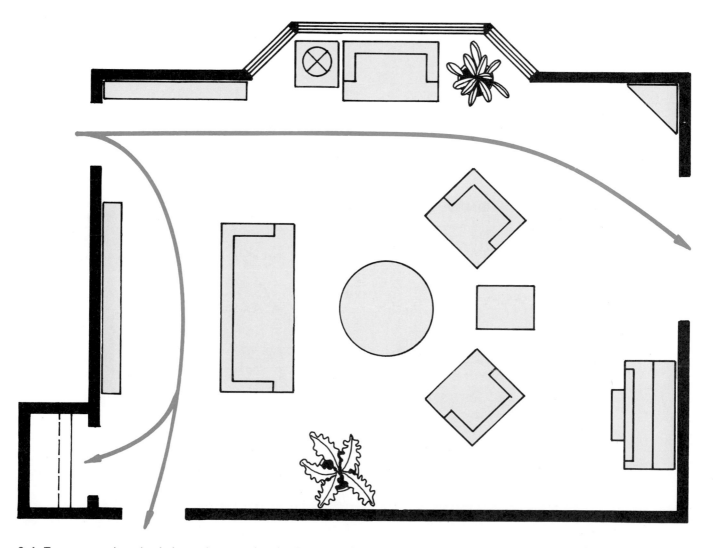

3-4 To accommodate circulation and a secondary furniture grouping, a living room width greater than 14 feet generally is needed.

THE BENNINGTON CO.

3-5 A secondary furniture grouping allows an area for quiet reading or more intimate conversation away from the main conversation circle.

people, 3-5. Or it may be a piano, a desk, or a reading chair for one person.

The ideal living room length allows enough space for the desired number of conversation circles and for circulation. A length of 6 to 18 feet is sufficient for one seated conversation area and circulation. A living room 18 to 22 feet long can easily accommodate a primary conversation area and a secondary furniture grouping.

A well planned living room avoids circulation across conversation areas. Circulation problems can be avoided by locating entrances strategically. For example, in 3-6, two doorways are located at one end of the room, and

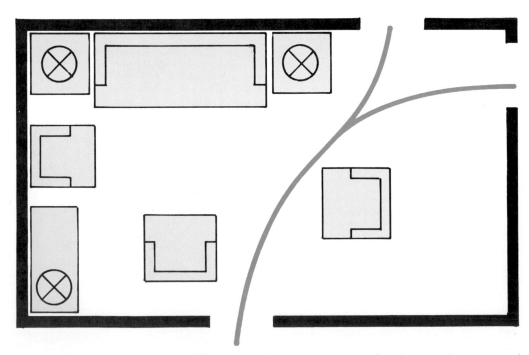

3-6 Poorly placed doors make it difficult to provide a good conversation circle that is not crossed by a circulation path.

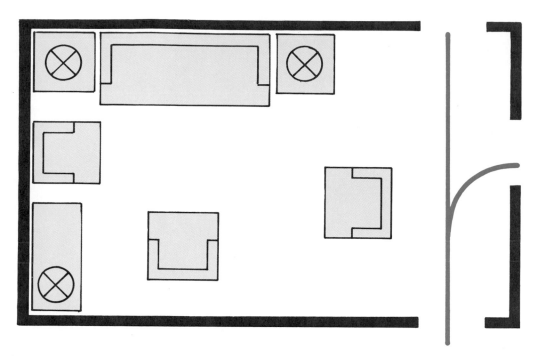

3-7 Well placed living entrances allow a direct circulation path that does not interfere with the conversation circle.

the other doorway is located in the middle of the opposite wall. This causes circulation to pass across the living room, interfering with conversation and/or television viewing. In 3-7, the doorways are located at one end of the room so that circulation passes along one side of the room.

If a living room has a fireplace, it should be located so that it can be seen by the people seated in the conversation circle, 3-8. There should be no circulation between the fireplace and the conversation circle.

GRABER CO.

3-8 A fireplace can become the focal point of a conversation circle.

DINING ROOMS

Many homes built today provide an area for informal dining in the kitchen and more formal dining in a dining room. Having a room set aside for dining is both functional and relaxing for many households. The decision to plan a separate dining room depends on the lifestyle of the household.

The primary purpose of a dining room is to set aside a place for eating. However, dining rooms may serve other purposes. A dining room may be used to display a household member's special interest such as a collection of unusual seashells or beautiful houseplants. Such displays make interesting topics for dining conversations.

A closed or open dining room plan may be selected. In a closed plan, the dining room is set apart from the living room or kitchen. In an open plan, the dining area is an extension of the living room or kitchen, 3-9. A home tends to appear more spacious with an open plan because there are fewer walls to divide the space.

Location

The dining room needs to be located near the kitchen to allow for the movement of food at serving time. It should also be near the living room so guests can move easily from the living room to the dining room. Therefore, an ideal location for the dining room is between the living room and the kitchen, 3-10.

Size and Arrangement

The ideal size for a dining room is determined by the number of people to be served at one time, the furniture intended, and the amount of space needed for circulation.

3-9 The open dining room plan gives a home a more spacious appearance.

The minimum dining area size for four people is 80 square feet. A dining room of about 120 square feet can comfortably seat four people and provide space for a buffet. A dining room of about 180 square feet seats four to eight people and has space for a hutch and a buffet, 3-11. A dining room over 200 square feet is considered very large; it has room for several pieces of furniture.

The basic pieces of dining room furniture are a table and chairs. The size and shape of the table is determined by the size of the household or the number of people dining and the size of the dining area or dining room. Approximately 2 feet in table length should be allowed for each person to be seated. A rectangular table 2 ft. 6 in. by 5 ft. 6 in. seats four to six people.

The required space for dining room chairs varies with the size and style of the chairs. (Large chairs and armchairs require more space.) For average size chairs, at least 32 inches is needed from the edge of the table to the wall or buffet or hutch to pull out a chair and be seated. About 36 to 44 inches is needed from the edge of the table to the wall or buffet or hutch for serving around an occupied table. See 3-12.

Other dining room furniture pieces are buffets, hutches, corner cabinets, and serving carts. They provide space for food and storage. Serving carts move wherever needed and take very little floor and wall space.

FAMILY ROOMS

Many households need space for more lively activities. Having a family room in addition to a living room makes possible the separation of active and passive activities. The living room can be used for conversational, reading, listening, and study activities. The family room can be used for games, hobbies, TV viewing, dancing, and active play. See 3-13.

Family rooms also may be referred to as playrooms, recreation rooms, or multipurpose rooms. Family rooms differ from living rooms in that they are usually informally furnished with durable and easily maintained furniture.

Location

No set rules exist for the location of a family room. In some homes, the family room is separated from the rest of the home. For example, many basements and attics are converted into family rooms. Basements are often good locations for family rooms because they are usually large enough for various types of activities. Basements also tend to contain noise well.

Family rooms also can be located in such a way that they provide an extension to living or service areas. For example, locating the family room near the living room provides overflow space. Locating the family room by the kitchen allows the household members involved in meal preparation to share in family room activities. In some homes, the family room is combined with the kitchen and is called a great room. See 3-14. A family room also may be located near a pool or outdoor recreation area. This provides a convenient arrangement for predominantly outdoor entertaining. Food, beverages, and guests who prefer to be indoors can be in the family room, close to the outdoor activities.

Size and Arrangement

The ideal size for a family room depends on the activities to be performed in the room and the number of people who will use the room. However, a space 12 by 16 feet or larger is recommended.

An important consideration for family rooms is storage. Storage will most likely be needed for games, hobbies, and other recreational activities. Storage units could be used to form a room divider, if desirable, to separate the activity area from the remainder of the room.

Furniture for the family room should be comfortable as well as durable and serviceable. A sturdy table with comfortable chairs could serve as an area for game playing, dining, or a variety of hobbies.

Floors, like the furniture, need to be durable, easy to clean, and suitable for activities. If noise or warmth is a consideration, carpeting may be practical.

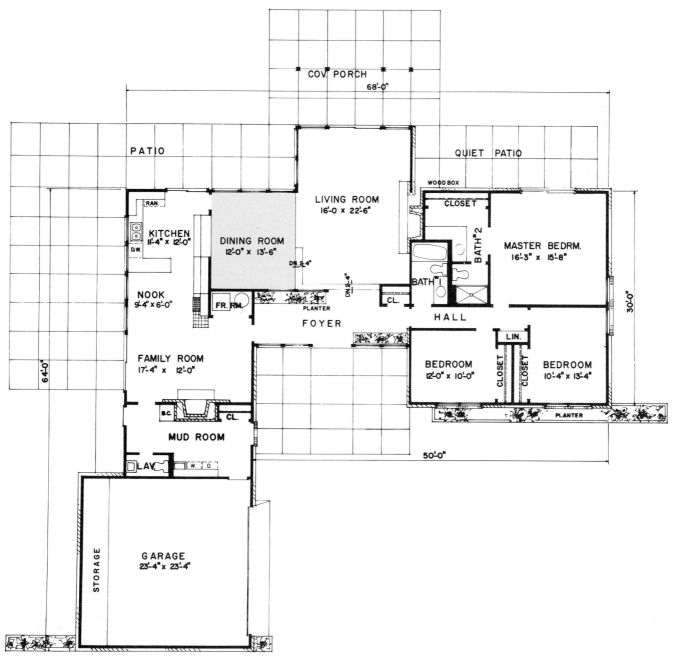

3-10 *In this floor plan, the dining room is located conveniently between the living room and the kitchen.*

3-11   This medium-sized dining room has ample space for a large dining room table, a hutch and a buffet.

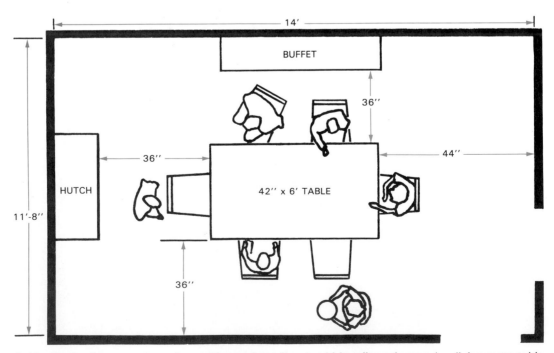

3-12   Ample clearance space for seating and service should be allowed around a dining room table.

ETHAN ALLEN, INC.

3-13 The family room may be used for special hobbies or activities, such as sewing or crafts. Family rooms generally have more casual furnishings than living rooms.

ARMSTRONG WORLD INDUSTRIES, INC.

3-14 A family room can be an extension of the kitchen.

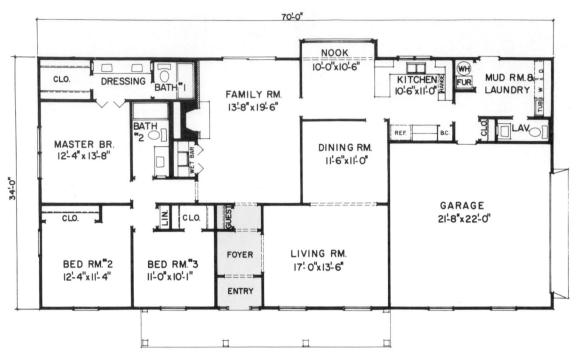

3-15 *A centrally located main entry helps in establishing good circulation patterns throughout a house.*

ROLSCREEN CO.

3-16 *A closet next to the main entrance is convenient for storing the outerwear of guests.*

ENTRYWAYS

Entryways control circulation to different parts of a home. From the entryway, guests or household members should be able to move to other parts of the home without interfering with activities in any area. Careful planning of entryways adds to the convenience and comfort that a family derives from their home. Entryways may be categorized into three groups: main or guest entries, special purpose entries, and service entries. (Service entries are discussed in Chapter 5.)

The main entry is the part of the home that most guests see first. An attractive main entry welcomes guests into a home and makes a good first impression.

In order to establish better circulation inside a home, the main entry is usually located near the center of the dwelling. The floor plan in 3-15 shows how a well located main entry provides access to various areas of a home.

A main entry that opens into an entry hall or foyer is preferred over one that opens directly into a living room. An entry hall or foyer lends privacy to the visitor and household. An entry closet is convenient for storing coats, hats, gloves, umbrellas, and other outdoor accessories. See 3-16.

Access to terraces, patios, and decks is provided by special purpose entries. See 3-17. Sliding glass doors and French doors are often used for this type of entry. These entries extend the use of the room to outdoor areas and make the room appear more spacious. Since special purpose entries are used less frequently and usually by fewer people, less clearance space may be needed.

The size of the dwelling and the number of people using an entry determine the space needed at an entry. The minimum space to allow for a door to swing plus one per-

3-17 A special purpose entry may provide access to a private garden or patio.

son to stand is 3 by 5 feet. An area 5 by 7 feet is more convenient and comfortable. The minimum foyer size is 6 by 6 feet plus closet space. Minimum closet size is 2 feet by 3 feet. However, a closet 2 1/2 feet deep and 4 feet wide is more desirable. For convenience and easy access, the closet should be located 4 to 5 feet from the entry door, not directly behind the door.

The floor in the entry hall or foyer and entry closet should be durable, water and soil resistant, and easy to clean. Slate, ceramic tile, asphalt tile, and vinyl floor coverings are popular and durable floor treatments. If carpeting is used, select a tight weave that is easy to vacuum. A doormat outside the door for cleaning shoes and boots reduces the amount of dirt carried indoors.

PATIOS, PORCHES, AND COURTS

Patios, porches, and courts extend the living areas of a home to the outdoors. They may be used for conversation, relaxing, playing, entertaining, dining, and cooking. Design, size, and location of patios, porches, and courts are determined by the size of the home and its intended purpose.

Patios

Patios are usually constructed at grade level with materials that are durable and maintenance-free. Brick, concrete, stone, and redwood are among the materials often used, 3-18.

Patios can be categorized by function as play patios, living patios, and quiet patios. Play patios are usually located adjacent to a family room or service area to provide an area for play activities. Living patios are located near the living areas of the home—the living room, dining room, and family room. If the patio is to be used for dining, then access to the kitchen or dining room is necessary. See 3-19. The living patio is usually the largest of the three types of patios and may be connected to or serve as a play patio as well. Quiet patios are located on

3-18 Pressure-treated redwood has become a popular material for patios.

3-19 A patio adjacent to the kitchen is convenient for outdoor dining.

3-20 A pool can be the center of activity for a patio.

The view as well as exposure to the sun should be considered in the design and planning of a patio. In cool climates, the sun is an important factor, and the patio should be placed on the south side of the home. In warm climates, shade is desired, and the patio should be placed on the north side of the dwelling.

Porches

Like patios, porches vary in shape, size, and purpose. Porches differ from patios because they are raised above ground and covered by a roof, 3-21. Uncovered porches are called decks. Porches built high off the ground are called verandas or balconies. See 3-22. Some are enclosed by screens, glass, or railings.

Porches are often located in front of the main entrance to provide shelter for guests and protection for the entry. A dining porch can be located off the kitchen or dining room.

The shape and size of a porch should fit the design of the dwelling. The lines and proportions of the porch should complement the lines of the house. A porch planned with the overall design of the house in mind appears to be a part of the house rather than having a "tacked-on" appearance.

Courts

Courts were an important part of early Spanish architecture and are still designed for homes today. Courts resemble patios; however, they are partially or completely

the quiet side of the dwelling, near the bedrooms. They are used for relaxing and even sleeping.

Patios vary in size and shape. The size of the patio is determined by the activities for which it will be used, the equipment and furnishings needed for the activities, and the size of the home. When an in-ground pool is designed for a home, it becomes an extension of the patio, 3-20.

3-21 Unlike patios, porches have a roof, providing shelter from the elements.

3-22 A veranda is generally located one story above the ground.

enclosed by walls. Courts are used for the same purposes as patios and porches—relaxing, entertaining, and dining, 3-23. Courts are more prevalent in warm climates where heating is not a major consideration.

PPG INDUSTRIES, INC.

3-23 This court is suitable for informal dining or entertaining. Privacy is its main feature.

REVIEW QUESTIONS

1. What activities take place in the living areas of a home?
2. What rooms are included in the living areas?
3. How can circulation through a living room be minimized?
4. What kind of furniture would you put in a 12 by 14-foot living room, and how would you arrange it? If the living room was 16 by 20 feet, how would you arrange it differently?
5. What might be placed in a secondary furniture grouping?
6. Why is it desirable to have a living room door placed at one end of the room?
7. Would you select a closed plan or an open plan for a dining room in a small home? Why?
8. What is an ideal location for a dining room within a house?
9. What size should a dining room be for a family of three? For a family of six?
10. What are some good locations for a family room in a home?
11. What type of furniture is appropriate for a family room?
12. Where would you locate the main entry of a house? Why?
13. If a house were in Texas, which side would be the best location for a porch or patio? If the house were in Minnesota, which side would be best?

4 Sleeping Areas

After studying this chapter, you will be able to:
- Describe the two main types of bedroom plans.
- Recognize a well-designed bedroom.
- Arrange bedroom furniture in a style that is attractive and functional.
- List the three main types of bathrooms and the fixtures they include.
- Recognize the need for special features in the bathroom due to heat and moisture.

All individuals, at times, require privacy. The purpose of the sleeping area of a home is to provide privacy for such activities as sleeping, bathing, and dressing.

Bedrooms, bathrooms, and dressing rooms constitute the sleeping area. For peace and quiet, these rooms need to be located away from circulation and other noise.

BEDROOMS

The number, sexes, and ages of family members determine the number and size of bedrooms needed. If possible, each individual should have his or her own bedroom or own space within a bedroom. Each person requires sleeping space, storage space for clothes and personal items, and dressing space. Space may also be needed for playing, studying, relaxing, and other activities. See 4-1.

DREXEL HERITAGE FURNISHINGS, INC.

4-1 This bedroom provides enough space for activities and storage in addition to sleep.

Location

Bedrooms may be located anywhere in the home as long as each bedroom has privacy of sight and sound. However, bedrooms are usually grouped according to one of two plans. One plan groups all bedrooms in one area of the home, 4-2. The other plan, called the split bedroom plan, separates the master bedroom from the remaining bedrooms, 4-3. A bedroom for overnight guests, live-in relatives, or employees may also be segregated from the remaining bedrooms.

A room that could be used as a bedroom should be considered for the first floor of a two-story home. Such a room would be convenient when caring for a sick or elderly person.

Another factor related to the location of bedrooms is accessibility. Ideally, each bedroom should open off a hallway instead of directly off another room. A person should not have to pass through one bedroom to reach another bedroom. Also, each bedroom should be close to a bath or have its own bath.

Size and Arrangement

The size needed for a bedroom depends on the number of persons who will use the room, their ages, the activities to be performed in the room in addition to sleeping and dressing, and the furniture. The more people sharing the room, the more activities performed in the room, and the larger the furniture, the larger the bedroom will need to be.

When arranging furniture in a bedroom, the placement of the bed should be the first consideration. This is because the bed is usually the largest and most used piece of bedroom furniture. Allow 22 inches of space on each side of the bed so a person can walk around it while making it. An exception is a twin bed that is going to be made from one side. Then only a 6-inch clearance is needed next to the wall to allow the bedspread to drape over the side. The amount of space recommended between twin beds is 22 inches.

Consider windows when positioning the bed. Early morning sun should not shine directly on the bed. Ventilation should be possible without a draft across the bed.

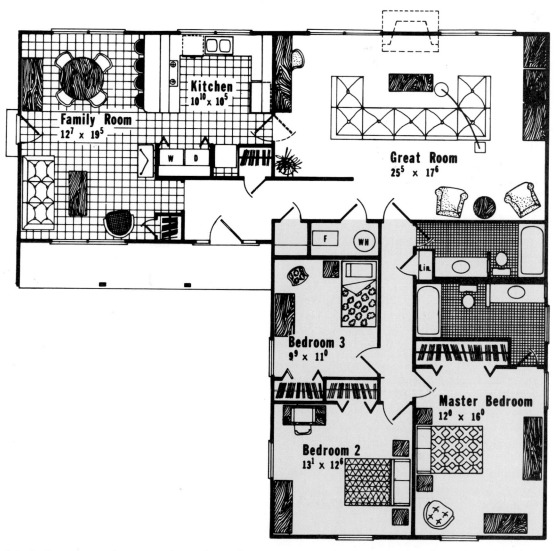

4-2 Bedrooms may be grouped together to form a compact sleeping area away from the noisier living and service areas.

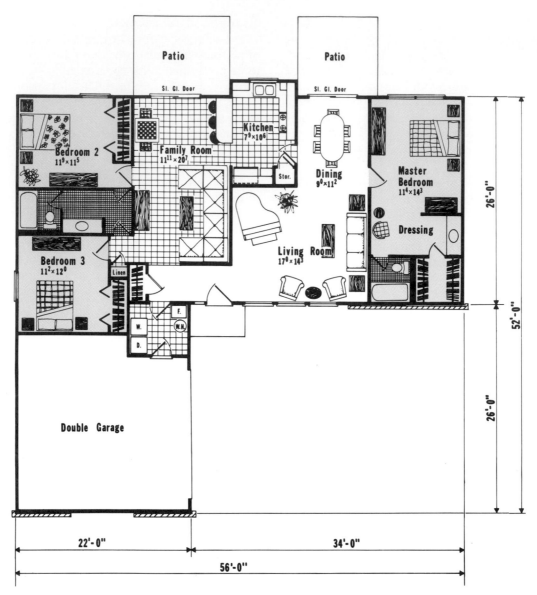

4-3 In the "split bedroom plan," the master bedroom is separated from the other bedrooms. This arrangement is desirable for many families.

When arranging the bed and other furniture, consider circulation into the bedroom. Neither the bed nor the other pieces of furniture should interfere with circulation into the room and to the bedroom closet.

Additional guidelines for furniture arrangement and clearance space make bedrooms more convenient and functional. Bedside tables should be the same height as the bed's mattress. Lamps on the tables should be at an appropriate height for reading. Sufficient lighting (natural and artificial) should be available for the dresser or makeup area.

In front of a chest of drawers or dresser, a space of 40 inches is recommended in order to pull out the drawers. In front of a closet, the recommended clearance space is 33 inches. For dressing, a 42-inch dressing circle is needed. See 4-4. The measurements given here are only guidelines. Some people prefer and can afford additional space and, thus, larger bedrooms.

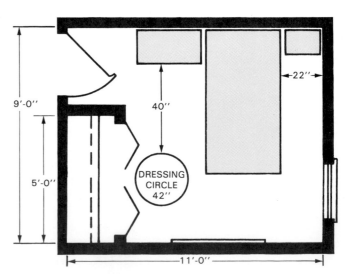

4-4 Space for a 42-inch dressing circle should be allowed in each bedroom.

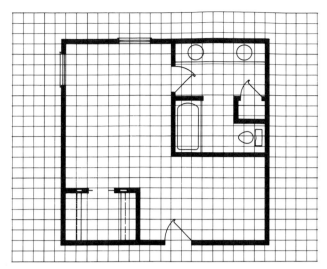

Step 1. Draw the dimensions of the bedroom on graph paper showing windows and doors in their correct positions.

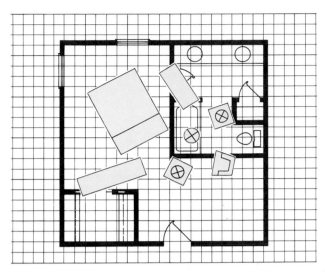

Step 2. Make scaled drawings of the furniture to be placed in the room, and cut them out.

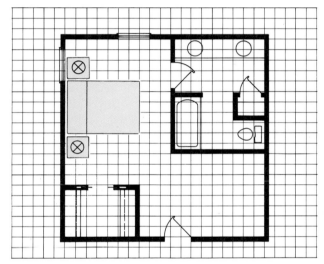

Step 3. Place the bed first.

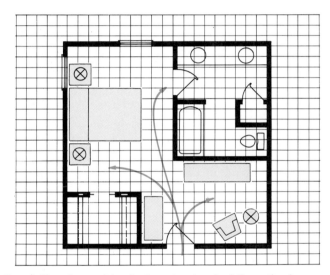

Step 4. Place the remaining furniture, keeping circulation paths clear.

SINGER FURNITURE

4-5 Follow these steps to plan the arrangement of bedroom furnishings.

The steps to follow when planning and arranging furniture in a bedroom are given in 4-5. The result of careful planning is shown in 4-6.

Closets, doors, and windows. Bedroom arrangement is affected by the location of closets, doors, and windows. The recommended location for a bedroom closet is adjacent to the room entrance. This location allows a person to reach the closet without having to walk around furniture. Closets can be placed along interior walls to provide insulation from noise between rooms and to provide more space on exterior walls for windows. Or closets may be placed on exterior walls to provide insulation from outside temperatures.

The minimum closet space recommended per person is 4 to 6 feet in length and 24 to 30 inches in depth. The two types of closets commonly found in homes are freestanding closets and built-in closets. Free-standing closets, also called wardrobes or armoires, are pieces of furniture,

4-7. They are not attached to or built into the walls as built-in closets are. Built-in closets deeper than 4 feet are usually considered walk-in closets. Some walk-in closets are large enough to accommodate a dressing area.

The recommended location for a bedroom door is in the corner of the room so it will not break up wall space. Each bedroom will have at least one entry door and possibly other doors leading to a bathroom, closet, or patio. The entry door should swing into the room, and space should be allowed for the door when it is open. To conserve space, a pocket door may be used for the entry, and sliding doors may be used for closet or patio doors.

Windows placed on two exterior walls are ideal for cross ventilation. High, *ribbon windows* (wide, short windows) provide ventilation and privacy, and they allow placement of furniture below. Ribbon windows also prevent drafts from blowing across the bed. Windows placed lower on the wall interfere with furniture arrangement. However,

49

4-6   Careful planning will produce a functional room layout like this one.

DREXEL HERITAGE FURNISHINGS, INC.

DREXEL HERITAGE FURNISHINGS, INC.

4-7   This period armoire provides an ideal storage place for clothes. Space inside is adjustable to accommodate various storage requirements.

they allow a person lying in bed to see out, and they can be used as fire escapes.

Master Bedrooms

The master bedroom may serve as a private retreat, 4-8. It may be personalized to accommodate activities other than sleeping. A conversation area, work area, or private garden may be part of the master bedroom. A master bath is convenient for personal bathing and grooming. The dressing area could be removed from the bedroom by planning a dressing room between the bedroom and bathroom. Special equipment or space for hobbies may be a part of the master bedroom as well.

Children's Rooms

The bedroom needs of children change as the children grow. Future needs should be considered when planning a child's room. A minimum-size bedroom should contain at least 100 square feet—enough to accommodate a single bed, a chest or dresser, and a bedside table or chair. This size is ideal for a nursery which can be converted to a child's bedroom in future years.

Young children need plenty of floor space for play. They also need child-high storage space for their toys and books. As children grow, their activities change. Older

DREXEL HERITAGE FURNISHINGS, INC.

4-8 The master bedroom may provide access to a private garden or include provisions for relaxing activities.

children may need higher shelves and more storage space as well as tables or desks for studying. They may have special needs if they have special hobbies.

Since children's bedrooms will have to change, flexibility and creativity are keys to planning. An "L" shaped room or room dividers could provide privacy for each child when the room must be shared. Twin beds offer flexibility in room arrangements, while captain's beds provide under-the-bed storage. Beds with bolsters may serve as couches for teenage children.

BATHROOMS

The trend in homes today is to have bigger bathrooms and more bathrooms. Although highly functional, today's bathrooms are also attractive and personalized, 4-9.

There are three main styles of bathrooms: half bath, three-quarters bath, and full bath. A half bath has only a water closet and a lavatory. A three-quarters bath has a water closet, lavatory, and shower. A full bath includes a water closet, lavatory, and tub with or without a shower.

Location

Bathrooms need to be located near the living areas of the home as well as the sleeping areas. If a home has only

ELJER PLUMBINGWARE, WALLACE-MURRAY CORP.

4-9 This bathroom is designed to be attractive and functional. Bathrooms can be personalized regardless of size or budget.

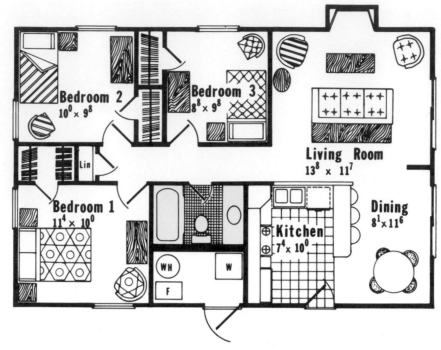

4-10 This three-bedroom cottage has just one bathroom, but its location is convenient to the living, sleeping, and service areas.

one bathroom, then it should be located in a place that is easily accessible to all areas of the home, 4-10.

The architectural style sometimes dictates the number and location of bathrooms in a dwelling. Ideally, a two-story home needs at least one and a half baths—a full bath upstairs in the sleeping area and a half bath downstairs near the living and service areas. A split-level home also needs one and a half baths—a half bath on the lower level and a full bath on the upper level. A ranch home that has the bedrooms located away from the living and service areas also needs one and a half baths. Houses with four or more bedrooms are more functional with two or more bathrooms.

Size and Arrangement

The size bathroom needed depends on the number of persons who will be using the bathroom and the activities to be performed there. Activities may include bathing, applying makeup, and dressing. More elaborate bathrooms may even provide space for exercising, sunbathing, or laundering.

The bathroom should be as comfortable and convenient as is necessary to meet the needs of those using it. For example, a bathroom that is shared by all family members should have ample storage and counter space for the grooming and hygiene supplies of each family member. A seldom-used guest bath would not require as much counter and storage space.

The basic fixtures needed in a full bath include a water closet, lavatory, and tub/shower. Saunas and jacuzzis also may be added. The proper arrangement of these fixtures and adequate space clearances make a bathroom convenient to use.

Water closets, like all bathroom fixtures, come in many sizes, shapes, and colors. They are available as floor-mounted units or wall-mounted units. See 4-11. Clearance space around a water closet should be at least 15 inches from the center of the stool to the side wall or to another fixture and 24 inches in front of the stool.

Lavatories are available in a vanity base or as a wall-hung unit. Twin lavatories are convenient when one bathroom must be shared by two or more people. The common size for a bathroom lavatory is 18 inches. A larger sink should be placed in the bathroom if it will be used for purposes other than grooming, such as hand-washing clothes.

Bathroom tubs come in many sizes and shapes, 4-12. They range in size from 54 to 72 in. long and 28 to 32 in. wide. Common shapes are rectangular, square, and round. A clearance space of 30 to 42 in. is needed between the front of the tub and the opposite wall.

Tubs are available with different features. Most tubs have a shower head installed above it. Some tubs have wide ledges that can be used as seats for leg or foot washing. For safety, some tubs have grab rails and non-skid bottoms.

Homes that have two bathrooms may have a tub/shower installed in one bathroom and just a shower stall in the other. A shower stall requires less space than a tub and lowers the cost of building a home. Shower stall sizes range from 30 by 33 in. to 36 by 48 in.

Saunas and jacuzzis are available for home installation. These may be placed in or near the bathroom. They should not interfere with general circulation in the bathroom. Saunas may be purchased as kits or custom installed. Some newer models are designed to accommodate one per-

ELJER PLUMBINGWARE, WALLACE-MURRAY CORP.

A

B

ELJER PLUMBINGWARE, WALLACE-MURRAY CORP.

4-11 Water closets are available as wall-mounted (A) or floor-mounted (B) units.

4-12 This square tub has a non-skid bottom and is available in several sizes and colors.

KOHLER CO.

4-13 This unit, called an Environment Masterbath, contains a sauna with a removable floor, a whirlpool, sun lamp, steam, and rain.

son and require no more space than a closet. Others contain a combination of a sauna, whirlpool, and steam bath, 4-13. Jacuzzis are available in ready to assemble wood kits or in precast units. Many are designed to double as a bathtub and a whirlpool. Skid-proof steps are generally placed outside the jacuzzi for easy, safe access, 4-14. At least 30 to 42 in. of clearance space should be allowed for entering and leaving a sauna or jacuzzi.

Storage space should be available in each bathroom. Storage may be needed for grooming supplies, medicines, grooming appliances, and towels and washcloths. A vanity and/or a bathroom closet can provide storage space.

Heat and Moisture Considerations

Ventilation can be obtained from an exhaust fan or from a window. Exhaust fans should be located near the water closet and tub. Electrical switches controlling fans and lights should be placed so that they cannot be reached from the tub.

Heat, high humidity, and frequent cleaning are factors to consider when choosing materials to finish bathroom walls, floors, and ceilings. Walls should be finished with materials that are waterproof and easily cleaned. See 4-15. If walls are finished with dry wall or plaster, a gloss or semi-gloss paint that resists soil and water should cover the surface.

Bathroom floors should not be slippery when wet. A bath mat or rug with no-slip backing can be used at bath times. Ceramic or vinyl tile floors are good for frequently-used bathrooms. Nylon acrylic carpeting is popular in master bathrooms.

CALIFORNIA REDWOOD ASSOCIATION

4-15 A clear, water-repellant containing mildewcide protects these redwood walls from water damage in this high moisture area.

REVIEW QUESTIONS

1. What are the two main plans for arranging bedrooms within the house? Why might one plan be chosen over the other?
2. What are the steps to follow when planning the arrangement of bedroom furniture?
3. What amount of space should be allowed for the following activities? Making a bed from one side. Making a bed by walking around the bed. Opening a dresser drawer. Opening a closet door. Dressing.
4. If two bedrooms had the same dimensions, why might one have more usable space than the other?
5. What is the difference between a free-standing closet, a built-in closet, and a walk-in closet?
6. What factors should be considered when planning a children's bedroom?
7. What are the three main styles of bathrooms? What fixtures do each of these contain?
8. In a small home, where should the bathroom be located? Where should bathrooms be located in a two-story home?
9. What is an advantage of a wall-mounted water closet?
10. What features might you add to a bathtub in the home of an elderly couple?
11. What items can be included in the bathroom to assure proper ventilation?
12. Why would flat-finish paint be a poor choice for a bathroom?

ALUMINUM GREENHOUSES, INC.

4-14 Carpeted steps allow easy and safe access to a jacuzzi.

5 Service Areas

After studying this chapter, you will be able to:
■ Describe the three centers of the work triangle, and plan an efficiently arranged kitchen using any of the six common floor plans.
■ Evaluate the efficiency of a laundry facility, considering its location and layout in relationship to the lifestyle of the household.
■ List possible uses and layouts of the basement.
■ Determine the best location on a floor plan for a garage or carport and for service entries.
■ List types and uses of special purpose rooms and storage units.

The service areas of a home sustain all the other areas of a home. The living and sleeping areas depend upon the service areas for many activities; consequently, much planning is necessary to make these areas as efficient as possible. The service areas may include the following: kitchens, laundry facilities, basements, garages, service entries, special purpose rooms, and storage.

KITCHENS

The kitchen is the center for meal preparation and clean-up. Although many homes have their kitchens in separate rooms, more and more kitchens open into a dining room, living room, or family room. Open kitchens make it more convenient to supervise or participate in nearby activities while working in the kitchen. The open design also helps small kitchens—like those in apartments or small homes—seem larger. See 5-1.

The kitchen itself may have facilities for dining, doing office work, or laundering in addition to preparing meals. A well-planned kitchen that meets the needs of household members should fit the lifestyle of the household. It should contain areas for each activity performed, ample workspace, and adequate storage.

Location

Ideally, the kitchen needs to be located near the service entrance of a home as well as the dining area or dining room, 5-2. If the household barbeques often, it is important to have the kitchen located near the patio or deck.

If there are young children in the home, it may be important to have the kitchen oversee the outdoor play area or be near the family or recreation room. In addition, the kitchen should have access to the main entry and the living room but be out of view from both. Circulation from the kitchen to the bathroom or bedrooms should not pass through the living room.

WOOD-METAL INDUSTRIES, INC.

5-1 An open kitchen helps a small apartment seem more spacious.

5-2 *The dining area of a home should be adjacent to the meal preparation area.*

5-3 *This large kitchen contains all the necessary features for the serious gourmet—plenty of counter space, abundant cabinet storage, and a pleasant decor.*

Size and Arrangement

The ideal size for a kitchen is determined by the kind and amount of food to be prepared and the activities which will take place in the kitchen. Smaller kitchens may vary in size from 60 to 130 square feet. A household that prepares gourmet food often may need a more spacious and elaborately equipped kitchen, 5-3. Extra space may be needed for eating, laundering, and/or a home office. Such kitchens may have as much as 300 square feet of space. Households that do not prepare much food from scratch or eat at home much may find a large, elaborate kitchen to be a waste of space.

Work Centers

A well arranged kitchen is designed around work centers. Most kitchens have three basic work centers: the *food preparation and storage center,* the *cooking and serving center,* and the *cleanup center.* Larger kitchens may have additional centers such as a mixing center, an eating center, a planning center, and a laundry center.

Food preparation and storage center. The food preparation and storage center focuses on the refrigerator-freezer. Cabinets and counter space beside the refrigerator are a part of this center. Wall and base cabinets are used for the storage of nonperishable foods, food containers, and serving dishes. A counter at least 18 inches wide is needed on the latch side of the refrigerator for setting out supplies and preparing food.

A small center for mixing is usually located beside the food storage area. Counter space at least 36 inches wide is needed for this activity. Storage in this area is needed for mixing bowls, measuring tools, baking utensils, small appliances such as an electric mixer and blender, and baking ingredients such as sugar and flour.

Cleanup center. Activity in the cleanup center takes place around the sink. The cleanup center may also include a dishwasher and food waste disposer. In this center, foods such as fresh produce are cleaned, and dishes and utensils are washed. The sink should be placed no more than 3 inches from the front edge of the counter. To the right of the sink, 36 inches of counter space is needed for stacking dirty dishes. To the left of the sink, at least 18 inches in needed for draining and stacking clean dishes.

If a dishwasher is present, it should be located to the left of the sink for easy right to left loading. See 5-4. Cabinet and drawer space is needed for the storage of

KITCHENAID DIV., HOBART CORP.

5-4 This cleanup center has plenty of counter space on either side of the sink for dirty and clean dishes. The dishwasher is placed to the left of the sink for ease in placement of dishes from the sink to the dishwasher.

ARIST-O-KRAFT

5-5 The cooking center in this home has plenty of cupboard space above and below the cooking surface. Counter space is available on either side of the cooking surface.

dishes, dishclothes and towels, and dishwashing detergent. Utensils for cleaning, cutting, and straining foods may also be located here.

Cooking and serving center. The focal point of the cooking and serving center is the cooking surface. The cooking surface may be part of a range or installed in a heat-resistant counter just as an oven may be part of a range or built into a wall. Above the cooking surface or within the surface, an exhaust system is needed to ventilate the air. A cooking surface should not be placed directly under a window since curtains are a fire hazard.

The cooking center requires at least 24 inches of heat-resistant counter space on each side of the range to hold ingredients and utensils needed for cooking. Wall and base cabinets are needed for storage of seasonings, cookware, cooking utensils, and pot holders, 5-5. Electrical outlets are needed for using appliances such as a countertop microwave oven, an electric frypan, or a toaster.

The work triangle. The focal points of the three work centers—the refrigerator in the food preparation and storage center, the sink in the cleanup center, and the cooking surface in the cooking and serving center—form a work triangle. The work triangle should follow the normal flow of food preparation. Food is taken from the refrigerator-freezer, cleaned at the sink, and taken to the range for cooking. Leftovers are returned to the refrigerator. This completes the work triangle.

The triangle should measure no more than 22 feet from the middle of the refrigerator, to the middle of the sink,

to the middle of the rangetop. See 5-6. A larger triangle would require too much walking to perform a task.

Appliances, Cabinets, and Counters

Kitchen appliances can be obtained in a variety of types, sizes, shapes, and colors. Figure 5-7 illustrates standard shapes, sizes, and symbols for major kitchen appliances.

When choosing appliances, the amount of usable space in the kitchen should be considered. Space should be

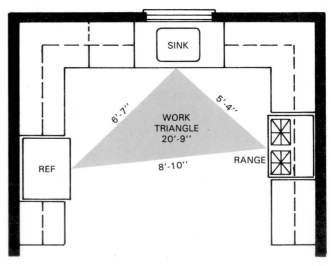

5-6 The sum of the three sides of the kitchen work triangle should not exceed 22 feet.

allowed for clearance as well as for the appliance itself. In order to store and remove food from a refrigerator comfortably, 36 inches of clearance is needed.

For a conventional range, 38 inches from the front of the range will allow a person to use the oven in a standing position. An additional 38 inches from the tip of an open oven door will allow room for a person to kneel in front of the oven. To load and unload a dishwasher, 42 inches in front of the dishwasher and 20 inches on either side should be allowed. See 5-8.

Cabinets can be custom-made or manufactured. Standard sizes of base cabinets are 36 inches high and 24 inches

deep. Widths range from 9 inches to 48 inches, in 3-inch increments. Typical base cabinets include a drawer and two shelves.

Wall cabinets generally range from 12 inches to 30 inches high and 12 or 13 inches deep. Those 12 to 18 inches high are useful over sinks, refrigerators, and ranges. Wall cabinets are generally available in widths of 12 to 48 inches, in increments of 3 inches.

A minimum run of 72 inches of cabinet space is recommended for ample kitchen storage. This does not include cabinet space under the sink since food products should not be stored there. Space under the sink could be used

REFRIGERATOR

Ft³	Width	Height	Depth
9	24″	56″	29″
12	30″	68″	30″
14	31″	63″	24″
19	34″	70″	29″
21	36″	66″	29″

UPRIGHT FREEZER

Ft³	Width	Height	Depth
9	26″	47″	26″
13	28″	58″	28″
15	28″	64″	27″
16	30″	66″	30″
20	33″	66″	28″
31	36″	73″	32″

STANDARD FREE-STANDING RANGE

Width	Height	Depth
20″	30″	24″
21″	36″	25″
30″	36″	26″
40″	36″	27″

DROP IN RANGE

Width	Height	Depth
23″	23″	22″
24″	23″	22″
30″	24″	25″

DOUBLE OVEN RANGE

Width	Height	Depth
30″	61″	26″
30″	64″	26″
30″	67″	27″
30″	71″	27″

BUILT-IN COOK TOP

Width	Height	Depth
12″	2″	18″
24″	3″	22″
48″	3″	25″

RANGE HOOD

Width	Height	Depth
24″	5″	12″
30″	6″	17″
66″	7″	26″
72″	8″	28″

DOUBLE COMPARTMENT SINK

Width	Depth
32″	21″
36″	20″
42″	21″

BASE CABINET

Height: 34½″
Depth: 24″
Width: 12″ to 48″
    in 3″ increments

SINGLE COMPARTMENT SINK

Width	Depth
21″	21″
24″	21″
30″	20″

WALL CABINET

Depth: 12″ or 13″
Width: 12″ to 48″
Height: 12″ to 36″
    in 3″ increments

PANTRY

Height: 84″
Depth: 24″
Width: 18″ to 48″
    in 3″ increments

DISHWASHER

Width	Height	Depth
18″	34½″	24″
21″	34½″	24″
24″	34½″	24″

TRASH COMPACTOR

Width	Height	Depth
15″	34½″	24″
18″	34½″	24″

5-7 Kitchen appliances are available in several standard shapes.

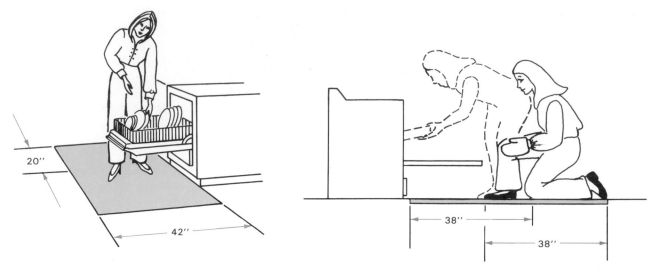

5-8 Space is needed for using a front-loading dishwasher and a conventional range.

for storage of cleaning products and a garbage can. Use of corner cabinet space can be maximized by using an L-shaped lazy susan, 5-9. The shelves rotate outward for easy access to stored items. Many standard cabinets also have shelves that pull out, 5-10.

Space between the wall cabinets and base cabinets is usually 15 to 18 inches. This distance provides space for portable appliances such as mixers. Above a range, cabinets should have 30 inches of clearance or a minimum of 24 inches if a hood is used. Cabinets above the sink should be placed above eye level.

Countertops are made to order in sections and generally about 25 inches deep and 1 1/2 inch thick. Countertops should be easy to clean and non-absorbant. Materials include ceramic, metal, wood, and laminated plastic.

Sufficient outlets for electric appliances and lighting should be provided in the kitchen. Lighting should be provided in a central location as well as above each work center.

Kitchen Floor Plans

Work centers may be arranged into a variety of floor plans. The six common plans are: the U-shaped kitchen, the L-shaped kitchen, the corridor kitchen, the peninsula kitchen, the island kitchen, and the one-wall kitchen.

The *U-shaped kitchen* is one of the most popular kitchen layouts and the most efficient. See 5-11. In this design, the work centers form a continuous line around three adjoining walls. There are two major advantages of this layout. It prevents circulation from passing through

QUAKER MAID

5-9 These lazy-susan shelves swing out for easy access to store goods.

HJ SCHEIRICH CO.

5-10 The heights of these sliding base shelves are perfect for storage of various dry goods. Any item is within easy reach.

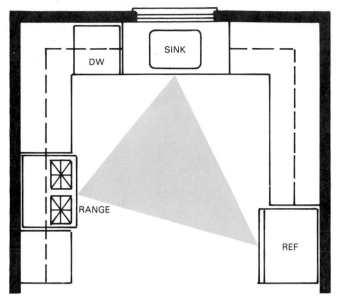

5-11 ''U''-shaped kitchen. The cleanup center is most functional at the base of the ''U'' with the preparation and storage center on the right sidewall and the cooking center on the left sidewall.

the work triangle, and it provides ample cabinet and counter space.

In an *L-shaped kitchen,* the work centers form a continuous line along two adjoining walls, 5-12. The L-shaped kitchen is a popular layout because it adapts to a variety of room plans. In a large room, this design allows space for an eating area. Another advantage of this plan is that it doesn't allow the work triangle to be interrupted by circulation.

A *corridor kitchen* is suited to a long, narrow room. It consists of two walls divided by an aisle 4 to 5 feet wide, 5-13. A compact work triangle is the major advantage of a corridor layout. Another advantage is that it may be located between two eating areas — an informal dining area at one end and a formal dining room at the other end. However, if the corridor is open at both ends, circulation through the corridor may interfere with the work triangle. If the room is very long, this will create a long, narow work triangle that requires many steps.

A *peninsula kitchen* is a U-shaped kitchen with a counter extending perpendicularly from one end of the U. See 5-14. This type layout is often used to separate the kitchen from an adjoining family room or a dining room. The peninsula can be used for extra storage space, as an eating area, or for space for a built-in appliance.

The *island kitchen* may be a variation of the U-shaped kitchen, the L-shaped kitchen, or the one-wall kitchen. This plan has a separate counter unit which stands alone, 5-15. A clearance of 4 feet should be allowed on each side of the island. An island, like a peninsula, can serve as a mixing center, a cooking and serving center, a cleanup center, a counter for informal eating, or just additional counter and storage space. An island also serves as a divider between the food preparation area and the rest of the room.

A *one-wall kitchen* is often used where space is limited such as in an apartment or cottage. In this type of layout, all of the appliances and cabinets are located on one wall, 5-16. When not in use the one-wall kitchen is often closed off from other rooms by a folding door. This plan is generally the least desirable because it does not provide enough cabinet or counter space, and it has a long, narrow work triangle.

LAUNDRY FACILITIES

Caring for clothes and linens is another important activity that is performed in the service area of a home.

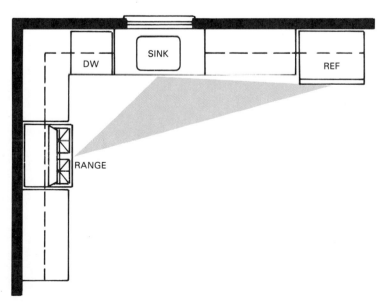

5-12 ''L''-shaped kitchen. This design provides several alternatives for efficient layout.

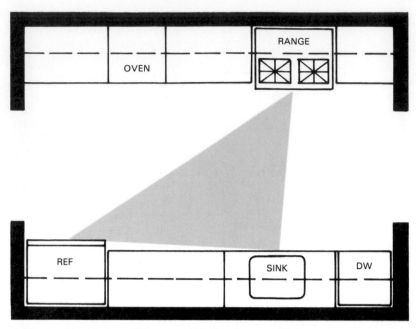

5-13 Corridor kitchen. This type of kitchen is most efficient when the preparation and storage center and the cleanup are on the same wall with the cooking center on the opposite wall.

Laundry facilities may vary from a washer and dryer tucked away in a closet to a separate laundry room with plenty of space for sorting, folding, and ironing clothes, 5-17.

The activites that are involved in laundering are: sorting and preparing clothes for washing, washing (by hand or machine), drying (air-drying or machine-drying), folding, and ironing.

LOCATION

No set rules exist for the location of laundry facilities in a home. However, the availability of hot and cold water lines, a gas line or 240-volt electrical outlet, and an outside wall for a dryer vent may limit the choice of locations. These features are expensive to have moved or

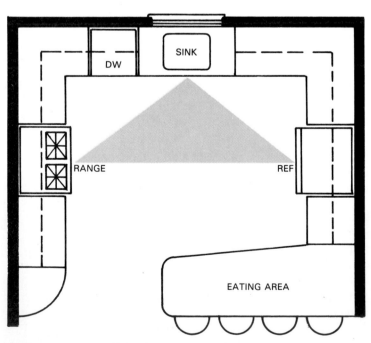

5-14 Peninsula kitchen. The peninsula layout adds extra counter space that could be used to house a range, sink, or refigertor. The peninsula is often used as an eating area. This plan prevents circulation through the kitchen to other areas of the home.

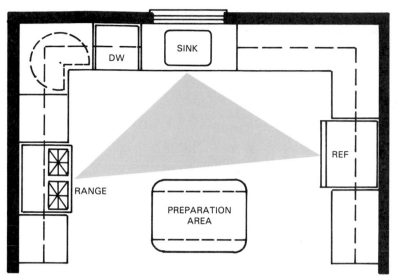

5-15 *Island kitchen. This island kitchen is a variation of the ''U''-shaped layout. The island area can be used like a peninsula.*

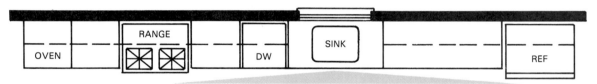

5-16 *One-wall kitchen. Since the refrigerator is on the right, work flows from right to left in this one-wall kitchen layout. Notice that countertop space is provided in each of the work centers.*

installed, and cost may outweigh other considerations.

Laundry facilities may be located in the kitchen, in a mud or ultility room, in the sleeping area, in the basement, or in its own room. Each location has its advantages and disadvantages.

The advantage of locating the laundry facilities in or near the kitchen is that kitchen and laundry duties can be supervised at the same time, saving steps between two separate locations. A disadvantage of a kitchen location may be lack of adequate space for folding and ironing.

Locating laundry facilities in a mud or utility room near the service entrance is also convenient, 5-18. In some families, soiled clothing is removed here. If the household has a washer, but no dryer, close proximity to the service entrance would be convenient for taking laundry outside to line dry.

The sleeping area is a practical location since this is the area where soiled clothes are removed and clean clothes are stored. However, a washer and dryer can be noisy, making this location less desirable to some households.

Another location for laundry facilities is the basement. Although this location removes the noise from the other areas of the home, it can be inconvenient. Unless there is a laundry chute, laundry has to be carried up and down stairs which requires more time and energy. In addition, having the washer and dryer in the basement makes it difficult to combine doing the laundry with other household activities.

AMANA

5-17 *A laundry facility should have counter space for sorting and folding clothes.*

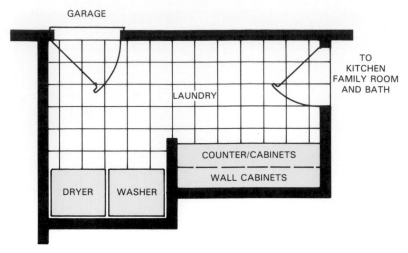

5-18 This laundry doubles as a mud room. Located adjacent to the garage, it is also the service entrance.

If space and expense are not limiting factors, a home could have a room just for laundry. A good location for a laundry room is between the kitchen and the bedroom area.

Size and Arrangement

The ideal amount of space needed for laundry facilities depends on the number and ages of the household. The more family members there are, the more space needed for sorting, folding, and hanging clothes.

The arrangement of the laundry facilities should be such that work flows in an orderly fashion, 5-19. Equipment required in the laundry area includes a sink or laundry tub, a washer, and a dryer. Counter space is needed in the sink area for pretreating stains and in the dryer area for folding clean clothes. Storage for supplies is also necessary. Space should be allowed for ironing and hanging clean clothes.

Washers and dryers range from 24 inches to 34 inches in width. Top opening washers require space above to

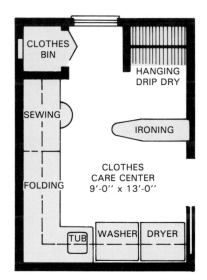

5-19 A well-designed clothes care center has facilities for collecting soiled clothes, sorting, pretreating, washing, drying, ironing, folding, mending, and storing. This center is 13 feet long and 9 feet wide.

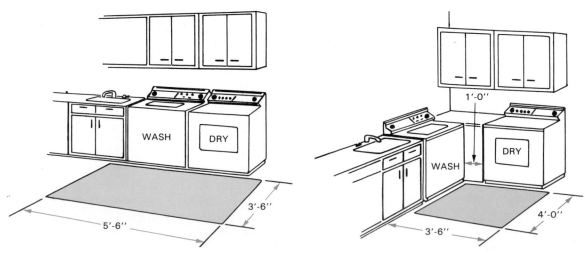

5-20 In the side by side washer-dryer location (left) a 3 ft. 6 in. by 5 ft. 6 in. clearance space is needed. In the right angle location (right), a 3 ft. 6 in. by 4 ft. clearance area is shared by both appliances.

open the door and to remove and insert clothes. A washer and dryer can be placed side by side or at right angles to each other. See 5-20.

In the side by side arrangement, an area 3 1/2 feet deep and 5 1/2 feet long should be clear in front. In the right angle arrangement, a 3 1/2-foot by 4-foot clearance area should be shared by both appliances.

The floor space required for ironing is an area 4 feet, 9 inches wide and 6 feet long. On the working side of the board, a 30-inch space is required, and a 6-inch space is needed on the opposite side. At the point of the ironing board, an 18-inch clearance space is needed.

BASEMENTS

Although basements can be living areas or sleeping areas, they are more likely to be part of the service area. Laundry facilities, a furnace or utility room, a workshop, and storage are often located in a basement, 5-21.

When part or all of a basement is used in a service capacity, an exterior entrance to the basement is helpful. An exterior entrance makes it easier to store tools and equipment that are used outside such as lawnmowers and garden tools. It also helps reduce traffic on the interior stairway.

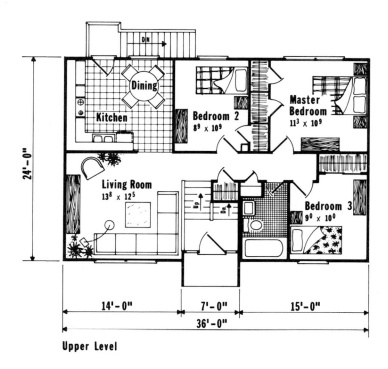

Upper Level

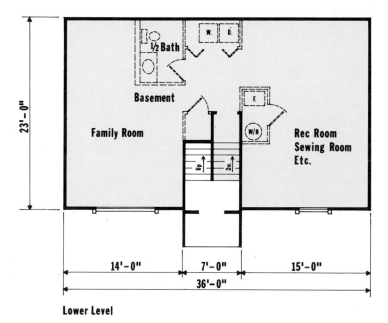

Lower Level

5-21 This small townhouse unit has a full basement with a family room, half bath, sewing or recreation room, utility area, and laundry planned.

The interior stairway to a basement should be located to accommodate the greatest amount of traffic that uses the basement. For instance, if the laundry facilities are the most used area of the basement, then the stairway should lead from the laundry area to the sleeping area. If the recreation room is the most used room in the basement, then the main floor stairway entrance should be centrally located. The basement stairway should be 36 inches or more in width to accommodate large items such as water heaters, furniture, and equipment.

Because of its location and construction, moisture is a primary concern in the basement. Dampness can damage any items stored in the basement, and it makes the environment uncomfortable for people. It can be reduced by providing proper ventilation and by using a dehumidifier. Insulating walls with moisture-resistant insulation also reduces the amount of dampness in a basement. Heating can be used to dry the air and provide a more comfortable environment.

CRAWFORD DOORS, JIM WALTER CO.

5-22 This overhead garage door is wide enough for two cars. Its design blends well with the design of the house.

GARAGES AND CARPORTS

Shelter for an automobile is the fundamental purpose of a garage or carport. However, they may also provide space for storage, laundry equipment, or a workshop.

Location

The garage or carport should be located at the service entrance so packages and groceries can be carried directly from the car into the kitchen. If possible, orientation to the sun and wind should be considered in the location of a garage. In cold climates, a garage located on the north side of a home will help insulate the home against northerly winds. A garage facing the west or south would help shade a home from the sun.

Size and Design

How a garage or carport will be used determines the size garage or carport needed. To store one car, a space 11 by 20 feet is needed. Storage space required for two cars is 21 by 21 feet. These dimensions include the space needed to open car doors and to walk around the car or cars. If other vehicles are to be stored such as campers, bicycles, motorcycles, or lawn mowers, additional space is needed. More space is also needed if a workshop or laundry room is desired.

The design of the garage or carport should complement the design of the home. Garage designs that extend the lines of the eaves can make a house appear larger.

Garage doors also should complement the overall design of the home, 5-22. Various types of doors are available. Overhead doors either slide back into the garage or project out when opened. Doors that swing outward, slide, or fold are also available. A door for a one-car garage needs to be at least 8 feet wide, 9 feet preferably. A door 16 feet wide is needed for a two-car garage. A door 18 feet wide is needed if the approach to the garage is not straight. To increase the clearance between cars, two single

doors may be used. A common height for a garage door is 7 feet.

Taller doors may be necessary for tall vehicles such as recreational vehicles. For greater convenience and safety, automatic garage door openers may be used on almost any type of overhead door.

SERVICE ENTRIES

The service entry usually leads to the work area of the home, namely, the kitchen. Groceries are brought in through this entry. Laundry may be taken in and out this entrance. Also, family members tend to use this entrance instead of the main entry, especially if they are wet or dirty.

Preferably, the service entrance should open into a mud room or utility room instead of directly into the kitchen. This type of room provides space for taking off and storing coats and other outdoor clothing which helps prevent family members from tracking mud, snow, or dirt throughout the home.

SPECIAL PURPOSE ROOMS

After primary areas of the home have been planned, consideration may be given to special purpose rooms. These areas may include a home office, darkroom, sewing room, arts and crafts studio, ham radio room, music room, billiard room, shop, and greenhouse. See 5-23.

When planning a specific area, the amount of space and privacy required should be considered. Some areas may be placed in the corner of another room.

Noise may be a consideration in determining location. A restoration shop or music room may be more functional if located away from bedrooms. Rooms requiring great privacy such as a darkroom should be placed in a remote

5-23 Special purpose rooms can be designed to meet the needs and tastes of any family member.

area to keep traffic away. Adequate storage for materials required should be provided.

Lighting is needed above work areas. Ventilation is an important requirement in a shop where fumes can form and in craft areas where toxic paints are used. Plumbing is a consideration in areas where water is needed such as a darkroom or shop. Electrical outlets should be available in all areas, and a 240-volt outlet should be placed in a shop for major equipment.

STORAGE

Approximately ten percent of the space in a house should be allocated for storage. Each family has different storage needs depending on family size and individual habits.

A good floor plan provides for storage throughout the home. Storage space should be sufficient and convenient. Floor plans can be used to determine how much built-in storage is provided and how much space is available for additional storage. Storage space should be flexible so that changes in space can be made as interests and family size change.

When planning storage for a specific activity, space should be allowed for the larger items first and the smaller items last. In a sewing area, for example, the sewing machine, ironing board, and cutting table are large items that should be planned for first. Smaller items, such as an iron, sleeve board, and pressing ham would be planned for next. See 5-24.

Two types of storage space are used in the home — built-in and freestanding. Built-in storage units are attached permanently to the walls, ceilings, and floors, 5-25. They usually require less space than freestanding units and utilize space more efficiently. However, they limit furniture arrangement possibilities and cannot be moved as easily.

The main advantage of freestanding units is that they can be moved easily. Freestanding units range in size from small, compartmental boxes to large wall units and are available in many styles and finishes, 5-26. Some freestanding units used in the home might include cabinets, shelf units, wall units, wardrobe closets, trunks, and storage racks.

HJ SCHEIRICH CO.

5-24 A well-planned sewing room has large closets and cabinets as well as storage areas for small items.

5-25 Built-in storage units can be designed to hold many different items.

REVIEW QUESTIONS

1. What are the three main work centers of a kitchen? What tasks are performed in each? What equipment is commonly found in each?
2. A designer was shown a floor plan for a kitchen with a 72-inch run of counter space. The designer felt that this was not adequate storage space. Why might this not be enough space?
3. Why is a U-shaped kitchen preferred over a one-wall kitchen? Why would a one-wall kitchen be chosen instead of a U-shaped kitchen?
4. What tasks are performed in the laundry area?
5. What are some possible locations for laundry areas? What are advantages and disadvantages of each?
6. What kinds of entrances are needed for a basement? Where should these be located?
7. Where should a garage be located in warm climates? In cold climates?
8. What size should a one-car garage be? What size door would be needed?
9. What is the best location for a service entrance?
10. What are some types of special purpose rooms that can be included in a house?
11. How does built-in storage differ from freestanding storage? What are advantages and disadvantages of each?

5-26 Free-standing units do not have to look awkward or temporary. Because they move, these units allow greater freedom in decorating.

6 Design

6-1 *The vertical lines of the paneling, cabinets, and bar stools add height to this snack area.*

After studying this chapter, you will be able to:
- Describe the various uses and effects of line, form, texture, and color.
- Evaluate a color according to hue, value, and intensity.
- Use a color wheel to plan various color schemes.
- Evaluate a room design according to its proportions, balance, emphasis, and rhythm.
- Use the elements and principles of design to plan a room design with appropriateness and unity.
- Evaluate the selection and placement of functional and decorative accessories according to the elements, principles, and goals of design.

A well designed home provides a pleasant atmosphere for those who live there. It is both attractive and functional. The study of design may be broken down into three main areas: the elements of design, the principles of design, and the goals of design.

ELEMENTS OF DESIGN

The elements of design are line, form, texture, and color. Each of these elements plays an important role in the overall success of a design, be it the design of a residential structure, a specific room in a home, or a piece of furniture.

Line

Lines give direction to a design. They can be used to emphasize a pleasing element or to disguise an undesirable one. Different types of lines have different effects on design.

Vertical lines lead the eye up, adding height, formality, and strength to a design. They can be seen in tall furniture; striped wallpaper; long, narrow draperies; and columns and pillars. Vertical lines can make a ceiling appear higher and rooms seem more spacious than they actually are, 6-1. They can also make the exterior of a dwelling seem taller and narrower, 6-2.

Horizontal lines lead the eye to the left or right, suggesting informality and restfulness. They can be seen in long, low roofs and in long, low furniture such as sofas and

AMERICAN PLYWOOD ASSOCIATION

6-2 Vertical lines help this long, low building seem taller and narrower.

CALIFORNIA REDWOOD ASSN.

6-3 The horizontal lines of these shelves give this storage unit a low, wide appearance.

chests. Horizontal lines can make buildings, rooms, and furniture seem wider and lower, 6-3.

Diagonal lines suggest action, movement, and excitement. Since diagonal lines can be overpowering and tiring, they should be used sparingly in design. Diagonal lines are present in gable roofs, cathedral ceilings, and staircases. See 6-4 and 6-5.

Curved lines add a softening, graceful effect to designs. See 6-6. However, too many curved lines create a busy look. Curved lines can be seen in doorway arches, ruffled curtains, curved furniture, and accessories.

In design, one type of line should dominate. Others may be added for interest. For example, horizontal lines may dominate a room. Accessories with diagonal or curved lines may be added.

Form

Form is the three-dimensional element of design. The form of a structure, a room, or an object should generally be determined by its function. The phrase, "form follows function," is a guildeline for good design. For example, a chair should be attractive, but its form should allow a person to sit comfortably.

The form of an object may convey a stable or fragile appearance, 6-7. Thinner, more delicate forms appear fragile, even if they are built of sturdy materials.

71

ARMSTRONG WORLD INDUSTRIES, INC.

6-4 *The use of diagonal lines adds interest to this family room.*

ROLSCREEN CO.

6-5 *The diagonal lines of the gable roof are the focal point of this exterior design.*

GRABER

6-6   The curved lines on the chairs and accessories in this room provide a soft, relaxing atmosphere.

Related forms tend to look better together than unrelated forms. A room is more pleasing if the form of dominant pieces is repeated in minor pieces and accessories within a room. See 6-8.

Texture

Texture is the way a surface feels to the touch or the way it *looks* like it would feel if it were touched. Thus texture appeals to sight as well as touch. Often, patterns or colors are used to create the illusion of texture. Ribbed, crinkled, rough, and smooth are some words used to describe various textures.

Texture can affect color by subduing or intensifying it. Smooth surfaces reflect more light than rough surfaces, making them look lighter and brighter. Rough textured surfaces absorb more light, making them look darker and less tense. For instance, red carpet looks darker and duller than red ceramic tile.

FINE WOODWORKING MAGAZINE

THE BENNINGTON CO.

6-7   Both of these chairs are made of sturdy, durable wood. However, the chair on the left appears fragile because of its thin form. The chair on the right appears to be more sturdy because of its thick, stocky form.

DREXEL HERITAGE FURNISHINGS, INC.

6-8 Rectangular forms are used throughout this bedroom. The bed, chest of drawers, nightstand, and desk are all rectangular forms. The bolsters, stereo, wall hangings, and window treatments harmonize with the rectangular forms of the furniture. The forms of the lamps and plants serve as accents.

A balance of textures is needed in a well designed room. A room decorated with the same texture throughout would be monotonous. However, too many different textures can give a design a disjointed and distracting appearance. Most well designed rooms have a dominant texture with accents of contrasting textures, 6-9.

Color

Color is the most exciting tool of the designer. It offers unlimited opportunities for decorating. Color can help to create a mood within a room. It can communicate excitement, romance, or solitude.

The way color influences human behavior has been the subject of many research projects. The results show that certain perceptions are linked to certain colors. Many color perceptions affect the way people feel about a room.

Red is associated with danger and power. It is bold, exciting, and warm. Research has shown red to stimulate the nervous system and increase blood pressure, respiration rate, and heartbeat.

Orange is cheerful, warm, and less agressive than red. It expresses friendliness, courage, hospitality, energy, and hope.

Yellow is cheerful, friendly, and warm. It has traditionally been associated with happiness, sympathy, prosperity, cowardice, and wisdom. Yellow rooms are light and airy.

GEORGIA-PACIFIC

6-9 Rough, earthy textures dominate this living room. The copper fireplace and accessories provide a smooth, shiny accent.

Green is refreshing. The color of nature, it is cool, peaceful, and friendly. Green is often associated with hope, envy, and the "luck of the Irish." Green mixes well with other colors and looks especially good with white.

Blue has the reverse effect of red. It is cool, calm, and reserved. Blue communicates serenity, tranquillity, and formality. However, too much blue in a room can be depressing.

Violet is the color of royalty, dignity, and mystery. It is dramatic, and it works well with other colors.

Black is mysterious, severe, and dramatic. It symbolizes wisdom, evil, and death. Small amounts of black help other colors to appear more vivid.

White is the symbol of youth, freshness, innocence, purity, faith, and peace. Like black, white can make other colors look cleaner and livelier.

When making color decisions for a home, the color preferences of all the family members should be considered. The social area of a home should be decorated in colors that will make all members feel comfortable. Individual color preferences can be used in the sleeping areas of the home.

The color wheel. The color wheel is the best tool for understanding color relationships in design, 6-10. The middle ring of the color wheel consists of three types of colors: primary colors, secondary colors, and intermediate or tertiary colors.

Yellow, blue, and red are the *primary colors*. By mixing, lightening, and darkening the primary colors, all other colors can be made.

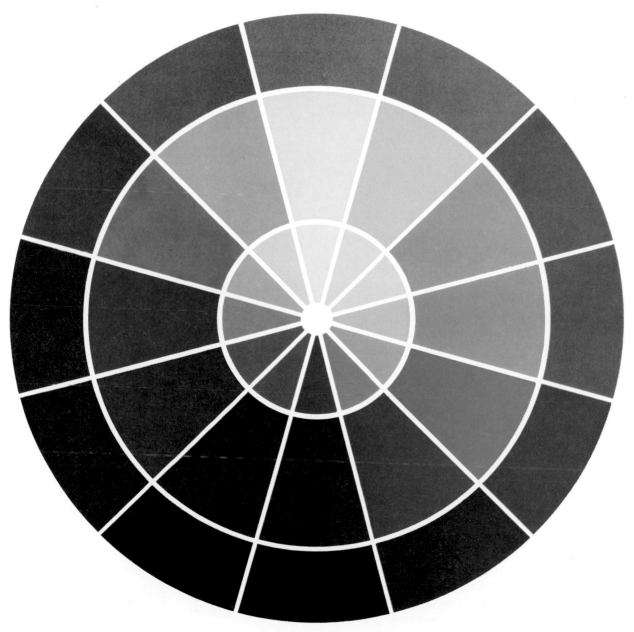

6-10 *The color wheel shows the primary, secondary, and tertiary colors. The middle ring shows the normal values of these colors. The inner ring shows tints of these colors. The outer ring shows shades of these colors.*

Orange, green, and violet are the *secondary colors.* These colors are made by mixing equal amounts of two of the primary colors. Orange is made by mixing yellow and red. Green is made by mixing yellow and blue. Violet is made by mixing blue and red. On the color wheel, each secondary color is positioned between the two primary colors used to make it.

The other colors on the color wheel—yellow-green, blue-green, blue-violet, red-violet, red-orange, and yellow-orange—are the *intermediate colors.* They are made by mixing a primary color with a second color. They are named after the two colors used to make them, with the primary color listed first.

Color characteristics. Each color has three characteristics: hue, value, and intensity. *Hue* is the name of a color such as red, green, or blue-violet. It is the characteristic that makes red different from green. A color may be lightened or darkened, brightened or dulled, but the hue will remain the same.

Value is the lightness or darkness of a hue. The normal values of hues are shown in the middle ring of the color wheel. All colors do not have the same normal value—some are lighter or darker than others. For example, yellow has the lightest normal value of the color wheel, and violet has the darkest.

The value of a hue can be made lighter by adding white. This produces a *tint.* For example, pink is a tint of red. It is made by adding white to red. For lighter tints, more white is added. Tints are shown in the inner ring of the color wheel.

A hue can be made darker by adding black. This produces a *shade.* Maroon is a shade of red. Shades are shown in the outer ring of the color wheel.

A value scale is shown in 6-11. It shows the full range of values for a hue, from the lightest tint to the darkest shade.

Intensity is the brightness or dullness of a color. The hues in the center ring of the color wheel are of normal intensity. The intensity of a hue may be lowered by adding some of its complement. The *complement* of a hue is the color directly opposite it on the color wheel. For example, red can be dulled by adding a small amount of its complement, green. See 6-12. Examples of high intensity colors include hot pink and fire engine red. Examples of low intensity colors include rust and smokey blue.

Warm and cool colors. Colors can be classified as warm or cool. Although the temperature throughout a home may be the same, some rooms may seem warmer or cooler because of the colors used in decorating. See 6-13.

Red, orange, and yellow are warm colors, with red being the warmest. They are considered warm because of their association with warm objects of the same color such as the sun and fire.

Warm colors are also called advancing colors because they make objects appear larger or closer than they really are. They can make a room feel warm and cozy.

Across from the warm colors on the color wheel are the cool colors. Green, blue, and violet are the cool colors.

Cool colors are associated with water, grass, and trees.

Cool colors are called receding colors because they make objects seem smaller and farther away. A small room can be made to look larger if it is decorated in cool colors. Cool colors make a room feel restful and peaceful.

Neutral colors. The neutral colors are white, black, and gray. White is totally absent of color, black is a mixture of all colors, and gray is a combination of black and white. Neutral colors are often used as background colors in rooms because they blend well with other colors.

Brown and beige are considered near neutral colors,

6-11 *The value of a color can be changed by adding different amounts of black or white.*

6-12 *The intensity of a color is lowered by adding some of the color's complement.*

A

DREXEL HERITAGE FURNISHINGS, INC.

B

KIRSCH CO.

6-13 The apparent warmth of a room is affected by the colors used to decorate it. Bedroom A seems cool because blue was used to decorate the room. Bedroom B seems much warmer because of the oranges and yellows in it.

AMERICAN OLEAN TILE

6-14 Near neutrals include brown and beige colors. They are often used in decorating because they blend well with each other and with other colors.

6-14. These also blend well with other colors. However, brown and beige colors are usually based on the hues red, orange, and yellow.

Color Schemes

When certain colors are used together in a pleasing manner, they create what is known as a color scheme or a color harmony. Color schemes provide guidelines for designing and decorating successfully with color. Seven common color schemes are the monochromatic, analogous, complementary, split complementary, triad, double complementary, and neutral color schemes.

A *monochromatic* color scheme is the simplest color harmony. It is based on a single hue of the color wheel, 6-15. Variation is achieved by changing the value and intensity of the hue and by adding accents of neutral colors.

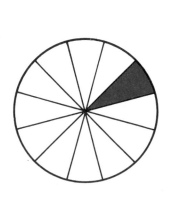

KIRSCH CO.

6-15 Monochromatic color schemes combine various shades and tints of one color. Accents of black or white are usually added.

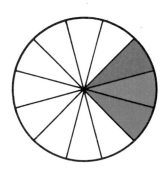

6-16 *This analogous color scheme has blue as the dominant color with blue-green and green as accent colors.*

A monochromatic color scheme can make a room appear larger and unified.

An *analogous* color scheme is made by combining related hues — hues that are next to each other on the color wheel, 6-16. Generally, three to five hues are used to form this color scheme. Examples are green, blue-green, and blue; and red, red-orange, orange, yellow-orange, and yellow. Analogous schemes tend to look best when one color is dominant and smaller amounts of the other colors are used to add interest.

A *complementary* color scheme is made by combining two colors that are directly opposite each other on the color wheel. Complementary (or contrasting) colors make each other look brighter and more intense, 6-17. When red is next to green, the red looks "more red" and the green looks "more green." For less contrast, the values and in-

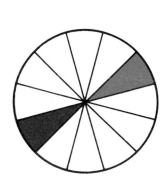

6-17 *Complementary colors intensify each other. This red and green color scheme looks vivid.*

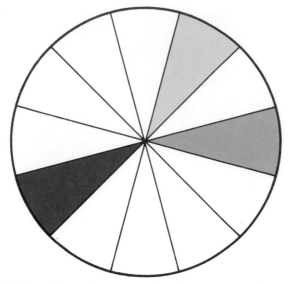

6-18 *The split complementary color scheme uses one hue, such as red, and the two colors beside its complement, such as yellow-green and blue-green.*

tensities of the two colors can be varied. Generally, one color is allowed to dominate, and various values and intensities are used to lessen the contrast.

In the *split complementary* color scheme, one hue is chosen, and the two hues on either side of its complement are used with it. See 6-18. For example, red, yellow-green, and blue-green form a split complementary color scheme. Red would most likely be the dominant color, and yellow-green and blue-green would provide contrast.

A *triad* color scheme is the combination of any three colors that are of equal distance from each other on the color wheel. For example, yellow, blue, and red—the primary colors—form a triad color scheme, 6-19. Any other three colors chosen the same way will also form such a color scheme. The three colors can be used in sharp contrast, or contrast can be lessened by changing values and intensities. Some skill is needed to achieve pleasing triad schemes.

The *double complementary* color scheme uses two complementary schemes together such as green and red with

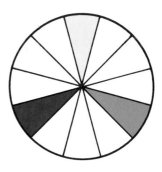

KIRSCH CO.

6-19 *The most popular triad color scheme uses blue, yellow, and red. The color combination gives a lively appearance to this child's bedroom.*

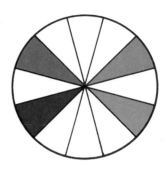

GORDON'S, INC.

6-20 The complementary colors, red and green and blue and orange, are used in this double complementary color scheme.

blue and orange, 6-20. Any combination of pairs may be used as long as each pair is composed of complementary colors.

Neutral color schemes are made by using combinations of black, white, and gray. Shades of brown, tan, and beige may also be used. Touches of accent colors are usually added for interest. See 6-21.

When planning color schemes, keep in mind the following guidelines:

Color schemes look best when one color dominates.

Exposure of a room affects color scheme choice. Rooms that face north or east and receive little sun can be warmed with reds and oranges. Rooms that face south or west and receive sun can be cooled with blues and greens.

Light values and cool hues make rooms appear larger.

Dark values and warm hues make rooms appear smaller.

Large areas look best when covered with colors of low intensity. The larger the area of color, the more intense it appears.

The differences between contrasting colors are emphasized when used side-by-side. For example, light colors appear lighter beside dark colors, and dark colors appear darker beside light colors.

Colors appear different under different lighting conditions. Artificial light softens colors. Colors that appear attractive under artificial light may not be pleasing in daylight.

Surfaces with rough textures make colors appear darker than surfaces with smooth textures.

HJ SCHEIRICH CO.

6-21 This neutral color scheme uses black and white to give this bathroom a crisp appearance. Small accessories provide accent colors.

PRINCIPLES OF DESIGN

Principles of design are guidelines to follow when working with the elements of design. Together, they can be used to create an aesthetically pleasing room design. Proportion, balance, emphasis, and rhythm are the four main principles of design.

Proportion

Proportion or scale is the ratio of one part to another part or of one part to the whole. Uneven proportions, such as 2:3, 3:5, and 5:8, are preferred over even proportions, such as 1:1 and 1:2. For example, a rectangle has more pleasing proportions than a square. A coffee table that is two-thirds the length of a couch is more pleasing than one that is the same length or half the length of the couch. See 6-22.

Furniture and accessories should be in proportion to the room in which they are placed, and they should be in proportion to each other. For example, a large canopy bed would look best in a large bedroom with a high ceiling. A small dining room table would look best with a small light fixture above it.

Objects should be in proportion to people as well as to the room. If a couch is intended for relaxation, it should be long enough for a person to lie on it comfortably. Kitchen counters should be at a proper height for efficient work.

Proportion is influenced by visual size. Two objects may have the same dimensions, but one may appear larger than the other because of its design. For example, a piece of furniture with bold lines, coarse textures, and large patterns appears to be larger than a piece with thin lines, smooth textures, and small patterns. Even though they are the same size, the first piece seems to take up more space in a room. See 6-23. Both the visual size and the actual size of furniture and accessories should be considered when choosing pieces for a room.

The visual size of an object is also affected by its frame of reference. For instance, a sofa with a high back will seem too tall next to a low window. The same couch will seem to be of normal height in a room with higher windows. Curtains with a large floral print may look odd on a small window, but they may look just right on a large picture window.

Balance

The purpose of balance in a design is to project a sense of equilibrium. Balance may be either formal (symmetrical) or informal (asymmetrical).

Formal balance is achieved through the placement of identical objects on either side of a central point, 6-24. This type of balance is used frequently in architectural designs and landscaping as well as in room designs, 6-25. Formal balance gives a quiet, orderly feeling to a room.

Informal balance is the placement of different, but equivalent, objects on either side of a central point. Various forms, textures, and colors can be used together

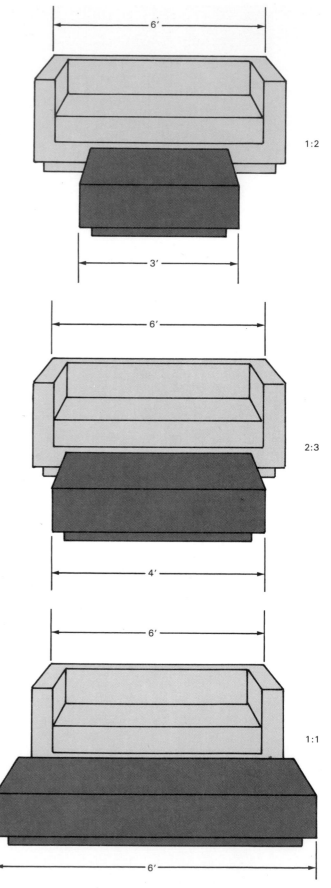

6-22 Objects in a room should be in proportion to each other. The center coffee table/couch combination is in a 2:3 ratio. This is considered more pleasing than a 1:1 or 1:2 ratio.

82

A

SINGER FURNITURE

B

SINGER FURNITURE

6-23 The visual size of an object affects proportion. The furniture in these bedrooms is about the same size. However, the bold lines and patterns in bedroom A give the furniture a large visual size. The furniture in bedroom B has a smaller visual size because of its thin lines and fine pattern.

KNOB CREEK

6-24 Here, formal balance is used to create a pleasing effect. The lamps and pictures on either side of the mirror are the same size and shape. The mirror and plant serve as a central point.

to achieve informal balance. See 6-26. For instance, a large object can be balanced with a few smaller ones. Since informal balance involves the arrangement of varied objects, it usually requires more thought and creativity to achieve than formal balance.

Emphasis

Emphasis refers to the center of attention or interest in a design. It is the feature that repeatedly draws attention. The center of interest in a room is usually a feature such as a fireplace, a work of art, or a dominant piece of furniture. See 6-27. Emphasis is also used in landscaping and exterior design.

To achieve effective emphasis, two guidelines need to be kept in mind. First, the point of emphasis should dominate, but it should not overpower everything else in the room or design. Second, no other features should compete with the focal point.

Rhythm

Rhythm leads the eye from one place to another in a design. Rhythm can be created through repetition, gradation, transition, and radiation.

6-25 Formal balance gives this Georgian house a stately appearance.

CALIFORNIA REDWOOD ASSN.

6-26 The two sides of this room do not mirror each other, but they are balanced. The large couch on the left is balanced by the two small chairs on the right. The lamp and accessories on the left are balanced by the shelf unit on the right.

THE ADAMS CO.

6-27 This unusual fireplace provides a point of emphasis for this room.

6-28 Repetition is used to lead the eye up this staircase. Although each vase is slightly different, the similar patterns of their dried floral arrangements lead the eye from one vase to the next.

Rhythm by *repetition* can be achieved by repeating color, line, form, or texture. See 6-28.

Gradation is rhythm created by a gradual change in color value, from dark to light, or a change in form, from large to small. See 6-29.

Rhythm through *transition* is created by curved lines that carry the eye over an architectural feature, 6-30. It is also used to carry the eye over rounded parts of furniture.

Radiation is rhythm created by lines that flow outward from a central point. It can be found in the lines of a flower arrangement, a light fixture, or the leg supports of a table, 6-31.

GOALS OF DESIGN

The elements and principles of design can be used to meet the goals of design. The goals of design include appropriateness and unity.

Appropriateness

Good design should be appropriate for its intended function and for the lifestyle of the household. For example, the furniture and accessories in a living room should be appropriate for the functions of relaxation, conversation,

THE LANE CO.

6-29 These urns illustrate the principle of rhythm by gradation. The eye is lead from the largest to the smallest.

ROLSCREEN CO.

6-30 The curve of this bay window provides rhythm through transition, leading the eye from one side of the room to the other.

THOMASVILLE FURNITURE

6-31 This dining room set illustrates the principle of rhythm by radiation. The plant leaves, table edges, and chairs all lead the eye outward from the center of the table.

6-32 The furniture and accessories in this room are appropriate for conversing and entertaining.

and entertaining. Comfortable chairs and soft lighting would be appropriate for these functions, 6-32.

Appropriateness for the lifestyle of a family should also be considered. A family with several small children would find durable, easy care furniture and carpeting most appropriate for their living room. A household member who designs pottery as a hobby may find a pottery display case in the living room appropriate. Good design is appropriate for personality, needs, and values of family members.

Unity

Unity is present in a design when all parts of the design look as if they belong together. In a room design with unity, the room is seen as a whole room, not just as a room full of furniture, accessories, colors, and patterns.

Unity is achieved by repeating certain elements of design. A dominant type of line, form, texture, and color,

should be apparent in the design. Contrasting lines, forms, textures, and colors can be used to add interest and variety, but they should not compete with the dominant elements. For example, light browns and beiges may be used throughout a room for unity. Splashes of blue may be used for accent. Curved patterns may be used throughout the room with a few rectangular patterns for accent. See 6-33.

ACCESSORIES IN DESIGN

Accessories complete the total room design. Accessories should reflect the personalities of the household members and give individuality to a design, 6-34. They may be functional, decorative, or both.

The elements, principles, and goals of design should be considered when choosing accessories. Items should repeat or accent the dominant line, form, texture, and color in the room. Accessories should be in proper proportion to other items in the room. Accessories can be used to achieve formal or informal balance. They may be used for emphasis in a design, or they may repeat patterns in other pieces for rhythm. Each accessory should be appropriate, and it should add to the unity of the overall design.

Functional accessories include such items as lamps, mirrors, clocks, screens, and fireplace tools. These items should be chosen and placed for functional purposes first and decorative purposes second. See 6-35. For example, if a lamp for reading is to be selected, only lamps that will provide enough light should be considered. An acceptable style should be chosen from those lamps.

Likewise, a lamp for reading should be placed near a chair or couch, not in a corner away from seating.

Decorative accessories include sculptures, figurines, pottery, crafts, plants, pictures, and other wall hangings. These items should be pleasing to the household members and expressive of their personalities.

Due to their decorative nature, these objects should be placed so that they are enhanced by their surroundings and easily seen. Table tops, shelves, display cases, and individual stands are often used for three-dimensional accessories.

Pictures and wall hangings should be hung carefully so they unify the room's design and their proportions seem

AMERICAN OF MARTINSVILLE

6-33 The goal of unity is met for each element of design in this bedroom. Curved lines are repeated in the furniture, hot tub, and lamp shades. The footstool, books, and mirror provide contrasting straight lines. The rectangular forms of the furniture are contrasted by the rounded hot tub and the vases. Most of the room is heavily textured, but a few smooth textures are used for contrast. The predominantly brown room is accented by the blue screen, hot tub interior, and pillows.

A

GORDON'S, INC.

B

GEORGIA-PACIFIC

6-34 Accessories say a lot about the personality and lifestyle of a household. They may indicate an interest in fine oriental art and cozy conversation (A), or an interest in literature and casual activity (B).

DREXEL HERITAGE FURNISHINGS, INC.

6-35 The brass lamp chosen for this room has a wide shade to provide ample lighting for conversation and reading. Its style and location blend well with the overall design of the room.

pleasing. Unless pictures are large and dramatic enough to be used alone on a wall, they should be grouped with furniture pieces in the room. Space between pictures and furniture should be small enough to make the pictures and furniture look unified. The furniture then serves as an anchor for the pictures, 6-36. A picture without an anchor appears to float on a wall, and it does not appear to be part of the overall design.

Picture groupings should be hung in a unified arrangement. The grouping should be based on one dominant horizontal line and/or one dominant vertical line. See 6-37. Hanging groupings in a stair-step fashion should be avoided; this arrangement carries the eye away from the grouping. One exception is on walls with a diagonal architectural feature, like a stairway.

Spacing between pictures should be small enough to unify the grouping. Even spacing should be used between all the pictures in the grouping.

Groupings of uneven numbers of pictures are more pleasing than groupings of even numbers of pictures. Groupings also tend to be more pleasing if one picture dominates the grouping. For example, one picture that is much larger than the others in the grouping is dominant. One picture showing activity in a group of formal portraits is dominant. Color and shape can also be used for dominance.

CALIFORNIA REDWOOD ASSN.

6-36 The fireplace serves as an anchor for this water color. The picture is in good proportion to the wall and the fireplace.

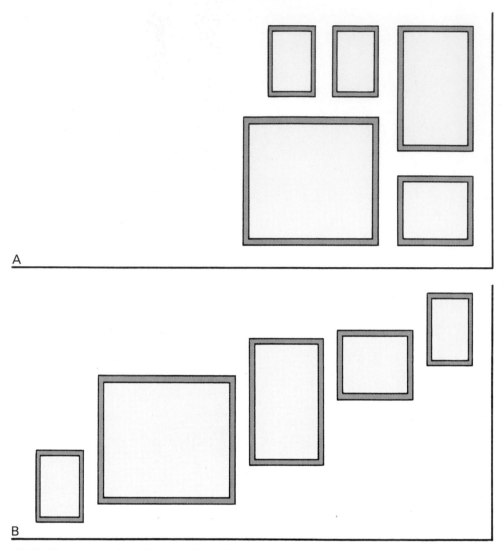

6-37 Picture groupings that are aligned on one or more sides (A) have a pleasing, unified appearance. Groupings that are not aligned (B) lead the eye away from the pictures.

A picture or grouping of pictures should be hung at eye level—with the center of the picture or grouping around 5 or 6 feet from the floor. Pictures and groupings above furniture should be in proportion to the furniture. A picture above a chair or sofa should be placed at least 6 to 8 inches above the furniture. This way, the head of a seated person will not touch the frame.

REVIEW QUESTIONS

1. What are the four elements of design? What guidelines should be followed when using them?
2. In a small bedroom with a high ceiling, would you prefer wallpaper with vertical, diagonal, or horizontal stripes? Why?
3. What effect do curved lines have on design?
4. In design, what is meant by the phrase, "Form follows function"?
5. How can texture affect color?
6. What feelings are created by the colors red, orange, yellow, green, blue, violet, black, and white?
7. Explain the three characteristics of color.
8. What is the difference between a warm color and a cool color? What are some examples of each?
9. A woman in a small apartment with a low ceiling was trying to decide between a tall china closet and low hutch for her dining room. Which would you suggest? Why?
10. How does formal balance differ from informal balance?
11. What are the two main guidelines for achieving emphasis in a room design?
12. What four methods can be used to create rhythm in design?
13. What are two goals of design? How can the elements and principles of design be used to meet the goals of design?
14. How does the selection and placement of functional accessories differ from the selection and placement of decorative accessories?
15. What are two guidelines to follow when hanging pictures above a couch?

7 Wood, Masonry, and Concrete

After studying this chapter, you will be able to:
- List the major characteristics and uses of hardwoods and softwoods.
- Identify the various kinds of wood materials used in residential housing.
- List the main types of wood finishes, and describe their characteristics and uses.
- List and describe the main types of masonry materials used in residential housing.
- Describe the characteristics and uses of concrete, and list types of decorative finishes that can be applied to concrete.

Many different materials are used in a house. Some materials are part of the structure while others are used for furnishings and decoration. The eight families of materials most commonly found in modern dwellings are wood, masonry, concrete, metals, glass, ceramics, plastics, and textiles. Metals, glass, ceramics, plastics, and textiles are discussed in Chapters 8 and 9.

This chapter discusses the basic properties of wood, masonry, and concrete. Some applications of these materials to residential housing are also presented.

WOOD

No other material is comparable to wood in its degree of workability, beauty, strength, durability, and versatility, 7-1. Wood has a higher strength to weight ratio than steel, concrete, or glass. It is easy to fabricate and repair. Wood is also one of the few housing materials that is replenishable.

Wood Classification

Woods are broadly classified as hardwoods and softwoods. *Hardwoods* are deciduous or broadleaf trees. These trees are noted for shedding their leaves at the end of their growing season. *Softwoods* are coniferous or cone bearing trees. These trees typically have needle shaped leaves and do not shed.

Generally, hardwoods are harder than softwoods, but there are exceptions. For example, yellow pine and yew are classified as softwoods, but they are harder than many

HJ SCHEIRICH CO.

7-1 Wood is used in many ways throughout the home. This kitchen has hardwood floors, veneered plywood cupboards, laminated composite board counters, and a ceiling constructed of timber beams and wood planks.

93

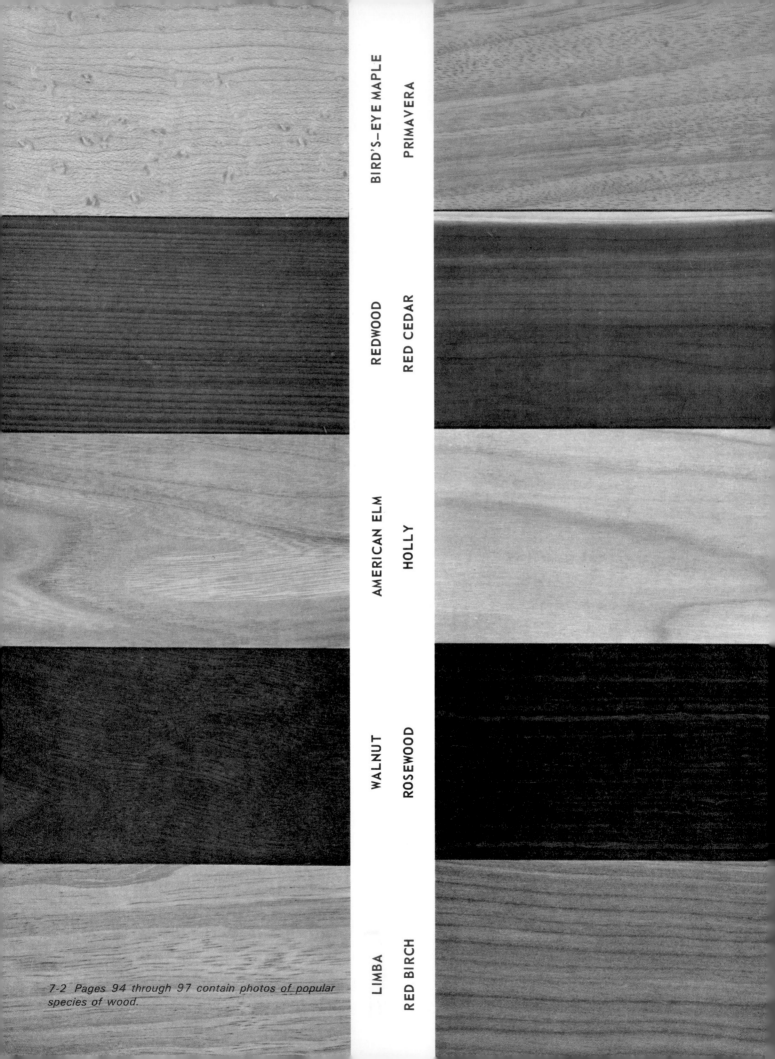

BIRD'S—EYE MAPLE

PRIMAVERA

REDWOOD

RED CEDAR

AMERICAN ELM

HOLLY

WALNUT

ROSEWOOD

LIMBA

RED BIRCH

7-2 Pages 94 through 97 contain photos of popular species of wood.

SATINWOOD

WHITE OAK

WHITE ASH

SUGAR PINE

TULIP

RED GUM

HICKORY

AMARANTH

BASSWOOD

CYPRESS

WORMY CHESTNUT

CHERRY

HEMLOCK

VERMILION

LACEWOOD

BALSA

PONDEROSA PINE

EBONY

BEECH

WILLOW

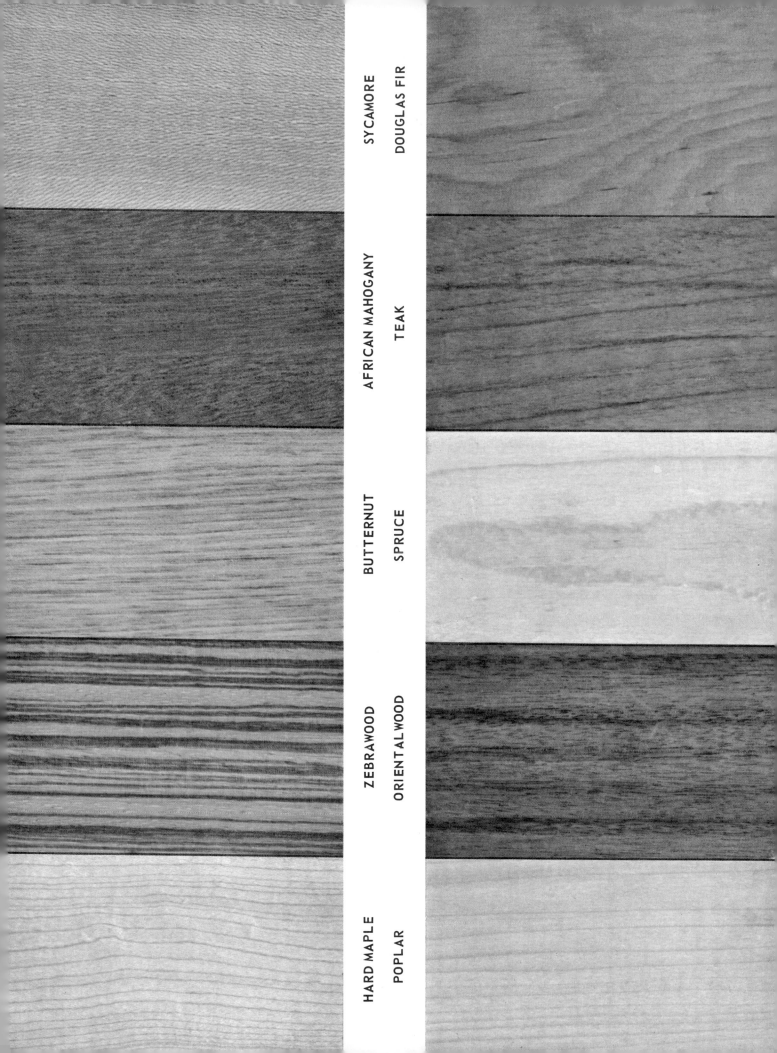

SYCAMORE

DOUGLAS FIR

AFRICAN MAHOGANY

TEAK

BUTTERNUT

SPRUCE

ZEBRAWOOD

ORIENTALWOOD

HARD MAPLE

POPLAR

PHYSICAL PROPERTIES AND USES OF COMMON WOODS

NAME	WOOD CLASSIFICATION	FOREST REGION OF GROWTH	PROPERTIES	USES
Ash, White	Hardwood	Northern and Central U.S.	Hard, creamy white to light brown in color, grain similar to oak, wears well, has medium tendency to warp.	Furniture frames requiring bending, veneer, handles.
Beech, American	Hardwood	Northern and Central U.S.	Hard and strong, white or slightly reddish in color, good for natural finish, medium tendency to warp.	Food containers, furniture, handles, veneer, curved parts, rocker runners, interior parts requiring strength.
Birch, Red	Hardwood	Northern and Central U.S.	Hard, heavy and strong, medium tendency to warp. Sapwood is white, heartwood is dark reddish brown.	Boxes, baskets, furniture, woodenware, flooring, veneer plywoods.
Cedar, Western Red	Softwood	Western U.S. and Alaska	Soft and weak, reddish brown to white in color, close grained, lightweight, easily worked, low shrinkage and warping, resists decay.	Shingles, siding, paneling, novelties, posts.
Cherry, Black	Hardwood	Central U.S.	Strong, durable and hard, light to dark reddish brown in color, close grained, low tendency to warp.	Furniture, carvings, woodenware, veneer.
Cypress, Bald	Softwood	Southern U.S.	Strong, light yellowish brown in color, silver gray when exposed, weathers easily, resists decay, low warpage.	Tanks, vats, gutters, siding, shingles, trims, posts.
Elm, American	Hardwood	Northern, Central, and Southern U.S.	Hard and heavy, light grayish brown tinged with red to dark brown in color, porous, open grained, high shinkage and warpage.	Baskets, boxes, crates, decorative veneers, curved parts of furniture.
Fir, Douglas	Softwood	Western U.S.	Soft, strong and heavy, yellow to reddish brown in color, coarse grained.	Plywood, framing, millwork, cabinets, low cost furniture.
Mahogany, Honduras	Hardwood	Central America	Medium hard and strong, almost white to light brown in color, dense, hard to work, low shrinkage.	Fine furniture, cabinets, veneer.
Maple, Sugar and Hard	Hardwood	Central and Southern U.S.	Hard, heavy and strong, almost white to light brown in color, dense, hard to work, low shrinkage.	Furniture, flooring, handles, woodenware, veneer.
Oak, Red and White	Hardwood	Northern, Central, and Southern U.S.	Hard and strong, workable, pale gray to reddish in color, open grained, carves well.	Furniture, flooring, millwork, handles, woodenware, veneer paneling.
Pine, Eastern White	Softwood	Northern and Central U.S.	Soft, white to cream in color, close grained, uniform, relatively weak, easy to work, medium warping and shrinkage.	Millwork, carvings, veneer, trim, cabinets.
Pine, Sugar	Softwood	West coast	Soft, white to cream in color, close grained, uniform, easy to work, low warping and shrinkage.	Cabinets, carvings, fancy woodwork, trim, doors, windows.
Poplar, Yellow	Hardwood	Eastern U.S.	Moderately soft and weak, white to yellowish brown, uniform texture, easy to work.	Siding, trim, inexpensive furniture, cabinets.
Redwood	Softwood	West Coast (California)	Soft and moderately strong, reddish brown in color, splinters easily, resists rot and decay, weathers to a silver gray.	Construction, millwork, vats, outdoor furniture.
Walnut, Black	Hardwood	Central U.S.	Hard, heavy and strong, light to dark chocolate brown in color, low warpage, good finish.	Fine furniture, veneers, cabinets, paneling.

7-3 These native American woods are used in housing construction and furniture making.

hardwoods. Basswood, balsa, and cottonwood trees are classified as hardwoods, but they have soft wood.

There are an estimated 150,000 species of hardwoods in the world. The species differ in grain pattern, color, strength, and other factors that affect their appearance and use, 7-2. The United States has almost 1200 species of trees. However, only 100 species have much commercial value. The physical properties and uses of several popular American woods are listed in 7-3.

Of the commercially important species in the United States, about 40 are softwoods. Softwoods are strong and resilient, but they do not accept finishes as well as most hardwoods. They are generally used in construction. The remaining 60 species are hardwoods. Oak is the most frequently used of these. Hardwoods tend to be more expensive than softwoods. However, they resist denting and scratching better than softwoods, and their surfaces yield smooth finishes with attractive grain patterns. Hardwoods are most often used to make flooring materials and furniture.

Wood Materials

Wood is defined as the hard, fibrous substance that forms the trunk, stems, and branches of trees. It can be processed to make lumber, plywood, or other wood products used in construction.

Lumber is the product of the sawmill. It is sawed from logs into boards of various sizes. The boards may be resawed or planed to standard dimensions. Resawing and planing also help to give the wood a smooth, even surface. Lumber also may be crosscut to various lengths.

After lumber is cut, it is *seasoned* or dried. This process removes most of the moisture from wood to help prevent shrinking, warping, splitting, and rotting in finished wood products. As moisture is removed, lumber shrinks. Since boards are cut to standard dimensions from green (unseasoned) wood, the actual dimensions of seasoned lumber are smaller than the nominal dimensions. For example, a "two-by-four" is actually about 1 1/2 by 3 1/2 inches when dry.

Lumber is not processed beyond sawing, resawing, planing, crosscutting, and seasoning. It may be used as is or processed further. *Timber,* or lumber that is five inches or larger in width and thickness, is used mainly as support posts or beams. Softwood lumber is frequently used as is for construction of housing, especially the structural framework. It also can be used to produce millwork. *Millwork* is processed lumber such as doors, window frames, shutters, trim, panel work, and molding. Hardwood lumber is generally used to make furniture or to produce millwork.

Plywood is made from thin sheets of wood—called veneers or plys—that are glued together to form a panel. The grain of each ply runs at right angles to the next ply, 7-4. This adds strength to plywood and reduces warping, shrinking, and splitting. The outer layers may be of fine, attractive veneer or of plain wood depending on how plywood is used. Plywood is used in construction,

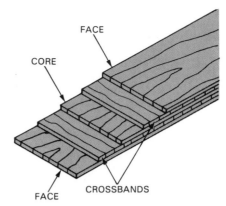

7-4 *Plywood has an odd number of plys with the grain of each ply running at right angles to the next ply.*

especially of floors and walls. It is also used to make furniture and paneling.

Laminated timber is constructed from layers of wood, 7-5. Because layers of wood are used, this type of timber is produced in shapes and sizes that are difficult to achieve with solid timber. Arches and beams are custom fabricated, and they are bonded together with glues stronger than the wood itself. The grain of each board in laminated timber runs in the same direction rather than at right angles to each other.

Composite board is fabricated from wood particles into panels. It may be covered with a thin veneer for some uses. The most common types of composite board are hardboard and particleboard. *Hardboard* is made from refined wood fibers that are pressed together. One or both sides may be smooth. *Particle board* is made from wood flakes, chips, and shavings that are bonded together with resins or adhesives. Panels can be produced in larger thicknesses than hardboard panels. Also, particle board is more readily covered with veneers and laminates than hardboard.

Composite board is less expensive than plywood, but it is strong enough to be used in many of the same ways.

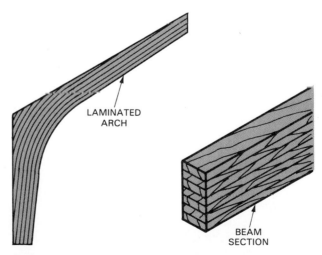

7-5 *Laminated timbers can support wide spans because of their construction.*

Left uncovered, composite board is suitable for floor underlayment and wall materials as well as for hidden parts of furniture. Laminated and veneered particle board is popular for doors, counters, and exposed parts of furniture.

Wood Finishes

Most woods require a protective finish or treatment to retain their beauty and usability. Finishes and treatments keep wood surfaces clean. They reduce the hazards of rot, decay, weathering, and insect damage. They also help keep the moisture content of wood constant so that wood will not warp, crack, or shrink. Typical finishing materials include bleaches, fillers, stains, clear finishes, and paints. One material or a combination of materials may be used to finish wood.

Bleaches. Bleaching removes the natural color of wood to give a pale or weathered appearance. It also evens the color of wood pieces with dark and light portions. Various acids or chlorine compounds are used to bleach wood. Bleaching must be done carefully, or the compounds may damage the wood. Instructions for using bleach should be followed carefully. Bleached wood may be treated with other finishes or left unfinished.

Fillers. Some types of wood, called *open grain wood,* have large, open pores. These include such woods as walnut, oak, and mahogany. Filler is often applied to open grain wood to even the surface. This prevents stains and other finishes from accumulating in the pores so that the finished surface has an even color and a smooth texture. Paste filler is the most common type used, but liquid and latex fillers are also available.

Stains. Stains add color to wood without masking grain patterns. They may be oil, alcohol, or water based. Oil based stains may be classified as pigmented or penetrating stains.

Pigmented oil stains contain insoluble pigments (like those in paint) that are permanent in color. They coat, but do not penetrate, the wood's surface. If applied too heavily, pigmented stain will obscure the wood grain. This product is especially useful in disguising the irregular grain pattern of softwood and in covering trim to match stained siding. See 7-6.

Penetrating oil stains, alcohol-based stains, and water-based stains contain soluble, organic dyes that penetrate the wood's surface. They have a clean, transparent appearance compared to pigmented stains, 7-7. They produce brighter colors but fade more quickly than pigmented stains. Penetrating stains should be properly sealed, or their color is likely to bleed into succeeding coats of varnish or lacquer. Penetrating stains are most commonly used on furniture and cabinets, but they may be used on any wood surface where a clear, bright color is desired.

Clear finishes. Clear finishes are used to protect wood, to enhance the grain pattern of wood, and to give a luster or gloss to the wood's surface. They may be used on plain, stained, or bleached wood. One type or a combination of clear finishes may be used. Varnish, shellac, laquer,

THERMA-TRU, DIVISION OF LST CORP.

7-6 Pigmented stains cover wood, but they allow some of the wood grain pattern to show through.

oil, wax, and other, synthetic finishes are the most common clear finishes.

Many kinds of *varnishes* are available for use as top coats on wood surfaces. Varnish is used to emphasize wood grain and deepen wood tones, 7-8. Different types are available to give from a slight luster to a glossy shine. Varnish is most often used on wood furniture and floors. Pieces with a good finish have several thin coats of varnish rather than one or two thick coats.

The two main types of varnishes are *spirit* varnishes and *oleoresinous* varnishes. Spirit varnish is made of a resin or gum dissolved in alcohol. Oleoresinous varnish contains a gum or resin dissolved in a drying oil.

Shellac is technically a spirit varnish, but it is designed specifically for sealing wood. It changes the character of wood very little, but it prevents moisture from entering or leaving wood. Shellac is used on stained wood to prevent stain from bleeding into the topcoat. It is used on plain wood to prevent topcoats from penetrating into wood. However, it does not provide an acceptable top coat if used alone.

Lacquer is a complex finishing material containing nitrocellulose. It forms a tough, durable surface for wood. Different formulas of lacquer are available to produce from a low gloss to a high gloss. Lacquer based sealers are also available; these should be used under lacquer finishes.

A   B   AMERICAN PLYWOOD ASSN.

7-7 Penetrating oil stains (A) are more transparent than pigmented oil stains (B).

Lacquer is used on furniture and other woodwork. It is especially popular as a finish for oriental style pieces because of its ability to produce a very high gloss. See 7-9. Lacquer is not intended for outdoor woodwork.

Oil finishes penetrate wood to bring out grain pattern, darken the wood, and produce a soft luster. They are used mainly on fine wood furniture. The most commly used oils are boiled linseed oil and tung oil thinned with turpentine. Between five and thirty coats are needed to produce a good finish. Oil must be reapplied periodically to renew the wood's surface.

Wax may be used over other finishes to produce a smooth luster or shine. It also may be used on plain wood to penetrate the surface, enrich the grain pattern, and darken the wood. Several kinds of wax are available from animal, vegetable, and mineral sources. Popular waxes include carnuba, beeswax, candelilla, Japan wax, and mineral waxes. Wax finishes are not very durable; they must be renewed frequently.

Many new finishes are made with synthetics for superior durability. Some have already begun to replace older finishes. *Polyurethane* is one synthetic, clear finish that is especially popular as a floor finish. It dries more quickly than traditional varnish, and it resists wear and abrasions well. It also has high resistance to chemicals, alcohol, and grease.

DREXEL HERITAGE FURNISHINGS, INC.

7-8 Varnish enhances wood grain patterns and gives a luster to wood.

DREXEL HERITAGE FURNISHINGS, INC.

7-9 Lacquer finishes are popular for oriental furniture.

Epoxy resin is another excellent floor finish because of its durability. It also may be used for furniture and exterior woodwork. Other synthetic coatings include polyester, polyamide, vinyl, acrylic, and silicone coatings. Most of these have excellent properties, but some are currently limited to narrow applications.

Paints. Paints are colored coatings that form opaque films. They contain pigment suspended in a liquid medium called a vehicle. The pigment provides color and hiding power. The vehicle provides the proper consistency for brushing, rolling, or spraying. A binder is also added to paint. This bonds pigment particles together to form a cohesive film during the drying process.

Paint is most commonly chosen to finish woods that do not have natural grain beauty such as pine, gum, poplar, and fir. It is used frequently to cover exterior wood siding and trim. Some homes also have painted interior wood doors and molding, 7-10. Although paint is used on some Early American and early Scandanavian styles of furniture, 7-11, most modern furniture is stained.

Paints can be oil or water based. They may be designed for interior or exterior use. When wood is covered with paint, no other finishing material is needed. Enamel is a special kind of paint made by mixing pigments with varnishes or laquers to produce a hard, smooth, long-lasting finish. Enamel is especially useful for surfaces that receive much wear.

CHAMPION INTERNATIONAL CORP.

7-10 *Paint is sometimes used to cover wood moldings, windows, and doors in homes.*

WESTERN WOOD PRODUCTS ASSN.

7-11 *Painted furniture captures the flavor of early furniture in Scandinavian countries.*

7-12 Brick is a popular building material because of its strength and ease of maintenance.

MASONRY

Through the years, the variety of masonry materials used in housing has greatly increased. Dozens of new shapes, textures, colors, and applications are now available. For example, brick alone is made in at least 10,000 different shape, color, and texture combinations. Masonry materials have grown in popularity because they are versatile, durable, and beautiful. Although masonry construction is often more expensive than wood construction, masonry products generally require less maintenance and last longer. The materials used in masonry construction can be classified as structural clay products, concrete masonry units, glass block, and stone.

Structural Clay Products

Structural clay products, sometimes called burned clay products, are made from clay or shale. These materials are made naturally as rock weathers. Shale is very dense and harder to remove from the ground than clay. Therefore shale products are more costly. Structural clay products may be divided into three main groups: brick, tile, and architectural terra cotta.

Brick. Brick is fireproof, weather-resistant, and easy to maintain. It is popular for fireplaces, chimneys, walls, and floors. See 7-12. The four classes of brick most commonly used in residential housing are *building or common brick, facing brick, paving brick,* and *firebrick.*

Building brick is used mainly as a structural material where durability and strength are more important than appearance. Facing brick is used on exposed surfaces where appearance is more important, 7-13. Paving brick is a harder brick that is highly resistant to abrasion and moisture absorption. It is used to pave walks and

7-13 Facing brick is used where an attractive finish is desired.

Unit Designation	Nominal Dimensions, in.			Manufactured Dimensions using 3/8 in. mortar joints		
	t	h	l	t	h	l
Standard Modular	4	2 2/8	8	3 5/8	2 1/4	7 5/8
Engineer	4	3 1/5	8	3 5/8	2 13/16	7 5/8
Economy 8 or Jumbo Closure	4	4	8	3 5/8	3 5/8	7 5/8
Double	4	5 1/3	8	3 5/8	4 15/16	7 5/8
Roman	4	2	12	3 5/8	1 5/8	11 5/8
Norman	4	2 2/3	12	3 5/8	2 1/4	11 5/8
Norwegian	4	3 1/5	12	3 5/8	2 13/16	11 5/8
Economy 12 or Jumbo Utility	4	4	12	3 5/8	3 5/8	11 5/8
Triple	4	5 1/3	12	3 5/8	4 15/16	11 5/8
SCR brick	6	2 2/3	12	3 5/8	2 1/4	11 5/8
6-in. Norwegian	6	3 1/5	12	5 5/8	2 13/16	11 5/8
6-in. Jumbo	6	4	12	5 5/8	3 5/8	11 5/8
8-in. Jumbo	8	4	12	7 5/8	3 5/8	11 5/8

7-14 Bricks are available in a variety of sizes.

driveways. Firebrick is used for places that become very hot. Examples are the inner linings of fireplaces, of brick ovens, and of outdoor barbecues.

Bricks are available in a variety of sizes. The lengths of most newer bricks are based on a module of four inches, although some older styles of brick are not. Common nominal lengths are eight or twelve inches. A list of common brick sizes is shown in 7-14.

Like wood, bricks are smaller in actual size than in nominal size. The nominal size of a brick includes the brick's actual dimensions plus the thickness of mortar used in a wall built with that brick. Nominal dimensions make it easier to determine how many bricks are needed to build a wall of a certain size. For example, if a wall is to be nine feet long and bricks with a nominal length of twelve inches will be used, nine bricks will be needed to form the length of the wall.

About 99 percent of all brick produced is in the color range of reds, buffs, and creams. Colors vary with the chemical makeup of the clay and the time and temperature used to fire the brick. Various textures of the brick surface are created by the method used to cut and mold the brick. The two most common finishes are a smooth surface produced by water (water-struck brick) and a sand-paper like surface produced by sand (sand-struck brick).

The appearance, durability, and strength of brick construction depends largely upon the *bond* used. The term bond refers to three different types of bonds. The *structural bond* is the way bricks are interlocked to provide support and strength. The *pattern bond* is the pattern formed by the masonry units and mortar joints on the exposed parts of construction. The *mortar bond* is the adhesion of mortar to masonry. A wide variety of designs is possible using different structural, pattern, and mortar bonds.

Mortar is used between masonry units to bond units together and seal spaces between them. It also is used to compensate for slight differences in the sizes of masonry units. Mortar joints can provide a decorative effect in the masonry wall, 7-15. The seven main styles of mortar joints are shown in 7-16.

Hollow masonry. Hollow masonry may be classified as hollow brick or hollow clay tile. Hollow brick has the appearance of brick in a finished wall. Both have less cross

7-15 Extruded mortar joints give a brick wall a rustic appearance.

7-17 Concrete building bricks have the appearance of clay brick, but they are lighter in weight and less expensive.

sectional area than solid bricks. Though the faces are solid, holes make up 25 to 40 percent of the unit's total mass. This makes hollow units lighter, easier to handle, and less expensive to transport than solid brick. Also, larger units can be used because of their light weight.

Like brick, clay tile is available in structural and facing units. The units are used like brick; however, special construction may be necessary to make hollow clay tile construction as structurally sound as brick construction. Clay tile is produced in interesting shapes for use in decorative masonry screens.

Architectural terra cotta. Architectural terra cotta is a custom-made product that can be produced in many shapes and colors. It is expensive and difficult to find, making it uncommon for modern homes. However, some older homes have masonry trim and chimneys of terra cotta. Terra cotta may be a desirable construction material for remodeling and restoring these homes.

Concrete Masonry Units

Concrete masonry units have become a popular housing material for both above ground and basement construction. Concrete masonry is less expensive than brick and fairly lightweight. It is also fire and weather resistant, and it requires little maintenance. Over 700 different concrete units are made throughout the United States. They may be classified as concrete brick, concrete block, and special units.

Concrete brick. The two main types of concrete brick are *building brick* and *slump brick.* Concrete building brick is similar in size, function, and appearance to clay brick. See 7-17. Slump brick or block are produced from a wet mixture which causes the bricks to sag or slump when removed from their mold. This results in an irregular face with the appearance of stone, 7-18.

Concrete block. Most of the concrete masonry units produced are concrete block. They are used mainly for foundation and basement walls. In some sections of the country, they are used for exterior walls as well. Concrete

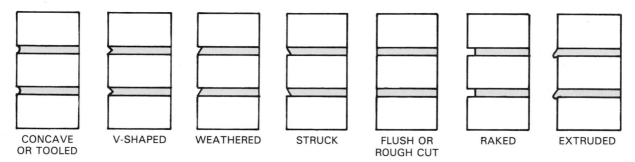

| CONCAVE OR TOOLED | V-SHAPED | WEATHERED | STRUCK | FLUSH OR ROUGH CUT | RAKED | EXTRUDED |

7-16 Several styles of mortar can be used in brick construction.

7-18 Slump brick has the appearance of stone.

7-19 Concrete block has great support strength.

block may be solid or hollow. Most types are capable of supporting heavy loads, 7-19.

Concrete blocks are generally produced in larger sizes than concrete or clay bricks. The most common size is 8 by 8 by 16 inches (nominal size). Half blocks and special application blocks are available for special uses.

Different pattern and mortar bonds can be used with concrete block to produce decorative effects. The most common patterns for concrete block are the running bond and the stacked bond, 7-20. For decorative effects, blocks may be projected from the surface. See 7-21.

Special units. Many types of concrete block are designed for special purposes. Most have a more decorative finish than ordinary concrete block, but some have special, functional uses.

Decorative units include ribbed, fluted, and stri-faced units. These have parallel ridges or grooves that form patterns when used in a wall. Split-faced units are made by fracturing units to produce a rough, stone-like surface, 7-22. Other types of blocks have more complex designs in a variety of patterns and colors.

Faced blocks are both decorative and functional. They have a ceramic type glaze finish on their face. This surface is less porous than concrete, making faced block more stain resistant and easier to clean than standard concrete block. Faced block is used mainly in kitchens, schools, and hospitals.

Screen blocks are often used for outdoor fences and walls. They have an open design to provide privacy and ventilation, 7-23.

Sound blocks have special cavities designed to absorb sound. They are useful for interior walls of noisy areas.

Glass Block

Glass blocks are hollow units of clear, rippled, or frosted glass. They are *partially evacuated,* meaning that some of the air has been removed from them to prevent condensation and improve insulative value. Standard glass block units are produced in 6, 8, and 12-inch squares. Custom made sizes are also available.

Glass blocks are often used in masonry walls where natural lighting is desirable, 7-24. They are more private and secure than standard windows. They are frequently

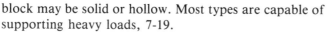

RUNNING BOND

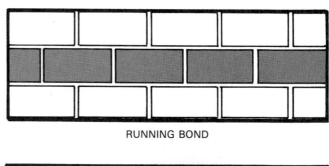

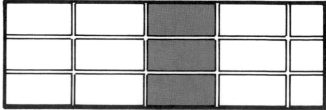

STACKED BOND

7-20 Concrete block is usually laid in the running bond or the stacked bond.

PORTLAND CEMENT ASSN.

7-21 Decorative effects can be produced by projecting concrete blocks.

PORTLAND CEMENT ASSN.

7-23 Screen blocks provide privacy but allow ventilation.

PORTLAND CEMENT ASSN.

7-22 Split-faced concrete block has a rough, stone-like appearance.

PITTSBURGH CORNING CORP.

7-24 Glass block is stronger than pane glass, but it allows light to enter a room.

PITTSBURGH CORNING CORP.

7-25 Glass block is popular for bathrooms, where security and privacy is desirable.

used in place of basement, entryway, and bathroom windows, 7-25. Glass blocks are also useful as decorative screens.

Stone

Stone is an ancient building material, once used as the main structural component of houses. Today it is almost always used in a nonstructural application — for facing, veneer, or paving. See 7-26. The varied color and texture of stone provide visual interest. Stone is fireproof and resistant to decay, and it gives a feeling of permanence and stability. Stone is, however, an expensive material. It is also more difficult to use in building, causing more expensive labor costs.

Several types of natural stone are commonly used in housing structures. They include granite, sandstone, limestone, marble, and slate. Manufactured stone and terrazzo are two other stone materials used in residential housing.

Natural stone. Granite is a hard, durable stone varying in color from almost white to black. It also can be found in shades of pink, green, and yellow. Fine granite has a salt and pepper pattern, 7-27. It may be given a smooth polish or left coarse. Granite is used for table tops, window sills, building stones, steps, paving, and wall veneers.

Sandstone is composed mainly of quartz grains cemented together with silica, lime, or iron oxide. Some sandstone is porous; it is prone to dampness and has a poor insulative value. It may require a special treatment if it is used in cold regions. Colors are in the brown, tan, and rust ranges, and texture ranges from smooth to granular. Popular varieties include bluestone, brownstone, silica sandstone, and lime sandstone. Sandstone is used for building stone, trim, fireplace hearths, decorative pieces, and wall veneers.

Limestone consists mainly of the mineral calcite and compact shells or crystalline rocks, 7-28. It varies widely in color from white to dark grays and tans. Probably the best known type of limestone is Bedford Limestone from Bedford, Indiana. Limestone weathers more rapidly in humid climates than in dry climates. It is used for building stones, fireplaces, window sills, trims, and ornamentation.

Marble is an expensive, luxurious looking stone formed from recrystallized limestone. It may be white, yellow, brown, green, black, pink, or a mixture of several colors, 7-29. Marble is hard and durable, but not as durable as granite. Therefore, it is used more for interior applications. Marble is generally polished for a smooth, shiny

7-26 Stone construction adds variety and interest to a house.

THE ADAMS COMPANY

7-27 Unpolished granite has a rough texture. The colors are usually in a salt and pepper pattern with some crystalline formation throughout the stone.

7-28 Limestone has a fine grain, giving it a smooth appearance.

PORTLAND WILLIAMETTE CO.

7-29 Marble is available in a variety of patterns and colors. This room has a fine, pink marble fireplace.

surface. It is used for wall veneers, floors, table tops, bath fixtures, sculpture, and landscape chips, 7-30.

Slate is a hard, somewhat brittle stone formed from compressed clay or shale. It is frequently blue-gray in color, but it may be green, red, brown, or black. Slate is split into sheets so that the surface often has patterned grooving. Slate is used mainly for flooring stones and roofing shingles, 7-31.

Manufactured stone. Manufactured stone is a veneer made from a lightweight concrete to give the appearance of natural stone construction, 7-32. Simulated stone also can be produced from fiberglass. It is colorfast and

weatherproof. Manufactured stone is available in several colors and textures for interior and exterior use.

Manufactured stone may be applied over stucco, concrete block, brick, cast concrete, or any other untreated masonry surface which is rough enough to provide a good mechanical bond. It may be applied over other wall surfaces such as plaster or wood, but special preparation of the wall is needed. Stone can be cut to various shapes as needed.

Terrazzo. Terrazzo is a very old material composed of marble chips bonded together with cement. It is expensive, but durable. It may be cast in place or precast into

VERMONT CASTINGS, INC.

7-30 An Italian marble fireplace and a white marble floor add elegance to this living room.

7-31 *Slate floors have a sleek appearance and are easy to maintain.*

7-32 *Manufactured stone looks like real stone, but it is lighter in weight and easier to use.*

desired shapes. The main use of terrazzo is as a floor finish. It is generally ground and polished to a smooth surface for interior floors, 7-33. Exterior patios and pathways are generally left rough, 7-34. Terrazzo with a rough surface is called rustic terrazzo. Terrazzo has become a popular material for precast shower receptors, window sills, stair treads, and wall veneers.

Concrete

Almost any home has some concrete in its structure. Concrete is used for footings, foundations, exterior walls,

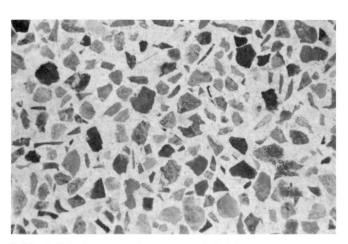

7-33 *Polished terrazzo has a smooth finish.*

PORTLAND CEMENT ASSN.

7-34 Rustic terrazzo is used for exterior applications.

floors, walks, and driveways, 7-35. Before concrete hardens—when it is in *plastic* form—it can be formed into unlimited patterns and textures. Hardened concrete is economical, tough, weather resistant, and long lasting.

7-35 Concrete is most commonly used for foundations and walks, but it also can be used for exterior walls.

Concrete is made from a mixture of portland cement, fine aggregate (sand), coarse aggregate (gravel or crushed stone), and water. Other materials may be added for special uses. The proportion of ingredients in a concrete mix determine its plastic and hardened qualities. Plastic concrete should be workable, consistent, and easy to finish. Hardened concrete should be strong, watertight, and wear resistant.

A wide variety of decorative finishes can be incorporated into concrete during construction. Decorative concretes include colored concrete, exposed aggregate concrete, and concretes with textured finishes or geometric patterns.

Colored concrete. Concrete may be colored using one of three methods. Color may be mixed into the dry batch before the concrete is mixed. It may be added to a top coating of concrete placed on a regular concrete bed. Or, color may be added to a plastic concrete slab just before it is smoothed.

Exposed aggregate concrete. Exposed aggregate is one of the most popular decorative finishes for concrete. Aggregate (such as pebbles or stones) may be chosen in an unlimited variety of colors and textures. Aggregate may be worked into the surface of poured cement, or it may be mixed into cement which is then poured and washed to expose the aggregate. Exposed aggregate surfaces provide slip resistance as well as an attractive, sturdy finish.

PORTLAND CEMENT ASSN.

7-36 Mortar can be applied to concrete to produce a travertine finish.

PORTLAND CEMENT ASSN.

7-37 Stamps can be used to give concrete the appearance of tile.

Textured finishes. Textured finishes may be produced on concrete slabs used for walls or floors while they are still wet. Slabs may be textured by using a broom, by putting rock salt on the surface to produce cavities, or by applying a dash coat of mortar to the surface, 7-36. Other methods can be used to produce more textures.

Geometric patterns. An endless variety of geometric patterns can be stamped, sawed, or scored into a concrete surface. Stone patterns are popular. The patterns of brick or tile may be applied with a stamping tool, 7-37. Wood or metal divider strips can be used to form patterns. To resist decay, wood strips should be of pressure treated lumber.

REVIEW QUESTIONS

1. How does a hardwood differ from a softwood? How do these differences affect the use of hardwoods and softwoods?
2. What steps are used to process wood into lumber? How is lumber used?
3. How does seasoning affect wood?
4. Why are plywood and composite board becoming more common than solid wood?
5. Would pigmented or penetrating stain be more common for use on oak furniture? Which would be more common for yellow pine siding?
6. How does shellac differ from regular varnish? Can either be used alone on wood?
7. What qualities make masonry products popular building materials?
8. How does mortar function in masonry construction?
9. What options are available for producing a decorative wall from concrete masonry?
10. What types of stone are available for use in residential housing? How are these most commonly used?
11. List the kinds of decorative finishes available to be used on concrete.

8 Metals, Glass, Ceramics, and Plastics

After studying this chapter, you will be able to:
- List the main properties and housing applications of iron, steel, aluminum, copper, brass, bronze, and lead.
- Describe the main properties of glass, and list the different types of glass products that are used in housing.
- List the main properties and housing applications of ceramics.
- Identify plastic products used in housing.

Metals, glass, ceramics, and plastics are used extensively in homes. They have unique characteristics that make possible a variety of applications. They are important materials although they are not used to the same extent in structures as wood, masonry, and concrete. These materials may be used in construction, furniture, appliances, and accessories. This chapter discusses the characteristics and applications of metals, glass, ceramics, and plastics.

METALS

Over the years, the amount of metal used in residential structures has increased at a steady rate. Today's average "wood" home contains about 8,000 pounds of various metals. This doesn't seem possible until you begin listing some of the metal products used in a residence. Such a list may include the main supporting beam of a house, wood and masonry reinforcements, water pipes, heating ducts, electrical wiring, roofing materials, gutters, nails, plumbing hardware, appliances, window frames, and doors. Cooking utensils, furniture, tableware, and other accessories could also be included.

Metals are versatile housing materials because they can be shaped in so many ways. They can be cast into complex shapes, rolled into sheets, extruded into standard shapes, machined, welded, bent, sawed, drilled, hammered, and spun. Metals are avaliable in a variety of natural colors. They can be coated with many materials for a wider variety of colors and for added protection. Metals are also strong, decorative, and good conductors of heat and electricity.

Although hundreds of different metals and *alloys* (mixtures of metals) are produced today, not all of them are used in residential housing. The seven metals most commonly used in housing are iron, steel, aluminum, copper, brass, bronze, and lead.

Iron and Steel

Iron and the iron-containing alloy steel are frequently used in the housing industry. Pure metallic iron is soft, *ductile* (able to be drawn into wire), and easily shaped. However, it is too weak for most uses. The addition of carbon gives iron a high level of strength, corrosion resistance, and wear resistance. Iron with carbon added also has great resistance to warping and cracking at high temperatures.

Two types of iron are used in the housing industry. They are *cast iron* and *wrought iron*. Cast iron—made of iron and 2 to 3.75 percent carbon—is melted in a blast furnace and cast into different shapes. It is used for wood-burning stoves, bathtubs, sinks, skillets, sewer lines, waste disposal systems, and gas pipes, 8-1. Wrought iron is nearly pure iron that is worked into various shapes. It is used in ornamental lawn furniture, lighting fixtures, fences, and porch railings.

Steel contains elements other than iron to make it stronger, more ductile, more *malleable* (able to be formed into sheets), and less brittle than pure iron. One negative aspect of steel is that it corrodes. However, elements such as copper and chromium may be mixed with steel to increase corrosion resistance. Steel is used to make I-beams, appliances, cabinets, bathtubs, sinks, knife blades, and cooking utensils.

Copper-bearing steel is steel with copper added to its mixture for improved corrosion resistance. It is used for sheet metal products such as siding, roofing products, and flashing (used on roofs at joints to prevent leaking), 8-2.

Weathering steel produces a protective oxide coating that resists rust and corrosion. The oxide coating formed is a rusty brown color. Weathering steel is generally used where accessibility is difficult, such as siding on multi-family structures. Also, it is used where the rust color is desirable for architectural reasons, such as on a part of a roof to provide an accent.

8-1 *Wood burning stoves are most often made of cast iron because iron does not warp or crack at high temperatures.*

Stainless steel is steel with chromium added to its mixture. It is hard and corrosion resistant over a wide temperature range. Stainless steel can be scoured over and over and maintain a pleasant appearance. Structurally, stainless steel is used for gutters, downspouts, architectural trim, window sills, railings, tubings, and pipes. Interior items made of stainless steel may include cooking

8-2 *Roof flashing is often made of copper-bearing steel because of its constant exposure to moisture.*

utensils, eating utensils, sinks, ranges, appliances, counter tops, and furniture, 8-3.

Stainless steel is more expensive than carbon steel. However, it is a better material for frequently-used items because it resists corrosion and tarnish, maintains a bright and shiny appearance, and holds a sharp edge longer than carbon steel.

8-3 *Stainless steel sinks are easy to maintain. They retain their original shine and do not show scratches over the years.*

Aluminum

Aluminum has been produced since the 1800's, but it has been accepted as a construction material only in the last fifty years. About 300 pounds of aluminum are used in a typical residence today. Aluminum's unique combination of properties make it one of the most versatile metals. Aluminum is lightweight and highly resistant to corrosion. It is an excellent conductor of electricity and a good reflector of heat and light. It can be easily formed into many shapes, and it is receptive to many finishes. Finishes may be added for decoration or for extra corrosion resistance. Some alloys of aluminum are even stronger than structural steel.

The three main methods of processing aluminum are extruding, casting, and rolling. Extruded aluminum is heated to a plastic state and then forced through a die opening to produce a desired shape. This process provides great flexibility of design shape and accurately sized, high quality aluminum products. The most common use of extruded aluminum is for window and door frames, 8-4. Louvers, railings, grilles, solar collectors, and builder's hardware such as door and window hinges can also be made of extruded aluminum.

Cast aluminum products are made by pouring hot metal into molds. Cast aluminum is used for decorative panels,

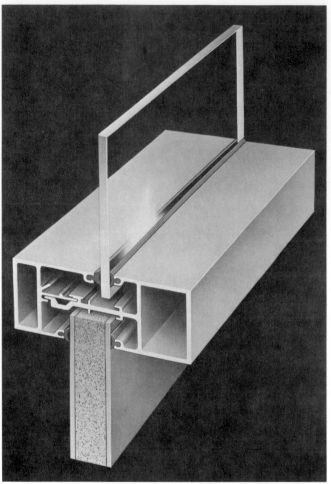

8-4 Extruded aluminum is often used for window and door frames.

lamp bases, trivets, plant stands, electrical fittings, grilles, handles, and cookware, 8-5.

Aluminum is rolled by running soft aluminum through steel rollers. Rolled aluminum products are generally not as straight or accurately sized as extruded aluminum products. Also, the surface finish of rolled aluminum is generally of poorer quality. Rolled aluminum may be used to make pipes, air ducts, awnings, garage doors, appliance cabinets, range hoods, and suspended ceiling supports.

Copper

Copper is used in residential structures in sheet, roll, and wire forms. Its most important qualities are electrical conductivity, heat conductivity, and resistance to corrosion. Its strength and ductility are affected by the mechanical and heat treatment that it receives. Copper that is heated and cooled slowly becomes brittle. Copper that is heated and cooled rapidly is malleable and ductile. When copper is exposed to moist air, it forms a thin coating of green carbonate. This coating protects copper against further corrosion.

Copper is used in housing construction primarily for wiring, tubing, pipes, roof flashing, and decorative nails and bolts. It is also an excellent, but expensive, roofing material, 8-6. Inside the house, copper may be used for cookware, range hoods, lamps, and decorative pieces. Since copper is a soft material, it lends itself to many finishes. It can be brushed, burnished, polished, sandblasted, or buffed.

Brass

Brass is an alloy of copper and zinc. Most brasses range in composition from 60 percent copper and 40 percent zinc

8-5 This cart has a cast aluminum base fashioned after an antique sewing machine.

8-6 The copper roofing over this bay window will last indefinitely. It forms an oxide coating that protects it from further corrosion.

BALDWIN HARDWARE CORP.

8-7 Brass hinges are attractive, and they are less likely to creak with age than hinges made of other metals.

to 90 percent copper and 10 percent zinc. Standard brass contains 67 percent copper and 33 percent zinc. Its color ranges from copper red to silvery white, depending on its copper content. Small amounts of tin can be added to help prevent corrosion or tarnishing. Brass also may be coated with clear enamel or another coating to prevent corrosion.

Brass may be formed by casting, hammering, stamping, rolling, or drawing. Brass is expensive, but its attractive color and strength make it a desirable housing material. It is used for weatherstripping, screws and bolts, nails, and wire, 8-7. It also is popular for furniture and decorative pieces, 8-8.

KNOB CREEK, INC.

8-8 Brass is popular for decorative pieces such as this lamp base.

Bronze

Bronze is an alloy of copper and tin. They usually contain from 75 to 95 percent copper and 5 to 25 percent tin. Tin increases the hardness of copper. The strongest bronze, called *Gun Metal* bronze, contains 90 percent copper and 10 percent tin. The term Gun Metal originated because this composition was used to make cannons.

Bronze is a beautiful and stately material that weathers well. Although expensive, it is the highest quality material available for thresholds, glass sliding door frames, window sills, screens, screws, and bolts. The best quality of plumbing valves and pipes are made of bronze, 8-9. Bronze is also used for interior decorative pieces, 8-10.

Lead

Lead is a heavy, yet workable, metal that is resistant to corrosion. Lead sheets are used extensively under showers, as liners for pools, and as flashing. It is sometimes used as a roofing material on curved or irregular shaped surfaces. Lead is the most useful material for pipes in high earthquake areas. Lead is also used to attach anchor bolts in concrete.

8-9 Cast bronze plumbing hardware will last indefinitely because it is almost completely corrosion resistant.

PRESIDENT BENJAMIN HARRISON MEMORIAL HOME

8-10 Bronze is an attractive material for art objects such as this statue of Beethoven.

One disadvantage of lead is its high expansion and contraction rate in changing temperatures, making it difficult to fasten into place. Another is that its weight limits the number of practical housing applications for lead.

Glass

Glass making has been an art for over 4500 years. However, until the early twentieth century glass could not be produced in large, flat sheets. The availability of flat glass has exerted a fantastic influence on modern lifestyles and architecture. While the colonial home had only a few small, divided windows, Modern homes may have entire walls of glass. See 8-11.

Glass is one of the only housing construction materials that allows the passage of light and a view. It does not conduct electricity, and it is almost completely corrosion resistant. Only a few chemical reactions can cause glass to break down.

Although strong, glass does break if enough force is applied to stretch or bend glass past its breaking point. The *tensile strength* of glass refers to the amount of force that glass can withstand. Tensile strength of glass can be increased by increasing its thickness or by applying certain production techniques to the glass. Tensile strength is decreased by scratches and imperfections and by improper production. It is also decreased by rapid temperature changes.

Flat glass. Most of the glass used in housing structures is flat glass. It is used for window and door panes, mirrors, table tops, and shelves, 8-12. About 95 percent of the flat glass in America is *float glass*. This glass is produced by floating molten glass over a bed of molten metal. This process yields an even sheet of glass that is smooth and polished on both sides. Float glass is produced in several strengths and thicknesses to fit different needs. The glass is distortion free and available in sheets large enough to create a wall-sized window.

Sheet glass and plate glass are types of flat glass produced by other methods. Sheet glass is often rippled, causing distortion and poor quality. It may still be found in older houses. Plate glass is of similar quality to float glass, but it is much more expensive to produce. Both types have been almost completely replaced by float glass.

JANCO GREENHOUSES

8-11 Older homes (left) had few windows with small panes of glass due to limited technology. Modern homes (right) may have entire walls of glass.

THOMASVILLE FURNITURE INDUSTRIES, INC.

8-12 Flat glass is used for the shelves and doors of this contemporary buffet. Several of the objects displayed in the buffet are handblown glass.

Decorative glass. Types of decorative glass include patterned, etched, cut, or enameled glass. Patterned glass has either a linear or geometric pattern embossed on one or both sides. This produces a translucent glass that allows privacy while admitting light. It is made in thicknesses of 1/8 and 7/32 inch and may be tempered to increase its strength. Patterned glass is used for partitions, in bathrooms, or in other areas where privacy is desired. Patterned safety glass is frequently used as a tub or shower enclosure.

Etched glass is treated with hydrofluoric acid to give glass a frosted effect. Various patterns can be used for a decorative effect, 8-13. Enameled glass has translucent or solid colors applied to its surface. Cut glass is produced by applying gem cutting techniques to glass. The cut surfaces catch and break up light.

Tinted glass. Tinted glass is made by adding a coloring agent to a batch of molten glass, 8-14. Gray and bronze are the most common colors. The addition of a tint can reduce light transmission from 25 to 75 percent, depending on the color and thickness of the glass. This helps to reduce heat transmission and glare.

Tinted glass is used most frequently in warm, sunny climates to provide a more comfortable interior. In cool climates, tinted glass may be used for eastern or western windows to reduce glare. However, they are not recommended for northern and southern windows because they interfere with the sun's ability to provide solar heat. Tinted glass can contribute to the architectural style of a house. It also is used for table tops and shelves.

Reflective glass. Reflective glass, also called environmental glass, is fairly new. It is even more effective than

tinted glass in reducing heat gain, 8-15. The glass has a transparent metal or metal oxide coating bonded to one surface of the glass. Frequently, the reflective material is laminated between two thicknesses of glass to protect the coating from abrasion. Coatings used include cobalt oxide, chromium, copper, aluminum, nickel, and gold. Glass may be neutral, copper, bronze, blue, or golden in color. Reflective glass is used primarily in warm climates to reduce air-conditioning costs.

PRESIDENT BENJAMIN HARRISON MEMORIAL HOME

8-13 Frosted patterns may be etched on glass for a decorative effect.

AMERICAN SOLAR HOMES

8-14 Tinted glass is used for windows where hot sunlight and glare is not desirable.

8-15 These large window wall panels are made from reflective glass to reduce interior heat gain in warm weather.

Insulating glass. Insulating glass is designed to reduce heat loss and gain. It contains two pieces of glass with either dehydrated air or a special dry gas in between. Insulating glass units are produced with metal or welded glass edges, 8-16. Metal edge units are generally available in a wide range of sizes and glass thicknesses. Welded glass edge units are generally limited to smaller sizes. The typical width of the air void in an insulated glass unit is from 1/4 to 1/2 inch. Insulated glass is widely used in housing structures and in some appliances to reduce heat loss or heat gain.

Handblown glass. Handblown glass is expensive but desirable for its beauty and individual character. It is produced by dipping a hollow metal rod into molten glass and blowing the glass into a bubble. The bubble is then formed into a shape by rolling, twisting, or shaping with tools while the glass is still hot and plastic. Handblown glass is used mostly for art pieces and vases, although it can also be used for fine *hollowware* (drinking glasses).

Molded glass. Molded glass products of excellent quality are available today, 8-17. They are less expensive and often more durable than handblown items. Molded pieces are produced by machine blowing molten glass into wood or cast iron molds. These pieces, like their handmade predecessors, may be decorated by etching, sandblasting, enameling, and cutting. Molded glass is used for storage containers, art pieces, and hollowware.

Leaded glass. Leaded and stained glass have gained renewed popularity. They are made by setting small pieces of clear or colored glass into strips of lead or copper foil, 8-18. *Leaded glass* usually refers to transparent or colorless glass. *Stained glass* refers to glass colored by pigments or

metal oxides that are fused to the glass. Leaded and stained glass are generally used in decorative windows, doors, and lampshades.

CERAMICS

Ceramic products have been used from the beginning of civilization, and they remain popular today. Ceramic

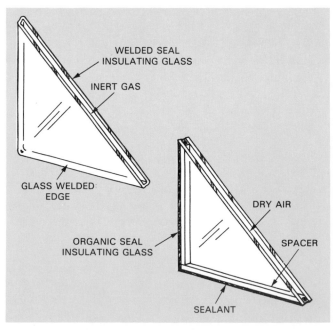

8-16 Both welded edge and metal edge insulating glass are more effective insulators than single-pane glass.

8-17 This molded glass dinnerware is similar in quality and appearance to handblown glass, but it is much less expensive.

materials are made from clay that is hardened with heat. A great diversity of ceramic products are available. Included are wall and floor tiles, roofing tiles, drain tiles, chimney flue liners, dishes, and sculptured objects.

Clay, in its plastic form, is easily shaped. When dried and fired, it is like porous stone. Firing clay in a kiln preserves its shape, color, and texture. Firing also makes clay resistant to heat, cold, moisture, acids, and salts. Clay

THERMA-TRU, DIV. OF LST CORP.

8-18 The varied patterns of the glass pieces give these leaded glass doors an intriguing appearance.

can be glazed, colored, and textured for decoration. Glazing also increases clay's strength and decreases its porousity, making it waterproof.

Ceramic Tile

Ceramic tile is made from clay or shale that is fired at high temperatures. It is manufactured in modular unit sizes. All ceramic tile products possess good abrasion resistance and a high degree of resistance to moisture. These properties make ceramic tile a perfect choice for areas exposed to heavy foot traffic, water, or corrosive chemicals. Tiles are produced in a variety of dimensions, properties, and appearances, 8-19. The main types of ceramic tile produced are glazed tile, ceramic mosaic tile, and quarry and paver tile.

Glazed tile is available for use on walls or floors. Those designed for walls usually have one coat of glazing, while those for floors generally have two or three coats. Tiles designed for very heavy traffic areas should be finished with a special crystalline glaze. Glazing gives tile a smooth, glossy finish that resists stains. Many different colors and textures of glazes are used on tile, making tile a versatile decorating tool, 8-20.

Nominal sizes of standard 5/16 in. thick glazed tile include 4 1/4 by 4 1/4 in., 4 1/4 by 6 in., and 6 by 6 in. Some glazed wall tile are sufficiently abrasion resistant for use on floors in light traffic areas. All glazed floor tile can be used on walls, however, floor tile is usually more expensive. Glazed tile is especially popular for bathrooms and kitchens, where high moisture resistance and ease of cleaning is especially important. However, new designs and colors have made glazed tile popular for other rooms such as living rooms and bedrooms.

Ceramic mosaic tile may be made of porcelain or natural clay. They are smaller than standard glazed tile and are generally available in vivid, solid colors. Areas covered with ceramic tile may be in all one color, in a random combination of colors, or in geometric or pictoral patterns, 8-21.

Porcelain mosaic tiles are brighter, smoother, and more water repellant than clay tiles. The clay mosaic tiles are generally in muted, earthy colors. Mosaic tile is generally

LIS KING

8-20   Triple glazed tile is durable enough for medium to heavy traffic areas. It is an attractive and easily maintained floor covering.

1/4 in. thick and is available in standard sizes of 1 by 1 in., 1 by 2 in., and 2 by 2 in. They are also made in hexagonal and round shapes. Mosaic tile is generally used on walls, floors, and countertops.

Quarry tile and *pavers* are the strongest of the ceramic tiles. They are made from natural clays and shales. Although quarry tile can be glazed, these tiles generally derive their color from the type of clay used, 8-22. This gives the tiles great long-lasting wear because the top color can't be scratched off.

Quarry tiles may be 1/2 or 3/4 in. thick and are available in 6, 9, and 12 in. squares. Pavers are produced in 1/2 in. thick tiles 2 3/4 by 6 in., 6 by 6 in., and 4 by 8 in.

Roofing Tile

Clay tile roofs are characteristic of Spanish and Mediterranean architecture, 8-23. Clay roofing tile is durable and attractive but very expensive. It also is more porous than other roofing materials.

Clay roofing tile is available in a flat or roll design. Flat tile are similar to shingles with interlocking edges. Roll type tile forms a corrugated design. Clay tile is generally fastened to the roof with copper nails because copper resists corrosion and lasts as long as the tile. A waterproof membrane is required under clay tile to prevent leaking.

Pottery

Pottery refers to ceramic objects such as dinnerware, jars, pots, and vases. Pottery making is an old art, but most pottery pieces today are manufactured rather than handmade. Pottery may be catagorized as earthenware, stoneware, and porcelain.

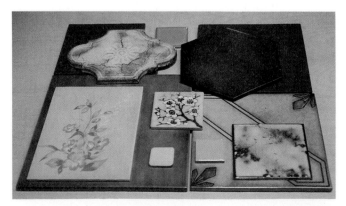

8-19   Ceramic tile is available in a variety of styles to suit almost any purpose.

LIS KING

8-21 *The ceramic mosaic tiles on this counter are arranged in a multicolored pattern of stripes.*

8-23 *Ceramic roofing tile is attractive and long lasting.*

Earthenware is the most casual type of pottery. It is made of coarse textured clay fired at a relatively low temperature (1800 to 2100°F). Earthenware products are porous, fragile, and opaque. Flower pots, casual dinnerware, and folk pottery are of earthenware, 8-24. They are generally red or brown in color. If they are glazed, the glaze generally has a rougher texture than those on stoneware or porcelain.

Stoneware is made of a finer clay than earthenware. it is usually gray or light brown in color. The clay is fired at a medium temperature (2100 to 2300°F) that causes the clay to vitrify and lose its porousity. This clay is used primarily for high quality, casual dinnerware, 8-25. Stoneware pieces are more durable and waterproof than earthenware pieces. Glazes on stoneware are generally in subtle colors with a matte finish.

Porcelain is fired at a high temperature (2250 to 2500°F) to a white, finely textured finish. The highest quality of pottery, it is completely vitrified and very hard. A chipped

ETHAN ALLEN, INC.

8-22 *Quarry tiles are suitable for heavy traffic areas. Their colors are warm and earthy.*

8-24 *Earthenware has a rough, somewhat porous finish.*

8-25 *Stoneware is more durable than earthenware. It is popular for casual dinnerware.*

area will not absorb moisture due to porcelain's nonporous nature. Porcelain items are often translucent, giving them a delicate appearance.

Expensive dinnerware and artwork are made of porcelain. Bathtubs, sinks, and other household fixtures also may be finished with porcelain, 8-26. Most porcelain is white, off-white, or pastel. Glazes on porcelain have a hard, glossy finish, and patterns are finely detailed, 8-27.

PLASTICS

Plastics are manufactured polymer materials. Plastic is a fairly new material; the first commerical plastic in the United States was developed around 100 years ago. Plastics are gaining use in housing due to their wide range of properties and their reasonable cost. For example, plastics are generally moisture and corrosion resistant, lightweight, tough, and easily molded into complex shapes, 8-28. They possess characteristics found in other, more expensive materials.

Plastics have a variety of uses in housing. They are replacing many natural building materials because of their low maintenance requirements and durability. Plastics are used for floor coverings, window frame and door coatings, siding, counter and table top laminates, safety windows, vapor barriers, insulation, furniture, and accessories, 8-29.

Plastics may be classified as *thermoplastics* and *thermosetting plastics*. Thermoplastic materials can be repeatedly softened with heat and hardened by cooling. Many

AMERICAN OLEAN TILE CO.

8-26 *Porcelain finishes are popular for bathroom fixtures. The finish is smooth, durable, and easy to maintain.*

8-27 *Decorative porcelain items like this doorknob often have finely detailed, painted designs.*

MICHIGAN BELL COMMUNICATIONS, AN AMERITECH CO.

8-28 Plastics allow the inexpensive production of durable, lightweight household items such as this phone.

thermoplastics are flammable. Thermosetting plastics are permanently shaped during the manufacturing process and cannot be softened again by reheating. They form a rigid, often brittle, mass that will not burn. Some characteristics, and applications to housing of several commercial plastics are listed in 8-30 and 8-31.

FORMICA CORP.

8-29 Plastic laminates are popular for kitchen and bathroom counters because they are durable, easily cleaned, and available in a wide variety of colors and patterns.

THERMOPLASTICS		
FAMILY	**IMPORTANT PROPERTIES**	**APPLICATIONS**
Acrylics	Weather resistant, colorable, transmits light, cements well, good electrical properties, good surface luster.	Skylights, translucent panels, lenses, carpeting, draperies, lighting fixtures, containers.
Polystyrene (PS)	Transparent, water resistant, softens at 212 degrees F., brittle, yellows with exposure, tasteless and colorless.	Tile, sheets for wall coverings, building insulation, molded furniture parts, appliance housings, packaging containers.
Polypropylene (PP)	Off-white in color, lightweight (will float), good flex life, good electrical and chemical resistance, easily colored, scratch resistant.	Bottles, fibers for carpeting, housewares, electrical parts, appliance housings, hoses, containers with integral hinges.
Vinyls	Good strength and toughness, average chemical resistance, can perform well at low temperatures, begins to soften at 130 degrees F.	Pipe and tubing, simulated leather, gutters, siding, storage tanks, adhesives, upholstery, outdoor furniture.
Polyamides (Nylon)	Tough, resists abrasion and chemical attack, not recommended for outdoor exposure, high surface gloss, colorable.	Textiles, drawer slides, rollers, hinges.
Cellulosics (CA) (CAB)	Very tough, good electrical properties, moderately heat resistant, good surface luster, colorable.	Household appliances, tool handles, safety glasses, plumbing fittings.
Tetrafluorethylene (TFE)	Highly resistant to chemical attack, wide temperature range, ''anti-stick'' quality.	Lining for pots and pans, electrical insulation, gaskets, tape.
Polycarbonates (PC)	Transparent, high impact strength, good heat resistance, weathers well, good chemical resistance.	Window glazing, lighting globes, bottles, housings for tools and appliances, covers for electrical panels.
Acrylonitrile-Butadiene-Styrene (ABS)	Chemical resistant, rigid, rough, will tolerate high temperatures, medium chemical resistance, tan in color, will burn.	Plumbing fittings and pipe, hardware, furniture, appliances.
Polyethylene (PE)	Flexible, tough, chemically resistant, feels waxy, fair weatherability, easily colored.	Vapor barriers in walls and floors, containers, electrical insulation, housewares, ice trays, bottles.

8-30 Thermoplastics can be softened with heat and hardened with cooling.

THERMOSETTING PLASTICS		
FAMILY	IMPORTANT PROPERTIES	APPLICATIONS
Alkyds	Opaque, may be colored, good weather resistance, tough, moisture resistant.	Paints and enamels, circuit breakers, electrical insulation.
Melamines (MF)	Hard, durable, abrasion resistant, chemical resistant, easily colored.	Decorative laminates, countertops, switch plates, dinnerware, doorknobs, appliance housings, adhesives for wood.
Polyesters	Weather and chemical resistant, stiff and hard, colorable, heat resistant.	Textile products, bathtubs and shower stalls, tool handles, appliance housings, prefabricated sections for roof and wall panels.
Silicones (SI)	Very stable, excellent corrosion resistance, good insulating properties, will stretch, wide temperature range, odorless, tasteless, nontoxic.	Coatings and sealants, fuel lines, gaskets, transformer insulation, masonry waterproofing.
Phenolics (PF)	Hard and brittle, low cost, chemically inert, excellent heat and insulating properties.	Fabrics, laminating veneers, telephones, tool housings, handles, impregnated wood.
Epoxies	Will adhere to most any building material, good chemical and moisture resistance.	Protective coatings for walls and floors, adhesive, high strength mortar.
Polyurethanes (UP)	Excellent thermal insulating properties, lightweight, resistant to moisture and decay, can be made fire-resistant.	Sponges, insulation, gaskets, shock impact devices, synthetic leather, furniture cushions.
Ureas	Good scratch resistance, low to medium chemical and heat resistance.	Molded hardware, electrical fittings, adhesive, insulating foam.

8-31 Thermosetting plastics are hard and flame resistant.

REVIEW QUESTIONS

1. How does cast iron differ from wrought iron? What are some uses of each in housing?
2. What are the main properties of steel? How does the addition of copper affect its properties? How does the addition of chromium affect its properties?
3. What are some uses of steel in housing?
4. What are the three main ways that aluminum is processed? For what housing products is each type used?
5. How do copper, brass, and bronze differ from each other? How is each metal used in housing?
6. What qualities make glass a desirable housing material? What qualities make it undesirable?
7. Two windows made of the same type and thickness of glass were hit with the same amount of force. Only one broke. Why might this have happened?
8. What different kinds of glass are used in housing? What are their main uses?
9. What types of ceramic products are used in housing? What qualities make these products popular?
10. What properties make plastics desirable materials? What are some plastic products used in housing?

GEORGIA-PACIFIC

Metals, glass, ceramics, and plastics have become important materials in home furnishings.

9 Textiles

After studying this chapter, you will be able to:
- ■ Describe the origins, qualities, and uses of natural and manufactured fibers.
- ■ Evaluate a yarn in terms of the method used to create it and its advantages, disadvantages, and uses.
- ■ Describe the various types of fabric construction in terms of the methods used to produce them, their quality, and their uses.
- ■ Evaluate the appropriateness of a fabric for a specific use within the home.

Textile products are used throughout the home to add color, texture, and comfort. Carpets, rugs, upholstery, and curtains are common textile products used in the home. Understanding the materials and methods involved in fabric construction will help you to choose fabrics that are attractive, durable, and appropriate for use in the home.

FIBERS

The basic element of most textiles is the fiber. Fibers are combined to form a continuous strand called a yarn. Yarns are woven, knitted, or fastened together to make fabric.

Fibers determine a fabric's strength, elasticity, texture, shrinkage, warmth, absorbency, and durability. They also determine a fabric's resistance to stains, fire, sun, mildew, and abrasion. The properties of a fiber depend on its source. Fibers are obtained from either natural or chemical sources. They are classified as natural fibers and manufactured fibers.

Natural Fibers

Natural fibers are derived from one of three naturally occurring substances: cellulose, protein, or mineral. See 9-1. *Cellulosic fibers* come from plants. Cotton and flax are two common cellulosic fibers. *Protein fibers* come from animals. Silk, wool, and specialty hair fibers such as cashmere and camel hair are protein fibers.

The only natural mineral fiber is asbestos; it is found in rocks. This fiber has been used for insulation, and it

NATURAL FIBERS

Cellulosic
- Cotton
- Flax
- Hemp
- Jute
- Ramie

Protein
- Silk
- Wool
- Specialty hair fibers
  - Alpaca
  - Angora
  - Camel hair
  - Cashmere
  - Guanaco
  - Llama
  - Mohair
  - Vicuna

Mineral
- Asbestos

9-1 These natural fibers can be categorized as cellulosic (plant), protein (animal), or mineral.

has been used in products where a noncombustible material is required. Manufactured products, however, such as glass and novoloid are replacing asbestos because of the health problems that have been linked to asbestos fibers.

Natural fibers are unique because they cannot be duplicated exactly by technology. Cotton, flax (linen), silk, and wool are the four common natural fibers. The uses of these fibers in home furnishings as well as their characteristics and care are given in 9-2.

Manufactured Fibers

Manufactured fibers also come from substances found in nature such as wood pulp and petroleum. Unlike natural fibers, however, these substances are not fibrous in their natural form. They are transformed into fibers through chemical engineering. First, they are made into solutions. Then fibers are extruded from the liquid and solidified.

FOUR COMMON NATURAL FIBERS			
FIBER	**USES**	**CHARACTERISTICS**	**CARE**
Cotton	Sheets Towels Bedspreads Draperies Upholstery Rugs	Absorbent. Easy to dye and print. Does not generate static electricity. Highly flammable unless treated with flame retardant finish. Wrinkles easily. Shrinks in hot water unless treated. Soils easily.	Wash or dry-clean. Avoid damp storage to prevent mildew. Avoid prolonged exposure to sunlight.
Flax **(Linen)**	Draperies Upholstery Tablecloths Kitchen towels	Strongest of natural fibers. Durable-withstands frequent laundering. Ages well. Lint free. Wrinkles easily unless treated. Flammable. Expensive if of good quality.	Wash or dry-clean. Iron on wrong side to prevent shining. Avoid damp storage to prevent mildew.

Silk	Draperies
	Upholstery
	Lampshades
	Wall hangings
		Strong but lightweight.
		Very absorbent.
		Dyes well.
		Smooth and lustrous.
		Resists wrinkling.
		Retains shape well.
		Soil resistant.
		Expensive.
		Yellows with age.
		Spotted by water unless
		  specially treated.
			Dry-clean (unless otherwise specified).
			Avoid prolonged exposure to sunlight.
			Avoid contact with silverfish—will attack
			  fibers.

Wool	Blankets Draperies Carpets Upholstery Rugs	Warmest of all fibers. Very absorbent. Wrinkle resistant. Holds and retains shape well. Creases well. Expensive.	Dry-clean (unless otherwise specified). Press with low, moist heat. Avoid contact with moths and carpet beetles—will eat fibers.

9-2 *The four most common natural fibers are used in many household fabrics. Their characteristics and care requirements help to determine which uses are best for a specific fiber.*

MANUFACTURED FIBERS

Cellulosic
  Acetate
  Rayon
  Triacetate

Non-cellulosic
  Acrylic
  Anidex*
  Aramid
  Azlon*
  Glass
  Lastrile*
  Metallic
  Modacrylic
  Novoloid*
  Nylon
  Nytril*
  Olefin
  Polyester
  Rubber
  Saran
  Spandex
  Vinal*
  Vinyon

*Not currently produced in the United States.

9-3 *These manufactured fibers may be categorized as cellulosic and non-cellulosic.*

The two basic types of manufactured fibers are cellulosic and non-cellulosic. See 9-3. Cellulosic fibers are derived from cellulose, the fibrous substance found in plants. Rayon, triacetate, and acetate are three cellulosic fibers.

Non-cellulosic fibers are made from molecules containing various combinations of carbon, hydrogen, nitrogen, and oxygen. The molecules are linked into long chains called polymers from which filaments (long strands of fibers) are produced. The chart in 9-4 identifies the uses, characteristics, and care of many of the manufactured fibers used in home furnishings.

YARNS

A yarn is the product of several fibers twisted together. The size and texture of a yarn depends on the types of fibers from which it is made, the tightness of the twist, and the number of plys it has.

Yarns are either made from short fibers called *staple fibers* or from continuous strands of fibers called *filaments*. All natural fibers except silk are staple fibers. Silk and all of the manufactured fibers are filaments, but they can be cut into staple fibers.

Spun yarns are made from staple fibers. These yarns have a fuzzy appearance because tiny fiber ends protrude from these yarns. The tiny fiber ends of spun yarns may cause fabrics to pill. *Pilling* is the formation of tiny balls of fiber or "pills" that appear on fabrics that receive a lot of use.

Monofilament yarns are made from a single filament. Multifilament yarns are made from a group of filaments. Silk and most manufactured fibers are made into multifilament yarns.

Many textiles today are blends or combinations of natural and manufactured fibers. A *blend* is the result of two or more different staple fibers spun together into a single yarn. A *combination* is formed by twisting two different single yarns into one yarn. Blends and combinations enable fabrics to have the best characteristics of the fibers used. For example, cotton/polyester is a blend commonly used for sheets. It combines the soft, absorbent properties of cotton with the wrinkle-resistant properties of polyester to produce comfortable, easy care sheets.

Twist in yarns is necessary to hold fibers or filaments together. Twist also can increase yarn strength. As the degree of twist is increased in a yarn, the yarn becomes harder, more compact, and less lustrous. An average to high twist is used for most yarns made from staple fibers; a low twist is used for most yarns made from filaments.

Yarns can be classified as single, ply, or cord. See 9-5. The twisting together of fibers or filaments forms a single yarn. Two or more single yarns twisted together form a ply yarn. Knitting yarn is an example of a ply yarn. Two or more ply yarns twisted together results in a cord yarn. Ropes are often made from cord yarns.

FABRIC CONSTRUCTION

Fabrics can be made by various methods. Weaving, knitting, and tufting are the most common methods of construction involving yarns. Other methods may be used to construct fabrics with or without yarns. Color and finishes may be added at several stages.

Weaving

Woven fabrics are made with two sets of yarns interlaced at right angles to each other. The two sets of yarns used in weaving are warp yarns and filling yarns. The direction the yarns run is called the grain. Warp yarns run along the lengthwise grain. Filling yarns run along the crosswise grain.

By passing the filling yarns over and under different numbers of warp yarns, different weaves can be created. Five weaves often used for the construction of home furnishings fabrics are the plain, twill, satin, jacquard, and leno.

Plain weave. The simplest form of weaving is the plain weave. It is formed by passing a filling yarn over and under one warp yarn, 9-6. The plain weave produces strong, durable fabrics. Broadcloth, percale, gingham, and grosgrain are examples of plain weave fabrics.

A common variation of the plain weave is the basket weave. It is made by passing two or more filling yarns over and under the same number of warp yarns. Monk's cloth and hopsacking are woven in the basket weave.

Twill weave. Fabrics woven in the twill weave have diagonal lines or wales, 9-7. A wale is formed when a yarn in one direction floats (passes) over two or more yarns in the other direction. Each float begins at least one yarn over from the last one. Like plain weaves, twill weaves form strong, durable fabrics. They also resist wrinkles and hide soil. Denim and gabardine are two examples of twill weaves.

The herringbone twill is a common variation of the twill weave. In this design, the wale changes direction at regular intervals to produce a zigzag effect.

Satin weave. The satin weave produces smooth and lustrous fabrics. The smoothness and shine is the result of long floats on the surface of the fabric. A float is made

COMMON MANUFACTURED FIBERS			
FIBER	**USES**	**CHARACTERISTICS**	**CARE**
Acetate	Bedspreads Draperies Fiberfill Upholstery	Easy to dye. Soft and luxurious. Drapes well. Inexpensive. Resistant to pilling, moths, and mildew. Nonabsorbent. Melts under high heat.	Dry-clean (unless otherwise specified). Avoid contact with acetone and other organic solvents.
Acrylic	Awnings Blankets Carpeting Draperies Fiberfill Rugs Upholstery	Resembles wool. Soft, warm, and lightweight. Colorfast. Retains shape well. Resistant to wrinkles, chemicals, moths, mildew, and sunlight. Nonabsorbent. Generates static electricity. Not resistant to abrasion, pilling, stretching, and soil.	Machine wash in warm water. Machine dry on low setting. Hand wash delicates in warm water. Use moderately warm iron.

9-4 Many manufactured fibers are used in the home. Each has unique characteristics and care requirements. (continued)

FIBER	USES	CHARACTERISTICS	CARE
Glass	Curtains Draperies Insulation batting	Strong and relatively heavy. Resistant to heat, flames, and most chemicals. Nonabsorbent.	
Metallic	Draperies Rugs Slipcovers Tablecloths Upholstery	Colorfast. Very durable. Resistant to moths, mildew, and shinking.	
Modacrylic	Awnings Blankets Carpeting Curtains Draperies Rugs	Warm, heavy, and bulky. Retains shape well. Flame resistant. Resistant to chemicals, moths, mildew, and shrinking.	Dry-cleaning or fur cleaning process suggested for deep pile. For washable items, machine wash in warm water. Machine wash on low setting. Use cool iron.
Nylon	Bedspreads Carpeting Curtains Draperies Outdoor furniture Mattress pads Rugs Slipcovers Tablecloths Upholstery	Very strong and durable. Lustrous and lightweight. Easy to dye. Drapes well. Retains shape well. Resistant to moths, mildew, and oily stains. Nonabsorbent. Generates static electricity. Not resistant to soil and pilling.	Machine wash in warm water. Machine dry on low setting. Use warm iron if necessary.
Olefin	Awnings Carpeting Carpet backings Doormats Outdoor furniture Mattresses Slipcovers Upholstery	Very strong, yet lightweight. Colorfast. Very durable. Quick drying. Resistant to abrasion, chemicals, moths, mildew, oily stains, and shrinking. Inexpensive.	Machine wash in lukewarm water. Machine dry on low setting. Do not iron 100% olefin fibers.
Polyester	Awnings Bedspreads Blankets Carpeting Curtains Draperies Fiberfill Mattresses Mattress pads Pillowcases Rugs Sheets Slipcovers Tablecloths Upholstery	Very strong and durable. Easy to dye. Colorfast. Retains shape well. Resistant to wrinkles, stretching, bleach, moths, and mildew. Nonabsorbent. Generates static electricity. Not resistant to oily stains, soil, and pilling.	Machine wash in warm water. Machine dry on low setting. Use moderately warm iron. Most polyester items are also dry-cleanable.
Rayon	Bedspreads Curtains Draperies Sheets Slipcovers Tablecloths Upholstery	Resembles cotton. Absorbent. Easy to dye. Colorfast. Drapes well. Resistant to moths and pilling. Wrinkles easily unless treated with a special finish. Shrinks in hot water unless treated. Highly flammable unless treated.	Hand wash in mild, lukewarm suds (unless otherwise specified). Do not wring or twist. Air dry. Press on the wrong side while damp.
Saran	Awnings Draperies Outdoor furniture	Colorfast. Very durable. Strong and heavy. Flame resistant. Resistant to chemicals, moths, mildew, oily stains, and sunlight. Softens at low temperatures.	Washable with soap and water.
Triacetate	Bedspreads Draperies	Colorfast. Easy to dye. Drapes well. Holds shape well. Resistant to moths, mildew, pilling, and shrinking. Wrinkle resistant.	Pleated items are best hand washed. Other items can be machine washed and dried. Can be ironed on high temperature setting if needed.

9-4 Many manufactured fibers are used in the home. Each has unique characteristics and care requirements.

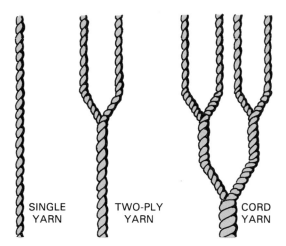

SINGLE YARN   TWO-PLY YARN   CORD YARN

9-5 A single-ply yarn is formed by twisting together fibers or filaments. When two single-ply yarns are twisted together, a two-ply yarn is formed. A cord yarn is produced by twisting together two or more ply yarns.

by passing a yarn in one direction over four or more yarns in the other direction, 9-8. Each float begins two yarns over from where the last float began.

The satin weave does not produce very durable fabrics because the floats tend to snag easily. However, durability can be increased if the yarns are woven closely together. The two fabrics woven in the satin weave are satin and sateen. In satin, the floats run in the warp direction. In sateen, the floats run in the filling direction.

Jacquard weave. Jacquard fabrics are characterized by intricate patterns, 9-9. These patterns are made by different arrangements of the warp yarns. The arrangements are determined by cards that are attached to the Jacquard loom. The complex process required to manufacture jacquard weaves makes jacquard fabrics expensive to produce.

Fabrics made on a Jacquard loom are damask, brocade, and tapestry. These fabrics are used for upholstery, tablecloths, and wall hangings. Jacquard fabrics tend to be less durable if they have long floats or if fine yarns are used.

Leno weave. The leno weave is characterized by paired warp yarns that are passed over and under the filling yarns in a figure eight configuration. This type of weave produces a meshlike fabric. Fabrics made by the leno weave are used to manufacture curtains and some thermal blankets.

Knitting

Knitted fabircs are made by interlooping yarns. The two methods of knitting fabrics are weft or filling knitting and warp knitting. In *weft knitting,* loops are formed by hand or machine as yarn is added in a crosswise direction. In *warp knitting,* loops are formed vertically by machine, one row at a time.

The only knitted fabrics used to any great extent in home furnishings are the Raschel warp knits. Rashcel knit fabrics are used in the making or curtains and draperies.

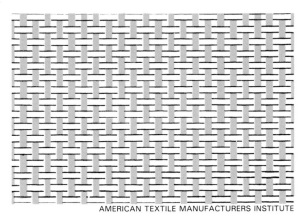

AMERICAN TEXTILE MANUFACTURERS INSTITUTE

9-6 A plain weave is formed by passing a filling yarn over and under one warp yarn. Textured curtain fabric can be made by combining thick warp yarns with thin filling yarns.

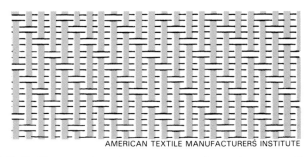

AMERICAN TEXTILE MANUFACTURERS INSTITUTE

9-7 Twill weaves have floats that form diagonal patterns. They are wrinkle and stain resistant.

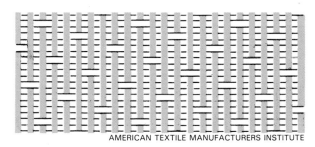

AMERICAN TEXTILE MANUFACTURERS INSTITUTE

9-8 The satin weave has long floats on the surface of the fabric. It is smooth and shiny, but not very durable.

9-9 Jacquard tapestry is a popular fabric to be used for upholstery. Upholstery tapestry is durable if the warp and filling yarns are of similar quality. Tapestry made with a combination of fine and coarse yarns is more likely to snag.

131

Tufting

Tufting is a construction method used to make carpeting. About 95 percent of all carpeting is tufted because tufting is an easier and less costly construction method than weaving.

Tufted carpeting and fabrics are produced by tufting machines. The machines have needles that loop yarns into a backing material. Since the needles go in and out of the backing in the same place, a latex coating is applied to the backing to hold the yarns in place, 9-10. To give body, a second layer of backing is often added.

Other Construction Methods

Some fabrics are made with methods other than weaving, knitting, and tufting. These include felt, nonwoven fabrics, films, foams, and leather.

Felt is a fabric made directly from wool fibers. Felting occurs when heat, moisture, agitation, and pressure are applied to wool fibers, causing the fibers to interlock permanently. Industrially, felt is used for padding, soundproofing, insulation, filtering, and polishing. Felt also is used for wall hangings and other decorative items.

Nonwoven fabrics are made by bonding fibers (other than wool fibers), yarns, or filaments by mechanical or chemical means, 9-11. Nonwovens are used to make many durable goods such as bedding, backing for quilts, dustcloths for box springs, carpet backing, and upholstered furniture. They are also used alone for draperies and mattress pads.

Films are made from synthetic solutions which are formed into thin sheets. Most household textile films and film coatings are made from vinyl or polyurethane solutions. Films may be used alone, or they may serve as a coating over some other fabrics. Products made from film and film-coated fabrics include tablecloths, shower curtains, draperies, upholstery, and wall coverings.

Foams are made from a rubber or polyurethane substance into which air is incorporated, causing the substance to foam. Foams are useful for their bulk and sponginess. They are available in a wide range of weights, densities, and resiliencies. Foams are used as carpet backings, padding for furniture, pillow and cushion forms, and foam laminates to fabric for household textiles.

Leather has no fibers but is used as a fabric. It is manufactured from the skins and hides of animals. Cowhide and steer hide are the most common leathers. In higher-priced furniture, leather is often used as an upholstery fabric because of its beauty, durability, and moisture resistance, 9-12.

Dyeing Fabrics

Color is a major part of any textile product. Dyeing is one way to add color to fabrics and other textile products. Fibers, yarns, or fabrics may be dyed.

One of two methods is used to dye fibers. Natural fibers are *stock dyed* by adding dye to the loose fibers. Manufactured fibers are *solution dyed* by adding dye to the thick liquid before it is extruded into filaments.

9-10 Tufted yarns are held in place by a latex backing.

9-11 Nonwoven fabrics do not have distinct patterns of woven yarns. Instead, fibers are fastened together by mechanical or chemical means.

WESTNOFA USA, INC.

9-12 Leather is a practical, yet attractive and comfortable, upholstery fabric.

In yarn dyeing, yarns are wound on spools and placed in a dye bath, 9-13. Plaid and striped fabrics are constructed from dyed yarns. Generally, yarn dyeing is less expensive than fiber dyeing but more expensive than piece dyeing.

Piece dyeing is the most common method of dyeing. Dye is added after the fabric has been constructed. Piece dyeing allows textile manufacturers to store undyed fabric and dye to order as fashion dictates.

Printing Fabrics

Printing is another way to color fabrics. With printed fabric, one side appears much lighter than the other. This is different from dyed fabric, in which both sides are the same color. Three common methods for printing fabrics are: roller printing, rotary screen printing, and block printing.

Roller printing (also called direct printing) accounts for the majority of fabrics printed. In this process, color is transferred directly to a fabric as it passes between a series of rollers, 9-14. Roller printing is a simple process used to produce large quantities of printed fabrics inexpensively.

In *rotary screen printing,* dye is transferred to a fabric through a cylinder-shaped screen which rolls over the fabric, printing the design, 9-15. A separate screen is required for each color. For many years, screen printing was done by hand. Now, it is one of the fastest printing processes.

Block printing is a hand process; it is the oldest technique for decorating textiles. A design is carved on a block and dye is applied to it. Then the block is stamped onto the fabric. Block printing is seldom done commercially because it is an expensive and time-consuming process.

Fabric Finishes

All fabrics receive one or more finishes during or after fabric construction. Most finishes are applied to add certain characteristics to fabrics. For example, a finish may increase the wrinkle or stain resistance of a fabric. Several fabric finishes are described in 9-16.

AMERICAN TEXTILE MANUFACTURERS INSTITUTE

9-13 Many spools of yarn are dyed at one time in this large vat.

AMERICAN TEXTILE MANUFACTURERS INSTITUTE

9-14 In roller printing, each engraved cylinder rolls over the fabric, imposing a multi-colored design.

AMERICAN TEXTILE MANUFACTURERS INSTITUTE

9-15 Rotary screen printing is one of the newest and fastest printing methods. A porous cylinder holds the design, and dye is forced through the holes in the cylinder leaving a colorful print.

133

TEXTILE FINISHES

Antistatic	Chemical treatment to prevent the buildup of static electricity.
Beetling	Mechanical process for linen fabrics which improves luster, absorbancy, and smoothness.
Bleaching	Chemical treatment to whiten natural fibers.
Brushing	Mechanical process to remove short fibers from a fabric's surface.
Calendering	Mechanical process in which heat and pressure are applied to produce a smooth, polished surface.
Crabbing	Process used to set wool fabrics.
Crease-resistant	Chemical process to help fabrics resist wrinkles.
Flame-retardant	Chemical finish to reduce the oxygen supply or to change the chemical makeup of fibers to reduce the chances of burning.
Fulling	Process to improve the appearance and hand of wool fabrics.
Mercerization	Chemical treatment for cotton and rayon fabrics which improves luster, strength, and absorbancy.
Mildew-resistant	Chemical treatment to prevent mildew from forming on fabrics.
Moth-repellant	Chemical treatment for wool fabrics which repels moths.
Napping	Process used to pull fiber ends from low-twist, spun yarns.
Preshrunk	Process in which moisture and heat are used to shrink fabric before it is sold to the consumer.
Sanforized	A trademark that insures that a fabric has been processed to reduce shrinkage to no more than one percent.
Scotchgard	A trademark that refers to a finish given to fabrics which resists water and oil stains.
Shearing	Mechanical process to remove loose fiber or yarn ends from the surface of a fabric.
Soil release	Chemical process to increase fabric absorbency so that soil can be removed.
Soil-resistant	Chemical process to make fibers less absorbant.
Water-repellent	Chemical process which coats fabrics with wax, metals, or resins to resist water.
Weighting	Chemical process which adds weight and crispness to silk fabrics.

9-16 Textile finishes enhance the quality of fabrics. Specific finishes and their purposes are listed here.

REVIEW QUESTIONS

1. What are the three naturally occurring substances from which natural fibers are derived? Give examples of each type.
2. Would you consider silk to be a good or poor choice for couch upholstery? Why?
3. What are the two basic types of manufactured fibers? Give examples of each type.
4. What is the difference between a spun yarn and a monofilament yarn?
5. Give an example of a blend or combination fabric. What advantages are there to using a blend or combination?
6. What are the five major types of weaves? How are they different from each other?
7. Would you choose a twill weave or a tapestry weave for a family room couch? Which would you choose for a seldom-used living room couch? Why?
8. Explain the tufting process. What household textile is most commonly tufted?
9. What are five main types of fabrics that are not produced by weaving or knitting?
10. In what stages can fabric be dyed? Which is the most expensive?
11. Describe the three main types of printing used on fabric.
12. List four possible functions of a fabric finish.

10 Furniture Styles

After studying this chapter, you will be able to:
- List the distinguishing features of furniture from the Late Renaissance, Baroque, Regency, Rococo, Neoclassic, Directoire, and Empire periods in France.
- Describe furniture of various styles from the Early, Middle, and Late Renaissance periods in England.
- List the distinguishing features of the furniture of Chippendale, Hepplewhite, Sheraton, and the Adam brothers.
- Describe the differences between Early American, American Georgian, and Federal furniture.
- List and describe the regional styles of furniture in America.
- List the main features of furniture in 20th century styles.

Furniture styles may be classified into the broad categories of traditional (or period) and 20th century. Within both categories, there are several styles. The term *style* refers to a distinctive manner of design. The primary characteristics of several furniture styles are presented in this chapter. Several terms used in the description of these styles are listed in 10-1.

TRADITIONAL STYLES

The traditional styles of furniture discussed in this chapter originated during historical periods in France, England, and the United States. Many European styles were inspired by rulers who commissioned cabinetmakers to produce designs that pleased them. For example,

Acanthus leaves	Large leaves used by the Greeks in decoration of architecture and artwork.	**Marquetry**	Wooden inlays used to create patterns in furniture finishes. Special woods in interesting grain patterns or colors are often used. Marquetry is sometimes cut into shapes such as flowers, or sometimes materials other than wood are used.
Arabesque	A scrolled leaf pattern, generally symmetrical in design.		
Bible box	A small box used in colonial times to hold the family Bible.		
Bun foot	A furniture support that is the shape of a flattened ball.	**Ormolu**	An alloy of copper and zinc with a gold-like appearance, used for furniture decoration.
Flemish	Features that are characteristic of the region of Flanders. In medieval times, Flanders was a country bordered by France and Belgium.	**Palmette**	A motif used on furniture resembling a fan-shaped palm branch.
Flemish foot	A furniture foot featuring a scroll design in an S or C shape.	**Ribband back chair**	A chair whose back has a pattern of interlaced ribbons.
Fluting	Parallel grooves used to ornament a surface. Fluting is commonly used on furniture supports and architectural columns.	**Spade foot**	A furniture foot with a squared-off, tapered shape. The spade foot is often set apart from the leg by a slight projection at the top of the foot.
Gothic	Term used to describe the arts of the middle ages. Cathedrals of this period, such as Notre Dame, are examples of this style. Gothic features are sometimes copied in furniture.	**Spooned back splat**	A vertical, spoon shaped strip of carved wood used as a chairback. The contoured shape is considered more comfortable than the shape of a flat splat.
Gothic tracery	Lacelike patterns cut in stone on Gothic architecture.	**Thimble foot**	A furniture foot with the same shape as a spade foot.
Gilded bronze	Bronze that is worked into very thin sheets and used as decorative overlays on furniture.	**Trestle**	A very plain table consisting of a wood slab for a top and a wood frame as a support.
Ionic capital	In ancient Greek and Roman architecture, a scroll shaped decoration used at the top of a column.	**Turning**	An ornamentation used on furniture legs and other pieces made by rotating wood on a lathe and shaping it with cutting tools.

10-1 Several terms are used in the description of furniture styles.

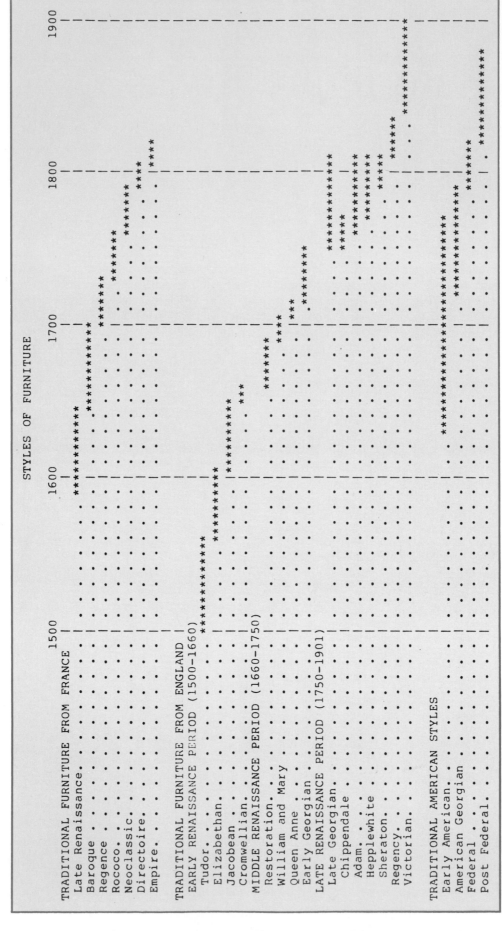

STYLES OF FURNITURE

10-2 Many traditional styles overlap in their time span of popularity.

10-3 *This Louis XIII cabinet is made of ebony. Although it has heavy proportions, several slender columns are used for support. The cabinet rests on bun feet.*

Napoleon inspired the French Empire style. Other furniture styles, like Queen Anne, were simply named after the reigning monarch. Still other furniture styles were named after the cabinetmakers who produced them. Chippendale and Hepplewhite are examples. A chart of traditional styles, their time periods, and their countries of origin is given in 10-2.

TRADITIONAL FURNITURE FROM FRANCE

Traditional furniture styles from France are often associated with the reigns of Louis XIII, XIV, XV, and XVI; the French Revolution; and the reign of Napoleon. However, the changes in furniture styles do not exactly correspond to the reigns of these rulers. The periods of French design are Late Renaissance, Baroque, Regence, Rococo, Neoclassic, Directoire, and Empire.

Late Renaissance (1589-1643)

The Late Renaissance period spanned the reigns of Henry IV and Louis XIII. Under these monarchs, both Italian and Flemish influence could be seen in furniture styles. Furniture was large and upright. Walnut, oak, and ebony were the primary woods used, 10-3. *Marquetry*, tortoiseshell, and gilded bronze were used for ornamentation, 10-4.

10-4 *This Louis XIII cabinet has intricate marquetry used on the doors and the inside chamber. Ormolu columns are used for decoration.*

Tall, slender columns and spiral *turnings* were used for supports and decoration. Bun feet and Flemish feet were typical of furniture during this period.

Baroque (1643-1700)

The Baroque period roughly corresponds to the reign of Louis XIV (1643-1715). The furniture of this period was massive, rectangular, and heavy in proportion, 10-5. Marble table tops were placed on elaborately carved, square legs. Upholstered chairs and sofas were covered in rich tapestries, brocades, and silks.

Moldings, carvings, and marquetry were still used, but new techniques to make more elaborate furniture were introduced by André-Charles Boulle. Boulle was master cabinetmaker to Louis XIV. He introduced the use of *ormolu,* an alloy of copper and zinc with the luster of gold, to use for ornamentation. He also created dazzling new inlays by using pewter, brass, and semitransparent tortoiseshell. This technique, known today as *boulle work,* was typical of Baroque furniture.

Regence (1700-1730)

The Regence period covered the later portion of the reign of Louis XIV. Furniture was still large, but more curves and lighter motifs were used in the designs, 10-6. The *cabriole leg,* a curved support in the shape of an animal leg, was introduced at this time, 10-7. Walnut and ebony began to be replaced by lighter woods. Regence was a transitional style between Baroque and Rococo.

10-6 Furniture of the Regence period is large, but not as severely rectangular as Baroque furniture. This Louis XIV chair represents a transition between the Baroque and Rococo styles. Curves and cabriole legs can be seen.

Rococo (1730-1760)

During the reign of Louis XV (1715-1774), intimacy and romanticism replaced the massive pomp of the Baroque style. Furniture was scaled down to more human proportions. Curves, flowing lines, and asymmetry replaced the

10-5 Baroque furniture was seldom in proportion to the people using it. This Louis XIV chair has massive proportions, square legs, and rich tapestry upholstery.

10-7 This Regence table has cabriole legs and ormolu ornamentation.

NATIONAL GALLERY OF ART

10-8 This Louis XV sofa is an example of the romanticism of the Rococo period. Flowing curves, floral garlands, and scroll feet are used for decoration.

rectangular Baroque shapes, 10-8. The carbriole leg, used in the Regence style, took on more elaborate form, and a scroll foot replaced the earlier goat's hoof.

Ornamentation was based on shapes of shells, foliage, shepards' crooks, and musical instruments. Inlaying and

NATIONAL GALLERY OF ART, WASHINGTON, DC

10-9 This Louis XV dressing table uses marquetry for a geometric herringbone pattern as well as for fish and floral decorations.

marquetry of exotic woods were used, 10-9. Painted furniture, in pale or neutral colors with contrasting molding, became popular at this time.

Marble or leather tops were common on furniture pieces. Chairs were thickly cushioned and covered in patterned fabrics, 10-10. Fabric designs harmonized with the curved forms of the furniture.

The Rococo style was the first traditional style that was truly French in origin. Italian influence of the Renaissance and Baroque styles was lost during this period. However, Chinese lacquer and Oriental motifs became popular components of Rococo furniture.

Neoclassic (1760-1789)

Neoclassic furniture was established in style just a few years before the reign of Louis XVI (1774-1789). Financial tension within France at this time led to a trend toward simplicity among aristocrats. Sometimes called the Classic Revival style, the Neoclassic style kept the intimacy of Rococo but returned to the straight lines of earlier styles.

Free curves and excessive ornamentation were replaced with straight lines, geometric curves, and symmetry, 10-11. Cabriole legs became less curved and eventually disappeared. Straight, tapered legs were emphasized with fluting and grooving, 10-12.

Ornamentation was of simpler carvings and marquetry. Motifs included roses, garlands, ribbons, and Cupid's bows and darts. Some Greek and Roman influences were seen toward the end of the period.

139

10-11 Neoclassic furniture kept the smaller proportions of Rococo styles but returned to straight lines.

Directoire (1789-1804)

The Directoire was the governmental body that ruled France for a short time after the French Revolution. The political upheaval disrupted the production of furniture. Those pieces that were built retained the graceful lines and proportions of the Neoclassic style associated with Louis XVI. However, symbols reminiscent of the French monarchy were rejected.

Motifs included military and agricultural forms such as arrows, spears, drums, stars, and wheat. Furniture woods were mainly native fruitwood, walnut, and oak.

10-10 Floral brocades were popular during the Rococo period. This Louis XV chair has thick cushioning.

10-12 Fluted legs and simpler marquetry were common for Neoclassic furniture like this Louis XVI writing table.

10-13 Greek motifs like this charioteer were popular during the Directoire period.

Greek and Egyptian forms were popular, 10-13. Chair backs that rolled back and sofa arms that curved out were borrowed from Greek styles. Furniture of this period is seen as a transition between the Neoclassic and Empire styles.

Empire (1804-1820)

Napoleon's political and military power inspired the Empire furniture style. He placed his mark on all aspects of the arts. Furniture became masculine with geometric shapes, absolute symmetry, and heavy, solid proportions,

10-14. Less carving and marquetry were used. Large surfaces featured plain, highly polished veneers, 10-15.

Ornamentation was mainly of bronze and ormolu. Motifs included military symbols; ancient Egyptian, Roman, and Greek symbols; and Napoleon's initial.

Styles were patterned after Greek and Roman designs, 10-16. These were chosen to emulate the power of Alexander and Caesar. Chairs and sofas of wood were designed to look like ancient stone and bronze ceremonial seats. Tabletops were of thick marble. The most popular wood was mahogany, but elm and maple were also used.

Toward the end of the Empire period, mass production began to take root in France. Factory techniques produced furniture that was of inferior quality but relatively inexpensive. Thus, the Empire style was the last of the great French traditional styles.

TRADITIONAL FURNITURE FROM ENGLAND: EARLY RENAISSANCE PERIOD

The first of three main periods of traditional furniture from England is the Early Renaissance period (1500-1660). Early Renaissance furniture styles include Tudor, Elizabethan, Jacobean, and Cromwellian. Each of these styles allowed a progressive tradition from *Gothic* to Middle Renaissance furniture. Often, this period is called the Age of Oak.

Tudor (1500-1558)

The Tudor style spanned the reigns of Henry VII, Henry VIII, Edward VI, and Mary. Italian Renaissance influence was not as strong in England as it was in other European countries. Dutch and Flemish designs were much more influential.

While lighter woods were being used throughout Europe, native oak remained the primary wood for

10-14 The plain, masculine design of this Empire couch was typical during Napoleon's reign.

SMITHSONIAN INSTITUTION PHOTO NO. 46933B

10-15 The plain veneer of this card table was common during the Empire period.

English furniture. Ornamentation included simple carving and inlaying. The Tudor rose and coat of arms and *arabesques* were common motifs. Overall appearance was large and heavy, and structural forms were rectangular as in the Gothic period.

Elizabethan (1558-1603)

The massive strength of the Tudor style remained during the reign of Elizabeth. Ornamentation was also similar, although a new type of decoration, called a *bulbous* form, was added to furniture supports. This melon shape was usually decorated with carvings or turnings.

Turned chairs and wainscott chairs were common during the Elizabethan period. A *turned chair* had a triangular seat with heavy, thick turnings for the back, arms, and legs. A *wainscott chair* had a rectangular, wooden seat with turned or column legs, and a carved or inlaid wooden back.

Jacobean (1603-1649)

Jacobean furniture was produced during the reigns of James I and Charles I. During this time, furniture became slightly smaller, lighter, and less ornamented, 10-17. Bulbous forms became more slender; carving was less pronounced; and more emphasis was placed on turning and fluting.

Motifs of acanthus leaves, intertwined circles, palmettes, and ionic capitals were used. Caricatures of human heads, called *romayne work,* were also used for decoration. *Split balusters,* or split spindles, (short, turned pieces of wood split in half) were often glued to surfaces. Upholstered chairs gained popularity, 10-18.

Cromwellian (1649-1660)

The Cromwellian period was a time of civil war, so furniture development was halted. Furniture of this time was plain and undecorated, 10-19. None of the European Baroque influence was felt at this time in England.

THE ST. LOUIS ART MUSEUM

10-16 Greek motifs decorate these Empire chairs. Concave legs were typical of chairs from this period.

10-17 Jacobean furniture had little ornamentation. The slender bulbous forms on the legs are the only decorations for this Jacobean stool.

10-19 This Cromwellian chair has little ornamentation.

10-18 This Jacobean side chair has a cushioned seat. Upholstered furniture became more popular during this period in England.

TRADITIONAL FURNITURE FROM ENGLAND: MIDDLE RENAISSANCE PERIOD

The second of three main periods of traditional furniture from England is the Middle Renaissance period (1660-1750). This period marked the close of the Age of Oak and the beginning of the Age of Walnut in England. Furniture styles include Restoration, William and Mary, and Queen Anne.

Restoration (1660-1689)

After the return of the monarchy, furniture became more extravagant again. Under the reigns of Charles II and James II, European styles—expecially Italian and French Baroque—influenced English furniture. Walnut became the popular wood.

Carvings and spiral turnings were still used, but marquetry and gilded metal gained popularity. Oriental lacquer was introduced at this time. Scrolls and floral patterns were common motifs. Caned chairs sported elaborate cushions with silk fringes.

William and Mary (1689-1702)

During the reign of William and Mary, furniture became simpler, more elegant, and less ornate, 10-20. Woods were highly polished. Oriental lacquer gained popularity, and a new, less expensive technique called

10-20 This William and Mary desk is an example of the simple, but elegant, furniture produced during this period. Small amounts of marquetry and metal are used for decoration. Bun feet support the desk.

japanning was used to imitate the finish. Marquetry continued to be used.

Caned chairs became unfashionable and were replaced by wooden chairs with stuffed and upholstered backs and seats. Some leg forms were squared; others had mushroom, bell, or inverted cup turnings. Many legs ended in bun feet.

Queen Anne (1702-1714)

During the reign of Queen Anne, a strong Oriental influence was seen in furniture design. For the first time, gracefully curved lines dominated English furniture styles, 10-21. The cabriole leg, inspired by Oriental design, replaced the earlier, turned legs. Motifs included scalloped shells and Oriental designs such as the lion mask. The claw and ball foot, adapted from a Chinese symbol, was used at the bottom of furniture legs. Spooned back splats in curved shapes added comfort to chair backs, 10-22.

Early Georgian (1714-1750)

Early Georgian styles are from the reign of George I. Styles of this period are so close to Queen Anne styles that they are often grouped as one style. Early Georgian furniture was heavier than Queen Anne furniture, and it further accented the curved line, 10-23. Large veneered surfaces were featured. Spooned backs, cabriole legs, and claw and ball feet were still common features.

10-21 This Queen Anne style highboy features shell motifs and cabriole legs. The Queen Anne period was the first in England to feature curved lines.

10-22 The chairs in this Queen Anne style dining room set have spooned back splats.

THE BIGGS CO.

10-23 Georgian furniture had more accented curves than Queen Anne furniture. Larger proportions also were used.

TRADITIONAL FURNITURE FROM ENGLAND: LATE RENAISSANCE PERIOD

The last of three main periods of traditional furniture from England is the Late Renaissance period (1750-1901). Styles of this period include late Georgian, Regency, and Victorian. The Age of Walnut and the Age of Satinwood occurred during the Late Renaissance period.

DIPLOMATIC RECEPTION ROOMS, US DEPARTMENT OF STATE

10-24 This Chippendale chair features the upholstery and curved lines that were popular in the late Georgian period. Carvings imitating Gothic tracery are used on the front legs.

Late Georgian (1750-1810)

The late Georgian period spans parts of the reigns of George II and George III. New prosperity during this period called for more elaborate furniture.

Styles of this period were influenced by England's master cabinetmakers and prominent furniture designers: Thomas Chippendale, George Hepplewhite, Thomas Sheraton, and Robert and James Adam.

Thomas Chippendale. A London cabinetmaker, Thomas Chippendale produced refined, high quality furniture that capitalized on styles of the times, 10-24. In 1754, he published *The Gentlemen and Cabinet-Maker's Director* which illustrated his Queen Anne, French Rococo, Gothic, and Chinese styles. See 10-25.

Chairs were some of Chippendale's best and most characteristic pieces. They had elaborately carved backs in many styles, 10-26. Patterns were taken from Gothic tracery, Chinese laticework, and Rococo motifs. The *ribband back chair* had an intricate design credited to Chippendale. Earlier chairs had cabriole legs, but later straight, square legs were used.

Chippendale worked almost exclusively in mahogany. Although Chippendale made many styles, his Chinese furniture was distinctive, and it is often labeled "Chinese Chippendale." See 10-27.

George Hepplewhite. In contrast to Chippendale's work, Hepplewhite featured slender lines and delicate proportions, 10-28. Subtle curves were incorporated. He used straight, tapered legs that were round or square. The legs ended in straight, spade, or thimble feet, 10-29. Chair backs were made in heart, oval, camel, wheel, and shield designs, 10-30. Satinwood was popularized by Hepplewhite for its lighter quality; however, he used mahogany as well.

Little ornamentation was used on Hepplewhite furniture. Carvings included wheat, oval patterns, ribbons, and fluting. Painted motifs were an innovation of Hepplewhite's, and they included the three-feathered crest of the Prince of Wales and floral designs.

Thomas Sheraton. Thomas Sheraton designed furniture that other cabinetmakers constructed. He published *The Cabinetmaker and Upholsterer's Drawing Book* in 1791, 10-31. The book presented the furniture styles of 1791-1793. Like Chippendale, Sheraton became established as a leader in the cabinetmaking industry because of his book's success.

Sheraton's designs were dominated by straight lines, 10-32. He replaced Hepplewhite's flowing curves with segmented curves joined by straight lines. Although his chair legs were like Hepplewhite's, his chair backs were rectangular.

Motifs for Sheraton's pieces included urns, swags, and leaves. He was the first in England to decorate furniture with porcelain plaques. Sheraton designed pieces that incorporated such mechanical devices as disappearing drawers, folding tables, and secret compartments.

The Adam brothers. Robert and James Adam were architects who employed cabinetmakers to build furniture

10-25 These drawings are taken from Chippendale's book, The Gentleman and Cabinetmaker's Director. *They illustrate features typical of Chippendale's work.*

10-26 This Chippendale chair features horizontal splats that are knotted in the center. This type of chairback is often called a "pretzel back."

10-28 Hepplewhite designs were typically more slender than Chippendale designs. This desk features painted motifs, an innovation of Hepplewhite's.

A

B

10-27 These Chinese Chippendale pieces have a distinctive Oriental design. The chair (A) is carved to imitate bamboo. The cabinet (B) features an Oriental lacquer finish.

10-29 *This drawing of Hepplewhite couch features spade or thimble feet. The drawing is taken from* The Cabinetmaker and Upholsterer's Guide, *published by Hepplewhite's wife after his death.*

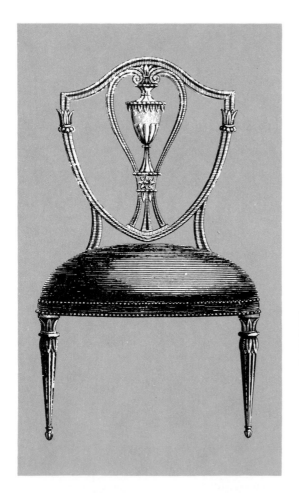

10-30 *These Hepplewhite chairs feature backs with shield designs.*

10-31 These drawings are taken from Sheraton's Cabinetmaker and Upholsterer's Drawing Book. *They feature more straight lines than Hepplewhite's furniture.*

10-32 *This Sheraton chair has segmented curves joined by straight lines. The chair back is rectangular.*

that would complement their architecture. Their styles were symmetrical and were inspired by Greek and Pompeiian designs, 10-33. The Adam brothers aided the transition from mahogany to satinwood as the preferred furniture wood.

Regency (1810-1837)

The Regency period marked the beginning of the decline of English furniture design. Cabinetmakers were drained of their ability to create new designs. Therefore, they drew upon ancient Roman, Greek, and Egyptian designs for styles and motifs. See 10-34 and 10-35.

Victorian (1837-1901)

Under the reign of Queen Victoria, furniture designs were *eclectic,* borrowing from several earlier styles, 10-36. As industrialism began to take hold, motifs from earlier periods were combined, altered, and adapted to machine processes. Light and dark woods were contrasted, and incised lines became more common than carving, 10-37. Furniture became less expensive and was geared toward a middle-class market.

TRADITIONAL AMERICAN STYLES

Furniture of early America was a mixture of many styles from many lands. Colonists imported furniture and the

10-33 These drawings are from The Works of Architecture of Robert and James Adam. *Their Greek and Pompeiian designs were used in furniture as well as architecture.*

COURTESY OF THE ART INSTITUTE OF CHICAGO

10-34 This English Regency chair is patterned after Roman or Greek designs. It features concave legs.

methods to make it from their native homelands. Therefore, traditional American furniture styles are belated reflections of European styles.

Traditional American styles of furniture may be placed in the following categories: Early American, American Georgian, Federal, and Post Federal.

DIPLOMATIC RECEPTION ROOMS, US DEPARTMENT OF STATE

10-35 This Regency mirror features symmetrical leaf designs like those in Greek art.

PHOTO NO. 76-9294

SMITHSONIAN INSTITUTION

A

THE ST. LOUIS ART MUSEUM

B

PHOTO NO. 73-6083

SMITHSONIAN INSTITUTION

C

10-36 Victorian Furniture was heavily eclectic, borrowing from Renaissance (A), Rococo (B), Gothic (C), and other styles.

10-37 This Victorian bed uses rosewood and satinwood for a contrasting design.

Early American (1630-1770)

Most Early American furniture was patterned after English Gothic and Jacobean styles. However, Early American styles were smaller and simpler. The American colonists were lower and middle class rural people who were not familiar with royal European furniture. They also lacked proper tools, skills, and wood to copy the intricate designs of Europe. Homes were smaller, and survival, not furniture, was the main concern.

Home furnishings, for the most part, were few and very basic. The most standard item was the chest. It ranged from a small Bible box to a large trunk with drawers, 10-38. Chests, as well as other Early American furniture, often served dual functions. For instance, a slanted Bible box could be used as a lap desk. A low trunk doubled as a seat.

10-38 This large chest has two drawers. Split spindles are glued on for decoration.

10-39 Chair tables were popular for tiny colonial houses because they saved space.

Tables were very plain; some were in the simple *trestle* style. To save space, drop-leaf and chair tables were often used. A chair table has a top that can be tilted back to make a chair. See 10-39. Many homes had only one chair and several small stools or benches for seating.

Chairs were straight and upright, with flat or caned seats, 10-40. Early chair backs often had vertical posts which ran across the back space. These chairs, called *slat-back* chairs, were rather uncomfortable, 10-41. Later, slat-backs were replaced with horizontal slats or split spindles. These kinds of chairs, called ladder back chairs, were more comfortable, 10-42. Large cupboards were important pieces in kitchens. Four-poster beds, trundle beds, and wooden cradles were used in the bedrooms, 10-43.

Furniture decoration included split-spindles, turnings, and bun feet. Geometric or floral patterns were carved in low relief. Painted decoration was sometimes added or used in the place of carving, 10-44. Pine, beech, and ash woods were used for furniture because they were plentiful.

By the end of the 17th century, colonists began to take greater interest in comfort and beauty. Styles began to change. Upholstered chairs and beds with curtains became more popular. Trained furniture makers had come to America, and they made furniture in the William and Mary style. Bun feet, and turnings in mushrooms, bells, and inverted cups were used. *Highboys, lowboys,* and *chests* were produced, 10-45. Walnut and mahogany became more popular woods.

American Georgian (1720-1790)

As the wealthy population grew in the colonies, people sought styles based on the English Georgian periods.

L & JG STICKLEY, INC.

10-41 The vertical posts of slat-back chairs made sitting uncomfortable.

Skilled American cabinetmakers, originally from England, began to reproduce English styles by copying from imported models and design books.

These cabinetmakers made some exact copies, but soon they varied the styles. American interpretations of English furniture are labeled with such names as "American Queen

L & JG STICKLEY, INC.

10-40 This Early American chair has an inexpensive, caned seat. A crude attempt was made to copy a Queen Anne style chairback.

SMITHSONIAN INSTITUTION PHOTO NO. 62.1760

10-42 Ladder back chairs were more comfortable than slat-back chairs.

10-43 This plain cradle is typical of colonial style furniture.

Anne" or "American Chippendale." See 10-46. Interpretations varied from region to region. Boston, Newport, New York, and Philadelphia emerged as design centers with their own distinct furniture styles.

American chairs were contoured to fit the human form. Many were styled after Chippendale, Hepplewhite, and Sheraton designs. Couches and upholstered chairs, like the wing chair, became very popular.

By 1760, the Windsor chair from England became a standard in the colonies. American versions seldom had cabriole legs and ornamental back splats. Instead slender, turned legs that slanted outward were used, and banister backs in several distinctive shapes replaced English splats. A popular variation of the Windsor chair was a rocking chair that originated in Boston, 10-47.

One version of a chest called a *secretary* became popular during this period, 10-48. It had drawers and a hinged writing surface. Highboys and lowboys became the most elegant storage pieces built in America, 10-49. Philadelphia designs became the most popular; these had cabriole legs, simple lines, elaborate decoration, and brass hardware, 10-50.

10-44 Carved furniture was rare in early colonial days. Instead, paint was used for decoration.

10-45 With trained cabinetmakers in America, furniture became more refined. This simple, but elegant, chest features marquetry, brass handles, and bun feet.

PHOTO NO. 76-1613

SMITHSONIAN INSTITUTION

A

C

DIPLOMATIC RECEPTION ROOMS, US DEPARTMENT OF STATE

B

DIPLOMATIC RECEPTION ROOMS, US DEPARTMENT OF STATE

10-46 During the American Georgian period, American cabinetmakers developed their own variations of English styles, such as American Queen Anne (A), American Chippendale (B), and American Empire (C).

PHOTO NO. 76-1615

SMITHSONIAN INSTITUTION

10-47 The Windsor rocker is an American version of the English Windsor chair.

Federal (1790-1820)

Little of any consequence to furniture designs happened during the American Revolution. As normal relations with England resumed, English styles were again adopted by American cabinetmakers. Cabinetmakers had refined their techniques by this time, and pieces of excellent quality

SMITHSONIAN INSTITUTION PHOTO NO. 72-4427

10-49 Highboys are chests that stand on tall legs. This highboy was made in Massachusettes.

SMITHSONIAN INSTITUTION PHOTO NO. 80-13975

10-48 The secretary has drawers, a hinged writing surface, and doors above the writing surface.

SMITHSONIAN INSTITUTION PHOTO NO. 46,936-A

10-50 This Philadelphia highboy features cabriole legs with claw and ball feet, intricate carving, and brass handles.

were produced. American furniture of this period was delicate and of excellent proportions, but not as elaborate as English styles, 10-51.

Federal style furniture was made from mahogany, satinwood, cherry, rosewood, maple, apple, and pear. Ornamentation was patriotic in nature. After the eagle was adopted as a national symbol, the motif was widely used to decorate furniture. Other symbols included cornucopias, fruit, flowers, and spiral turnings, 10-52.

In the late 1700's, the French Revolution brought an influx of aristocrats to America, and French-American bonds were strengthened. The American Directoire furniture style was inspired by this French influence. Chairs and sofas were modeled after Greek and Roman designs. Furniture legs were often concave, 10-53. Motifs include lion heads, acanthus leaves, lyres, swags, and festoons, 10-54.

Duncan Phyfe was considered the outstanding cabinetmaker of the Federal period. He designed his own interpretations of the Sheraton, Directoire, and Empire styles, 10-55. He worked primarily in mahogany and satinwood. Phyfe sets the standards for other cabinetmakers of the time.

Regional styles. Although the English and French dominated American design, other immigrant groups brought distinctive styles to the New World. The Germans, Scandinavians, and Shakers had distinct furniture styles that were eventually adopted by other Americans.

The German Masonites settled in Pennsylvania and used furniture that was simple and sturdy, but cheerful. They decorated their furniture with brightly painted or stenciled

10-52 Motifs of fruit and flowers are painted on this chair from the Federal period. Spiral turnings are used on the chair legs.

designs. The motifs included tulips, hearts, birds, and leaves in bright, cheerful colors. These people and their furniture styles were mistakenly called Pennsylvania "Dutch" instead of "Deutsch" which means German.

Scandinavians settled in the Midwest, mostly in Minnesota and Wisconsin. Their furniture styles were similar

10-51 This Federal style chair is similar to Hepplewhite designs, but it is simpler. Fewer curves are used, and painted designs are used in place of intricate carving.

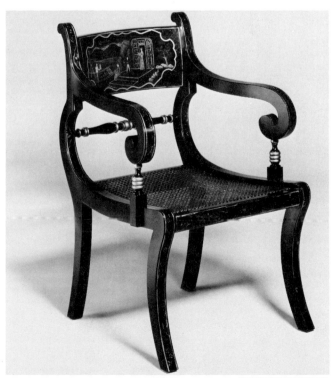

10-53 This American Directoire chair features concave legs.

10-54 Influence of the French Empire style can be seen in this Federal worktable with concave legs and a lyre motif.

to those of the Pennsylvania Dutch, but they used animal and human motifs. The Scandinavian painted designs were more realistic than those of the Pennsylvania Dutch and did not have as much popular appeal.

The Shakers were a religious group from England who valued cleanliness, order, and functionalism. They were strict, hard-working people, and their thoughts about lifestyle influenced their furniture designs. Their furniture was lightweight, simple, easy to clean, and completely void of ornamentation, 10-56. Much of their furniture was built into the room, and many pieces served more than one function. The Shaker concept that every object should have a function is considered the forerunner of modern design concepts.

Post Federal (1820-1880)

During the Post Federal era, America began to develop a large class of wealthy industrialists. This group called for furniture that demonstrated their wealth even if the furniture was not well designed.

From 1820 to 1840, the American Empire style was popular. This furniture had heavy proportions and cumbersome lines. Furniture from this period is considered to mark the decline of American furniture styles. Duncan Phyfe is said to have referred to his furniture from this period as "butcher furniture."

From 1840 to 1880, American designs were patterned after English Victorian styles. American Victorian, like

A

B

10-55 Duncan Phyfe patterned his work after styles such as Sheraton (A) and Federal (B).

WALTER TUCKER

10-56 Shaker furniture is simple and unornamented.

its English counterpart, borrowed heavily from past designs. Often, several designs were mixed on one furniture piece resulting in a cluttered look, 10-57. As in England, American designs were adapted to mechanization.

20TH CENTURY STYLES

The cluttered Victorian styles of the late 1880's caused furniture designers to react with simpler lines and forms. Styles popularized in the 20th century include: Art Nouveau, Frank Lloyd Wright, Bauhaus, Scandinavian, and Contemporary.

Art Nouveau

The Art Nouveau style was based on a rebellion against the ornamentation of the Victorian style, 10-58. Almost no ornamentation was used, and inexpensive woods

SMITHSONIAN INSTITUTION PHOTO NO. 72-2960

10-57 This post-Federal desk mixes different types of wood. Pieces were made using mechanization.

PHOTO NO. 79-7677

SMITHSONIAN INSTITUTION

10-58 This Art Nouveau chair is much simpler than Victorian chairs of the time. Later Art Nouveau chairs are similar in shape, but the backs and legs are almost completely unornamented.

PHOTO NO. 72-10527

COURTESY OF THE ART INSTITUTE OF CHICAGO

SMITHSONIAN INSTITUTION

10-59 Frank Lloyd Wright furniture is rectangular and unornamented. The simple design gives emphasis to the natural grain patterns of the wood used.

HERMAN MILLER

10-60 The Bauhaus principles of simple design were used to make this Eames chair. Leather is stretched over a metal framework. Leather cushions are added for comfort.

replaced mahogany and satinwood. The idea of Art Nouveau was to create furniture that was beautiful for its artistic merit, not its cost.

Furniture was designed to work with mechanization, not against it. Furniture of this time was based on flowing, natural lines ending in a curve similar to the bud of a plant. Art Nouveau furniture is still popular, and pieces may be seen in many restaurants, night clubs, and cafes.

Frank Lloyd Wright

In the early 20th century, Wright designed and built a series of homes which he called Prairie Houses. They represented the beginning of modern home design, and they offered innovations in furniture design.

Wright architecture placed more emphasis on nature and used fewer lines and forms. Wright believed that a structure, its surroundings, and its furnishings should be parts of a whole. He tried to accomplish this by blending the structure into its surroundings and integrating the furniture into the structure wherever possible.

Furniture was composed of geometric shapes, slats, and flat surfaces, 10-59. It is often regarded as architectural sculpture. Surfaces were usually natural and void of ornament.

Bauhaus

Walter Gropius founded a school known as the Bauhaus in Germany in 1919. The school focused on the design of buildings, furniture, textiles, and household articles which were made by machine. The guiding principle was to simplify the design of objects.

One of the first examples of the Bauhaus thrust was a tubular steel chair, designed by Hungarian Marcel Breuer in 1925. The chair had canvas or leather straps stretched across metal tubes to form the seat, back, and arm rests. There have been many adaptions of this chair, 10-60.

Mies Van der Rohe became director of the Bauhaus in 1930 and worked to spread the machine oriented point of view in Europe and the United States. Styles were based on the philosophy that form follows function. Only those features that directly concerned function were included in Bauhaus design.

Scandinavian

Scandinavian design was influenced by traditional Nordic methods used to make molded skis. Wood was curved by applying heat or steam to many veneers of wood, 10-61. Scandinavian white birch, a light, highly resilient wood, was commonly used, 10-62. As mechanization reached Scandinavia, these techniques were applied to furniture production. The result was a sleek, clean-lined style of furniture which was both elegant and functional.

Contemporary

Contemporary furniture styles are the very latest designs. They contain the new, the unclassified, and the experimental. No rules or guidelines apply to contemporary furniture design, and it is impossible to know which

WESTNOFA USA, INC.

10-61 *This unique Scandinavian dining set was made by curving the veneered wood pieces.*

WESTNOFA USA, INC.

10-62 *Birch is a popular wood for Scandinavian furniture.*

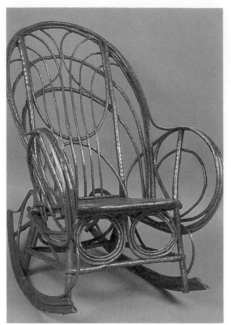

10-63 This contemporary rocking chair is made from bent willow branches painted gold.

contemporary designs of today will become the classic styles of tomorrow.

Many contemporary designs incorporate plastic, metal, glass, canvas, or wood, 10-63. Materials are often combined, 10-64. Furniture designers may be inspired by

10-65 These modular shelving units are lightweight and versatile. They can be arranged in many ways to fit in a room or to fill different functions.

10-64 Wood, metal, and glass are materials that are combined in this contemporary desk.

10-66 The bean bag chair originated in the 1970's. It has remained popular because it is colorful, lightweight, inexpensive, and comfortable.

anything from abstract art to everyday objects. Most contemporay designs cater to a middle class, mobile market. They are therefore inexpensive, versatile, and lightweight, 10-65. Some, however, are created simply for the artistic pleasure of the designer.

Some innovations that have remained popular include modular furniture units, folding canvas chairs, bean bag chairs, and waterbeds, 10-66.

REVIEW QUESTIONS

1. What is marquetry?
2. What types of ornamentation were popular for Baroque furniture? What metal was introduced during this period?
3. What kind of furniture leg was introduced during the Regence period in France?
4. What were the main features of Rococo furniture? How did Rococo furniture differ from Baroque furniture?
5. How did the motifs of the Neoclassic period differ from motifs of the Directoire period?
6. What earlier styles were copied in Empire furniture?
7. How did Jacobean furniture differ from Tudor and Elizabethan furniture?

8. What type of furniture finish became popular during the reign of William and Mary?
9. What features were typical of Queen Anne and Early Georgian furniture?
10. How did Chippendale furniture differ from Hepplewhite furniture? How did Hepplewhite furniture differ from Sheraton furniture?
11. What were the most common furnishings in Early American homes? How was the furniture decorated?
12. What furniture styles became popular during the American Georgian period?
13. What motifs were popular during the Federal period?
14. What features were typical of German, Scandinavian, and Shaker furniture?
15. How did mechanization affect furniture production in France, England, and America?
16. What features are most common in 20th century furniture styles?

ACKNOWLEDGEMENTS

pg. 137, 10-3. The Detroit Institute of Arts, gift of friends of K.T. Keller in honor of his 70th birthday, 55.458.

pg. 137, 10-4. The Detroit Institute of Arts, gift of friends of K.T. Keller in honor of his 70th birthday, 55.458.

pg. 138, 10-5. The Metropolitan Museum of Art, Fletcher Fund, 1929 (29.21).

pg. 138, 10-6. The Detroit Institute of Arts, gift of Miss Catherine Oglesby, 54.465.

pg. 141, 10-13. French, Jacob Freres, cabinet, ca. 1796, thuyawood and ebony with ormolu mounts, 40 1/2 in. by 45 1/2 in. by 25 1/2 in., purchased from the bequest of Cornelia Conger, 1974.251, © The Art Institute of Chicago. All rights reserved.

pg. 143, 10-19. Great chair, Boston, ca. 1660, maple, oak, and Russia leather, 38 in. by 23 5/8 in. by 16 3/8 in., Seth K. Sweetser fund, 1977.711, Museum of Fine Arts, Boston.

pg. 144, 10-20. American, Boston area, Massachusetts, desk, 1690-1720, walnut veneer on white pine, 43 1/2 in. by 36 1/4 in. by 20 1/4 in., Antiquarian Society through the following funds: Mrs. Harold T. Martin, Joyce Martin Brown, Melinda Martin Vance, Lena T. Gilbert Trust, 1979.1453, © The Art Institute of Chicago. All rights reserved.

pg. 151, 10-34. American, New York City, side chair, one of a pair, 1810-1820, mahogany (ash secondary wood), 35 in. by 18 1/2 in. by 17 1/2 in., gift of Mrs. Emily Crane Chadbourne, 1929.168, © The Art Institute of Chicago. All rights reserved.

pg. 160, 10-59 (left). Frank Lloyd Wright, library table, designed for Ray W. Evans house, Beverly Hills, Chicago, Illinois, 1908, oak, 28 3/4 in. by 36 in. by 66 in., 70.432, © The Art Institute of Chicago. All rights reserved.

11 Furniture Construction and Selection

After studying this chapter, you will be able to:
- List and describe the types of woods used in furniture construction.
- Evaluate the type and quality of a furniture joint.
- Describe the methods and materials used in the construction of upholstered furniture.
- List ways in which metals and plastics are used in furniture.
- Evaluate the usability of furniture according to its quality, cost, style, size, and maintenance requirements.

Furniture is of major importance to any housing unit. It is a chief factor in physical comfort and in the design of a home. Furniture increases the usefulness of an area and expresses the personality of household members. It

THOMASVILLE FURNITURE INDUSTRIES, INC.

11-1 This dresser is an example of case goods. It is made from maple in a New England style.

can make you feel at ease or uncomfortable in your surroundings.

Furniture is expensive and should be chosen with much care and thought. Price and quality of furniture is affected by the materials and methods used in construction. This chapter provides background information in furniture construction. It also shows you how to use this and other information to evaluate and select appropriate furniture.

Materials and construction are critical factors in the quality of furniture. Well-built pieces from appropriate materials will provide years of useful service, but if either is shortchanged, the results will be less than satisfactory.

Wood, metals, plastics, and fabrics comprise the primary materials used to make furniture. Construction

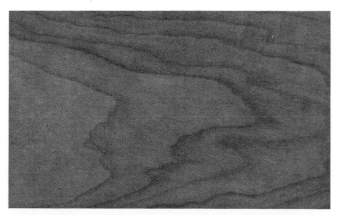

BLACK CHERRY. Fine, closed grained wood, machines well, may be sanded to a smooth finish, moderately hard, heavy (36 lbs./ft.³), reddish-brown in color, beautiful grain pattern, fine furniture wood.

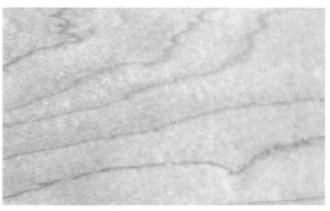

SUGAR MAPLE. (Also called Hard Maple), hard, strong, heavy (44 lbs./ft.³), fine texture, nice grain pattern, light tan color, machines well, fine furniture wood.

PECAN. Great strength and toughness, hard and heavy (50 lbs./ft.³), open grained, light brown in color, machines well, moderate gluing properties, popular furniture wood.

WHITE OAK. Very durable, strong and heavy (47 lbs./ft.³), heartwood is grayish-brown, open grained, glues well, used for quality furniture.

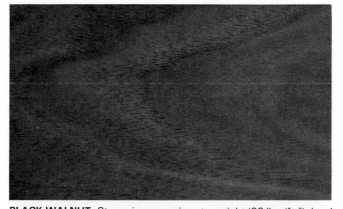

BLACK WALNUT. Strong in comparison to weight (38 lbs./ft.³), hard and dense, excellent machining properties, fine textured, beautiful grain pattern, heartwood is chocolate brown in color, sapwood almost white, very popular quality furniture wood.

11-2 These native hardwoods are used for fine furniture construction.

techniques are mainly concerned with methods of fastening pieces together to form a sturdy assembly that will hold its shape for a long time.

WOOD FURNITURE

The most common material used in furniture is wood. Wood may be the main material used in a piece of furniture. This type of furniture, called *case goods*, includes chests, dressers, tables, headboards, and desks, 11-1. Wood also may be used as a structural framework to be covered by other material as in upholstered furniture.

Wood Types

Various species of wood have different qualitites that make them more suitable for some uses than others. Solid

COCOBOLA. Dense, hard, oily, dark red color, from Central America, tight interwoven grain, somewhat difficult to work, used for fancy cabinetwork.

ROSEWOOD (Brazilian). Very hard, large irregular pores, dark brown with black streaks, also comes from India, Ceylon, Madagascar and Central America, quality furniture material.

MAHOGANY (Honduras). Medium hard and dense (32 lbs./ft.³), stable wood, even textured, open grain, beautiful grain pattern, excellent machining qualities, carves well, used for high quality furniture.

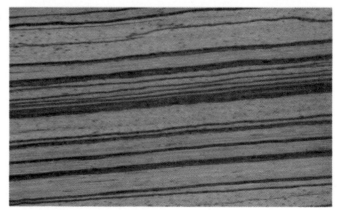

ZEBRAWOOD. (Also called Zebrano), hard, heavy, open grained, medium texture, light golden color with narrow streaks of brown, highly decorative, produces spectacular effect when quarter sawed, from Central and West Africa, excellent furniture material.

TEAK. Hard and strong, brown with a yellow cast, oily, grown in Burma, India, Thailand and Java, fine furniture material.

11-3 These imported woods are used in more exotic quality furniture.

woods, veneers, and processed woods may be used in furniture of different types and qualities. Wood finishes also may vary with the type and quality of a piece.

Woods may be classified as hardwoods or softwoods. *Hardwoods* have been defined as wood coming from trees that lose their leaves in the winter. Wood from trees that bear cones and needles and remain green in all seasons are classified as *softwoods*.

Hardwoods. Hardwoods are generally preferred over softwoods for quality furniture because they have greater dimensional stability, less pitch, and more durability. They are usually harder than softwoods, so they hold nails and screws better and are less likely to dent. However, hardwoods are generally more expensive than softwoods.

The native hardwoods most commonly used for fine furniture are cherry, maple, pecan, oak, and walnut. See

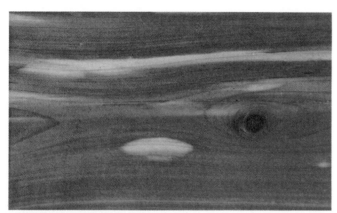

EASTERN RED CEDAR. Close grain, durable, medium dense (34 lbs./ft³), heartwood is red, sapwood is white, nice aroma, used mainly for chests and closets.

CYPRESS. Lightweight (32 lbs./ft³), soft, coarse texture, easily worked, durable, excellent exterior furniture wood, light yellow with brown streaks.

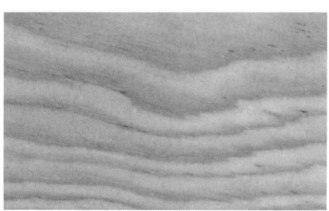

PONDEROSA PINE. Lightweight (28 lbs./ft³), soft, uniform texture, easily worked, rather weak, little warpage, cream to reddish-brown in color, used for rustic furniture.

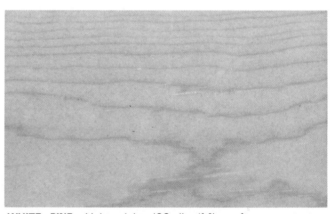

WHITE PINE. Lightweight (28 lbs./ft³), soft, even texture, cream colored, available in knotty pine grades, used for rustic furniture.

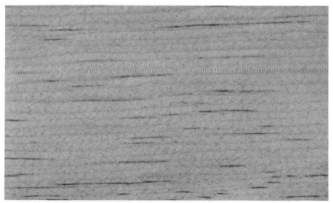

SUGAR PINE. Lightweight (26 lbs./ft³), soft, uniform texture, light brown in color with tiny resin canals, straight grain, warp resistant, easily worked, used for rustic furniture.

REDWOOD. Lightweight (28 lbs./ft³), soft, usually fine and even grained texture, reddish-brown in color, sapwood is lighter, easy to work, durable, used for outdoor furniture.

11-4 These softwoods are commonly used for less expensive or outdoor furniture.

11-2. More exotic, imported woods include cocobola, mahogany, rosewood, teak, and zebrawood, 11-3.

Softwoods. Softwoods generally develop checks and cracks with changing moisture conditions and have less strength than hardwoods, but they are less expensive. Cost may outweigh other considerations depending on how the wood is used.

Softwoods are sometimes used as back panels on case goods, since beauty and strength are not essential. They are also used to make processed woods.

Softwoods are often preferred for rustic or outdoor pieces. For example, pine develops checks and cracks that are considered attractive for country furniture. Redwood is coarse and splintery, but it withstands weather very well and is popular for outdoor furniture.

Popular furniture softwoods include cedar, cypress, pine, and redwood. Their qualities are listed in 11-4.

Wood veneers. Wood veneers permit the use of rare and expensive woods in furniture that would otherwise be too expensive or impractical. *Veneers* are thin slices of wood cut from a log in various ways.

Five basic methods of cutting veneers are used: *rotary cut, flat slicing, quarter slicing, half-round slicing,* and *rift-cut,* 11-5. Most softwood veneers are cut using the rotary cut method. Here, the log is mounted in a lathe and thin layers of wood (veneer) are pulled off as the log is turned producing a bold, variegated, rippled figure pattern.

Flat slicing produces a variegated, wavy figure by slicing parallel to a line through the center of the log. Quarter slicing produces a series of stripes. Here the growth rings are approximately at a right angle to the knife. Half-round slicing has characteristics of both rotary cut and plain sliced veneers. The cut is slightly across the annual growth rings of the log. Rift-cut veneer is used for oak and other woods which have ray cells radiating from the center of the log. This method emphasizes these cell patterns.

Veneer patterns may be obtained by matching pieces of veneer in various ways. The most common patterns are the: *book match, slip match,* and *special match,* 11-6. In book matching, every other sheet is turned over like leaves of a book. Therefore, the back of one veneer sheet meets the front of the adjacent veneer. This produces a matching joint design with a mirrored image look.

Slip matching results when adjacent sheets are joined side by side, without turning, to repeat the same grain pattern. Special matching may be used to produce a variety of patterns—diamond, reverse diamond, "V", herringbone, checkerboard, and others. All of these patterns are used in furniture today.

Veneer figure patterns are greatly affected by the part of the tree used. Although most veneer is cut from the trunk of the tree, some of the most interesting and valuable patterns are cut from the crotch, burl, or stump, 11-7. Veneers cut from a crotch have plume-like designs.

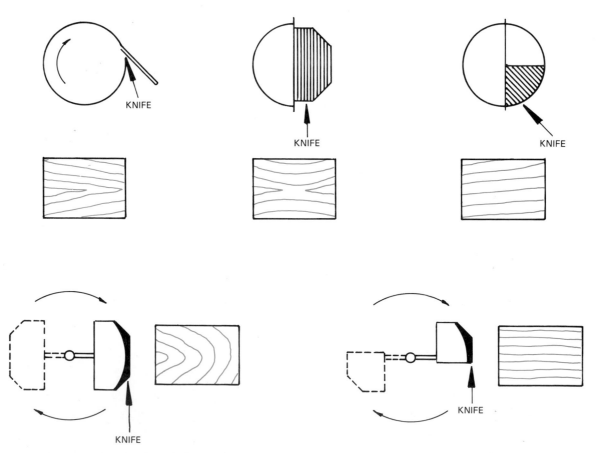

11-5 Different methods of cutting veneers produce different visual characteristics in the veneer. The five basic cutting methods are shown with their typically resulting grain pattern.

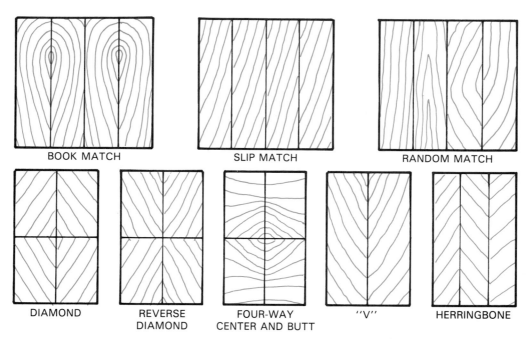

| BOOK MATCH | SLIP MATCH | RANDOM MATCH |

| DIAMOND | REVERSE DIAMOND | FOUR-WAY CENTER AND BUTT | "V" | HERRINGBONE |

11-6 Various methods of matching veneer pieces produce different patterns.

Burls produce veneers with a pattern of swirls, and stumps yield rippling patterns with sharp contrasts.

Veneered furniture is made by gluing together layers, or plies, of wood to make *plywood*. The outer layer is of a better veneer, and less expensive veneers or pressed wood are used as inner layers. Usually three, five, or seven layers are bonded together. The layers are placed so that the grain of one layer is at right angles to the grain of the layer next to it.

Most fine case goods, especially cupboards, chests, and tables, have veneered wood for exterior construction. Veneers are practical when solid wood would be too expensive, like rosewood, or too heavy, like ebony.

Solid wood. If a case good is made from solid wood, any exposed parts are made from the same wood. No veneer is used, but the unexposed parts of the piece may be made from different wood.

Solid wood has a greater tendency to crack, warp, and swell than a well-constructed veneered wood. It is also more expensive than veneer. For these reasons, solid woods are more often used for framework, and veneered wood is used for side, top, front, and back panels. Maple, pine, cherry, and birch are most commonly used for solid wood furniture.

Composite board. New technology has made it possible to make wood boards from wood particles. These processed woods are less expensive and often more durable than solid woods or veneered plywoods. For these reasons, composite board is becoming a common material in furniture.

The two main types of processed woods are *hardboard* and *particle board*. Both are formed by combining wood particles, various resins, pressure, and heat.

Hardboard is made from wood fibers into all-wood panels. The fibers are extracted from wood chips by steam or chemical processes, then they are compressed under heat. Hardboard is exceptionally strong; it is resistant to splits, cracks, splinters, abrasion, and moisture. Its surface can be smooth, or it can be textured to imitate the look of wood grain. However, surface designs cannot

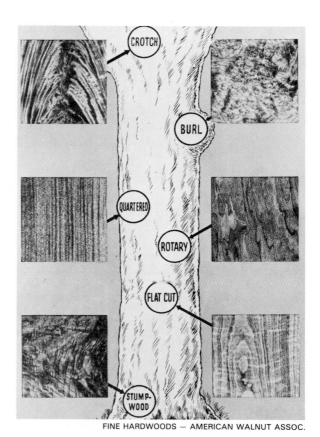

FINE HARDWOODS — AMERICAN WALNUT ASSOC.

11-7 Wood grain cut from different parts of the tree produces different grain patterns.

perfectly match the pattern of fine wood, so hardboard may not be suitable for some furniture uses. Hardboard is considered an excellent material for furniture door and drawers parts, tabletops, and the backs of bookcases, cabinets, and chests in less expensive furniture.

Particle board is made from wood shavings that are pressed together with heat and adhesive. Usually, several kinds of soft woods are used in the same piece of particle board. Fur, poplar, pine, hemlock, and aspen are most commonly used. Like hardboard, particle board is sturdy and versatile.

Particle board is often used as the core wood for cabinets and other furniture of low quality. The surface may be covered with laminated plastic or wood veneer. Uncovered surfaces can be identified as particle board by an irregular crystallized pattern.

Wood Finishes

Fine quality wood furniture should be properly treated and finished. Added color should come from several layers of finishing materials which work with the natural grain of the wood. Polishing, sanding, and rubbing will produce a *patina* — a mellow glow with richness and depth of tone.

Stains, oils, waxes, glazes, or sealers may be used during the finishing process. Good finishes will produce a smooth surface and protect wood from heat, moisture, and scratches.

Poor quality furniture is often finished with thick, stained varnish or one coat of varnish that is dried quickly. Brush marks may be evident on the surface. The shine will be hard and glossy instead of mellow and rich. Such finishes do not last as long as fine finishes.

Wood Furniture Construction

Most furniture today is made using modern machinery, but no piece is entirely "machine-made." Assembly or some finishing details are still performed by hand on quality furniture. The techniques used to fasten the various pieces together are just as important as the materials used in the furniture.

A piece of furniture is no stronger than its joints. Quality joining is expensive and time consuming and frequently hidden from view. Many different techniques and kinds of joints have been developed over the years to produce quality furniture. Several types of joining methods are listed here.

The *butt joint* is the most simple type of joint to construct. It is made by butting the end or edge of one board against the end or edge of another, 11-8. The joint is generally held together with glue, screws, or nails. The surfaces being joined should fit closely and be square with each other. The butt joint is a weak joint.

A *rabbet joint* is formed by cutting a recess in one or both pieces to be joined. The recess may be cut along an edge or on the end, 11-9. Rabbet joints are easy to make and are generally used on the corners of boxes, cases, drawers, and back panels of case goods. Glue and screws

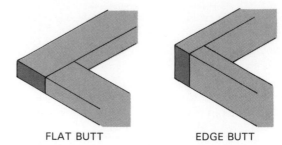

FLAT BUTT   EDGE BUTT

11-8 Butt joints are considered weak joints.

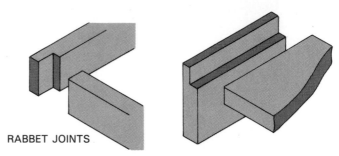

RABBET JOINTS

11-9 The cutting and fitting of a rabbet joint makes it stronger than a butt joint, but it is still relatively weak.

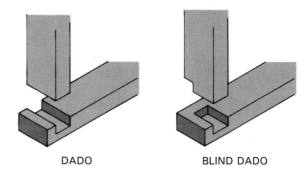

DADO   BLIND DADO

11-10 Dado joints are very strong when properly fitted and glued.

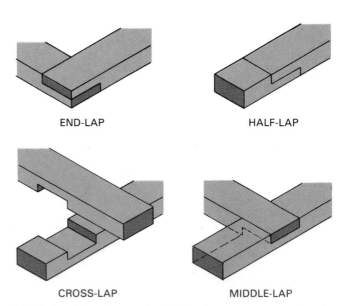

END-LAP   HALF-LAP

CROSS-LAP   MIDDLE-LAP

11-11 Lap joints are used widely in furniture construction for frames and crossed exterior pieces.

or nails may be used. The rabbet joint is stronger than the butt joint.

A *dado* is a rectangular recess cut across the grain of the wood. The dado is cut to the width of the piece to be joined and that piece is fitted into the dado. These joints are used for installing shelves, frames, and partitions in cabinets. They form strong joints when properly glued and carefully fitted. See 11-10.

Several types of *lap joints* may be used in furniture construction. They include: end-lap, half-lap, cross-lap, and middle-lap. Lap joints are made by cutting away an equal amount of wood from each piece so that when they are fitted together their surfaces are flush, 11-11. Lap joints may be used for corners of furniture frames, and they are often used to join exterior pieces of wood which cross each other. Glue and screws (when hidden) may be used to secure the joint for a strong connection.

Dowel joints may be used with several other types of joints such as the butt, rabbet, dado, or lap joints. They are used when extra strength is desired. Dowels are generally made of birch and range in size from 1/8 to 1 inch in increments of 1/8 inch. Length and diameter depend on the size of the pieces being joined. Glue is used to secure the dowels, 11-12.

The *mortise-and-tenon joint* is a very strong type of joint. Three main forms are used: blind, open, and haunched. Their construction is shown in 11-13. They may be used to join legs or rails to tables, benches, and chairs.

A *tongue and groove joint* is used along the common edge of two boards. The tongue is cut on one board and the matching groove is formed on the edge of the other board. The joint may be glued, but usually it is not when used in panel construction. More than one tongue and groove joint may be used on a thick piece of material. This joint forms a solid connection between the pieces, 11-14.

Spline joints may be used along the edges or at the corner of two pieces. A spline joint is a simple butt joint with a thin piece of wood inserted in a groove to strengthen the joint. See 11-15. For greater strength, the grain of the spline should be perpendicular to the groove.

Dovetail joints are used to fasten corner joints especially those on drawers. A high degree of precision is necessary to make a tight-fitting dovetail joint, but it provides maximum strength. Several variations of the dovetail joint are possible such as the lap dovetail, through dovetail, and half blind dovetail. The principle technique is similar, however, in all variations. A typical dovetail joint is shown in 11-16.

Blocking consists of small pieces of wood attached between the adjacent sides of two pieces for added strength. It is used at inside corners such as where a table leg is fastened to a rail and along the rail where it is attached to the table top. Blocking may be used where it would not be unsightly and where more strength is required. Blocks are usually glued and/or screwed in place, 11-17.

All of the joints used in furniture construction may be glued. Modern glues develop tremendous strength and generally exceed the strength of the wood.

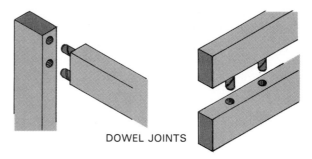

DOWEL JOINTS

11-12 Dowels may be used with several types of joints to improve their strength.

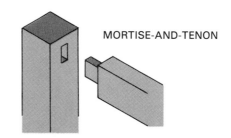

MORTISE-AND-TENON

11-13 Mortise-and-tenon joints form very strong joints and are useful in attaching furniture legs and rails.

TONGUE AND GROOVE

11-14 Tongue and groove joints are used along the common edge of two boards.

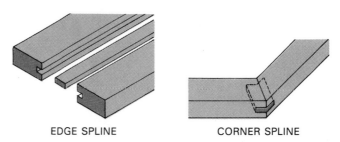

EDGE SPLINE   CORNER SPLINE

11-15 Spline joints are used to increase the strength of other joints.

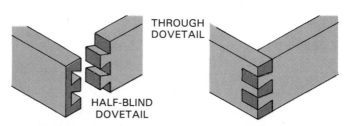

THROUGH DOVETAIL

HALF-BLIND DOVETAIL

11-16 Dovetail joints are used on high quality construction to provide maximum strength.

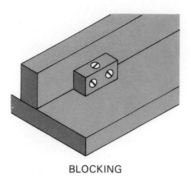

BLOCKING

11-17 Blocking is used to enforce other joints, but it should be located in areas which are not visible.

UPHOLSTERED FURNITURE

Upholstered furniture incorporates some type of frame, cushioning material, and covering, 11-18. Pieces such as sofas and chairs are frequently upholstered. This furniture must be examined carefully if the quality is to be accurately judged, because so much of the construction is hidden.

Upholstery Fabrics

Upholstery fabrics should be functional as well as attractive. How a piece of furniture is to be used will help determine what types of upholstery are most suitable. Overall, fabrics should be comfortable, durable, attractive, and soil resistant.

Plain or twill weaves are recommended for furniture that is used frequently. Pile weave fabrics such as velvet and corduroy show wear much more quickly. Brocades and tapestry fabrics are beautiful, but the threads of these fabrics catch and snag easily. These fabrics may be more suitable for seldom used living room furniture.

Both natural and synthetic fibers are used in upholstered furniture. While natural fibers are attractive, the addition of synthetic fibers such as rayon and nylon may increase a fabric's strength and stain resistance.

Non-woven fabrics such as leather and vinyl may be used for upholstery. They are sturdy and easily cleaned. Leather is durable and attractive, but it is very expensive. Vinyls may be made to resemble leathers; they are less expensive.

Construction

An upholstered piece will have a *frame* of some type. Generally, the frame should be made of kiln-dried hardwood. Wood that is not properly dried will be more likely to split and buckle. The joints should be strengthened with dowels and glue blocks. Padding on the frame is desirable where it would come in contact with a wear surface. The manufacturer's tag or literature should provide useful information about the frame construction. Remember that if the piece has a weak or poorly constructed frame, durability will be less than satisfactory.

The part of a chair or sofa that serves as the platform for cushioning materials is called the *seat base*. Several

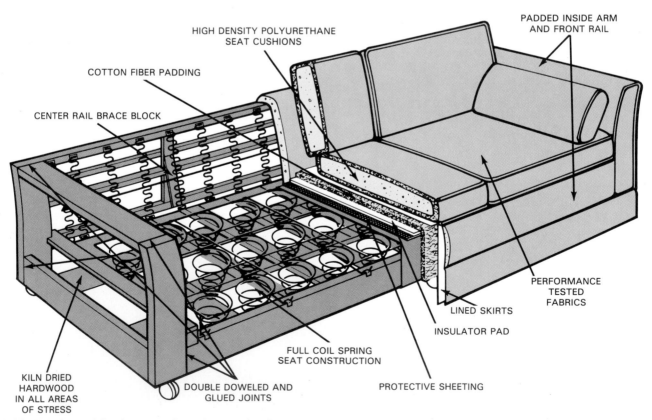

11-18 Upholstered furniture consists of a wooden frame and spring supports covered with padding and upholstery. The main construction of an upholstered piece is hidden from the view of the consumer.

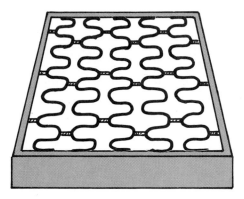

11-19 The S-type spring is used on a seat base when a minimum of bulk is desired.

11-20 Coil springs of heavy weight which are properly anchored provide a comfortable, resilient seat base.

types of springs are used in seat bases. One type is the *serpentine* or S-type spring, 11-19. This flat spring is nailed, screwed, or stapled to the frame at equidistant points from other flat springs. Springs are linked together with tiny coiled springs called *helicals*. This type of construction produces a minimum amount of bulk.

Another type of seat base construction which is frequently used is the *coil spring* type. See 11-20. Several coil springs are attached to webbing or steel bands. An average size chair would generally have nine to twelve springs per seat. The springs are tied as frequently as eight times per spring in quality pieces.

A thick layer of cushioning material should be applied directly over the springs and frame. Several materials are used such as cellular foams, fiberfill, feathers, and down. The most expensive furniture has feathers or down while the least expensive probably has some type of fiberfill. Polyurethane foam is used on most furniture today for cushioning.

The outer covering is the most visible part of an upholstered piece. The seams should be straight and tight with no loose threads. *Welting* or cording sewn into the seams adds strength, 11-21. Buttons and zippers should be secure.

Bedding

Innerspring mattresses are similar in construction to upholstered furniture. See 11-22. They contain a series of springs covered with padding. The springs vary in number, size, placement, and gauge (thickness of wire). Coils may or may not be individually *pocketed* or covered with padding.

A good quality mattress should have at least 300 heavy coils that are firmly anchored, good padding and insulation placed over the between coils, and a tightly woven cover with a nonsag border.

FLEXSTEEL INDUSTRIES, INC.

11-21 The welting on this couch is attractive, but it also adds strength to the seams.

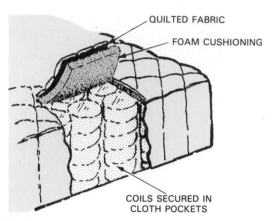

11-22 A good mattress consists of heavy gauge coils that are individually pocketed. They should be firmly anchored and covered with a tightly woven fabric.

Foam mattresses are made of latex or polyurethane foam. They are lightweight and less expensive than innerspring mattresses. A good foam mattress is about 6 inches thick. It has holes or cores in it which make the mattress more comfortable. Foam mattresses are often used by people with allergies.

Mattresses are usually supported by springs. The support may be *box springs, coil springs,* or *flat springs,* 11-23. Box springs are the most expensive, but they provide the most support. They consist of a series of coils attached to a base and covered with padding.

Coil springs have the same construction as box springs, but they are not covered or padded. They are of medium expense and quality. Flat springs are the least expensive and provide the least support, but they are lightweight and

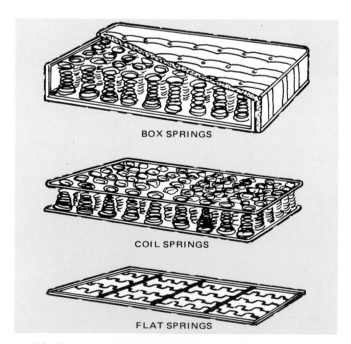

11-23 Box springs are coil springs that are padded and covered. Coil springs are anchored to a frame, but have no padded covering. Flat springs are attached to a frame and may have metal support strips banded across them.

take up little space. Flat springs are likely to sag and become uncomfortable with time.

METAL FURNITURE

There are many types and styles of metal furniture available today. Steel, aluminum, and iron account for the majority of structural metals used. Several metal coatings or platings are also popular.

Many modern furniture pieces are made from steel tubing, 11-24. These pieces are strong, lightweight, and fairly inexpensive. They may be assembled with mechanical fasteners, or they may be welded.

Aluminum tubing is used frequently for lawn furniture. It is lighter in weight and less expensive than steel. However, it is not as strong and tends to bend and dent.

Wrought iron is used to make decorative and outdoor furniture, but cast iron, steel, and aluminum are more popular. The cast metals use forms in the shape of wrought iron, 11-25. Since casting is more easily adapted to mass production, cast furniture is less expensive. Cast iron is heavy and brittle. Iron is usually coated or plated to protect it from rust. Cast metal is also used for furniture hardware.

Some metal furniture is plated. Chrome, brass, nickel, copper, and zinc are common plating materials, 11-26. *Plating* may be used for added protection or attractiveness. Often, a less expensive metal is plated with an attractive metal. Sometimes, using a solid metal such as copper would produce a weak or heavy piece of furniture, so plating with the metal is more practical.

Brass and copper plating are costly, but they are valued for their appearance. They have a tendency to tarnish and must be polished frequently. Some manufacturers place a protective coating of clear lacquer or enamel over these metals to help prevent tarnishing.

Baked enamel coatings have expanded the popularity of metal furniture, 11-27. A wide variety of colors are available in finishes that can be washed and are weather resistant. Kitchen cabinets, outdoor furniture, doors, and bathroom cabinets are examples of pieces made of enameled metal.

PLASTIC FURNITURE

Plastics possess an almost infinite variety of characteristics. They may be made to imitate almost any other material, or they may display a unique character of their own. Plastic furniture is lightweight, durable, inexpensive, and easily cleaned, 11-28.

Some of the broad families of plastics that have been used in furniture include vinyls, styrenes, polycarbonates, cellulosics, nylons, polyurethanes, polyesters, and acrylics.

The ability of plastics to be manufactured in solid shapes or produced as foam further enhances their desirability. Transparent and translucent plastics have special qualities which enhance some furniture designs. Plastics will probably replace many traditional materials used in furniture production.

WEYERHAEUSER CO.

11-24 Steel tubing plated with chrome was used for the framework of these barstools and this coffee table.

GRABER

11-25 This patio furniture has the look of wrought iron, but it is made from cast steel.

KIRSCH COMPANY

11-26 This dinette set is made from steel tubing with chrome plating. The plating protects the steel tubing and provides a durable and decorative finish.

BROWN JORDAN

11-27 Baked enamel forms a durable coating for these outdoor pieces made from steel tubing.

SMITHSONIAN INSTITUTION PHOTO NO. 76-5831

11-28 The tulip chair designed by Eero Saarienen, is a modern chair that makes use of plastic's ease of molding.

FURNITURE SELECTION

When selecting furniture, personal taste should be a primary consideration; however, other information will help you make more satisfactory choices. It is helpful to know the names of furniture pieces and their proper definitions. The glossary of furniture terms in 11-29 will help you to communicate properly when discussing furniture with a dealer.

Quality and cost, style, size, and maintenance requirements are important points to consider. Guidelines provided in this section will help you choose furniture that will provide satisfaction for several years.

Quality and Cost

Furniture is expensive, so care must be taken to get the best quality possible for the price paid. Knowledge of furniture materials and construction will help you know what to examine when judging quality. Much of furniture construction is hidden, however, so it is important to buy from a dealer who stands by his or her products.

The Federal Trade Commission has instituted Trade Practice Rules for the Household Furniture Industry. These rules prohibit furniture manufacturers and dealers from providing false or misleading information about their furniture. Any manufacturer's tags and labels with information about materials and construction cannot be removed by the dealer.

These rules also require manufacturers to state what types of outer coverings and stuffings are used on upholstered furniture. Leather and leather imitations must be marked as such. Manufacturers must indicate if vinyl, other platics, or marble dust are used in an imitation of leather, wood, or marble.

Descriptions of wood furniture follow strict guidelines. If a label states that a piece is made of one wood, any exposed parts must be made of that wood. Labels must state that a veneered piece is veneered.

Specific terms used to describe wood must conform to meanings determined by the FTC. *Solid* means that all exposed wood is of the same solid wood through the entire thickness of the piece. No veneers are used. *Genuine* means that the exposed parts are of the same wood, but that they are veneered.

If veneered wood is made from *plywood,* the layers will be placed with the grain at right angles to each other. *Laminated* wood refers to plywood where all of the layers have their grain in the same direction.

Combination is a term used to describe furniture with more than one type of wood used in the exposed parts. If a piece is of *all-wood construction,* the wood exposed is the same throughout the entire thickness of the piece.

Labels are helpful in evaluating furniture, but they don't tell you everything. Before any piece of furniture is taken home, it should be examined carefully by the buyer.

With case furniture, rub your hand over the surface. It should be smooth with no rough spots, splinters, or protruding nails. Check the back and inside surfaces as well. Stains should be even in color throughout the piece. Construction should be solid. Tap the panels of the furniture. If you hear a dull thud, the construction is solid. Pieces that sound hollow are probably constructed from thin panels of wood attached to wooden frames.

All furniture should have a sturdy base. Place firm pressure on the top or side of a piece to see if it wobbles. Make sure all working parts work. Doors should open and shut easily, and they should fit squarely into their frame. Hinges should be properly aligned and should not squeak.

Drawers should roll smoothly when open and shut. Avoid drawers that jar, catch, or slide without rollers. Keep in mind what will be stored in the drawers. Dresser drawers must be free of surface flaws which might catch on clothes.

When examining upholstered furniture, open and close all zippers to make sure they work smoothly. Also, look to see if upholstery fabric is underlined. Sit or lay on all chairs, sofas, and beds. Make sure that sitting down and standing up are not awkward or difficult tasks. You should not be able to feel an individual spring through the cushioning material.

When pricing furniture, solid construction should be a primary consideration. Intricate carvings, heavy shaped

Armoire	A large piece, usually of wood, with doors and used in place of a closet for storing clothing or household linens.
Barcelona Chair	A classic, contemporary chair design characterized by a stainless steel frame and upholstered leather back and seat.
Bentwood	Furniture pieces made from wood that has been steam bent into soft, curved shapes.
Bergére	An upholstered armchair with closed, upholstered sides and visible wood frame.
Bombé Chest	A Regency or Louis XV commode with bulging sides, front, or both.
Breakfront	A wide, tall cabinet with wood doors and drawers on the bottom and glass doors on the top. This piece is similar to the modern china cabinet.
Camelback	A chair or sofa that has a curved hump along the back.
Campaign Furniture	Furnishings with metal corners and handles patterned after military chests.
Chesterfield	An overstuffed sofa with upholstered ends.
Club Chair	A comfortable, heavily upholstered chair with a cushioned seat.
Coffee Table	A long, low table, generally placed in front of the sofa, used to hold books, magazines, ashtrays, etc.
Commode	A low chest of drawers that is generally set against the wall.
Console	A versatile table that can be used in most any location. It was originally a shelf attached to the wall.
Couch	Synonymous with sofa, but originally referred to as a sofa with a low back and one raised end.
Credenza	(Also called sideboard.) A storage piece, usually designed for the dining room, about chair-rail height with doors and drawers. May be used in other rooms as well.
Davenport	An upholstered sofa which may be made into a bed.
Director's Chair	A folding wooden frame chair with a canvas seat and back.
Divan	The divan bed has a concealed mattress which pulls out from the seat. It offers dual-purpose seating and sleeping. The divan is generally a living room piece.
Etagere	Standing set of shelves with sides open or closed depending on the design. A very versatile piece that may be used singly or in multiples. May be used to form modular wall units for living, dining, or bedroom.
Fauteuil	A French open armchair with wooden arms and caned or upholstered seat and back.
Gateleg Table	A space-saving table with hinged leaves and legs that swing out like a gate to support the leaves when raised.
Hutch	A chest or cabinet on legs with an open shelf above.
Lounge	A type of couch with no back but one high end for reclining.
Lounge Chair	A comfortable, roomy chair available in several styles.
Loveseat	A small sofa for two people.
Modulars	Uniform structural components that can be grouped together, used separately, or arranged in a variety of combinations. Usually three or four standard modules are used to form the system.
Morris Chair	A large armchair with loose cushions and a movable back.
Occasional Table	A small table usually placed at the end of a sofa which may provide shelves or drawers for additional storage. May serve as a lamp table, but generally a little shorter than a lamp table.
Parsons Table	A classic square or rectangular table with apron and legs the same width.
Pedestal Table	Any table that is supported by a single post rather than four legs.
Poster Bed	A bed with four decorative posts.
Savonarola Chair	An Italian Renaissance chair with a carved wood back and a frame composed of interlacing curved shapes.
Sawbuck Table	Any large table with two X-shaped supports.
Sectional	A piece of seating furniture made up of sections that can be used separately or together.
Semainier	A tall, narrow chest, originally French, with seven drawers. They may be used in small bedrooms, dens, or guest rooms.
Settee	A light double seat, upholstered piece with a back and sometimes arms.
Settles	A Colonial piece similar to a settee, but made of wood.
Side Chair	An armless dining chair.
Sofa	A broad inclusive term that refers to a seat for two or more people.
Sofa Bed	A sofa with a back that folds back flat to form a bed area. It has no regular mattress. It requires less space than the divan.
Studio Couch	A living room sleeper which has an upholstered mattress resting on an upholstered steel unit. Bolsters are used to form the back.
Studio Lounge	A single sleeper of a slab construction with flat springs and foam rubber padding.
Trundle Bed	A low bed on casters that may be rolled under a full height bed.
Wing Chair	An overstuffed chair that has projecting sides on the high upholstered back.

11-29 *The proper names of furniture pieces should be mastered if one is to be able to communicate accurately when referring to furniture.*

SINGER FURNITURE

11-30 Intricate carving, specially matched veneer, and metal latticework all add to the price of a furniture piece. Although they may be beautiful, these extras are not necessary on durable, quality furniture.

GRABER

11-31 Furniture may be made with different materials and contain different colors than the other items in a room. However, the basic style or mood of the room should be continued in its furniture.

THOMASVILLE FURNITURE INDUSTRIES, INC.

11-32 A king size, four poster bed may look great in a furniture show room, but it could be overpowering in a small bedroom. Check room measurements carefully to make sure that there will be ample clearance space left in the room after the furniture is placed. Make sure that there will be enough wall space without a window for tall pieces.

moldings, deep patinas, and curved construction all add to the beauty and price of a piece, but they are not essentials, 11-30. When looking for inexpensive but durable furniture, it is wise to choose pieces without these features. Your dollars will be invested in solid construction.

The price of furniture is also affected by the type of retailer that sells the furniture. Some bargains may be of quality comparable to more expensive pieces. However, service may be limited or sales may be final. Items that are being discontinued are often good buys, but it will not be possible to buy matching pieces later. When a price is cut, there are often disadvantages to buying. These may be in quality or service. Make sure you know what the disadvantages are and whether or not you can accept them.

Style

There are no set rules for choosing a furniture style, but it is important for furniture to blend with a room's overall design and mood. When shopping for furniture, it is helpful to carry swatches of fabrics, paint chips, or other color samples with which furniture must be coordinated. Individual pieces do not have to match, but they should blend with the other pieces in a room, 11-31.

In common rooms such as a living room, the tastes of all family members should be considered. Items that are particularly displeasing to any one member should be avoided, since all family members will use the room. Bedrooms and other private rooms allow for a more individualized style choice.

Size

Furniture size is important from two aspects. First, the furniture must fit into your house or apartment. Doors, stairs, and halls may present problems. The size of these openings should be measured before choosing furniture. An item of the proper color and style is useless to you if you can't get it in the front door.

Second, furniture should be of the appropriate scale for its use and location. The seat of a chair or couch should be slightly lower than the back of your knee—around 15 to 18 inches. If a seat is higher, your feet will not be able to rest on the floor comfortably. If it is lower, sitting and standing will be difficult.

Chairs to be used at tables or desks should be streamlined to fit well and allow free movement. A couch should be long enough to allow you to stretch out comfortably, but a longer couch would not be suitable for intimate conversation areas.

Furniture should be in proportion to the dimensions of the room in which it will be placed, 11-32. There should be ample room for circulation after all the furniture has been arranged in a room. Putting too many pieces of furniture, or furniture that is too big, into a room will detract from the overall plan and hinder the use of space. A diagram of standard furniture sizes is given in 11-33.

Maintenance

How much time and money must be spent in the upkeep of furniture is an important consideration. Fine wood furniture requires special cleaners and must be waxed

179

FURNITURE CUTOUTS SCALE: ¼" = 1 FT.

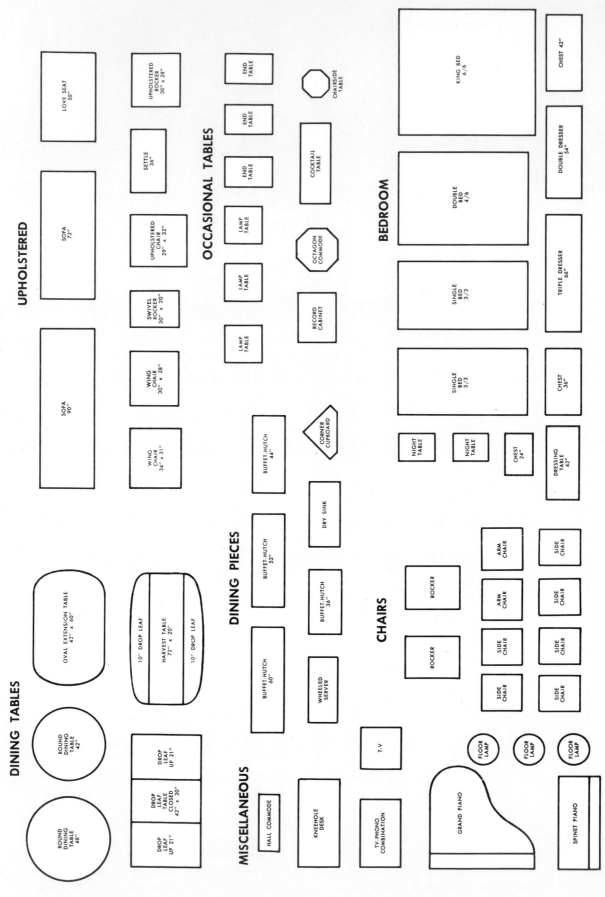

DINING TABLES

ROUND DINING TABLE 48"

ROUND DINING TABLE 42"

OVAL EXTENSION TABLE 42" x 60"

10" DROP LEAF
HARVEST TABLE 72" x 20"
10" DROP LEAF

DROP LEAF UP 21"
DROP LEAF TABLE CLOSED 42" x 30"
DROP LEAF UP 21"

UPHOLSTERED

SOFA 90"

SOFA 72"

LOVE SEAT 50"

WING CHAIR 34" x 31"

WING CHAIR 30" x 28"

SWIVEL ROCKER 30" x 20"

UPHOLSTERED CHAIR 29" x 32"

SETTLE 36"

UPHOLSTERED ROCKER 30" x 28"

OCCASIONAL TABLES

LAMP TABLE

LAMP TABLE

LAMP TABLE

LAMP TABLE

END TABLE

END TABLE

END TABLE

END TABLE

CHAIRSIDE TABLE

COCKTAIL TABLE

OCTAGON COMMODE

RECORD CABINET

DINING PIECES

BUFFET-HUTCH 60"

BUFFET-HUTCH 52"

BUFFET-HUTCH 44"

WHEELED SERVER

BUFFET-HUTCH 36"

DRY SINK

CORNER CUPBOARD

MISCELLANEOUS

HALL COMMODE

KNEEHOLE DESK

TV-PHONO COMBINATION

T-V

GRAND PIANO

SPINET PIANO

CHAIRS

ROCKER

ROCKER

ROCKER

SIDE CHAIR

SIDE CHAIR

SIDE CHAIR

SIDE CHAIR

ARM CHAIR

ARM CHAIR

ARM CHAIR

SIDE CHAIR

SIDE CHAIR

SIDE CHAIR

FLOOR LAMP

FLOOR LAMP

FLOOR LAMP

BEDROOM

KING BED 6/6

DOUBLE BED 4/6

SINGLE BED 3/3

SINGLE BED 3/3

NIGHT TABLE

NIGHT TABLE

CHEST 24"

DRESSING TABLE 42"

CHEST 36"

TRIPLE DRESSER 66"

DOUBLE DRESSER 54"

CHEST 42"

THOMASVILLE FURNITURE INDUSTRIES, INC.

11-33 Standard sizes of furniture pieces are useful when planning purchases.

regularly. Upholstered furniture may be vacuumed, but occasional steam cleaning may be necessary. Stain removal may be difficult if upholstery fabric is not easily removed from the furniture.

Features that aid in cleanability include smooth surfaces with very little carving or grooving. Woods may be treated with special coatings to make them more resistant to stains and easier to clean. Removable slip covers can be washed by machine and are easily replaced when they wear out. Treated fabrics resist stains. Plastic, metal, and vinyl furniture surfaces are resistant to stains and are easily cleaned.

Cleanability and maintenance requirements should be compatible with your family's lifestyle. For instance, a working couple with young children should choose furniture with easily cleanable upholstery and smooth case goods with protective coatings. A family with no children may choose furniture with plush upholstery and fine wood case goods with intricate carving.

REVIEW QUESTIONS

1. What are the qualities of hardwoods? How do they differ from softwoods? Which would you prefer for a china cabinet? For a lawn chair?

2. What are the five methods of cutting veneers? What kind of pattern does each type produce?

3. Would you consider veneered wood to be of superior or inferior quality to solid wood? Why?

4. How are processed woods used in furniture?

5. Name five types of joints used in wood furniture. What is the weakest of these joints? How do these joints differ from each other?

6. What type of upholstery fabric would you recommend for a family with seven young children? What would you recommend for a couple with no children? Why?

7. Develop a list of questions that you would ask a furniture sales person in reference to a couch that you consider purchasing.

8. What are some metals used in furniture production? How are they used? What are their advantages and disadvantages?

9. What are some of the requirements of the Federal Trade Commission that are helpful to furniture consumers?

10. How would you examine a piece of wood furniture before purchasing it?

11. Before you leave the house to buy furniture, what information and materials should you gather to take with you? Why?

12 Walls

After studying this chapter, you will be able to:
■ Describe the basic construction techniques used in building frame, masonry veneer, and masonry walls.
■ Evaluate the appropriateness of an exterior wall in relationship to its style, maintenance requirements, and ability to withstand weather conditions.
■ List and describe various types of wall treatments.
■ Choose a wall treatment that is appropriate for both the function and decoration of a setting.

Walls form one of the three basic elements of any room—walls, floors, and ceilings. They serve both aesthetic and practical functions. They define space, assure privacy, keep out the elements, and provide protection. Their area is so large that they play an important part in determining the character of a home or room. Floors and ceilings are discussed in Chapters 13 and 14.

This chapter examines the types of walls found in housing structures and provides a basic understanding of their construction. The properties of several types of wall treatments are discussed. Guidelines for choosing a wall treatment are also provided.

WALL TYPES

The main types of walls used in residential housing construction are frame walls and masonry walls. They both have different characteristics with their own advantages and disadvantages.

Walls may be described as bearing or nonbearing. A *bearing* wall supports some weight from the ceiling or roof of a structure. A *nonbearing* wall does not support any weight from the structure in addition to its own weight.

Frame Walls

Frame walls may be used as interior or exterior walls, depending on the type of material that is used to cover them. Interior frame walls are called partitions to distinguish them from exterior walls. Exterior frame walls are usually bearing walls. While some main partitions also are bearing walls, most interior walls are nonbearing.

Frame wall construction consists of regularly spaced studs attached to a sole plate at the bottom and a plate at the top, 12-1. Most studs are 2 by 4 inch wood boards, but studs are also available in aluminum and steel.

A typical frame wall is 8 feet high, finished floor to finished ceiling, with studs placed 12, 16, or 24 inches apart. The 16 inch spacing is most generally used.

Frame walls are made from kiln dried lumber with a moisture content of 15 to 19 percent. The moisture content should correspond to the atmospheric moisture level at the structure's location to reduce the chances of shrinking and warping. Construction grade lumber of douglas fir, southern yellow pine, hemlock, spruce, and larch are most generally used.

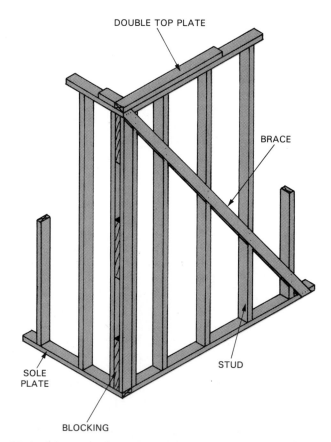

12-1 A frame wall consists of evenly spaced studs attached to a sole plate at the bottom and a plate at the top. Braces help to make the wall more secure.

182

12-2 Drywall is made from a highly compressed core of gypsum covered with heavy paper surfaces. It is lightweight, easy to cut, and very porous.

A frame partition is composed of studs covered by some type of sheet product. The most frequently used material is *gypsum wallboard,* more commonly called drywall. This board product has gypsum, a chalk-like material, as a core and it is covered with heavy paper surfaces, 12-2. It is available in large sheets from 4 by 7 ft. to 4 by 14 ft. Thicknesses available include 1/4, 3/8, 1/2, and 5/8 in. When a single thickness of drywall is used on a wall, 1/2 in. board is usually applied. A typical interior frame wall with drywall is 4 1/2 in. thick—the thickness of the stud plus two thicknesses of 1/2 in. drywall. See 12-3.

Openings in frame walls for windows and doors require special construction. An example of how openings are framed to provide extra strength is shown in 12-4. Each

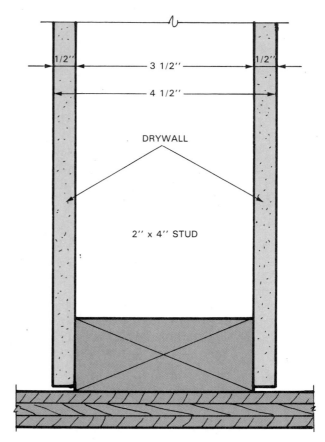

12-3 An interior frame wall covered with drywall is 4 1/2 in. thick.

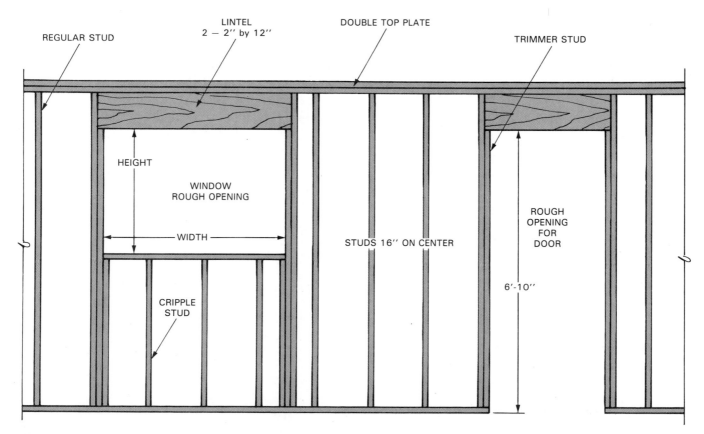

12-4 A lintel is required to support the weight above a window or door opening.

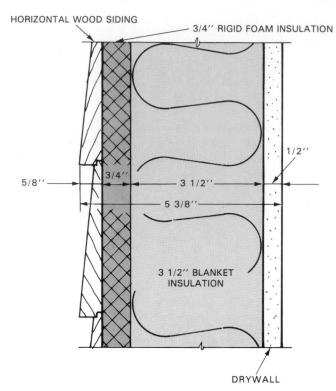

HORIZONTAL WOOD SIDING

3/4'' RIGID FOAM INSULATION

1/2''

5/8''

3/4''

3 1/2''

5 3/8''

3 1/2'' BLANKET
INSULATION

DRYWALL

12-5 A 5 3/8 inch thick exterior wall allows space for 3 1/2 inches of blanket insulation and 3/4 inches rigid foam insulation. The blanket insulation usually has a vapor barrier on the inside surface to reduce moisture loss in the winter.

opening has a heavier member, called a *lintel,* over the opening to support the weight above. Construction is similar for interior and exterior openings.

Exterior frame walls are composed of the same type of studs as partitions. They are covered with drywall or paneling, but several other materials also are applied. Generally, 3 1/2 in. of insulation is placed between the studs to reduce heat loss during cold weather and heat gain during warm weather. The outside face of the wall has a protective layer, or *sheathing,* nailed to the studs to help weatherproof the wall. However, in warmer climates or summer homes, sheathing is sometimes eliminated. Typical sheathing materials are: 1/2 in. plywood, 1/2 in. weatherboard, or 3/4 in. rigid foam insulation. A layer of building felt is placed over the sheathing, then siding is applied.

Several types of exterior siding are available; they are discussed in the wall treatments section of this chapter. Thickness of siding seldom exceeds 1 in. The thickness of an exterior frame wall with rigid foam sheathing and 5/8 in. siding would be 5 3/8 in. total. See 12-5. The nominal size frequently used on construction drawings is 6 inches.

Veneer walls. Brick or other masonry may be used as a covering for a frame wall. When masonry is used in this way, a *veneer wall* is built, 12-6. Masonry on a veneer wall does not provide structural support. The veneer is tied to

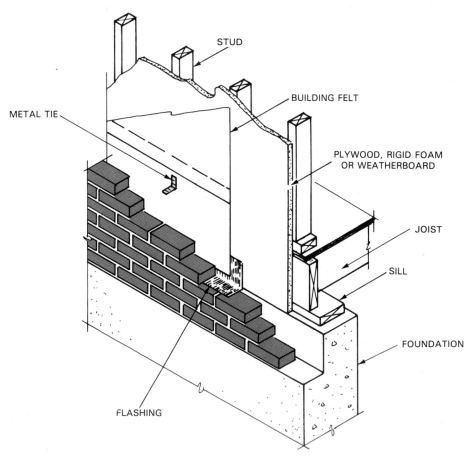

STUD

BUILDING FELT

METAL TIE

PLYWOOD, RIGID FOAM
OR WEATHERBOARD

JOIST

SILL

FOUNDATION

FLASHING

12-6 A brick veneer is attached to a frame wall using metal ties every 2 square feet.

the frame wall with metal ties that are spaced so that each 2 square feet of wall area has one tie.

An air space of about 1 inch is left between the sheathing of the frame wall and the masonry. This air space provides insulation and allows moisture to collect and escape at the bottom of the wall.

Veneer units are generally about 4 in. thick, but stone is frequently 6 in. thick. The thickness of a brick veneer wall is about 9 3/4 in. thick (1/2 in. drywall, 3 1/2 in. stud, 3/4 in. rigid foam, 1 in. air space, and 4 in. brick). The nominal size generally used on a drawing for this type of wall is 10 in.

Masonry veneer walls are very popular and appear to be more expensive than they are. They provide the advantages of a solid masonry wall with few disadvantages. For example, the installation of plumbing and electrical facilities is more difficult and costly in solid masonry than in masonry veneer.

Wood foundations. Currently some basement walls are built using pressure treated lumber. This type of basement wall is called a *wood foundation*. Wood foundations are most likely to be found in northwestern areas with dry climates. Building of wood foundations is relatively new, and it is not approved in some local codes.

Research has shown that lumber which has been treated with preservatives can resist rot for many years and therefore should be quite serviceable as a foundation material. Wood foundations are much less expensive than traditional concrete foundations.

Masonry Walls

A true masonry wall is constructed entirely of brick, concrete block, stone, clay tile, or a combination of these materials. With the exception of basement walls, few exterior walls are constructed using only masonry materials. Most brick structures are made of veneer walls. Concrete block, however, is used as an exterior masonry wall in many sections of the country. A typical concrete block wall is shown in 12-7.

Masonry walls for residential construction are generally about 8 inches thick. A proper wall can be made by using two thicknesses of regular brick or one thickness of 8 inch thick concrete block. Walls that require more than one thickness of masonry must be bonded together. They may be bonded using a *header course* every 16 inches vertically or using corrugated metal ties placed between the mortar joints. A header course is a row of bricks or blocks that are laid across both thicknesses of the wall. See 12-8.

If the interior of a masonry wall is to be covered, *furring strips*—strips of wood about the width of a stud—are required on the inside of the wall, 12-9. Drywall, plaster, or paneling is used to cover the wall. Insulation is frequently placed between the furring strips, then the covering is attached to the strips. If furring strips and a wall

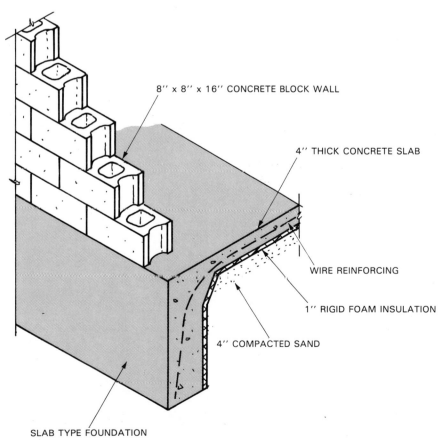

8'' x 8'' x 16'' CONCRETE BLOCK WALL

4'' THICK CONCRETE SLAB

WIRE REINFORCING

1'' RIGID FOAM INSULATION

4'' COMPACTED SAND

SLAB TYPE FOUNDATION

12-7 A slab type foundation with concrete block walls is common for ranch-style homes with no basement.

185

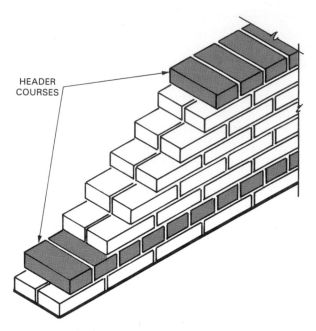

12-8 A header is a brick that is laid across a row. A course is a row of bricks. Placing a header course every sixth course will sufficiently bond an 8 inch thick wall.

12-9 Furring strips must be attached to a masonry wall if paneling or drywall is installed. Insulation with a vapor barrier may be stapled to the furring strips before the surface material is installed.

covering are not used, a masonry wall feels cold and damp.

Many interesting colors, textures, and designs are possible with masonry materials, 12-10. These materials may be used for exterior or interior walls, but adequate foundation support must be provided because these materials are very heavy.

Concrete walls are used mainly for *foundations walls,* but they may be used for exterior walls above grade. A foundation wall is normally the part of the dwelling that extends from the first floor to the footing, 12-11. A *footing* is a wide projection at the base of the foundation wall. It distributes the load of the wall's weight to a wider area.

Foundation walls are generally made from concrete cast in forms or from concrete blocks laid up to form the wall. The thickness of a foundation wall is dependent on several factors: the type of structure to be built on it, the height of the wall, and the ground pressures exerted against it. In general, however, a 10 inch thick foundation is used under a frame or concrete block structure. For a structure of brick veneer on a frame, a 12 inch thick foundation is commonly used. An 8 inch thick concrete block wall is acceptable for a one-story structure with a crawl space underneath it.

If a wall is unusually long or high, or if it will be expected to resist strong earth pressure, reinforcing steel is added to strengthen the wall. The same effect can be accomplished by making the wall thicker or by adding several *pilasters* along the wall. Pilasters are thickened sections built into the wall from the footing to the top of the wall. See 12-12.

Basement walls should be dampproofed on the outside to prevent groundwater from seeping through the wall. Poured concrete walls are generally painted with a heavy coat of hot tar, two coats of cement based paints, or a

12-10 Fluted concrete blocks produce a highly textured wall with strong, vertical lines.

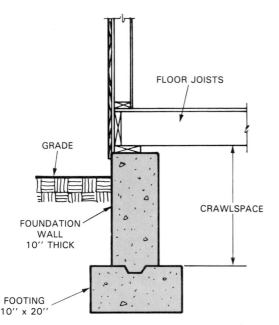

12-11 A typical cast concrete foundation spans from underneath the floor joist to the concrete footing. If a crawlspace is under the structure rather than a basement, its minimum height is 18 inches.

commercially prepared coating especially designed for that purpose. Concrete block walls frequently have a thick coat of cement mortar applied before painting with one of the materials listed above.

These techniques are very helpful in reducing moisture, but good drainage at the base of the wall is essential. A drain tile surrounded by a bed of gravel is the typical method of providing drainage, 12-13.

WALL TREATMENTS

Several types of wall treatments are available for both interior and exterior use. Some types of wall treatments may be used for interior or exterior surfaces. Treatments that are used mostly for exterior surfaces include wood siding, manufactured siding, and mineral fiber shingles. Wood shingles, decorative masonry, stucco or plaster, and paint are treatments that may be used for the interior or exterior. Interior wall treatments include wallpaper, fabric, paneling, tile, and mirrors.

Wood Siding

Wood siding is the most prevalent exterior wall treatment. Horizontal wood siding consists of wood boards that overlap. Most commonly, boards are beveled, or narrower on one edge than the other. Beveled siding is usually 3/16 in. thick on one edge and 1/2 to 3/4 in. thick on the other edge. Beveling helps to reduce the apparent thickness of an exterior wall.

Horizontal wood siding is considered attractive; many homeowners prefer the look of horizontal lines on their home. It is relatively inexpensive; however it requires much maintenance and upkeep compared to other exterior wall coverings. Wood is subject to rotting and shows wear from outdoor exposure more easily than other substances. It must be repainted every few years to protect it from weathering.

Other types of wood siding include vertical siding and plywood siding. Usually, these types of siding are not painted; they are treated for protection and may or may not be stained for a rustic appearance. Wood sidings of these types are usually more expensive than standard wood siding, but they require less maintenance.

Vertical siding may be used to set off entrances, but it also is used as a main wall covering. It may also be placed at an angle for added interest. See 12-14. Exterior plywood may be used to achieve the look of vertical siding. It may be applied more quickly and easily because it is in large panels.

Manufactured Siding

Manufactured substances such as aluminum, vinyl, and fiberglass are being used as alternatives to wood siding

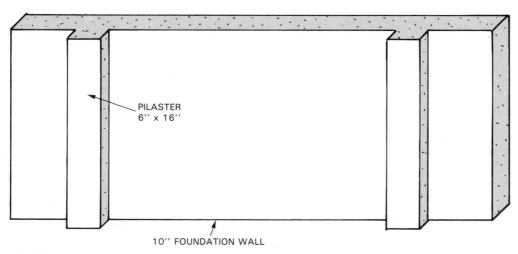

12-12 A long basement wall may be strengthened to resist earth pressure by pilasters about every 12 feet.

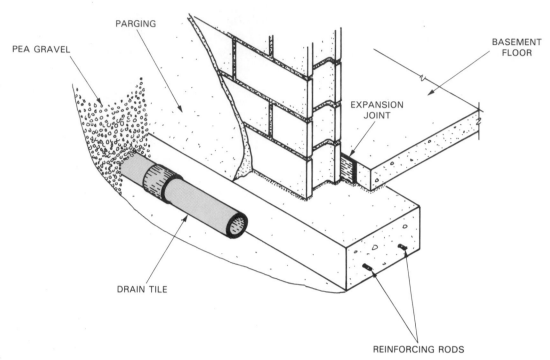

PEA GRAVEL

PARGING

BASEMENT FLOOR

EXPANSION JOINT

DRAIN TILE

REINFORCING RODS

12-13 Drain tile should be placed as low as possible to remove groundwater around a basement wall.

in some areas, especially those with cool, harsh climates. See 12-15. These substances imitate the look of wood, but offer low maintenance and high durability.

Aluminum siding is imprinted with a wood pattern and coated with a special, protective paint. Some companies may use a vinyl coating for color and added protection. Aluminum siding is durable and does not need repainting; however, some types dent. Aluminum also conducts elec-

tricity, so homes with aluminum siding must be properly grounded.

Vinyl siding is similar to aluminum siding in appearance, but it is less likely to dent and does not conduct electricity. Vinyl siding is usually as thick as wood siding or backed with foam padding. Both aluminum and vinyl siding provide more insulation value than wood siding.

CALIFORNIA REDWOOD ASSN.

12-14 Vertical siding may be applied at an angle for a dramatic effect.

12-15 This aluminum siding looks like traditional wood siding, but it lasts longer, requires less maintenance, and provides more insulative value.

Fiberglass is used to make products that look like natural wood shingles. they are long lasting and do not require painting or treating.

Mineral Fiber Shingles

Mineral fiber shingles are available as an exterior wall covering; however, they are not used extensively due to possible health hazards related to them. Mineral fiber shingles are made from asbestos and concrete. They are long lasting and completely fire resistant. Nails that may rust or corrode should not be used because shingles may loosen and fall off with age.

Older homes are most likely to have mineral fiber shingles. The shingles are fairly safe since they are outdoors, but they may be damaged. Painting will help to seal any exposed asbestos fibers. Any major repair work should be done by a professional who knows how to work properly with asbestos products.

Wood Shingles

Wood shingles may be made in a variety of styles. The most popular type of wood used in cedar. Shingles may be nailed on individually or applied in premanufactured panels.

Red cedar shingles have long been a trusted exterior material. They will last for over 50 years as a roofing material and indefintely as an exterior siding. Shingles of red cedar also help to create superior interiors because of cedar's blend of beauty and character. They are rustic and casual. The dimensional structure of wood shingles adds depth to an otherwise flat wall. In addition to being beautiful, cedar shingles are practical, requiring little maintenance, 12-16.

Cedar shingles may be allowed to mellow naturally with age, or they may be painted or stained any color. A semi-transparent stain will allow the wood's natural grain to show through. Other finishes include: linseed oil, lacquer, varnish, stain, wax, and paint.

A very rustic appearance is possible using handsplit shakes. The textures of shakes is exceptional, but they are more costly and more difficult to install than shingles. Their rough texture lends itself best to larger areas.

Decorative Masonry

Most decorative masonry wall treatments generally must be chosen before the wall is completed, but some treatments are possible, using very thin veneers, for existing walls, 12-17. Wall texture with lots of depth may be accomplished by projecting and recessing masonry units or using blocks with sculptured faces, 12-18.

A wall may be given form by omitting some units. Form can also be achieved by using perforated units to form

12-16 Red cedar shingles add texture and interest to this exterior. Shingles may be used for interior walls.

a grill or screen over an existing wall or to form a wall by itself. These units may be typical brick or special block or tile designed for this purpose.

Pattern bonds (the way masonry units are arranged) may be used to develop a series of interesting designs. These patterns may be used on exterior as well as interior walls or floors.

Mortar joints between masonry units may be used to add another dimension to a masonry wall. Joints may be tooled into different shapes, or they may be colored to complement the design scheme or accent the masonry units themselves.

Stucco or Plaster

The term *stucco* has traditionally been applied to exterior plastering, but today it may refer to the final finished coat of the plastering process either on an interior or exterior surface. Interior plaster generally uses a gypsum material while exterior stucco is formed with a portland cement material. Different materials are used because exterior stucco must be more durable to withstand outdoor weather conditions.

Stucco can be applied directly to concrete and masonry surfaces. Wood and metal framing that has been covered with a fine wire mesh or other material which will provide a good bond also can be covered with stucco. It is fairly inexpensive but has a tendency to crack and chip,

12-17 Very thin brick veneer was used to decorate these walls. This wall covering was designed to give interior walls the appearance of solid brick.

12-18 Strong texture is accomplished with these split-fluted concrete blocks.

especially when used for an exterior treatment. Stucco exteriors are most popular in dry, hot climates such as southwestern areas of the United States. It also is used to create a Mediterranean or Spanish style appearance for a house or room.

Stucco, as a wall treatment, refers to the finish coat that provides the texture and character of the wall, 12-19. The finish coat may be up to 1/4 inch thick and applied in many designs. Following are some of the typical stucco textures that are common:

Float finish—surfaces formed with a piece of carpet or a rubber-faced float.

Wet dash finish—coarse aggregate mix is dashed on with a brush.

Dash-troweled finish—high spots of dashed surface are troweled smooth.

Stipple-troweled finish—surface is stippled with a broom, then high spots are troweled smooth.

Pebble-dash finish—small, decorative stones are thrown against the wet surface to create an exposed aggregate finish.

Combed finish—surface is formed with a notched template.

Smooth troweled finish—surface is troweled very smooth.

Sand finish—surface is produced with a wooden float.

Acoustical finish—surface is machine sprayed and very textured.

Swirl finishes—swirls are produced with brush, trowel, or other objects.

The range of textures available with stucco is almost limitless. A style that is compatible with most any design scheme is possible. Color may be added to the stucco material itself, or the surface can be painted. Highly textured stucco on interior walls is gaining in popularity.

Paint

Paint is the most popular wall treatment because it is inexpensive, quick and easy to apply, and available in a wide variety of colors. Also, it is easily changed later.

Paint is easily coordinated with colors in a piece of furniture or in an accessory to be placed in a room. Matching colors can be approximated by mixing paints.

Paints are categorized as *latex* (water-based) or *alkyd* (oil-based). Each is preferred for different kinds of applications, and each is produced in matte, gloss, and textured finishes. They may be designed for exterior or interior use.

Exterior paints are usually called house paint. Oil-based paint is the most commonly used type of house paint, but water-based paints are available as well. House paints are usually self-cleaning. This means that the paint will develop a chalky surface at a controlled rate. This chalky surface will wash away with surface dirt when it rains, leaving the paint clean and fresh looking. Because of this chalking quality, house paint is not recommended for stairway rails or other surfaces that are touched frequently, since the chalk will rub onto other surfaces which come in contact with it.

Primer should be used before paint is applied to any new surface, interior or exterior, but it is especially important for exterior surfaces. Primer prepares a surface for paint and helps it to remain durable and retain its color.

Water-based paints are easy to apply with a roller and dry quickly. Uneven painting is less noticeable than with oil-based paint, and equipment used will come clean with water. One disadvantage, however, is that hiding power may not be as great as that of an oil-based paint.

Oil-based paints stand up to heavy scrubbing and are logical choices for bathrooms and kitchens. These paints require a solvent thinner and take longer to dry. Also, they usually give off more fumes than water-based paints. Equipment used for painting is more difficult to clean.

High-gloss, semi-gloss, and flat finishes are choices for aesthetics as well as practicality. High-gloss enamals are attractive on woodwork because of the high reflectance, durability, and ease in cleaning, 12-20. They are also used on decorative walls where a lacquered look is desired.

Semi-gloss finishes also resist stains and are easily cleaned. They can be used on walls or woodwork.

Flat finishes are porous and do not resist stains very well. They are very popular, however, as a wall paint because of their soft appearance. Flat paints are not recommended for woodwork. Texture paints add another dimension in addition to color, 12-21. They may be applied with a brush, roller, sponge, broom, or sprayer. This

12-19 A textured stucco wall can be easily applied to interior surfaces. This type of stucco has an acrylic base that does not harden quickly and allows time to experiment with textures.

THERMA-TRU, DIVISION OF LST CORP.

12-20 Three different types of paint are used in this room. Flat white is used on the walls, semi-gloss is used on the door, and enamel is used for the trim.

SINGER FURNITURE

12-21 A sponge was used to apply texture paint to these bedroom walls. Several other effects are possible by applying the paint with different methods.

type of paint is very useful for hiding imperfections in a wall's surface. However, once a textured paint is applied it is difficult to change or repaint the surface.

Wallpaper

Originally, wallpaper was used by the poor to copy the expensive textiles used by the rich, but today wallpaper is used by people of all income levels to decorate walls. Wallpaper is economically practical and can be used in any room. It completely covers old wall treatments.

Many colors, patterns, and textures can be produced on wallpaper, 12-22. Wallpaper may even imitate other materials. Test samples are available to help you choose appropriate patterns for a room. Patterns should coordinate with the color and design of furnishings and accessories in a room. See 12-23. Many types of wallpapers

have prepasted or self-adhesive backs and can be applied without the help of a professional.

When selecting a wallpaper, be sure to consider the conditions it must endure in a proposed location. For example, flocked paper is not a good choice where grease or dust is present. A washable paper is better for these locations.

Wallpaper is ideal for disguising odd-shaped architectural details. A busy, random pattern is best for this purpose because it will blend the lines of a room together with the pattern.

Fabric

Fabrics can be used to provide unique texture for a wall. Fabrics are available in a wide range of colors and patterns. They may be attached to the wall with glue, tacks,

12-22 *A broad assortment of wallpaper designs is available. Stock wallpaper is available to match almost any color or design scheme.*

194

LIS KING

12-23 The two wallpaper patterns in this room coordinate with each other and blend well with the floral pattern of the couch. Use of two patterns also helps to make this alcove seem separate and more private.

or double-faced carpet tape. They may also be fastened to a frame and then mounted to the wall, 12-24.

The best types of fabric for wall covering are those that are thick enough to prevent glue from showing through. They should be resistant to staining, fading, mildewing, and shrinking. Fabrics such as grass cloth and burlap are popular.

12-24 Fabric mounted to frames and set into walls provides a decorative wall accent. Wall fabric can be matched to other fabrics in a room.

Carpeting is sometimes used as a wall covering. It provides great texture and continuity between the wall and the floor. Carpeting on the wall also is functional as sound insulation.

Paneling and Boards

Wood paneling and boards are available in a wide range of colors, grains, and species. Few materials rival the beauty of wood. Whether it is used in the form of panels or narrower pieces called boards, it has a character all its own. It is most frequently chosen for its aesthetic qualities, but paneling is a practical wall treatment, 12-25.

New processes have made modern paneling very resistant to wear, easy to clean, and colorful. Many types of plywood paneling designed for exterior applications are also effective when used as an interior wall treatment. Roughsawn and brush textured panels are popular. When finished with a transparent, colored stain, they produce a warm, inviting atmosphere.

Paneling or boards are practical for many reasons. For example, insulation is easily added to a wall that will be paneled. Furring strips can be nailed to the existing wall, and insulation can be placed between the strips. Paneling over this will produce a new wall and reduce noise and heat transfer.

Paneling also is practical for repairing a damaged wall or for building a new partition. Paneling is economical and can be installed by the homeowner with a few tools and moderate skill.

Paneling and boards are durable and require little maintenance. These qualities make paneling popular for family rooms, game rooms, and kitchens.

Several types of siding boards are produced that may be used on interior walls. Most can be installed vertically, horizontally, or at an angle, 12-26. Some of the types of boards include beveled, channel, shiplapped, and tongue and grooved.

Another type of paneling that is gaining greater acceptance is hardboard. Hardboard is a pressed fiber product manufactured in a broad range of face patterns and textures. Many types can be used in any room including the bath or other high moisture area.

Plastic laminate paneling is surfaced with a material similar to that used on countertops. It is especially practical in areas of hard use, such as kitchens and baths. It also is available in simulated wood and in various patterns and colors. Plastic laminate paneling is very durable.

Ceramic Tile

Ceramic tile may be used as an attractive, durable, and easily cleaned wall covering. It has wide appeal for baths, kitchens, and other high use areas, but in recent years the variety and beauty of these tiles have brought them into all areas of the home. Their many colors and shapes make them usable with a variety of design styles.

Glazed tile is the most practical type of tile for walls in kitchens and bathrooms, 12-27. It has a smooth, hard surface that is easily cleaned. Unglazed tile is porous and

GEORGIA-PACIFIC

12-25 Paneling is a practical surface for this kitchen since it is easily cleaned and requires little maintenance, but it is attractive enough to use in the living room as well.

does not resist stains, but it provides a cool, earthy look suitable for some room decors. Ceramic tile is relatively expensive, but it is very long lasting and requires little maintenance.

Mirrors

Mirrors can be an effective wall treatment; they are often used to cover one wall in a room for accent. Mirrors can make a small room appear large, 12-28. Squares that are 12 by 12 inches can be used to cover a wall, or mirrors can be purchased in large dimensions. Distortion-free glass should be used for large mirrors.

Mirrors are expensive, but they produce a dramatic affect and are easy to maintain. Several styles are available including clear, smoked, and patterned.

Mirrored walls can be attractive, but they are not always appropriate. If the view that will be reflected is undesirable, mirrors are not appropriate. They should not be placed on a wall that is not a true plane, because the

image reflected will be distorted. Often, a series of strips of mirrors placed at eye level are sufficient to produce the effect of making a room seem more spacious.

SELECTION OF WALL TREATMENTS

Walls account for more space than any other single element in a home. The selection of treatments for these walls deserves special consideration. The type of treatment used should vary according to the function and decoration of a home.

Function

Wall treatments should enhance the function of a room. Each type of treatment has qualities that may enhance or detract from a room's function. The formality level, amount of visual interest, texture, and absorbancy level of a wall treatment are qualities that should coordinate with the function of a room.

12-26 Clear grade redwood boards were used for this dramatic effect. A clear, protective finish has been applied to emphasize the natural beauty of the wood.

12-27 Glazed ceramic tile is a practical wall covering for bathrooms because it is moisture resistant and easily cleaned.

12 28 The closet doors in this bedroom are covered with floor to ceiling mirrors. They help to give the effect of a more spacious room.

LIS KING

12-29 The formality of this dining room is accented by the symmetrical wallpaper design, wainscotting, and wooden molding.

The formality level of a room's wall coverings should fit the room's atmosphere and use. A formal living room or dining room requires formal walls. Formality is achieved through symmetrical balance and precise, stable forms. Wall treatments that include wainscoting or cove molding set the stage for formal design. A *wainscot* refers to the lower 3 or 4 feet of a wall when it is finished differently from the rest of the wall. Using a symmetrical pattern or texture can produce a formal appearance, 12-29.

An informal wall might be used in a game room, a child's bedroom, or a casual living room. Random wallpaper patterns or graphic designs painted on the wall add to the informality of a room.

The amount of visual interest of a wall may be described by using the terms active and passive. A wall that suggests movement and attracts attention is *active*. This can be accomplished by the use of design, texture, or color. A brightly painted accent wall or a boldly patterned treatment produces an active wall, 12-30. A *passive* wall is used as a background element and does not attract attention.

Off white wall treatments and wallpaper with fine prints are passive.

Active and passive wall treatments are more suitable for some rooms than for others. For example, bedrooms should be restful and quiet. Passive wall treatments can play a role in accomplishing this effect. Active walls would be more functional in a play room.

Texture adds to function and helps to create an overall atmosphere for a room. Formal walls are more likely to be smooth, while informal walls may be textured, 12-31.

A smooth, easily cleaned surface should be used in an area where dust or grease is stirred, such as a crafts room or a kitchen. A music room would be more functional with textured walls because sound would be absorbed better.

Absorbent or reflective qualities may add to or detract from the functionality of a room. Absorbant wall treatments that reduce the sun's glare should be selected for rooms that are mainly used in the daytime. Reflective room treatments work better in artificially lit rooms. A small room will seem larger if one wall is highly reflective.

HJ SCHEIRICH CO.

12-30 The bright, graphic design on this dining room wall adds visual impact and produces a feeling of motion. The active wall adds interest to both the kitchen and the dining room.

VERMONT CASTINGS, INC.

12-31 The texture of this painted brick wall blends well with the informal atmosphere of this family room.

12-32 *The large, bold pattern of this wallpaper is too strong and busy for the small walls of this bath. The effect is overpowering and all depth is lost.*

Decoration

Using principles of design can help to create walls with a pleasing appearance in a room. One factor to consider is the scale of the wall. Large, bold patterns are overpowering on a small wall, 12-32. A tall wall appears lower if the color of the ceiling is extended to the molding on a wall.

Small scale patterns in light colors make a wall appear larger. Mirrors create an illusion of more space. Scenes in perspective lead the eye beyond the wall for the same affect, 12-33.

If a room is very large, dominant colors and designs will make the walls appear closer. Vertical stripes will make a wall appear taller; this effect is useful in rooms with low ceilings.

The type of wall covering chosen should coordinate with the types of furnishings in a room. If furnishings for a room are traditional, then wall coverings should reflect the style of that period. See 12-34. If the furnishings are modern, then plastic, metal, or graphic wall treatments may coordinate well.

Colors should coordinate with, but not overpower, furniture. Walls that exactly match the color or pattern of the furniture will make the furniture blend into the walls.

Choosing a dominant feature in a room will help determine what type of wall covering should be used. If a room will contain several choice pieces of furniture, then the walls should serve as a passive background. If only a few

ENVIRONMENTAL GRAPHICS

12-33 *A wall mural such as this lake scene can create the illusion of space beyond the wall of the room. This scene is made of eight panels and covers an 8 ft. 6 in. by 13 ft. 8 in. area.*

12-34 *Using wallpaper from the same period and style as the other pieces in the room helps to unify the room's overall design.*

pieces of average furnishings are planned, then a dominant wall treatment may be more effective.

An art wall or collection display can produce a dominant wall. Bright, abstract colors and shapes also form an accent, 12-35.

REVIEW QUESTIONS

1. What is the difference between a bearing wall and a nonbearing wall? In what situations is each most likely to be used?
2. Describe the construction of an exterior frame wall and the construction of a partition. How are they different?
3. What is the difference between a brick veneer wall and a masonry wall? Which type of brick wall is most common today?
4. What kind of construction is necessary in order to apply paneling or drywall to a masonry wall?
5. Describe the basic construction of a concrete foundation. What techniques can be used to protect a foundation from water seepage?
6. How does manufactured siding differ from wood siding? To whom would you recommend each type of siding?
7. What types of wall treatments are available to someone who wants to add texture to a wall?
8. Name the two main types of paint and the types of finishes in which they are available. For what types of uses is each appropriate?
9. What types of wall treatments require little maintenance and can be easily cleaned?
10. What are the four qualities of a wall treatment that should be considered when determining whether a wall treatment is appropriate for a room?
11. How could you use wall treatments to make a small room appear larger?

12-35 *Bright colors and textured boards arranged in a bold graphic pattern make this a striking accent wall.*

13 Floors

After studying this chapter, you will be able to:
- ■ Describe the materials and construction methods used to make concrete floors and wood frame floors.
- ■ Describe the construction methods used in laying flooring materials and floor coverings.
- ■ Describe the appearance, texture, and maintenance requirements of various flooring materials and floor coverings.
- ■ Evaluate the appropriateness of a floor treatment for a room according to principles of function and design.

Floors constitute an important element of every area of the home. They support a home's furnishings and occupants, provide decoration, and supply space for movement within the structure. The basic types of floor con-

struction and typical floor treatments are discussed in this chapter.

FLOOR SYSTEMS

Floor systems for housing structures may be classified as wood floors or concrete floors. Most dwellings contain both. Methods of floor construction vary from one section of the country to another, but basic construction components are the same.

Wood Floor Construction

Wood floor systems are composed of several structural elements. These generally include support beams, joists or trusses, a subfloor, and a finished floor, 13-1. Wood floors are generally built over a crawlspace, basement, or

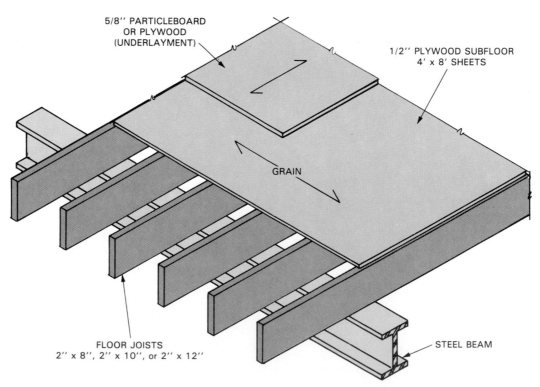

5/8" PARTICLEBOARD OR PLYWOOD (UNDERLAYMENT)

1/2" PLYWOOD SUBFLOOR 4' x 8' SHEETS

GRAIN

FLOOR JOISTS 2" x 8", 2" x 10", or 2" x 12"

STEEL BEAM

13-1 The typical components of a wood floor system are the supporting beam, the floor joists, the plywood subfloor, and the underlayment.

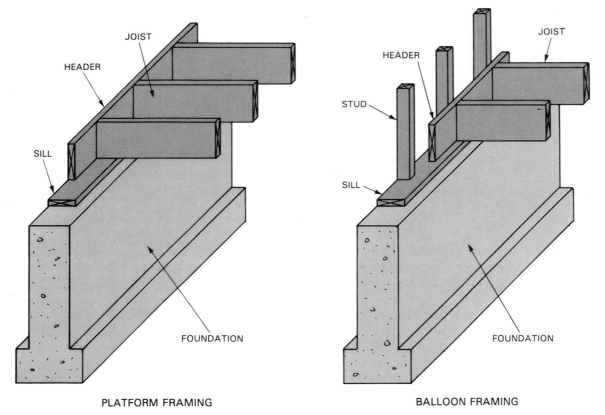

PLATFORM FRAMING   BALLOON FRAMING

13-2 Frame floors are placed directly on the foundation in platform framing. In balloon framing, the floor frame is fitted into the wall.

lower main floor level. All floor systems are supported by a foundation wall which also may be a basement wall.

Two types of floor framing are used. They are platform framing and balloon framing. With *platform framing,* the floor is placed on a sill that is connected to the top of the wall below it. The floor acts as a platform. The walls above the floor are constructed separately and placed on the platform.

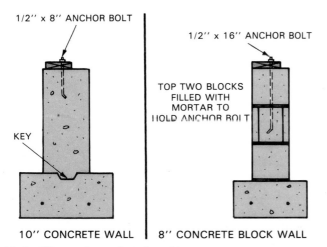

10" CONCRETE WALL | 8" CONCRETE BLOCK WALL

13-3 Sills may be anchored to either cast concrete or concrete block foundation walls. Cast concrete walls require an 8 inch anchor bolt, while the anchor bolt for a concrete block wall should be 16 inches. The longer bolt is needed to reach the second course of block for a secure anchor.

With *balloon framing,* the wall is continuous from the sill to the top of the wall, and the floor joists are attached to the studs. Figure 13-2 shows how these framing techniques differ. Platform framing is used more widely today than balloon framing. Balloon framing is an older technique that was used extensively in homes 100 years ago. It may be a concern when remodeling some older homes. Except for the differences mentioned, both frames are of basically the same construction.

The sill plate forms the connection between the foundation wall and the floor itself. A sill is usually made of 2 by 6 inch or 2 by 8 inch construction lumber. It may be attached to the foundation wall with anchor bolts or straps, 13-3. The size and spacing requirements vary from area to area; local building codes list specific requirements.

Joists or trusses rest on the sill plate and are fastened to it with nails or other fasteners. Traditionally, wood floor systems have used joists to support the floor. Joists are construction boards ranging in size from 2 by 8 inches to 2 by 12 inches in cross-sectional size. Joists are spaced 12, 16, or 24 inches apart with 16 inch spacing most common.

A *live load* (weight of furniture, people, etc.) of 30 lbs./ft.^{2} is considered standard for bedrooms and other light-loaded rooms. Kitchens, living rooms, and some other rooms are designed to support heavier loads. A design weight of 40 lbs./ft.^{2} is used in these areas.

Size and spacing of joists is related to the span required and the load to be supported. Spans that can be supported

JOIST SIZE	MAXIMUM LENGTH OF SPAN TO SUPPORT 30 lb./ft.²	MAXIMUM LENGTH OF SPAN TO SUPPORT 40 lb./ft²
2″ by 8″	14′ 9″	13′ 6″
2″ by 10″	18′ 3″	16′ 9″
2″ by 12″	21′ 9″	19′ 11″

13-4 Joists listed here can support different spans of weight. Length of spans are based on joists spaced 16 inches apart.

by various sizes of joists under live loads of 30 lbs./ft.² and 40 lbs./ft.² are listed in 13-4.

If the span required for a floor is greater than that which the joists can support, extra support must be provided. Typically, a beam or bearing wall is used for extra support. Figure 13-5 shows a basement that is too wide for joists to span without added support. A beam is used in the example on the left. On the right, a bearing wall supports the joists. If a floor were required to cover a very wide span, several beams or walls could be used for support.

A newer technique for supporting wood floors is to replace joists and beams with engineered wood floor trusses. These structural members are designed to span longer distances and, thereby, eliminate the need for posts,

beams, and bearing walls in the basement or crawlspace, 13-6. For example, typical 12 inch floor trusses spaced 24 inches apart can support 40 lbs./ft.² over a span of 25 feet. They are produced in a large variety of sizes, usually from 2 by 4 inch pieces fastened together with metal plates. As large structural lumber becomes harder to find and as the price continues to rise, more floor trusses will be used in construction.

Once the joists or trusses are in place, the subfloor is attached. In the past, a covering of 1/2 inch plywood has been used to provide a large work area for people and equipment until the floor is finished. After the walls and roof are completed, then an underlayment of 5/8 inch particleboard or plywood is nailed and glued over the subfloor. Recently , a new approach has been gaining acceptance. The subfloor and underlayment are combined into a single thickness to save labor cost. Three-fourth inch tongue-and-grooved plywood, 13-7, is nailed and glued to the joists or trusses. Either method is acceptable.

Once the structure is enclosed and much of the interior work is completed, the finished floor can be put in place. Types of floor finishes are described in the floor treatments section of this chapter.

Concrete Floor Construction

The use of concrete slabs for floors in homes and garages is common throughout the United States. This

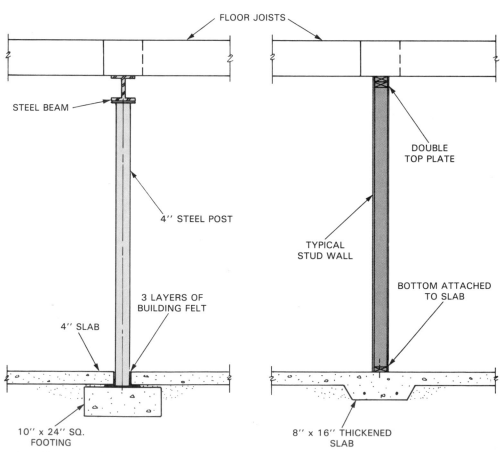

FLOOR JOISTS

STEEL BEAM

4″ STEEL POST

DOUBLE TOP PLATE

TYPICAL STUD WALL

3 LAYERS OF BUILDING FELT

BOTTOM ATTACHED TO SLAB

4″ SLAB

10″ x 24″ SQ. FOOTING

8″ x 16″ THICKENED SLAB

13-5 Either a beam or bearing partition may be used to support joists when the span is too great. Steel posts are used to support the beam if needed.

Floors

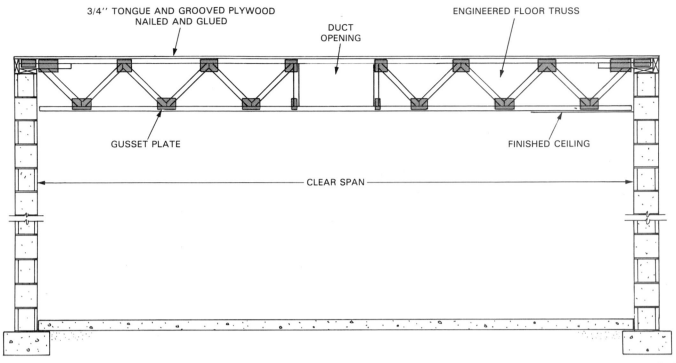

13-6 *Floor trusses are engineered to span long distances with support only at the ends. Plywood decking is glued and nailed at the top of the trusses. Typical ceiling materials may be attached to the underside.*

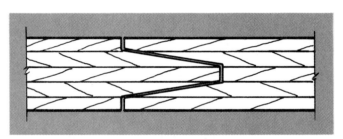

13-7 *Plywood sheathing may be joined by using tongue and groove joints. These joints do not have to be centered over floor joists.*

type of construction is generally economical. It produces a satisfactory floor system if designed and built properly.

Two types of concrete floor systems are commonly used for residential structures. The first combines the slab and foundation into a single unit. This is called a *thickened-edge slab*. The second type is a *floating slab*. A floating slab is separate from the foundation wall. In both cases the slab rests on undisturbed earth or compacted fill. However, the thickened slab is supported along the edges. The floating slab is only supported by the soil below it. See 13-8.

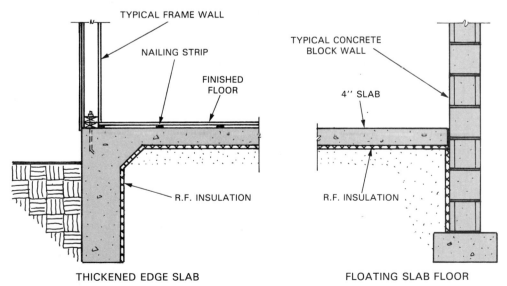

THICKENED EDGE SLAB   FLOATING SLAB FLOOR

13-8 *Concrete slabs may be supported along the edge, or they may rest on sand fill. Both types of construction are used in housing structures.*

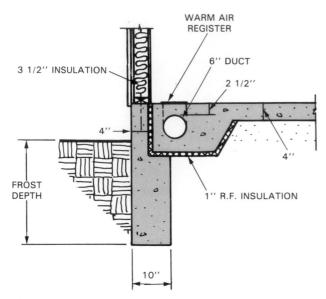

13-9 *This type of insulated, thickened-edge slab has the heating duct cast in the slab. Rigid foam insulation is used to prevent heat loss through the concrete.*

Heating ducts, conduits, and water pipes are frequently cast into the floor of structures with a thickened-edge slab since this type of construction does not have a basement or crawlspace. The edge of the slab may be enlarged to accommodate heating ducts. See 13-9.

Electrical conduits and water pipes must be planned accurately so they will be in the right location once the floor is in place. A disadvantage of this type of floor is that these utilities are inaccessible.

Whether and how a concrete floor will be finished may affect preliminary construction. For example, nailing

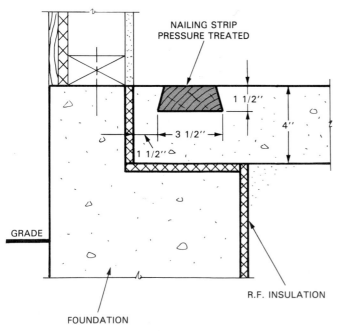

13-10 *A nailing strip for carpet or other attachments is easily included when the concrete is being poured. The beveled edges on the strip hold it tightly in the concrete.*

strips may be embedded in the slab during construction if the floor is to be carpeted, 13-10. Some treatments such as slate or flagstone require a mortar bed to compensate for materials of varying thicknesses. See 13-11. This process adds height to the floor, so extra height should be allowed in preliminary building. Planning the type of floor treatment before casting the slab helps to eliminate later problems.

FLOOR TREATMENTS

Floor treatments may be categorized as flooring materials and floor coverings. *Flooring materials* refer to materials that are used as the top wearing surface of a floor and are structurally a part of the floor. They are usually more permanent than floor coverings. *Floor coverings* are placed on top of the structural floor; although they are attached, they are not a part of the structure.

Flooring Materials

The flooring materials commonly used in residential housing include wood, ceramic tile, concrete and masonry, and terrazzo. Flooring materials do not include underlayment or subfloor, but the finish floor material may require special consideration of these elements.

Wood. Wood flooring, especially hardwood, has been one of the most used materials for floors. It is beautiful, wear resistant, readily available, and economical. Even though many new materials are now produced for floors, wood is still popular. Hardwood species that are frequently chosen include oak, birch, beech, and hard maple. Some softwood species also are used for flooring. They include fir, larch, hemlock, and southern pine. Softwoods are durable if quarter sawed lumber is used so that the edge grain is exposed. Standard style flooring boards are available in most of these species.

Standards for the quality of hardwood flooring have been established by organizations such as the National Oak Manufacturers Association, Maple Flooring Manufacturing Association and the National Bureau of Standards. Softwood flooring strips are graded according to rules established by groups such as the Western Wood Products Association and the Southern Pine Association.

Grading is based on length of pieces, their appearance, and the number of imperfections in the pieces. The highest grades usually have the most even coloring and contain few knotholes or other imperfections. They are more expensive than lower grades of wood. Lower grades generally have a rustic appearance.

The three main types of wood flooring used in housing structures are strip flooring, wood planks, and parquet. Strip flooring consists of pieces cut into narrow strips of varied lengths, 13-12. It is available in widths from 1 1/2 to 3 1/4 in. and thicknesses of 3/8, 1/2, and 25/32 in. Most strip flooring has tongue and grooved edges and ends. Strip flooring usually is concave, or it has grooves cut on the back side. This feature allows each strip to lay flat even if the subfloor is uneven.

Floors

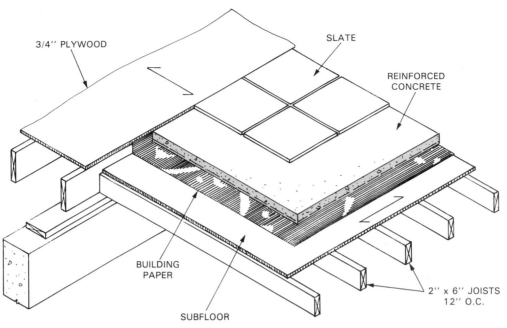

3/4" PLYWOOD

SLATE

REINFORCED CONCRETE

BUILDING PAPER

SUBFLOOR

2" x 6" JOISTS 12" O.C.

13-11 *Masonry floors typically have reinforced concrete subfloors.*

SINGER FURNITURE

13-12 *This hardwood floor is an example of strip flooring. The boards are narrow pieces of various lengths. They are held together by tongue and groove joints.*

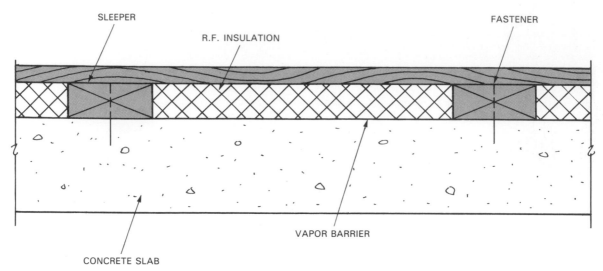

SLEEPER

R.F. INSULATION

FASTENER

VAPOR BARRIER

CONCRETE SLAB

13-13 *When wood flooring is used over a concrete slab, treated furring strips should be used to prevent decay.*

Strip flooring may be applied over a wood subfloor or concrete slab with imbedded furring strips or *sleepers*, 13-13. The strips are generally nailed into the floor below. If application is over concrete, then the strips are nailed to the sleepers which are secured to the concrete. It is a good idea to use a vapor barrier between the concrete and flooring because concrete may become damp. Some expansion space should be allowed between hardwood strips because they swell with moisture changes. The strips may buckle or move a partition wall if expansion space is not allowed.

Floor boards wider than 3 1/4 in. are called planks. Planks are usually 25/32 in. thick, but they are available in a 33/32 in. thickness. Widths range from 4 to 8 in. and lengths range from 4 to 16 ft. Floor boards are generally attached to a wood subfloor with screws covered with wood plugs. They also may be attached to concrete with a mastic (a thick type of adhesive). Planks are designed to simulate colonial flooring, 13-14.

Wood block flooring, more commonly called parquet, is produced in three different types: unit blocks, laminated blocks, and slat blocks. Unit blocks and laminated blocks

13-14 *Wood planks are wear resistant, rustic flooring materials. They are attached to a plywood subfloor with screws, and plugs are used to cover them.*

HARRIS MFG. CO.

13-16 *This type of flooring is made from blocks that are combined in a construction similar to plywood. Each square is butted up next to the adjacent square.*

HARRIS MFG. CO.

13-15 *Each square of this wood block floor is made up of several short strips of wood that have been glued together. Tongue and grooved edges hold the blocks together securely.*

are factory-joined pieces that are usually 6, 8, 9, or 12 inch squares. Unit blocks are made from several short lengths of 3/4 inch thick strip flooring, 13-15. This type of parquet is often referred to as solid parquet. Laminated blocks are made from three thin plies of parquet block to form a block 1/2 inch thick. See 13-16.

Slat block is a third type of parquet that comes as individual slats of hardwood from 3/4 to 3 inches wide and from 4 to 7 inches long. These pieces are square edged and may be laid in several different patterns, 13-17. All types of parquet flooring may be attached to wood or concrete floor with a mastic.

Most types of wood flooring are available with a factory applied finish. This type of finish is considered superior to on-the-job applications because the conditions can be more accurately controlled. Much care must be taken with installation, however, since hammer marks will damage the finish.

Wood floors offer design flexibility because wood is an ageless material. It complements any decor and any lifestyle and adds warmth and character to any room.

HARRIS MFG. CO.

13-17 *The herringbone pattern is one design that can be made with slat block flooring. Each piece of wood in the floor is individually laid.*

LIS KING

13-18 Glazed floor tile provides an attractive bathroom floor that is easily maintained.

Wood floors do require some special care such as cleaning and waxing, but they are long lasting and may be refinished to coordinate with different decors.

Ceramic tile. Ceramic tile is a popular flooring material because it lasts indefinitely and requires little maintenance. However, tile is expensive to install and cool to the touch. The three main types of tile—glazed tile, ceramic mosaic tile, and quarry and paver tile—are discussed in Chapter 8, "Metals, Glass, Ceramics, and Plastics."

Glazed tile is available in a variety of colors and patterns. Although some types cannot take heavy abuse, newer styles are double or triple glazed for extra durability. Glazed tile does not require waxing or special care to maintain its shine. Glazed tile is especially popular for bathroom floors, 13-18. However, new styles are being used in kitchens, dining rooms, living rooms, and other areas, 13-19.

Ceramic mosaic tile is popular for bathroom and kitchen floors, 13-20. Mosaic tile for floors are generally back or face mounted to squares of paper or of another material. These larger units may be installed more quickly and easily.

Paver and quarry tile are designed for traffic areas. Since their color is continuous throughout the tile, wear from heavy traffic does not show. These tiles also are frostproof, so they can be used outdoors. Their color and texture are suitable for informal decoration, 13-21.

Grout is used to fill the joints between tiles. It may be cementitious, resinous, or a combination of both. The type

AMERICAN OLEAN TILE CO.

13-19 Glazed tile is used in the dining room and the greenhouse area of this home.

AMERICAN OLEAN TILE CO.

13-20 Ceramic mosaic tile is used for the floor of this bathroom.

CALIFORNIA REDWOOD ASSN.

13-21 Quarry tile was chosen for this high traffic family area. The earthy color is attractive, yet the tile is practical.

of group used depends upon the requirements of the different kinds of tile and their applications.

Cementitious grouts consist of portland cement modified to provide qualities such as whiteness, uniformity, hardness, flexibility, and water retention. Resinous grouts (epoxies) possess special properties such as high bond strength and resistance to chemicals. However, they are harder to apply and more expensive.

Concrete and masonry. Concrete and masonry floors have a high resistance to abrasion. They may be designed using several patterns, textures, and colors. They are suitable for indoor and outdoor floors. Indoor floors may be waxed for a warmer, more polished look. The basic types of concrete and masonry floors used in housing structures include concrete, brick, slate, and flagstone.

Concrete floors may have a smooth or textured surface, and color may be added. The most common treatment of concrete as a floor material is to trowel it smooth. The surface produced is serviceable for garage, porch, and patio floors. This type of floor is functional rather than decorative. Color or texture may be added, however, for an interesting design, 13-22.

Brick floors are popular in traditional as well as contemporary homes, 13-23. Many patterns are possible and color combinations are almost endless. Regular brick or special pavers may be used to form a brick floor using regular mortar joints. Brick pavers are thinner than conventional brick. Some are glazed, but most are not. Pavers

PORTLAND CEMENT ASSN.

13-22 This concrete patio has exposed aggregate and a decorative color design to add interest.

DREXEL HERITAGE FURNISHINGS, INC.

13-23 Brick flooring adds a rustic charm to this traditional home. It may be left natural or waxed for a subtle glow.

are frequently 1 1/4 by 3 5/8 by 7 5/8 inches in size. Brick floors are more practical if installed over a concrete slab rather than on a wood floor base.

Slate floors add a touch of class to a room. Slate is expensive, but it is durable and luxurious looking, 13-24. It may be used anywhere a tile or brick floor is desirable. Slate is frequently a blue-gray color, but is available in green, red, brown, or black. The same type of bed is required for slate as for ceramic tile. If the thinset method (no mortar bed) is used, then slate of equal thickness is needed. A variable thickness material may be used with the thickbed method where mortar is used to even out the slate. Slate may be cut to form regular patterns of rectangular shapes, or it may be used in random shapes and patterns, 13-25. A thin mortar joint of 1/4 inch is best with slate and should be consistent throughout the floor area.

Flagstone floors are very popular for patios and other exterior applications, 13-26, but they produce a practical and serviceable interior floor as well. Random shapes and colors best describe a flagstone floor. Native stone is selected and split to be used in these floors. Usually, sedimentary type stone is used because it may be split into large, flat pieces. These are ideal for paving a floor.

Flagstone floors may be left rough and highly textured or ground smooth. They are expensive but attractive. This floor material may be used in any room or area of the

ARIST-O-KRAFT

13-24 One-foot squares of slate have been used to add a luxurious but durable touch to this kitchen.

13-25 This attractive, formal patio is surfaced with slate of various shapes and sizes.

house. It is easy to maintain and lasts indefinitely. Cleaning with a damp mop is all a stone floor requires to maintain its beauty.

Masonry floors are usually more expensive than other floors, but they are highly durable and always in style. As new masonry materials are developed, the range of choices increases and applications are broadened. Concrete and masonry are materials of permanence; they should be chosen with care because they cannot be changed easily.

Terrazzo. The term *terrazzo* is derived from the Italian word "terrassa" which means terrace on the roof. Originally, decorative chips from mosaic work were saved and used to make colorful and durable indoor and outdoor floors. Today, mainly marble chips are used with a portland cement binder to form terrazzo floors. When the cement hardens, the surface is ground smooth and polished. Rustic terrazzo is also popular. It contains colorful gravel in addition to marble chips, and its finish is left rough, 13-27.

Terrazzo floors are hard and smooth, and they only require damp mopping to maintain their luster. They may, however, be waxed for a more polished surface. They last indefinitely and are popular in heavy traffic areas. A wide range of colors and chip sizes is available. Terrazzo is a permanent type floor material that is expensive due to labor required for installation. These floors require a solid base of concrete under the terrazzo topping. Topping thickness is at least 1/4 inch. Divider strips of brass or other non-corrosive material are used to control shrinkage,

13-26 The rustic character of flagstone blends well with the traditional motif of this home.

PORTLAND CEMENT ASSN.

13-27 Rustic terrazzo is generally made from smooth stones. It is not ground to a polish like indoor terrazzo floors.

cracks, and form designs in the finished floor. Terrazzo is an old floor material, but it is still popular today because of its beauty, durability, and low maintenance requirements.

Floor Coverings

Floor coverings play a large and important role in the total design of a room or area. Although they may be changed more frequently than flooring materials, they last several years and require a substantial investment. Therefore, floor coverings should be chosen with care. The main types of floor coverings used in residential housing include soft floor coverings and resilient products.

Soft floor coverings. Soft floor coverings include carpeting and rugs. Carpet is fastened directly to the floor. It is sold by the roll in standard widths of 27 inches to 18 feet. It usually covers a floor from wall to wall. Rugs are not fastened to the floor, and they usually do not cover the entire floor.

A soft floor covering's characteristics are determined by its fibers, construction, texture, and density. The type of padding used with carpeting also affects its characteristics.

About 90 percent of the carpets and rugs produced today are made from four manufactured or synthetic fibers.

They are nylon, acrylic, polyester, and olefin. Wool is still used as a fiber, but it has been replaced extensively by manufactured fibers. No single fiber is perfect for all types of carpeting. Its durability, resilience, ability to maintain color, and ease of cleaning are factors to consider when choosing a soft floor covering.

Wool produces a highly durable, luxurious carpet. It has good resistance to abrasion and excellent resiliency. It has superior resistance to soil and fading, so it retains its original appearance for years. Static buildup is not a problem with wool fibers. Wool is the most expensive of the popular carpet fibers.

Nylon has a reputation for tough, long-lasting wear. It is highly resistant to crushing and matting; however, it may pill. Nylon fiber does conduct static electricity unless an anti-static finish is applied. It is easy to clean, but its color will fade under prolonged exposure to light.

Of the synthetic fibers used in carpet, acrylic fiber looks and feels the most like wool. It accepts dye well and has a color retention similar to wool. It is soft to the touch and has good elasticity, but it does not resist crushing as well as wool. Acrylic accumulates very little static buildup.

Polyester has a feel somewhat similar to wool. It resists wear but does not resist crushing as well as other fibers. However, it is economical for use in heavy duty carpets. Of the manufactured fibers, polyester generates the least amount of static electricity.

Olefin is very tough and highly water resistant. It is very resistant to fading and staining, but it is difficult to dye. Also, it is not very resilient. Olefin is most commonly used for indoor/outdoor carpeting. It is a good fiber for carpets used in high traffic areas as well. Olefin is also used in computer rooms and other similar areas because it reduces static electricity.

The method of construction used in making a rug or carpet is a factor in appearance, wearability, quality, and price. One method is not necessarily better than another; there are various grades within each method. Five basic construction techniques are used to make soft floor coverings. They are tufting, weaving, knitting, needlepunching, and flocking. The characteristics of each of these methods are outlined in 13-28.

Textures of a soft floor covering are produced by the pile of yarns. The yarns may be cut, uncut, set in different length, twisted, or untwisted. The five basic types of carpet texture are cut pile, level-loop pile, multi-level loop pile, cut and loop pile, and shag pile. Their characteristics are outlined in 13-29.

The density of pile of a soft floor covering is a key factor in determining the quality of a carpet. Density of carpets can be compared by finding the number of tufts to each square inch of surface area. Carpet with more tufts per square inch will probably wear longer, 13-30. Type of fiber, construction, and backing are other factors to use when determining quality. For example, a tight-loop construction of a good, abrasion-resistant fiber will wear longer than a plush construction of the same fiber. The strength of the backing is important because no matter

TUFTED CARPET

TUFTING. Pile tufts are inserted by needles threaded with yarn into a prefabricated backing material. Tufts are locked into place with a latex adhesive. Yarns may be looped, cut, or both. A second layer of backing is used for dimensional stability. Tufting is used for over 90% of the total production of carpets.

WOVEN CARPET

WEAVING. Backing yarns (warp and weft) and surface yarns (pile) are interlocked simultaneously creating a single fabric. There are three main types of woven carpets. A wilton weave produces many patterns and colors in cut or loop pile. The axminster weave is produced in cut pile only, with each individually set. This permits a great variety of patterns. A velvet or plush weave is generally monochromatic with all pile cut to the same length.

KNITTED CARPET

KNITTING. The backing yarn, stitching yarn, and pile yarn are looped together with three sets of needles. Knitting produces an uncut, loop pile. A latex backing is applied for added body.

NEEDLEPUNCHED CARPET

NEEDLEPUNCHING. A web of fibers is interlocked through the use of felting needles. They have a felted or flat-textured construction. A latex backing is added for strength. This type of construction is used mainly for indoor/outdoor carpeting.

FLOCKED CARPET

FLOCKING. Short, chopped fibers are attached to adhesive backed fabric using an electric charge. Fibers are embedded vertically to produce a single level, cut pile surface similar to velour. Colored patterns may be printed on flocked carpet.

13-28 The construction technique used to make soft floor coverings affects their appearance and durability.

how wear-resistant a fiber is, if the backing deteriorates the life of the carpet will be reduced.

Carpet padding or cushion protects a carpet and provides more comfort for the user. It also improves the carpet's appearance and length of life. The main purpose of padding is to prevent the pile from being crushed by traffic. It also smooths out any irregularities that may be in the subfloor. The five main types of padding are hair or felt, rubberized felt, sponge rubber, polymeric foam, and attached lining.

Hair or felt padding gives long wear and firm support. However, it may stretch and shed and is not mildew resistant. Usually, this type of carpet backing is not recommended by the carpet industry. Rubberized felt has the same advantages as hair or felt, but it has a layer of rubber attached to reduce stretching. Hair or felt padding is not recommended for damp climates.

Sponge rubber is produced in flat or bubble forms. It is available in several thicknesses. Sponge rubber resists mildew, and it is mothproof. This is the most popular

| VELVET PLUSH | SAXONY PLUSH | FRIEZE |

CUT PILE

CUT PILE. The pile loops are cut leaving two individual yarns in place of each yarn loop. There are three basic types. Velvet plush has very little twist in the yarns for an elegant, level sweep of color. Saxony plush has two or more yarns twisted together so that each tuft is distinguishable from the surface. Freize is made up of tightly twisted, well defined yarns, producing a pebbly effect.

LEVEL LOOP PILE

LEVEL LOOP PILE. All pile loops are left uncut and at equal height. The pattern produced is smooth, level, and long wearing.

MULTI-LEVEL LOOP PILE

MULTI-LEVEL LOOP PILE. Loops are left uncut, but are at different heights. Usually, there are two or three different heights in one carpet for a sculptured look.

CUT AND LOOP PILE

CUT AND LOOP. Cut pile and loop pile are combined in the same carpet. Many patterned surface textures are possible.

SHAG

SHAG. Cut pile is very long. Different lengths are available. Shags produce a casual, highly textured effect.

13-29 Various pile textures are produced by using different construction techniques.

13-30 One characteristic used to judge the quality of a carpet is the density of pile. The carpet sample on the top of this picture has more tufts per inch than the sample on the bottom.

carpet padding. Polymeric foam is a cellular type of structure that is resistant to mildew, fungus, and moths. Rubber backing may be used in any location.

An attached lining is usually foam rubber attached to the carpet. It is less expensive than other types of padding. Carpet with attached lining may be applied directly to concrete or other subfloor material.

Quality padding can increase the life of a given carpet by 100 percent over the same carpet using a low quality or improper pad. Padding is especially important for carpets because carpets are usually more permanent and more expensive than rugs.

Rugs are constructed similarly to carpets; however, they are manufactured in different sizes. Rug sizes may be categorized into three types of size: room size rugs, area rugs, and scatter rugs.

A rug is considered to be room size when it leaves a 3 to 12 inch border of the floor below it exposed. This frames the floor area and defines space, 13-31. Room size rugs are available in standard sizes such as 9 by 12 ft., 12 by 12 ft., and 12 by 15 ft. Room size rugs do not require special installation and are relatively easy to remove and send out for cleaning. They sometimes can be turned to equalize wear. Room size rugs may be moved to a new room or location more easily than wall-to-wall carpeting.

DREXEL HERITAGE FURNISHINGS, INC.

13-31 A room size rug provides a decorative floor covering while still revealing the natural floor surface. The bare floor helps to frame the room.

13-32 The area rug in this room is used to unify the furniture grouping.

13-33 Scatter rugs are often used to add color to a room. On smooth floors, they also may provide a slip-proof area for standing.

Area rugs are available in a wide variety of colors, textures, sizes, and shapes. They are not designed to cover the entire floor, but to emphasize or define areas of the room. They also can emphasize separate functions in a dual-purpose room. Area rugs are often used to unify a furniture grouping, 13-32. They also may serve as a focal point in a room's design. They can be used in almost any room of the home, especially to make a large room seem smaller or a small room seem cozy.

Scatter rugs are generally smaller and less formal than area rugs. They are used to reduce wear in heavy traffic areas or to provide accents of color, 13-33. Scatter rugs are good covers for surfaces that are prone to dirt or spills because they protect the permanent surface and they can be cleaned easily in the washing machine.

Resilient floor covering. Resilient floor coverings are smooth, hard materials that return to their original shape. They are made in either sheet or tile form. The main types of resilient floor coverings are asphalt, cork, rubber, vinyl, vinyl asbestos, and poured seamless floors.

Tiles (9 by 9 in. and 12 by 12 in.) are usually cemented or taped to the floor, but sheet materials may be laid loose or attached. Tiles usually waste less material, because extra tile is not wasted when allowing for irregularities. Worn areas also can be replaced without replacing the entire floor covering. However, the newer tiles are generally brighter in color than those not replaced.

Sheet floor covering comes in rolls with standard widths of 6, 9, and 12 ft. It has the advantage of being seamless. Therefore, it is favored for areas where spills may seep into the cracks between tiles. It also may be continued up

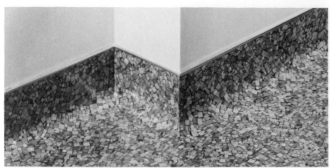

ARMSTRONG WORLD INDUSTRIES, INC.

13-34 Continuing seamless resilient floor covering up the wall helps prevent dirt from accumulating where the floor and wall meet.

the wall for a few inches to eliminate dirt traps where the wall meets the floor, 13-34.

Asphalt tile is durable and moisture resistant, but it may be damaged by grease. Also, it does not recover well from indentation. It is a good floor covering for below grade, concrete floors. Asphalt tile is the least expensive of all permanent, smooth floor coverings. Tiles may be plain or marbleized and come in a full range of lighter hues. The surface is slippery when wet and moderately hard.

Cork tile is a luxury floor covering for light traffic areas. It is quiet and comfortable, but it damages easily. It is not resistant to grease or stains, and it requires careful wax maintenance. Cork tile is moderately expensive. Its texture patterns range from fine to coarse and its color ranges from light to dark brown.

Vinyl cork tile is made by sealing cork under a clear, plastic covering. It is more resistant to dents and dirt than cork tile, and it is easier to maintain. However, it is not strong enough to hold well under heavy traffic. Vinyl cork tile may be used at any grade level.

Rubber tile is more common in commercial use than residential use, but it may be used in a home. It is quiet, comfortable, and very resilient. It has good resistance to denting and staining, although some types are not resistant to grease. Rubber tile requires a moderate amount of maintenance. It is available in bright, clear colors that may be plain or marbleized.

Vinyl tile is made of solid vinyl, 13-35. It resists damage from alcohol, petroleum products, ammonia, bleaches, household cleaners, stains, and grease. It is very durable and suitable for most home traffic areas. Vinyl tile requires a moderate amount of care; some types have no-wax finishes that make care even easier. Vinyl tile is moderately expensive. Its wide range of styles, patterns, and colors

ARIST-O-KRAFT

13-35 Solid vinyl tile is a good choice for a kitchen because of its damage resistance and low maintenance requirements.

13-36 Vinyl asbestos tile is reasonably priced, attractive, and functional.

and high level of durability have made it one of the most popular resilient floor coverings for residential use.

Vinyl asbestos tile, sometimes called reinforced tile, is highly durable and strong. It has a high resistance to

13-37 Cushioned, printed vinyl floor covering has good durability, but it is more comfortable and warmer than other hard floor coverings and materials.

grease, household acids, stains, and oils. Vinyl asbestos tile is inexpensive. It has good color and pattern clarity, 13-36. However, due to health problems associated with asbestos, this tile is not as commonly used as it was in the past.

Rotovinyl is made by printing a pattern on a vinyl sheet and covering the sheet with a layer of clear vinyl. It is suitable for light traffic areas. It also is available with a cushion backing for extra wear and comfort, 13-37.

Inlaid vinyl sheets have their color and pattern extended from the surface to the backing of the sheet. The color and pattern will remain as long as any of the product remains. They are available with or without a cushioned back.

Sheet vinyl is available with a no-wax finish. This floor covering has a special, clear urethane coating that provides high shine without waxing, 13-38. The surface resists scuffs and can be cleaned with a damp mop. Vinyl no-wax floors are very durable.

Poured seamless floors consist of an epoxy base and a hard, urethane finish. They can be used over many surfaces such as concrete, wood, vinyl rubber, or asphalt tiles. They are stain resistant as well as dent and scratch resistant. The surface is easy to maintain with a damp mop, and gloss may be restored by applying a new coat of clear finish.

SELECTION OF FLOOR TREATMENTS

Floors are no longer treated as bland, practical spaces with no design interest. In recent years, floors have been decorated in different, new colors, textures, and materials. The result has been positive and widely accepted.

ARMSTRONG WORLD INDUSTRIES, INC.

13-38 No-wax floors retain lustrous shines and require only damp mopping for maintenance.

Function

Floors have an important function role in a living space. They make it possible for us to move from one area of the structure to another, define space, support the furnishings, and shield the occupants from the earth below. These are important factors to keep in mind when considering various design treatments. For example, a beautiful white carpet is not practical for families with children and pets. Floors receive the most wear and dirt of any surface in the house or apartment. The challenge is to be both practical and design conscious so that the floors can make a positive contribution to the overall beauty and function of the home.

Various floor treatments have strengths and weaknesses to consider when selecting one for a specific application. For example, halls, foyers, baths, and kitchens are heavy traffic areas where dirt and moisture are prevalent. A durable, smooth floor treatment—such as ceramic tile or a resilient floor treatment—is practical for such areas. See 13-39.

Another factor to consider is the amount of time to be spent in caring for a floor treatment. Many people prefer the beauty of all wood floors, but they do not want to spend their time waxing and caring for such a floor. Some floor treatments have special coatings or treatments that make them easier to maintain. Colors can hide or emphasize dirt. Light colored floor treatments show dirt more easily than dark colored floors. Multicolored or patterned treatments such as a tweed carpet act as a camouflage to dirt, 13-40.

KITCHENAID DIV., HOBART CORP.

13-39 Tile floors like this one are popular for kitchens because they are attractive and easily cleaned.

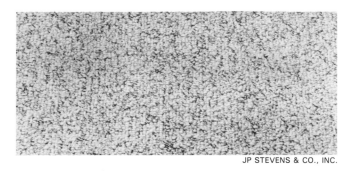

13-40 A tweed carpet does not show dirt or lint as much as a solid colored carpet might. It is a good choice for high activity areas of a home.

Cost of a floor treatment may limit your choices. However, it is important to consider the length of wear in relationship to cost. For example, flooring materials such as wood and ceramic are more expensive than floor coverings such as vinyl tile or carpeting, but they also are longer lasting.

The degree of hardness or softness of a floor is another consideration when choosing a floor treatment. Soft flooring usually feels warmer and is more comfortable than hard flooring. However, hard flooring is usually more durable and easier to clean.

Decoration

Different types of floor coverings convey different moods. Each type blends better with some decors than others. The floor of a room unifies the other components of a room. It should blend with the color, style, and formality level of furnishings within a room.

A floor may be dominant if bold patterns or intense colors are used. These types of floors can be focal points in rooms with few or simple furnishings. Simple patterns and light or neutral colors are more suitable for rooms with dominant furnishings or accessories.

13-41 The light carpet in this room helps to give an open, airy impression.

The intensity of a color increases with size. Therefore, a small sample of a floor treatment will appear much lighter than an entire floor of that treatment.

The type of floor covering used can convey a warm or cool feeling. Generally, smooth treatments generate a cool atmosphere, and more textured treatments such as carpeting convey a feeling of warmth. Warm colors can make a room seem cozy. Cool colors have a calming affect.

Floor coverings can make a room appear larger or smaller. Dark colors can pull elements together and make the room look smaller. Light colors produce a spacious effect, 13-41. Use of one floor treatment in a room gives an illusion of space because of the large, unbroken expanse that it provides.

REVIEW QUESTIONS

1. What are the components of a platform frame floor? How is it constructed?
2. What is the difference between a thickened-edge slab concrete floor and a floating slab concrete floor?
3. List and compare the appearance and construction of strip flooring, wood planks, and parquet.
4. What are some advantages and disadvantages of ceramic tile as a flooring material? For what rooms would you recommend ceramic tile?
5. What types of masonry materials may be used as flooring materials? What type of construction is recommended for floors under masonry?
6. What fibers are most commonly used in carpet production? What are the outstanding features of each?
7. How are the weave and pile of a carpet related to its texture and strength?
8. How can room size rugs, area rugs, and scatter rugs be used within a home?
9. What are the main types of resilient floor coverings used in residential homes? What are their care requirements?
10. What types of floor treatments would you recommend for a kitchen of a home with small children? For a kitchen in a home with just adults? For a living room? Why?
11. How can floor treatments be used to make a room convey the following feelings: A. Smaller. B. Larger. C. Warmer. D. Cooler.

14 Ceilings and Roofs

After studying this chapter, you will be able to:
- Describe the construction methods and materials used to build a roof.
- Evaluate ceiling surface materials according to their ease of placement, cost, and treatment requirements.
- Explain how a roof is constructed and identify the major parts of the roof.
- Identify the style of a roof.
- List and describe various types of roofing materials.

Ceilings and roofs help to confine the space within a house and to protect the house from the elements. Each room within a home has a ceiling. The ceiling defines the height of a room, provides support for lighting fixtures, and adds to the decoration of a room or area. The roof of a house protects the home from heat, cold, rain, snow, wind, and other elements. It also serves as an integral part of the exterior style of a home. This chapter outlines the construction and treatment of ceilings and roofs.

CEILINGS

Like walls and floors, ceilings help to define the limits of a room. Standard ceiling heights of modern homes are much lower than those of older homes. Homes built in the late 1700's have ceilings as high as 12 to 14 feet. Early twentieth century homes may have 9 foot high ceilings. Today, the standard ceiling height in first and second floor areas is 8 feet. Finished basement ceilings are often 7 feet high because space is needed to enclose heating ducts, beams, and plumbing. The lower ceiling heights save on construction costs. They also make heating the home less expensive.

Ceiling Construction

Most residential ceilings have a frame construction similar to that of floors, 14-1. A ceiling, however, uses lighter joists because it does not have to support much weight. Rafters above the joists support the roof. For many rooms, the floor above serves as a ceiling for the room. The ceiling cover for these rooms may be attached directly to the floor joists.

If a ceiling spans a very large distance, a beam may be needed for extra support. Roof trusses also may be used as a ceiling frame. Like floor trusses, roof trusses use small pieces of lumber fastened together with metal plates, 14-2. They eliminate the need for a separate ceiling frame. Also, they can span greater distances than traditional ceiling joists.

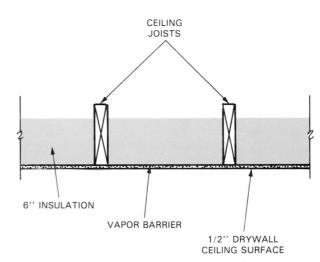

14-1 Like floors, ceilings are constructed of joists. The ceiling surface material is attached to the ceiling frame.

Ceiling joist spacing is typically 16 inches, but spacings of 12 and 24 inches are also used. Trusses are generally spaced 24 inches apart.

Cathedral ceilings also may be used in residential housing, 14-3. This type of ceiling has exposed beams and a surface covering that is attached to the rafters. Since no surface covering is placed below the support beams, ceiling joists are not needed.

Ceiling Surface Materials

Several different materials are commonly used to form the ceiling surface. The most typical are gypsum board, plaster, wood boards, and suspended ceiling materials. See 14-4. These materials provide surfaces that may be covered with a ceiling treatment or left untreated.

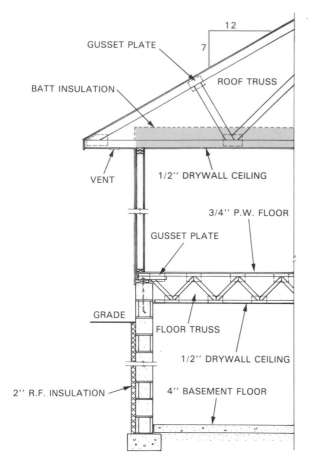

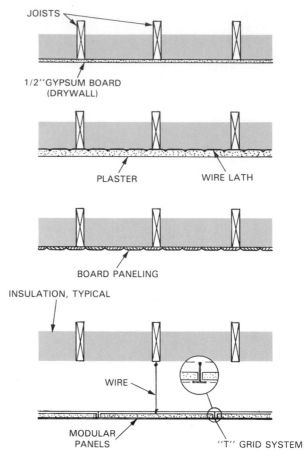

14-2 Ceiling surface materials can be applied to roof trusses without adding a joist ceiling frame.

14-4 The most common ceiling surface materials are gypsum board, plaster, wood panels, and suspended ceiling materials.

Labels in figure 14-2:
GUSSET PLATE
BATT INSULATION
ROOF TRUSS
VENT
1/2'' DRYWALL CEILING
3/4'' P.W. FLOOR
GUSSET PLATE
GRADE
FLOOR TRUSS
1/2'' DRYWALL CEILING
2'' R.F. INSULATION
4'' BASEMENT FLOOR
12
7

Labels in figure 14-4:
JOISTS
1/2''GYPSUM BOARD (DRYWALL)
PLASTER
WIRE LATH
BOARD PANELING
INSULATION, TYPICAL
WIRE
MODULAR PANELS
''T'' GRID SYSTEM

BOYNE FALLS LOG HOMES

14-3 A cathedral ceiling has exposed beams, so joists are not necessary.

226

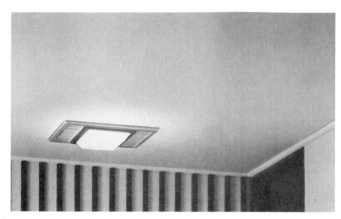

14-5 Gypsum provides a smooth ceiling surface that can be painted.

Gypsum board ceilings. Gypsum board can be used for ceiling surfaces as well as for walls, 14-5. It has replaced plaster as the most used ceiling material in housing structures. It is less expensive than plaster and it can be installed more quickly. Gypsum board can be finished with several types of treatments. It is also fire resistant.

When used as a ceiling surface, gypsum board is attached to joists or trusses using nails and adhesive. The adjoining edges are covered with a perforated tape and gypsum compound. This procedure forms a smooth surface suitable for painting or other treatment. Two thicknesses of drywall can be used to form a ceiling of superior quality. This type of construction is less likely to show cracks from shrinkage and loose nails as the ceiling ages.

Plaster ceilings. Gypsum plaster is a traditional ceiling material. It is durable, economical, fire resistant, and structurally rigid. It is also a good sound insulator. Plaster can be applied to curved as well as flat surfaces, and it can be molded into shapes, 14-6.

Some sort of base must be attached to the ceiling before plaster can be applied. The base material is called a *lath*. Commonly used laths are of gypsum, perforated gypsum, insulating fireboard, and expanded metal. Two or three coats of plaster are applied over the lath. The first coat is called the *scratch coat*. It is applied directly to the lath. When it has hardened some, it is raked or scratched to provide a good bond for the next coat. When three coats are used, the second coat, called the *brown coat,* forms

FOCAL POINT INC.

14-6 Plaster can be molded into decorative ceiling coves and used as a ceiling surface material.

a base for the finish coat. The finish coat may be troweled smooth or given a textured finish, 14-7.

The total thickness of plaster on a ceiling should be at least 1/2 inch. Plaster on a masonry surface or a metal lath is usually thicker. Plaster may be applied by hand or with a plastering machine. Paint is often used as a treatment for plaster ceilings.

Paneled ceilings. Wood boards or sheet products can be used as a ceiling surface material, 14-8. Solid wood paneling boards are available in several designs that can be used on ceilings. They range in widths from 4 to 12 inches and are usually 3/4 inch thick. However, thinner styles are available. Boards are nailed directly to joists or trusses. They may be stained, painted, sealed with a clear finish, or left untreated.

Plywood paneling also may be nailed directly to joists or trusses. Many types are prefinished and require no further treatment. Paneled ceilings are durable and need little maintenance.

Suspended ceilings. Suspended ceilings are popular for kitchens, bathrooms, and basements, but they may be used in any location of the home. Suspended ceilings use a metal framework designed to support ceiling panels. The supports form a grid pattern that commonly holds either 2 by 2 ft. or 2 by 4 ft. ceiling panels, 14-9. The grid is suspended from joists or trusses by wires.

14-7 Several methods can be used to produce textured patterns in plaster.

DESIGN BY ELENOR FIELD AND CATHERINE SAUNDERS

14-8 Red cedar boards are one type of paneling that can be used as a ceiling surface material.

CONWED CORP.

14-9 Suspended ceilings consist of a metal grid that supports ceiling panels. Clear panels can be used for an illuminated ceiling.

Standard, prefinished panels for suspended ceilings are available in a wide variety of styles, 14-10. Translucent panels can be used to form luminous ceilings. These are popular for bathroom and recreation room ceilings. Flourescent lighting is placed above the ceiling panels.

Ceiling Treatments

Many ceiling surface materials are prefinished, and they require no further treatment. Gypsum board and plaster, however, require some form of ceiling treatment. Paint and ceiling tiles are the most common treatments.

Paint. Paint is a popular ceiling treatment. It is easy to apply and provides a passive background for a room. White and light colors are most common. These help to reflect diffused light in a room. They also make a ceiling seem higher. Dark colors may be used in homes with very high ceilings. Flat, interior wall paint is most commonly used on drywall and plaster ceilings. Wood ceilings may also be painted. Enamel or semi-gloss paint may be used on kitchen and bathroom ceilings to make cleaning easier.

Textured paints can be used to add interest to a ceiling. They are also good for covering cracks and other imperfections in a ceiling surface. Textured paint can be patterned in many ways. Various swirled, stippled, and troweled patterns can be used. Some paints have course

229

14-10 Panels for suspended ceilings are available in many prefinished patterns.

ARMSTRONG WORLD INDUSTRIES

14-12 Ceiling panels with tongue and groove edges are less likely to come loose with age.

sand for a rough texture. Patterns should complement the design scheme of a room, 14-11. Highly textured ceilings help to absorb sound and soften light reflection.

Ceiling tiles. Ceiling tiles can be applied directly to furring strips or to any smooth ceiling surface. The most common size for ceiling tiles is 12 by 12 inches. They may have smooth or tongue and groove edges. Tiles with tongue and groove edges tend to stay more secure, 14-12. Tiles may be applied to the ceiling using adhesive, nails, or staples.

Ceiling tiles are prefinished and come in a variety of styles. Tiles with bold patterns make the ceiling seem lower. Less prominent patterns make the ceiling seem higher. Accoustical tile can be used to contain sound in high noise areas such as recreation rooms and music rooms.

KIRSCH CO.

14-11 The pattern of this ceiling covered with textured paint complements the informal design of the dining room.

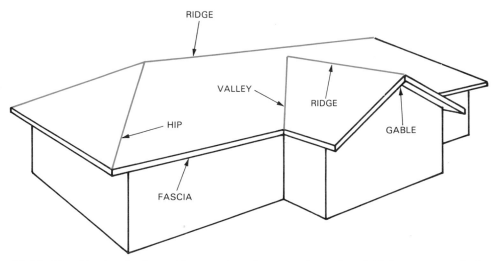

14-13 The ridge is a horizontal intersection of two sections of roof. Valleys are angular intersections of two sections of a roof.

ROOFS

Roofs protect the interior of a house from the elements. The same basic construction methods are used to build roofs of any style. Some styles are more difficult and expensive to construct, but they may enhance the architectural style of the exterior. Roofing materials vary in cost, durability, and style. They also affect the exterior's appearance.

Roof Construction

The roof framing is constructed of rafters that are arranged to provide support and structural form for the roof. Like ceiling or floor joists, rafters form the structural base for the roof surface. They may be placed in a variety of layouts depending on structural requirements and the style of roof desired.

Rafters are arranged to form sections of roof that extend from the top of the exterior walls to the ridge. The *ridge* is the horizontal line at which two sections of roof meet. The rafters are joined to the ridge board that runs along this line. The roof sections are placed at an angle to the ceiling so that the ridge is the highest point of the roof. Some roofs have a complicated structure with ridges perpendicular to each other. The sections of roof that slope down from the ridges meet and form an angular intersection. This intersection is called a valley. See 14-13.

The size and arrangement of rafters is determined by the span of the building and the desired slope of the roof, 14-14. The slope of the roof represents the ratio between the rise and run of the roof. The rise is the longitudinal distance from the top of the wall to the ridge. The run is the horizontal distance from the outside of a wall to the ridge. The span is the distance from the outside of one

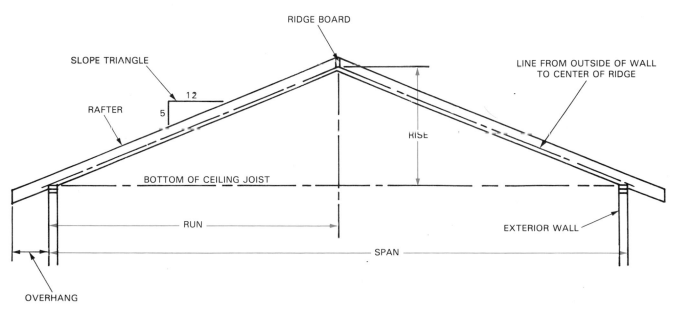

14-14 The rise, run, and span are used to determine a roof's construction.

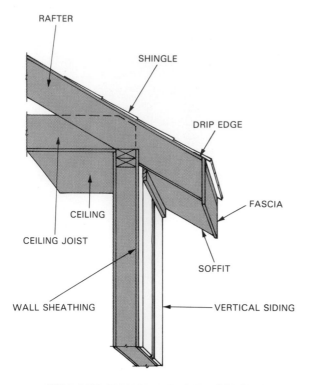

WIDE BOX CORNICE WITHOUT LOOKOUTS

14-15 A sloping soffit has a soffit board attached directly to the rafters.

to shade the house and prevents water from running down the exterior walls. The overhanging area of the roof is called the *cornice*. The underside of the cornice is called the *soffit*.

Most residential homes have boxed cornices. The rafters of a boxed cornice are enclosed by a soffit board. The soffit board may be attached directly to the rafters for a sloping soffit, 14-15. For a horizontal soffit, the board is attached to the wall at a point directly across from the end of the overhang. Horizontal support members may be added for wide soffits. See 14-16. Some rustic or contemporary houses have open cornices. These have exposed rafters, 14-17.

Some roofs are also extended horizontally past the end walls of the house. These extensions are called gable ends or rakes, 14-18. Generally, rakes are also enclosed with soffit boards.

Once the roof frame is built, it is covered with sheathing. The addition of sheathing makes the roof stronger and more rigid. It also serves as a base for nailing the roof covering material. Particleboard, waferboard, oriented strand board, shiplap, and plywood composite are typical sheathing materials.

Flashing is a wide strip of metal used over sheathing where leaking could cause problems. Weather resistant materials such as galvanized sheet metal, aluminum, or copper are used. Flashing is used around chimneys, at valleys, and where the roof intersects a wall, 14-19. A metal drip edge is usually used at the eave line and the rakes to preserve the soffit boards and to prevent water from getting under the roofing materials, 14-20. Gutters and downspouts are used to prevent water from running

exterior wall to the outside of the opposite exterior wall. On most homes, the run is half the span.

On most roofs, the rafters extend past the edge of the exterior wall to provide an overhang. The overhang helps

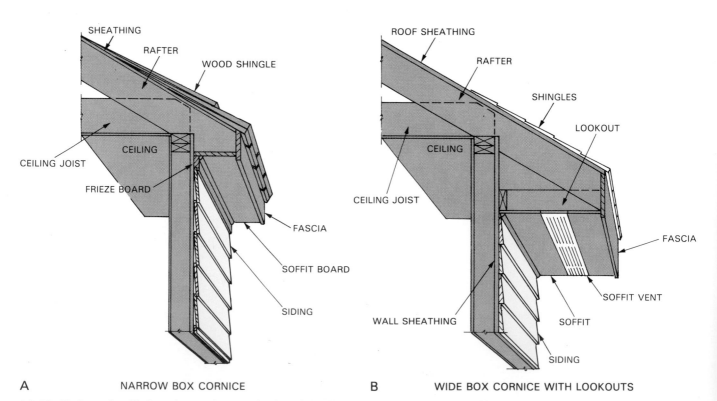

A NARROW BOX CORNICE

B WIDE BOX CORNICE WITH LOOKOUTS

14-16 Horizontal soffit boards may be attached to the rafters (A), or nailed to horizontal members (B).

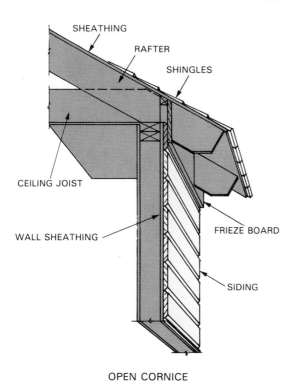

OPEN CORNICE

14-17 An open cornice has exposed rafters.

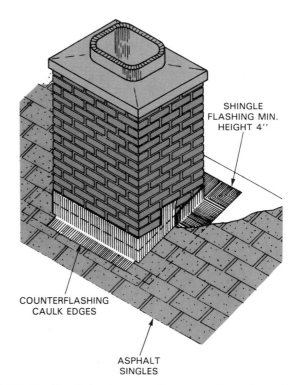

14-19 Flashing helps to prevent seepage through cracks.

directly off the eaves, 14-21. This prevents water from settling around the foundation and splashing on the house.

Provisions must be made in the roof structure for ventilation. Ventilation helps to prevent moisture from forming on the underside of sheathing. It also is needed for general circulation within the attic. Vents are generally placed on the underside of the roof overhang. Vents also may be extended through the roof. See 14-22.

Roof Styles

Roofs can be built in several different styles to enhance the overall appearance of the house. The most popular residential styles are shown in 14-23. The gable roof is one of the most popular styles for modern residential houses. It is simple and economical to build. It allows good ventilation and does not allow water and snow to build up on the roof.

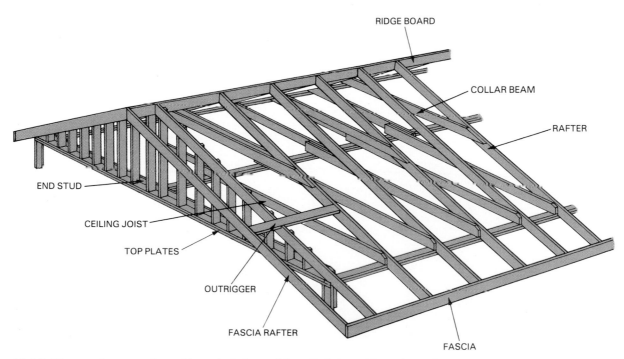

14-18 The overhang on the gable end of the roof is called the gable end or rake.

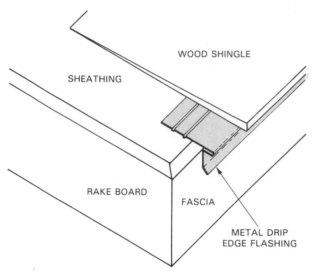

14-20 *Flashing at the eave line prevents water from getting behind shingles.*

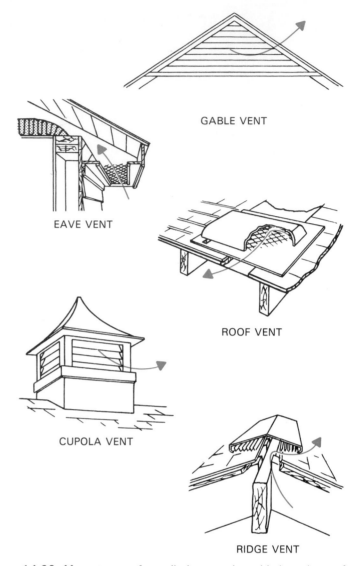

14-22 *Many types of ventilation can be added to the roof structure.*

The hip roof has a more complicated construction than the gable roof. It provides a cornice on all four sides of the house. However, ventilation is not good with this style. The Dutch hip has a gable added to each end of the hip roof. The gable creates a more interesting roof line. It also allows better ventilation.

The flat roof is one of the simplest, most economical roofs to build. It is most practical in areas where little or no snow falls. Flat roofs may have wide overhangs to provide shade. Most flat roofs have a slight slope of 1/8 to 1/2 inch per foot for drainage. Flat roofs are not covered with traditional roofing materials. Instead, a built up roof is made of layers of roofing felt and tar covered with gravel.

The shed roof is much like the flat roof, but it has more slope. Shed roofs with a slope less than 3:12 use a built

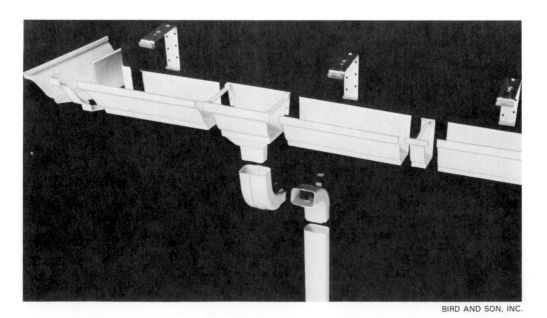

14-21 *Gutters and downspouts protect the walls and foundation from water.*

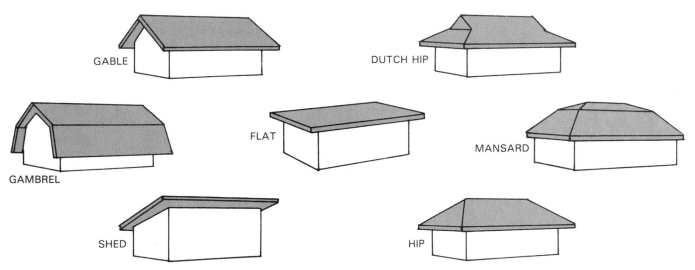

14-23 Several styles may be used for residential roofs.

up roof covering. Roofs with more slope may be covered with traditional materials. The shed roof is often used with other roof styles on a house. It is a common roof for additions to houses.

The gambrel roof is often called a barn roof because it was traditionally used on barns. It is common on Dutch colonial style houses. The gambrel construction permits added headroom to the top level of a home. The mansard roof also allows extra space on the top floor of a home. It is much more complex to build than the gable or hip roof.

Roofing Materials

Roofing materials help to protect the structure from elements such as rain, sun, dust, and wind. The appearance of a dwelling also is enhanced by roofing materials.

Common materials include asphalt roofing, wood shingles and shakes, tile, slate, and concrete materials, and metal.

Asphalt roofing. Asphalt roofing is available in shingles, roll roofing, and saturated felts. Asphalt shingles are the most common roofing material for residential structures, 14-24. Roll roofing has the appearance of shingles once attached to the roof, but it can be applied in strips. Both shingles and rolls last approximately twenty years. Saturated felts are used for built up roofs. They also can be used as sheathing under shingles.

Wood shingles and shakes. Modern wood roofing materials are more fire resistant than older wood roofing products. They are treated with fire-retardant chemicals. They are also decay resistant, lasting as long as fifty years. Shingles and shakes are commonly made of redwood, cypress, and western red cedar. They give a house a rustic

14-24 Asphalt shingles are the most popular roofing material.

14-25 Wood shakes give a house a rustic appearance.

14-27 Copper is an elegant but expensive roofing material.

appearance, 14-25. Wood roofing materials are more expensive than asphalt materials.

Tile, slate, and concrete materials. These materials are expensive, but they can enhance the architectural style of a home. They are heavy and require special roof construction to support the weight. Concrete materials have an appearance similar to tile and slate, but they are lighter in weight and less expensive, 14-26. These materials are very durable and will last for the life of the structure.

Metal. The most popular metal used for roofing is copper. It is seldom used to cover an entire roof because it is very expensive. However, copper roofing can be used in smaller quantities to accent the style of the house, 14-27. Copper is the most durable roofing material used.

REVIEW QUESTIONS

1. How do ceiling joists differ from floor joists? How are they the same?
2. Would gypsum board or plaster be more practical for a flat, rectangular ceiling? Which would be better for a curved ceiling?
3. How is a suspended ceiling constructed? For what rooms is this type of ceiling popular?
4. What are the two most common ceiling treatments?
5. What is the ridge of the roof? How is the ridge formed?
6. How is the slope of a roof determined?
7. Why is flashing used on a roof? Where is it normally located?
8. What are the seven main styles of roofs?
9. How do the roofing materials for flat and shed roofs differ from the materials used for other styles of roofs?
10. What are the main types of roofing materials used? What kind is the least expensive? What kind lasts the longest?

14-26 Concrete shingles have the appearance of slate and tile, but they are less expensive.

15 Windows and Doors

After studying this chapter, you will be able to:
- List standard types of windows available for residential use, and cite their .advantages and disadvantages.
- Evaluate the quality of a window's construction in terms of appearance, function, and insulative value.
- Select and place windows in a home so that optimum lighting, ventilation, privacy, and appearance is achieved.
- List and describe various types of window treatments.
- Distinguish among various types of doors by their appearances and methods of operation.
- Describe the construction of a door.
- List possible treatments for interior and exterior doors.

Windows and doors influence the interior and exterior appearance of the home. They provide both a physical and visual connection between two areas. They shield an opening from the elements and provide privacy while allowing light, ventilation, and a broadened view. Windows and doors should be planned to provide their optimum contribution to the function and design of a structure.

WINDOWS

Windows serve many functions. They provide natural light, ventilation, and privacy; contribute to the atmosphere of a room; add detail to a decorative scheme; and give balance and design to the exterior of a structure, 15-1.

ROLSCREEN CO.

15-1 Windows play an important role in the exterior design of this home. Informal balance is achieved between the large bay window on the left and the smaller windows on the right.

ANDERSEN CORP.

15-2 Double-hung windows are the most popular window used in residential housing.

GRABER

15-3 Double-hung windows can be opened or closed without interfering with draperies.

Window Types

Sliding windows, swinging windows, and fixed windows are the three basic types of windows used in housing construction. Combination windows and overhead windows also are used. The kind selected depends on the functions to be performed, architectural style of the structure, construction considerations, building codes, and personal taste.

Sliding windows. The most common type of sliding window is the *double-hung window.* See 15-2. It is a classic design that has remained popular since colonial times. The window opens vertically from the bottom, the top, or both. Two main glass areas, called *sashes,* are held in the window frame. When slid up or down, each sash is held in place by friction, springs, or weights. Double hung windows are usually taller than they are wide, and both sashes are the same size.

Several advantages are associated with double-hung windows. They are readily available and produced in a wide variety of sizes. They are easy to install and rarely warp or stick. They do not project inside or outside to interfere with draperies or traffic, 15-3. The horizontal lines of double-hung windows are considered more attractive and less distracting than the lines of other types of windows.

Double-hung windows are difficult to clean on the outside. However, many newer types of sashes are removable, or they are easily pivoted inward for cleaning. No protection from the rain is offered from open double-hung

MARVIN WINDOWS

15-4 Casement windows provide a good view, and they swing out to provide good ventilation.

windows. They are sometimes difficult to operate when furniture is placed in front of the window.

Horizontal sliding windows move on tracks at the bottom and top of the windows. They generally contain two movable sashes, but only half of the window area can be opened at one time. Screens are mounted from the outside. A wide range of premanufactured sizes are available.

Swinging windows. Types of swinging windows include casement, awning, hopper, and jalousie windows. Casement windows usually have two sashes hinged at the side to swing outward. Cranks are generally used to open and close casements, but push bars or handles may be used.

Casement windows, 15-4, are great ventilators. Because the sash swings out, air that would otherwise pass the opening is directed inward. Casements are opened easily with a crank even when they are located above a kitchen counter or behind furniture. Screens and storm sashes are easy to install and remove because they are located inside.

Casements do have some disadvantages. They project outward and may be bumped into easily, so they should not be used near walks or play areas. They collect dirt easily because of their construction and do not keep out rain when open. The vertical lines of these windows may be considered distracting by some.

Awning windows are hinged at the top and swing outward, 15-5. They are manufactured as single or multiple units stacked in a single frame, 15-6. The sashes are

DREXEL HERITAGE FURNISHINGS, INC.

15-5 An awning window swings out from the bottom to protect a room from rain while providing ventilation. Awning windows do not interfere with furniture placement.

MARVIN WINDOWS

15-6 Awning windows may be stacked to provide maximum ventilation and view.

opened with a crank or push bar and provide good ventilation and rain protection. Screens are located inside; they may be easily removed for window cleaning.

Awning windows, like casements, should not be located where they might interfere with pedestrian traffic, such as between the house and carport. They also collect dirt when open.

Hopper windows are hinged at the bottom and swing into a room. They are opened by a lock handle positioned at the top of each unit. Designed for low placement on a wall, hopper windows improve air movement and do not interfere much with draperies. They are frequently used as basement windows as well.

Hopper windows are usually manufactured as one unit. They are easy to clean, but they interfere with inside room space near the window. Screens must be removed from the outside.

Jalousie windows consist of a series of narrow glass slats (3 to 8 inches wide) that are held by a metal frame. The slats operate in unison, similar to venetian blinds. They open outward, but produce little interference due to their narrow slats. The amount of ventilation provided may be adjusted using a crank. Screens and storm windows are located inside when used with jalousie windows.

Jalousies are used where ventilation is a major concern. They do not seal well and allow substantial air infiltration when closed. They are difficult to wash because of

PPG INDUSTRIES, INC.

15-7 *Fixed windows are used in areas where view or lighting is more important than ventilation.*

ROLSCREEN CO.

15-8 *A bay window has a projected area of fixed glass with double-hung windows on either side.*

the small glass sections. Jalousie windows are produced in a variety of sizes ranging in widths from 18 to 48 inches in increments of 2 inches. Lengths are available from 17 to 99 1/2 inches in increments of 2 1/2 inches.

Fixed windows. The purpose of fixed windows is to admit light and provide a view, 15-7. They do not permit ventilation. Picture windows are generally used in less private rooms and take advantage of a view that enhances the room. Window walls are another type of fixed window. They are popular for special garden rooms or enclosed patios, particularly on the south side of a house.

Fixed windows are more likely to be custom made than bought in a standard size. Since the windows do not open, weatherstripping, hardware, and screens are not required.

Combination windows. Fixed windows may be used as units with sliding and swinging windows. Such units are called combination windows. For example, hopper windows are often combined with an upper, fixed window. A three section window may have fixed glass in the center and casements on either side. Awning windows may be placed above or below a fixed window. Combination windows allow an unobstructed view and ventilation.

Bay and bow windows are combination windows with their sections at angles so that the window projects out from the structure. Bay windows generally use two double-hung windows with a fixed window in the center, 15-8. The side windows are normally placed at 45° angles to the exterior wall.

Bow windows are usually constructed with casement and fixed windows. Standard combinations of four to seven units are common. These window units form an arc that extends beyond the outside wall, 15-9.

Skylights and clerestory windows. Skylights and clerestory windows are used to admit light into areas of a structure that have little or no natural light. Skylights are usually located on the roof or ceiling; clerestory windows are placed high on a wall. Their use can achieve dramatic lighting effects in a room. Some skylights and clerestory windows may be opened for ventilation.

Skylights are available in several basic shapes and sizes as well as unlimited custom design. Clerestory windows may be custom-made fixed windows or a series of standard windows, 15-10.

Window Construction

Windows consist of a frame, one or more sashes, and any necessary weatherstripping or hardware. Sashes may have dividers called muntins and bars across them to separate the glass into several rectangular panes. Frame materials include wood, metal, vinyl, and metal or vinyl clad wood.

Wood as a window framing material is a good insulator. It is considered attractive and blends well with most interiors. However, wood expands and contracts with different moisture conditions. This may cause gaps and sticking at different times of the year. Also, wood needs a protective coating of paint or vinyl that must be properly maintained.

ANDERSEN CORP.

15-9 A bow window provides a panoramic view and adds interest to the exterior design of a house.

NATURALITE, INC.

15-10 Skylights and clerestory lights give a room an airy appearance.

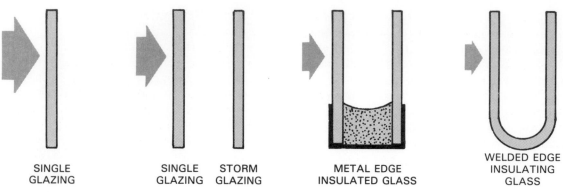

SINGLE GLAZING

SINGLE GLAZING

STORM GLAZING

METAL EDGE INSULATED GLASS

WELDED EDGE INSULATING GLASS

15-11   The type of glazing used in a window affects how much heat is lost through it. The size of the arrows represents the relative amount of heat lost through various types of windows.

Metal window frames usually are made from aluminum, although steel, brass, and bronze windows are also made. Aluminum windows are less expensive than wood and require less maintenance. Aluminum is very strong, allowing a thinner, lighter frame than is possible with wood. It is usually coated for an attractive, maintenance free finish. It can be left plain if desired because it naturally forms an oxide coating that needs no other treatment. Aluminum is not a good insulator, however, and condensation may form on it when interior temperatures differ greatly from exterior temperatures. Vinyl frames are similar to metal frames, but they are better insulators.

Metal clad wood frames are covered with aluminum on the exterior side or on both sides. This type of window offers the low maintenance of aluminum and the insulating value of wood. Those windows covered only on the exterior side also allow an interior wood finish.

Each style of window is constructed differently, and construction will vary with different manufacturers. Details of construction can be obtained from the window manufacturer.

Heat loss. As the cost of home heating rises, heat loss around windows and through glass becomes a major concern. Proper sealing and weather stripping helps to prevent drafts or loss or gain of heat.

Heat loss or gain through glass can be minimized in several ways, 15-11. A single paned glass window is not a good insulator, but its insulation value can be nearly doubled by adding a storm window. Dead air space between storm windows and regular windows acts as an insulator.

Insulating glass works on the same concept of using air as an insulator. The window consists of two panes of glass (double glazing) with a space containing air or another gas ranging from 1/4 to 5/8 inch in width. Insulated glass panes are produced as sealed units with metal or welded glass edges. The air between the panes is dehydrated to prevent condensation. New types of dry gas are being used for even better insulative value. Some manufacturers add a third pane (triple glazing) to insulated glass. Insulated glass may be used in combination with storm windows for reduced heat loss or gain.

Reflective coatings may be used on glass to reduce heat loss or gain. They usually are applied by the manufacturer, but special films also may be used to cover premanufactured windows. The coatings may be transparent or tinted.

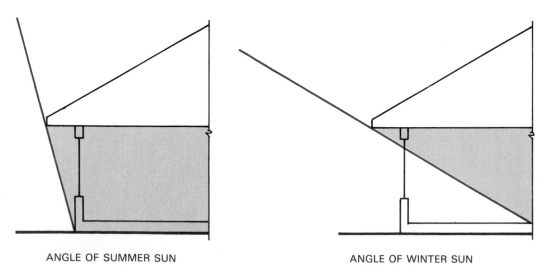

ANGLE OF SUMMER SUN

ANGLE OF WINTER SUN

15-12   When an overhang is properly designed, the sun is shaded from a room in the summer and shines into a room in the winter.

In the winter, when the sun is low and shining directly into a window, quality windows can transmit sunlight into a home and then trap its heat. Solar gain may even exceed heat loss through glass if the window has a southern exposure. A proper roof overhang will shade the higher, summer sunlight from a window. Then the properly insulated window will reduce heat gain in the home. See 15-12.

Window symbols. Standard window symbols are used on construction drawings to communicate the type and location of windows in the structure. Figure 15-13 shows some of these symbols with an elevation view. The sill below the window is shown where one is used. There is generally no sill on basement windows and some modern picture frame type windows used in frame construction.

Window Selection and Placement

Uniform lighting is desirable in a room. Proper placement and selection of windows helps to eliminate very dark or very bright areas. Generally, when the glass area is 20 percent of the floor area in a room, adequate natural light

is provided even on cloudy days. Draperies or blinds may be used to shield light out on extremely sunny days.

Windows that face south provide more light than windows facing other directions. One large window provides more even lighting than several smaller ones. Windows on more than one wall distribute light better than windows on a single wall. Windows placed high on a wall allow more light to enter a room than windows placed low on a wall.

Natural ventilation in a living space is necessary throughout the year. Windows are a prime source of ventilation, especially during warm weather. Adequate ventilation will be provided if openings are equal to about 10 percent of the floor area of a house and if they are placed in a way that takes advantage of breezes. The type of ventilation provided by different window placements is shown in 15-14.

Privacy is a concern in the placement of windows. Different types of windows provide varying amounts of sound and sight privacy. Closed windows provide a barrier that helps to keep exterior noise out and interior noise in. In

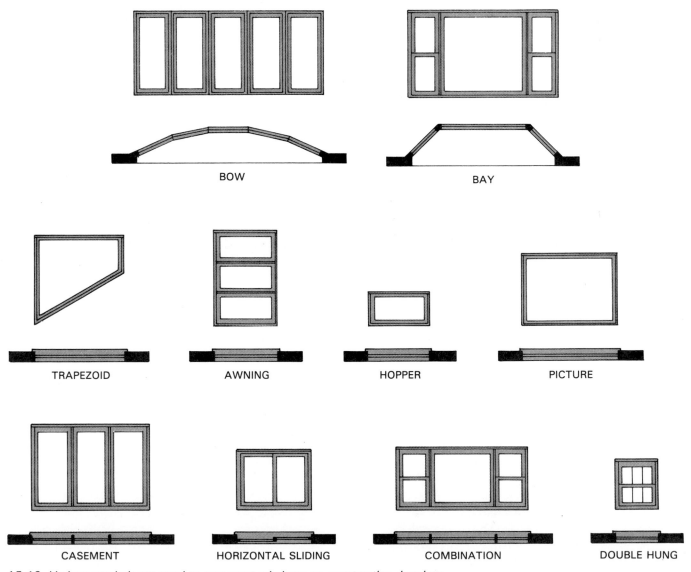

BOW

BAY

TRAPEZOID

AWNING

HOPPER

PICTURE

CASEMENT

HORIZONTAL SLIDING

COMBINATION

DOUBLE HUNG

15-13 Various symbols are used to represent windows on construction drawings.

243

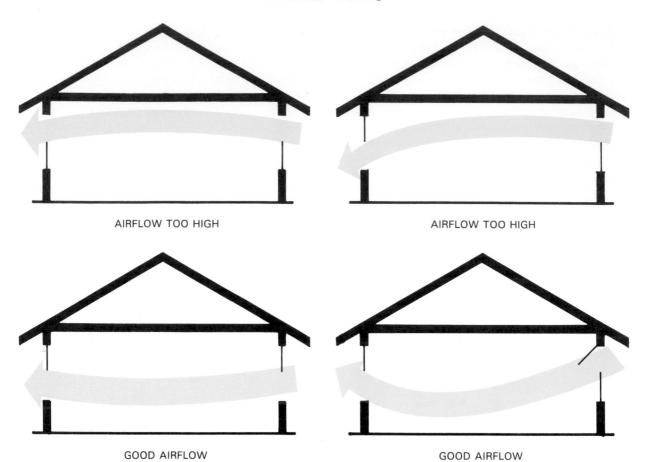

AIRFLOW TOO HIGH   AIRFLOW TOO HIGH

GOOD AIRFLOW   GOOD AIRFLOW

15-14 Window placement affects airflow through a living space.

AMERICAN SOLAR HOMES

15-15 The windows of this solar home are a focal point of its simple architectural style.

louder surroundings, insulated glass windows can provide sound reduction while still providing natural light.

Visual privacy may be more desirable for some areas of the home than others. Textured or colored glass, or windows that are higher than eye level, will increase privacy in bedrooms, bathrooms, or other private areas. Outdoor shrubbery and fences can help obstruct the view from public areas into a window. The use of window treatments allows the amount of privacy within a room to be easily changed.

Windows may help to create an atmosphere within a structure. They may serve as a frame for an attractive view which will add to a room's overall appearance. A window can be scaled to fit the proportions of a view. Vertical windows accent a narrow view, while horizontal windows allow a panoramic view. Even without an exceptional view, windows help to give a feeling of open space by extending the line of vision past the wall. When a window is used for aesthetic value and is not required for ventilation, fixed glass is appropriate.

Windows have a dominant effect on the exterior appearance of a structure. Exteriors are becoming simpler through elimination of costly, unnecessary decoration. As this happens, windows become more important to the architectural character of the structure, 15-15. Although windows should first meet interior requirements, adjustments may be desirable to create a more acceptable exterior. A properly designed exterior should provide continuity between wall and window areas, 15-16.

WINDOW TREATMENTS

The purpose of window treatments is twofold. First, they control light and air and provide privacy. Second, they complement the design scheme and, therefore, help to beautify the interior space. Frequently, one purpose will take preference over the other.

Before selecting a window treatment for a room, you should first consider the style of living in that room or area—informal, formal, or a mixture. Just as important as how the room will be used is the role that the window is to play in the total design scheme. For example, will the window be treated as a focal point or a background element? A large window with a view should be a focal point; but if the view is depressing or at least not impressive, then the window may become background for other room elements.

Window treatments can be chosen to correct poor design situations. If windows are out of proportion to the rest of the room—too narrow, short, or irregular in size—the proper window treatment can change their appearance.

Another consideration when selecting window treatments is the direction that the window faces. North windows receive no direct sunlight; they usually require a different treatment than south or west windows that receive much direct light.

Finally, window treatments must be able to withstand the conditions of moisture, strong sunlight, and frequent use to which they will be subjected. Only materials that

VANDE HEY'S ROOFING TILE CO., INC.

15-16 This house, patterned after a Tudor cottage, has windows that blend well with its architectural style.

will retain their original quality under these conditions should be used.

Interior Window Treatments

Several basic interior window treatments are possible. They include draperies, curtains, shades, blinds, shutters, panels, and other treatments. One or more of these treatments should coordinate with most design schemes.

Draperies. Draperies are generally defined as heavy material with pleated panels that can be drawn across the glass area or placed at either side for decorative purposes, 15-17. Draw draperies may open and close at the center of the window (center draw) or pull as one unit across the entire window area (one way draw). When open, either type will stack to one or both sides of the window. Stationary panel draperies, positioned at the side of a window, may be used when privacy is not essential and the view is important.

Tier draperies utilize several tiers of short draperies. Each tier may be controlled individually, providing great variability in the level of natural light in a room.

Sheer casement draperies are see-through type draperies. They provide some privacy and filter sunlight, but not to the extent of typical heavier fabrics.

GRABER

15-17 Draperies can be distinguished from curtains by their heavy, pleated panels. These draperies are hung on a decorative rod.

KIRSCH CO.

15-18 Double-draw draperies have a set of sheers close to the window and heavier draperies set out from the window.

Still another type of draperies are double-draw draperies. They generally have sheer draperies that hang close to the glass and draperies of a heavier, more opaque fabric positioned a little further out from the wall, 15-18. They provide filtered light when the heavier draperies are open and maximum privacy when they are closed.

Draperies are frequently topped with *cornices, valances,* or *lambrequins.* A cornice is a horizontal decorative treatment across the top of the window, 15-19. It usually is made of wood, padded, and then covered with fabric. A valance is also a horizontal decorative treatment across the top of the draperies to provide a finished appearance and hide hardward and cords. Valances are generally made from fabric. Lambrequins are cornices that extend down the sides of the draperies.

Curtains. Curtains are usually considered less formal than draperies. They add to the casual charm of any room. Popular types of curtains include *shirred, ruffled,* and *cafe curtains.*

Shirred curtains are gathered directly on rods and hang straight down, 15-20. They may be attached both at the top and at the bottom.

Ruffled curtains are edged with ruffles on the hem and sometimes the sides. They are frequently finished with

15-19 This valance accents the Oriental design of this room.

15-20 Shirred curtains are usually gathered at the top and bottom. When made of a lightweight fabric, they allow light to filter into a room.

15-21 Ruffled curtains help to create a pleasant informal atmosphere in a room.

KIRSCH CO.

ruffled valances and tiebacks, 15-21. A tieback is a device used to hold back a curtain on the sides. Priscilla type curtains cross at the top and are generally made of sheer or semisheer fabrics that are ruffled on three sides.

Cafe curtains are straight curtains hung from rings that slide along a rod. They may be used in tiers to cover an entire window, or they may cover the window bottom with or without a matching valance at the top, 15-22. The curtain tops may be looped, scalloped, or pinch pleated. Cafe curtains are considered the most informal of the curtain types.

Shades. Window shades are second in use only to curtains as a window treatment. The primary purpose of shades is to control light by filtering it or by excluding it entirely. Many people use shades in combination with decorative curtains to protect the curtains from fading and to block out light without moving the curtains. Shades are also effective in reducing heat loss in winter and heat gain in summer.

The main types of shades include roller shades, Roman shades, Austrian shades, and pleated shades. The roller shades are composed of a strip of material hung on a roller from the top of a window, 15-23. The strip is pulled down to close the shade, and it rolls up by a spring mechanism to open the shade. Roller shades are available in translucent and opaque styles. They are produced in regular and reversed roller types. Reversed roller shades roll towards the window.

Roman shades do not roll up; they are pulled up by cords. They are made from decorative fabric and are generally used alone as a window covering. Roman shades hang flat when closed, but fold into horizontal pleats when raised, 15-24.

Austrian shades are designed to operate the same as Roman shades. However, they have scallops of sheer fabric between the vertical cords. They are often used in formal rooms where they provide an elegant accent.

Pleated shades are relatively new. They are generally of a solid fabric that is folded into horizontal accordian pleats. They may be raised or lowered using cords. Although sheer, most pleated shades have a special lining to improve their insulative value, 15-25.

GRABER

15-22 Cafe curtains are the most informal type of curtain.

KIRSCH CO.

15-24 Roman shades are drawn up by cords into folds.

SEARS, ROEBUCK, AND CO.

15-23 Roller shades may be used alone or with another treatment.

SEARS, ROEBUCK, AND CO.

15-25 Although translucent, most pleated shades are good insulators.

15-26 The narrow slats of these modern wooden blinds are both functional and attractive.

Blinds. Horizontal venetian blinds and vertical blinds are popular window treatments. New materials, patterns, and colors have made them versatile decorating tools.

A venetian blind is a series of slats supported by tapes and operated by cords. The slats may be made of wood, metal, or plastic. Contemporary venetian blinds have very narrow slats that are smooth when closed and nearly invisible when open, 15-26. Blinds may even be designed to fit between double glass panes, 15-27.

Vertical blinds consist of a series of vertical slats that hang from only an upper track or may be held in a lower track as well, 15-28. The slats may be metal, fabric covered plastic, wood, or split bamboo. They may be angled to control the amount of light entering a room or shut completely. Some types may be drawn open as well. Vertical blinds are useful for creating a feeling of height in a room. Dust does not collect on them as quickly as on horizontal blinds.

Shutters. Shutters are available in both traditional and contemporary styles. Traditional shutters have louvered or fixed slats. Contemporary shutters utilize fretwork inserts combined with a backing of fabric or some other opaque material. Shutters are attached with hinges so they

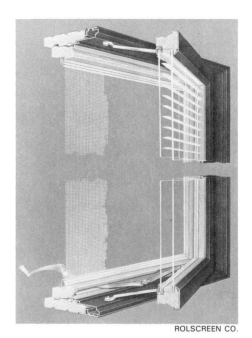

15-27 Venetian blinds may be placed between two panels of glass in some types of windows. This eliminates the need to clean the blinds.

DREXEL HERITAGE FURNISHINGS, INC.

15-28 Vertical slat blinds are elegant and practical, and they help to make a window appear taller.

can be opened to admit light and more ventilation. One or more units may be connected to cover several windows or a single wide window.

Shutters may be used in combination with curtains and blinds or other window treatments. They can be painted to match any color scheme or decor. They provide privacy and ventilation which makes them good choices for bedrooms and bathrooms.

Sliding panels and screens. Sliding panels and screens may provide a spectacular room focus. Wood panels, fabric panels, and sliding screens can be dramatic window treatments. Wood panels may have latticework or carving backed with translucent or opaque material. They may be stained or painted to match the room's decor.

Fabric panels are made by stretching fabric over a wooden frame. These may be premanufactured or custom made with fabrics that match or complement other pieces in the room. Some panels have painted scenes that serve as a focal point.

Sliding screens may be used in place of draperies or curtains. They frequently are used to cover sliding glass doors and windows. They also may be used with casement windows that swing outward. These screens require a series of tracks at the top and bottom as well as space beside the door or window if they are to be fully opened.

Other treatments. Privacy and shade from sun is not always necessary for all types of windows. Stained glass or etched glass windows are highly decorative with no other treatments, 15-29. Decorative wood frames may be

FOCAL POINT, INC.

15-29 Stained glass windows are highly decorative and require no further treatment.

15-30 A tastefully designed plant window provides a refreshing view from the interior and exterior of a home.

15-31 An awning shades a room from direct sunlight, and it can be rolled up when shade is not needed or desired.

15-32 These decorative shutters accent the windows of this Georgian style home.

used to accent a window. Houseplants, on shelves or hung, and potted trees provide partial coverage and a refreshing appearance, 15-30.

Exterior Window Treatments

Exterior window treatments have two advantages. First, they enhance the exterior appearance of the house. Second, they do not require interior wall space or interfere with interior furniture. Some of the more popular exterior window treatments include awnings, shutters, trellises, and grilles.

Awnings. Awnings are available in metal or in weather resistant fabrics. They protect the window from rain and wind and produce soft lighting inside the home, 15-31. Some awnings are stationary while others may be rolled up. The selection of awnings should be coordinated with other exterior elements to avoid an added on look.

Shutters. Functional shutters are not used nearly as often today as they were in the past. When they can be used to cover the window, they provide much protection against heavy weather. Most shutters on homes today are decorative; they are attached to the wall on either side of the window and cannot be closed, 15-32.

Trellises. Trellises are popular for providing shade. They may be designed to complement the architectural style of any house. Climbing plants may add to the appearance of a trellis.

Grilles. Grilles are usually considered stationary window coverings. They may be made from wood, plastic, metal, or masonry. Grilles are effective for providing privacy, shading, and ventilation.

DOORS

Doors are necessary for connecting one area to another while providing protection and privacy. The main types of doors used in residential construction are flush, panel, swinging, sliding, folding, and garage doors.

Flush doors. Flush doors are more common than panel doors in current construction. They are manufactured in woods such as birch, mahogany, and oak as well as in metal and vinyl. These materials are used as panel coverings for flush doors. The coverings result in a smooth, plain surface, 15-33.

Hollow core flush doors are made of a framework core covered with a wood, metal, or vinyl veneer. Regardless of the covering, the core is usually made of wood. Hollow core doors are lightweight and relatively inexpensive. Their strength and insulation value are low, however, so they are used almost exclusively as interior doors.

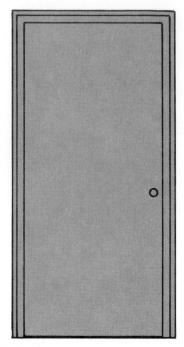

15-33 *A flush door has a smooth surface. It may have a hollow core or a solid core.*

Solid core flush doors consist of solid particleboard or tightly fitted blocks of wood covered with a veneer. These doors are heavy and strong. They also are good insulators. Solid core doors are more expensive than hollow core doors, so they usually are used as exterior doors.

Standard interior flush doors are 1 3/8 in. thick and 6 ft. 8 in. high. Widths range from 2 to 3 ft. in increments of 2 in. Wider or narrower doors can be made to fit special needs. Exterior flush doors are produced in widths from 2 ft. 6 in. to 3 ft. 6 in. in 2 in. increments. Heights include 6 ft. 6 in., 6 ft. 8 in., 7 ft., 7 ft. 6 in., and 8 ft. Standard exterior doors are 1 3/4 in. thick; however, larger doors are usually 2 1/4 in. thick.

Stile and rail doors. Stile and rail doors are constructed with a strong, heavy frame around the perimeter of the door. Vertical frame members, called stiles, and horizontal members, called rails, provide support across the center of the door. The space between the stiles and rails are filled with thinner panels that are set into the framework. See 15-34. These panels are most commonly made of glass or wood. Many different styles are possible by altering the size, shape, and arrangement of the panels.

Panel doors are stile and rail doors that use thinner wood panels between the framework. They are solid and provide complete sight privacy and good sound privacy when closed. Sash doors are the same as panel doors except that one or more of the panels are glass. French doors are sash doors with all glass panels, 15-35. Sash doors provide privacy, but they also allow light and a view.

Louver doors have a series of wooden slats set between the stiles and rails. These doors are not solid, so they are not practical for exterior use. They are appropriate where good ventilation is desirable or where privacy is not important. Louver doors are commonly used for closets, laundry rooms, or space divisions.

Swinging doors. If a door is placed on hinges so that it swings out from the wall, it is a swinging door. Swinging doors are the most convenient to operate for passage from room to room; they are also the most secure. However, ample space must be allowed for the door to swing out from the wall.

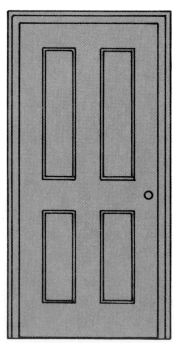

15-34 *A variety of styles is possible with a stile and rail door. The panels may be arranged in a variety of geometric patterns.*

THERMA-TRU, DIVISION OF LST CORP.

15-35 *French doors are stile and rail doors with all glass panels.*

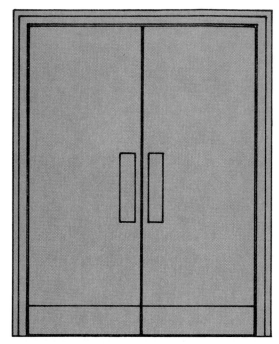

15-36 Double-acting doors are easy to open, and they swing shut automatically.

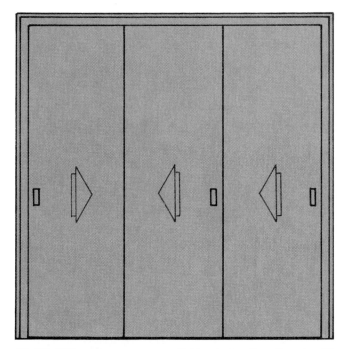

15-38 Sliding doors are on parallel tracks to allow them to slide past each other.

Most swinging doors only open in one direction, but special hinges may be used so the door will swing in a 180° arc. This type of door is called a *double-acting door,* 15-36. It has a spring in the hinge which returns the door to its closed position.

Double-acting doors are used between rooms which have lots of traffic but require that the door remain closed most of the time. They may be single or double doors.

15-37 Dutch doors are swinging doors with independently moving top and bottom halves.

Space must be allowed on both sides of these doors so that the door can swing freely.

A *Dutch door* is a swinging door with independently moving upper and lower halves, 15-37. The top half may be open for free movement of air, while the bottom half will serve as an enclosure for small children and pets.

Sliding doors. Sliding doors are set on a track and may be opened or closed by gliding along the track. Glides on the floor keep the doors from swinging. They are useful because they do not require extra clearance space for opening. The three main types of sliding doors are bypass, pocket, and surface sliding doors.

Bypass doors are the most commonly used type of sliding door. They are popular for closets and other large openings. The doors are set on adjacent, parallel tracks so that they pass each other when moving. Door handles are recessed so they do not interfere with passage. The most common sets of bypass doors have two doors, but more can be used to cover a larger opening, 15-38. One disadvantage of this type of door is that the total opening is obscured by the width of one door even when fully opened.

These doors may be purchased in standard widths from 2 to 3 ft., a height of 6 ft. 8 in., and a thickness of 1 3/8 in. They may be flush or stile and rail of wood or metal construction.

Glass sliding doors are a type of bypass door popular for exterior use, 15-39. Usually two glass panels are used with one that is stationary and one that moves. They allow a broad, unobstructed view as well as passage between the interior and exterior of a house. They may have a bronze, aluminum, wood, or steel frame. Standard widths of glass sliding doors include 6, 8, 9, 10, 12, 15, 16, 18, and 20

CARADCO CORP.

15-39 Sliding glass doors permit access to the outside while providing a broad view.

feet. Heights include 6 ft. 8 in., 8 ft., and 10 ft. Sliding screen doors may be used with the doors. The door units may be constructed of a single thickness of glass or of insulating glass.

Pocket doors are sliding doors that fit within the wall when open, 15-40. They are useful where space is not available for a swinging door. They are more difficult to operate than swinging doors, and they require the wall space beside them to be hollow. It is difficult to use this space for mounting objects such as wall cabinets and telephones.

Surface sliding doors run on a track that extends onto the wall beside the doorway. This type of door requires free wall space for moving the door.

Folding doors. The most common types of folding doors are bifolding, multi-folding, and accordian doors. They are hung on overhead tracks with nylon rollers or glides, like sliding doors. Folding doors fold back into a stack when open.

Bifolding doors are made of two units. They may be of flush or of stile and rail construction. The units are joined with hinges, 15-41. They are usually installed in pairs that open from the center. If more than two units are joined, a *multi-folding door* is made. These can be used to cover larger openings.

Bifolding and multi-folding doors may be slightly thinner than typical flush or panel doors. Wood doors are 1 1/8 inches thick, and metal doors are 1 inch thick. They may be purchased in either 6 ft. 8 in. or 8 ft. heights. The most common use of these doors is for closets. They require less operating space than a typical flush or panel door, but the panels swing out from the wall, so some clearance space is needed.

Accordian doors are generally used to close large openings where other types of doors would be impractical. They consist of very narrow panels that fold back and require very little space when open, 15-42. They may be

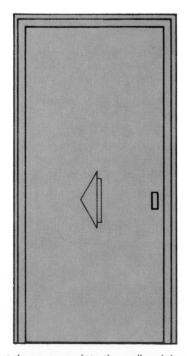

15-40 Pocket doors recess into the wall and do not require any clearance space in a room.

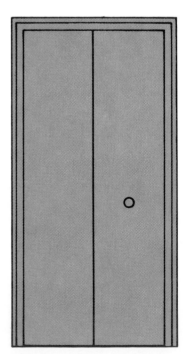

15-41 Each unit of a bifold door contains two panels that are hinged together and fold back when open.

15-42 *Accordian doors are useful for large openings where little clearance space is available for opening a door.*

CRAWFORD DOORS

15-43 *Overhead sectional garage doors have several panels that are hinged together so that the door can follow a curved track when opening.*

made of wood slats, plastic, or other sturdy, flexible materials. They are available in sizes to fit almost any opening.

Garage doors. Two basic types of garage doors account for most doors used today. They are the overhead sectional, 15-43, and the one piece overhead door, 15-44. These doors are produced in wood, metal, and fiberglass.

Garage door sizes are keyed to single car and double car garage openings. Typical widths are 8, 9, and 10 feet for single car doors, and 16, 17, and 18 feet for double car doors. Standard heights are 6 ft. 6 in. and 7 ft. Commercial garage door sizes may be required to accommodate motor homes or travel trailers.

If an automatic garage door opener is to be installed, proper space and wiring should be allowed in planning the garage. Adequate headroom is necessary to mount the motor drive on the ceiling above the door when it is open, and an electrical outlet is required to operate the motor.

DOOR CONSTRUCTION

A door is typically mounted in a *door jamb*. A jamb is a door frame that fits inside the rough opening in a wall. It allows the door to fit securely into the wall when closed. Door jambs are constructed of wood in most residential homes, although metal may be used.

Door jambs consist of two side jambs and a head jamb across the top, 15-45. Most exterior doors require a sill at the bottom to prevent drafts and leaks. Garage doors are an exception. Door sills may be made of wood, brick, stone, or concrete. Many styles and types are ready-made, but frequently they are custom-made on the job.

Exterior door jambs are usually 1 1/8 inches thick while interior jambs are 3/4 inches thick. The door stop—a strip usually of wood, around the door jamb that prevents the door from passing all the way through the opening—is

MANVILLE BUILDING MATERIALS CORP.

15-44 *One piece overhead doors are of a single unit that swings up and out when opened.*

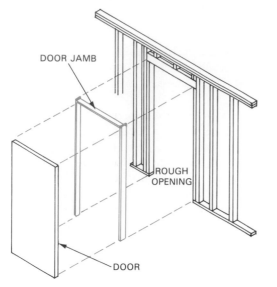

15-45 A door jamb is fitted into the rough opening of a wall. It provides a secure fit for a closed door.

rabbeted into an exterior jamb, but it is nailed to the face of an interior jamb.

Door jambs for interior and exterior doors are available as a preassembled unit with the door already hung and ready for installation. These units are called pre-hung doors. Rough openings must be sized properly to these units since little adjustment is possible.

Door symbols. Standard door symbols are used on construction drawings to communicate the type and locations of doors in a structure. Some of the accepted symbols are shown in 15-46 with an elevation view to help clarify the type of door shown. Sills are shown on all exterior doors except garage doors.

Door Treatments

Doors are sometimes given little attention in the total planning and decorating scheme of a home. However,

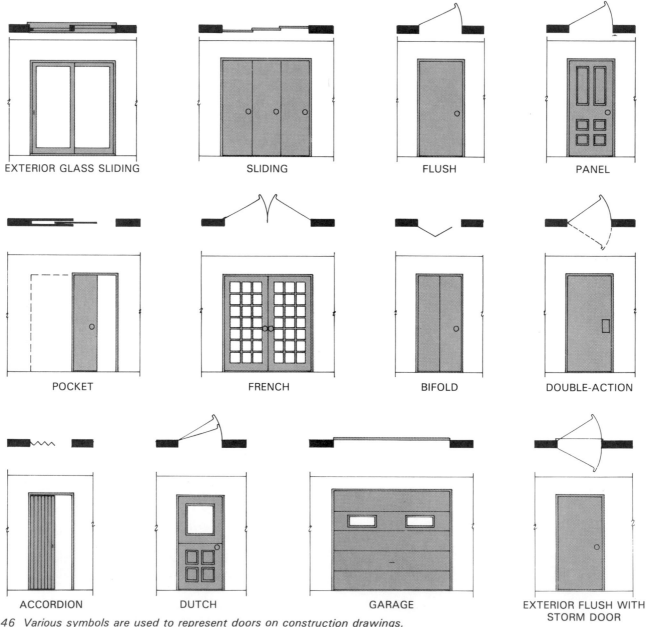

15-46 Various symbols are used to represent doors on construction drawings.

GEORGIA-PACIFIC

15-47 The stained glass on this exterior door blends with the interior of this home as well as the exterior.

their treatment should be given careful consideration. A main entry door may be the focal point of a home's exterior. Interior doors may serve as an accent to a room's decor.

Main entry doors should be attractive on both the outside and the inside, 15-47. Many treatments may be applied to the exterior of a plain, flush door. These include accent painting, molding, or decorative hardware, 15-48. Manufactured or custom-made doors may have decorative carvings or stained glass inserts. Panel doors are attractive when painted in two colors to accent the panels.

Although many interior doors are of stained wood, other treatments are possible. Doors may be decorated to complement a room's design, but it should first be considered whether the door will be opened or closed all of the time.

The effect of a door may be softened by covering it with the same treatment used on the walls. Wallpaper, paint, or fabric are common wall treatments that can be used on doors. Panel doors may have coordinating fabric or wallpaper inserts. Some older homes may have too many doors to make furniture arrangement practical. A door may to temporarily closed off with fabric, screens, or wall units.

REVIEW QUESTIONS

1. What are the main advantages and disadvantages of sliding windows, fixed windows, and swinging windows?
2. What types of units are available as combination windows? For what uses are combination windows appropriate?
3. What are the advantages and disadvantages of wood and metal window frames?
4. What types of glazing are available in standard windows? Which types are the most energy efficient? What type is the least energy efficient?
5. How many windows, of what dimensions, would you put into a living room that was 10 by 16 feet? Assuming that two adjacent walls of the room were exterior walls, where would you place the windows? Why?
6. What is the difference between curtains and draperies?
7. What types of window treatments would you recommend for someone who wanted to completely block sunlight from a room? What would you recommend for someone who wanted filtered sunlight?
8. What types of exterior window treatments are available for residential use?
9. How does the construction of a flush door differ from the construction of a stile and rail door?
10. How is an interior door constructed differently from an exterior door?
11. What type of door would you recommend for a doorway where there is no room for clearance of a swinging door? Why?
12. Other than staining, what are some treatments that can be used to decorate doors?

THERMA-TRU, DIVISION OF LST CORP.

15-48 Decorative moldings on a flush door add interest to its plain surface.

16 Stairs and Halls

After studying this chapter, you will be able to:
- Describe the six basic design shapes used for stairways, and evaluate their appropriateness for various applications.
- Evaluate a stairway in terms of comfort and safety.
- Apply basic design principles to the choice of stairway treatments.
- Evaluate a hallway in terms of function, durability, and decoration.

Stairs and halls are designed to provide access to various living areas of a structure. They make it possible for a person to pass from one room to another without interfering with activities in those rooms. Hallways provide passage between rooms on one level of a structure. Stairs are used to connect different levels.

STAIRWAYS

A stairway is a series of steps that leads from one level to another in a structure. *Landings* also may be used as a part of the stairway. A landing is a flat floor area that may be used at any point along a staircase. Steps and landings may be combined into a variety of designs to fit different structural, functional, and decorative needs. A list of terms used to describe stairways is offered in 16-1.

A housing unit with a first and second floor has a *main stairway* between those levels. Dwellings with two levels, of the split foyer design, have a main stairway between the upper level and the foyer and another between the lower level and the foyer. Structures with basements have a *service stairway* from the first level to the basement. Main and service stairways are usually constructed differently and do not have the same degree of visibility in a home.

Main stairways are generally assembled with prefabricated parts produced in a mill or cabinet shop. The finest types are made from hardwoods or other wear-resistant materials such as terrazzo, stone, or tile. The main stairway is commonly used as a focal point in a decorating scheme, 16-2. Therefore, decoration as well as safety and convenience are concerns.

Service stairways are generally not visible to guests and, as a result, receive less design emphasis than main stairs. These stairways are usually constructed on site from typical construction materials—usually softwoods. The main concerns when constructing service stairways are safety and convenience.

Balusters	Vertical members that support the handrail on open stairs.
Enclosed stairs	Stairs that have a wall on both sides. Also known as *closed, housed,* or *boxed* stairs.
Headroom	The shortest clear vertical distance measured between the nosing of the treads and the ceiling.
Landing	A flat floor area at either end of the stairs and possibly at some point in between. They are commonly used in L and U stairs.
Nosing	The projection, usually rounded, of a stair tread that extends past the face of the riser below.
Open stairs	Stairs that have no wall on one or both sides.
Rise	The distance from the top surface of one tread to the top surface of the next.
Riser	The vertical face of a step.
Run	The horizontal distance from the face of one riser to the face of the next.
Stairwell	The opening in which a set of stairs is constructed.
Stringer	A structural member that supports the treads and risers. *Housed stringers* are routed or grooved to receive the treads and risers. *Plain stringers* are cut or notched to fit the profile of the stairs.
Total rise	The total floor to floor vertical height of the stairs.
Total run	The total horizontal length of the stairs.
Tread	The horizontal member of each step.

16-1 *In order to understand a discussion of stairways, it is helpful to know the definitions of these terms.*

Stair Designs

Six basic design shapes are used for stairways. They are the straight run stairs, L stairs, double L stairs, U stairs, winder stairs, spiral stairs, and circular stairs.

Straight run stairs, 16-3, are used more frequently than any other type. Generally, they are the simplest and the

16-2 *A main stairway is usually visible from public rooms in a home, so it should be attractively designed.*

CE MORGAN

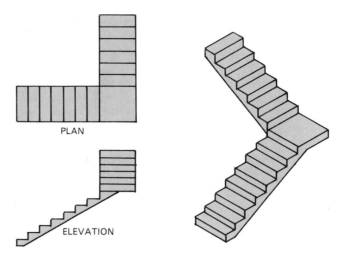

16-4 *L stairs may be used where sufficient length is not available to construct straight run stairs.*

most economical to build of all designs. Straight run stairs have no turns or landings between the ends.

L stairs have one landing at some point along the flight of stairs and change direction to the right or left at that point, 16-4. If the landing is near the top or bottom of the stairs, the term *long L* is used to describe the design. The L stair design is used when the space needed for a straight run stairway is not available or when a change in direction is desired.

Double L stairs have two landings, each with a 90° turn, along the flight. This design type is used when neither the straight run nor the L stairs may be used, 16-5. They are much more expensive to build and, as a result, are not frequently used.

U stairs have two flights of steps parallel to each other with one landing between them. Two types of U stairs are possible — *wide U* and *narrow U*. Wide U stairs have a well hole between the two sets of steps, 16-6, while narrow U

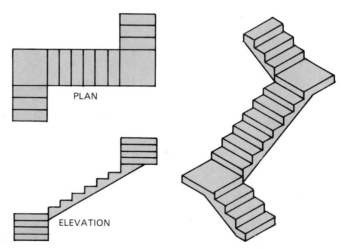

16-5 *Double L stairs have two turns. They are not used frequently because of excessive cost.*

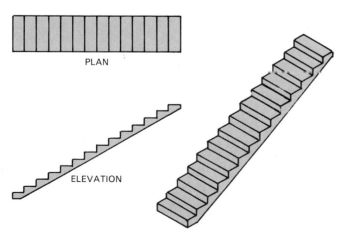

16-3 *Straight run stairs connect two levels without a turn or landing between the stairs.*

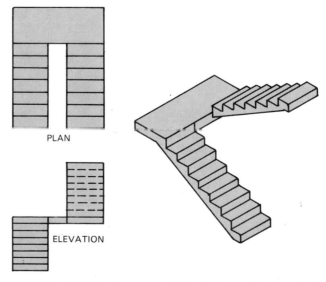

16-6 *Wide U stairs have a well hole between the two flights of steps. They require more space to construct than other designs.*

stairs have little or no space between the flights, 16-7. These stairs are more compact.

Winder stairs have wedge shaped steps that are substituted for a landing, 16-8. Winder stairs are unsafe because of the varied and narrow tread width at the winding area. This design should be avoided whenever possible.

Spiral stairs consist of a number of wedge shaped steps that may be fastened together to form a cylindrical stairway. They take up very little floor space, but they are more difficult to walk on than straight stairs. Manufactured kits have made this design popular, 16-9.

Circular stairs are custom-made, using trapezoid shaped steps. The basic shape of the stairs is an arc or irregular curve. These stairways are impressive in very large homes, 16-10.

Stairway Comfort and Safety

A safe and comfortable stairway is based on the stride of an average person stepping up the height of a riser and forward the depth of a tread. Based on this guideline, the ideal stair should have a riser height of 7 1/4 inches and a run of 10 1/2 inches. These dimensions produce a stair slope angle of about 34°, 16-11. Some variation is permitted. Generally, a riser height between 7 and 7 5/8 inches and a run between 10 and 11 inches is acceptable if the angle of stairs is between 30° and 35°.

Each riser height and tread width should be the same for every step of the stairway. Uniform steps help prevent tripping or stumbling.

Stair width is another factor to be considered. The minimum acceptable width of either a main or service stairway is 36 inches, but widths of 38 to 42 inches are preferred. Frequently, main stairs are slightly wider than service stairs, but both need to be wide enough to carry large furniture pieces from one level to another and to allow passage along the stairway. Stairways with turns

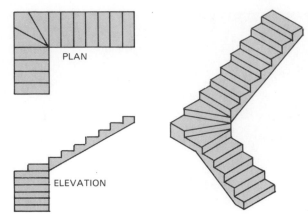

16-8 Winder stairs have wedge shaped treads instead of a landing. They are generally considered unsafe because of the varied tread width.

should be wider than straight stairways to provide the same degree of accessibility.

Safety is also dependent on good lighting, adequate handrails, non-skid treads, and plenty of headroom. All stairways should have at least one lighting fixture located so that it will light each step. Switches at both ends of the stairs are necessary to use the light each time is it needed.

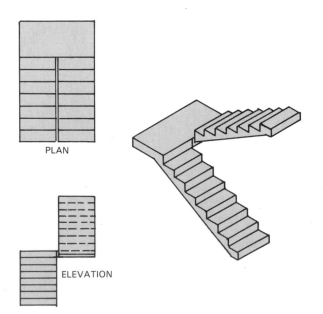

16-7 Narrow U stairs are similar in design to wide U stairs, but they do not have as much space between the flights.

AMERICAN GENERAL PRODUCTS, INC.

16-9 Spiral stairs are useful where limited space is a major concern.

AMERICAN GENERAL PRODUCTS, INC.

16-10 Circular stairs may be the main focal point of a large, formal entryway.

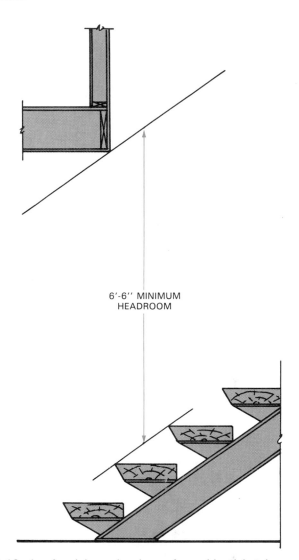

6'-6'' MINIMUM HEADROOM

16-12 A safe minimum headroom for residential stairways is 6 feet 6 inches.

Handrails are required on at least one side. They should continue the entire length of the stairs including landings. The recommended height of handrails along the stairs is 30 inches above the nosing of each step and 34 inches above the floor on landings. Rails may be attached to one or both sides of the stairs as desired. Railings are very important around open stairwells. They should be strong enough to prevent falls into a stairwell opening.

A non-skid covering on each tread is a desirable feature. Carpeting is safe on properly designed stairways with a

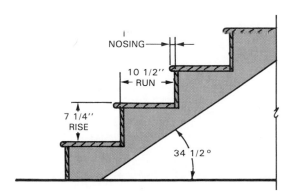

NOSING

10 1/2''
RUN

7 1/4''
RISE

34 1/2°

16-11 Stair dimensions should fit the stride of the average adult for safe use.

moderate slope angle and wide treads; but when it is placed on narrow treads of steep stairs, the stairway may be slippery and unsafe.

A safe stairway also has adequate headroom for the average person. A vertical distance of 6 ft. 6 in. is the accepted minimum headroom. It is measured from the nosing line of each step to the ceiling, 16-12. Headroom is not a problem when one stairway is located directly above another as in a two-story building with a basement. This arrangement also saves floor space, 16-13.

STAIRWAY TREATMENT

Stairways should be decorated to add interest and enjoyment to the living space. Generally, the theme of the room where the stairway shows the most is chosen for the stairs also, 16-14. For example, if the main stairway begins in the foyer, then the color scheme and carpeting may be continued up the stairs. Hints of the scheme of the upper floor may be added. If your foyer color scheme were white, blue, and green and the upper hall were mainly yellow, you could use green carpeting on the stairs. Walls could be covered with green and white wallpaper with touches of blue and yellow.

Sometimes a stairway may be very beautiful or unique in design and workmanship, 16-15. A unique stairway should become a focal point with wall treatments and other decorations that accent the stairway.

As already mentioned, stair coverings should be skid proof. They also should be durable. Carpeting with short, tight pile is best. Padding should not be too thick so that a firm footing is possible. If steps have a good wood finish, but carpeting is still desired, then exposed wood on both sides of the carpet will echo the wood handrails and enhance the design scheme. Non-skid strips or finish are available for exposed wood stairs.

When materials such as stone, terrazzo, or tile are chosen for stairways, 16-16, it is usually a continuation of the same materials used in a connecting room. These materials may function as structural members as well as decoration.

HALLS

Hallways are necessary elements of most homes. They provide main avenues for traffic circulation and access to the various parts of the living space. Each member of the household passes through the halls many times each day, so halls should be pleasant and functional.

Standard residential hallways range in width from 36 to 42 inches. Proper width is dependent on the length,

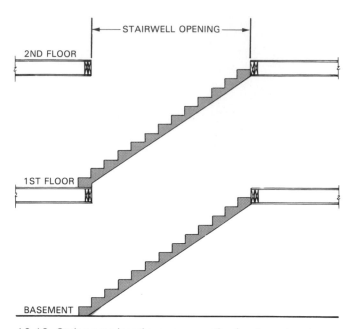

16-13 Stairways placed over one another in a two-story house saves floor space and eliminates the problem of allowing extra space for headroom.

shape, and expected use of a hall. Only very short halls should be 36 inches wide. Longer halls no wider than 36 inches appear too narrow. Halls with right angle turns need to be wider than 36 inches if they are to provide room for moving furniture. If a hall is used frequently by several people, space should be provided so that two people can

KEMPER-TAPPAN

16-14 The natural wood theme of the kitchen is continued up this stairway to the loft. This helps to tie the two areas together visually.

16-15 This spiral stairway is a focal point for the room because of its unique design.

16-17 A brick floor is both attractive and practical for a frequently used hallway. Wear does not show, and the floor is easily maintained.

16-16 Stone stairs are used in this home to accent the design of the stone walls.

pass each other comfortably. Less frequently used hallways may be narrower.

The floor covering for hallways is important. It should be durable, since halls have frequent traffic in a concentrated space. See 16-17. Coverings such as cork tile, low quality carpeting, and less durable types of vinyl tile are not recommended for hallways.

Walls along hallways also experience heavy wear. Washable wallpaper, paint, or other treatments are appropriate, especially if small children are in the home. Patterns that do not show dirt and handprints help to keep the hallway looking clean.

The color of the hallway should coordinate with the rooms that open into it. Often, the wall and floor coverings used in a main room are continued through the hallway.

REVIEW QUESTIONS

1. How do main stairways differ from service stairways?
2. What are the six basic design shapes used for stairways?
3. What type of stairway would you use in a two-story home with very little floor space? Why?
4. What points of construction should be considered when making sure a stairway is safe?
5. What factors should be considered when determining how wide a hall should be?

17 Lighting

After studying this chapter, you will be able to:

■ Explain how natural light can be used to enhance the decor of a home.

■ List the advantages and disadvantages of incandescent and fluorescent light.

■ Explain the difference between general lighting, local lighting, and accent lighting, and list types of fix-

tures which can be used to create each type of lighting.

■ Evaluate the appropriateness of lighting sources for the activities of a room.

Lighting affects the beauty and efficiency of a home. Proper home lighting allows a person to perform tasks

LIS KING

17-1 Sunlight brings out warm, flattering tones in objects. It also emphasizes textures by creating sharp, contrasting shadows.

safely and efficiently without eyestrain. Well planned lighting also enhances the mood and decorative scheme of a home. To utilize light sources fully, a person should understand how different forms and arrangements of light affect their surroundings. Both natural and artificial light should be considered when planning a residential lighting scheme.

NATURAL LIGHT

Natural light is provided by the sun. Along with making colors seem sharper and brighter, sunlight generates a feeling of well-being. The amount of natural light that enters a room is controlled by the size, number, and arrangement of windows; by the type of window treatments used; and by the placement of rooms.

Natural light gives objects warm, flattering tones, 17-1. However, strong sunlight may produce harsh shadows and glares. Rooms that receive much full sunlight should not be decorated with many smooth or shiny surfaces. Such a room would cause eyestrain and create an uneasy atmosphere due to glare.

Direct sunlight—from a rising or setting sun, for instance—will be less likely to cause glare if windows are not at eye level. Skylights and clerestory windows create pleasant effects, 17-2. Window treatments can be used as filters, making sunlight less intense.

Exterior foliage is also useful for filtering light, 17-3. Deciduous trees, which have leaves in the summer and shed them in the winter, are especially effective in front of windows with a southern exposure. They temper summer sunlight but allow more exposure to sunlight in the cold, winter months.

Rooms that would be enhanced by natural light should be placed strategically. For example, a kitchen or breakfast area used in the morning would benefit from an eastern

HJ SCHEIRICH CO.

17-2 Skylights allow sunlight to enter without producing glare.

267

17-3 Deciduous trees help to filter hot, summer sunlight.

17-4 A well designed room can be enhanced by a combination of natural and artificial light.

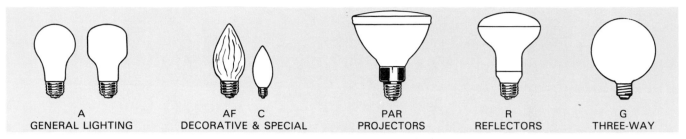

17-5 *Incandescent bulbs come in a variety of shapes to fit different functions.*

A	AF	C	PAR	R	G
GENERAL LIGHTING	DECORATIVE & SPECIAL		PROJECTORS	REFLECTORS	THREE-WAY

exposure. A living room or family room could receive steady sunlight throughout the day if it had a southern exposure.

In some rooms, natural light may not be necessary, or it may be a hindrance. Household members who do not prefer a bright bedroom may want their rooms to face north. A northern exposure is also useful for rooms that should not have a wide variation in lighting, such as an art studio.

Sunlight can only be used as a light source during the day, and its intensity during the day is not always predictable. Therefore, rooms utilizing natural light usually have artificial light as well, 17-4. Most artificial light changes the appearance of colors and textures. The appearance of a room in both types of light should be considered when planning the room's decoration.

ARTIFICIAL LIGHT

Artificial light is predictable and controllable. It may come from an incandescent source or a fluorescent source. These sources are available in various types of light bulbs. Different bulbs and fixtures can be used to produce light suitable for different uses.

Incandescent Light

Incandescent light is produced when electricity is passed through a fine tungsten filament in a vacuum bulb. Light is produced when the electricity causes the wire to become so hot that it glows. The intensity of light emitted can be varied by altering the size, wattage, shape, and surface treatments of the bulb, 17-5.

Small, 6 watt bulbs are commonly used for decorative purposes or as night lights. Incandescent bulbs for general use are larger and range from 25 watts to 150 watts. Larger bulbs are available for situations where unusually bright light is needed. Three-way bulbs contain two filaments that may be operated simultaneously or independently to offer three different levels of light.

The most common incandescent bulb is the pear-shaped, general service bulb. Several decorative shapes are also available, including round bulbs and bulbs shaped like flames. Cone shaped bulbs are designed for use as flood lights or spotlights.

Bulbs may have a variety of surface treatments. Clear bulbs allow light to shine at full strength. They produce glare, making them unsuitable for most activities unless they are covered. However, small, clear bulbs used in chandaliers or for other decorative purposes produce a brilliant sparkle.

A bulb with a frosted treatment disperses light more evenly and decreases glare. This is the most commonly used type of bulb. Shadows are softened in its light, and the surface of the bulb is cooler than an untreated surface. A shade should be used with a frosted bulb.

An opaque silver coating is often used on the top portion of spotlights and floodlights. These lights are usually set in reflective bases, and light from the bulb is reflected from the base. Light bulbs also may have colored coatings.

Incandescent lights are less expensive to install and replace than fluorescent lights. They do not hum or flicker, and they do not interfere with other electrical devices. The light from an incandescent source is more flattering to skin tones. However, incandescent lights use more electricity than flourescent lights, making them more expensive to operate. They also produce more heat.

Fluorescent Light

Fluorescent light is produced in a glass tube by releasing electricity through a mercury vapor to make invisible ultraviolet rays. A coating of fluorescent chemicals on the inside of the glass tube transforms the rays into visible, white light.

Fluorescent tubes may be straight or circuline, 17-6. Straight tubes range in length from 12 to 48 inches and in power usage from 13 watts to 40 watts. Circuline tubes vary in diameter from 8 1/4 to 16 inches and in power usage from 22 watts to 40 watts. U-shaped tubes are also available.

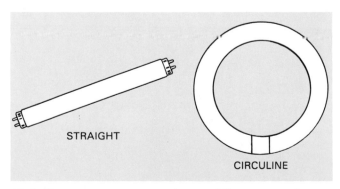

STRAIGHT

CIRCULINE

17-6 *The two most common shapes of fluorescent tubes are the straight tube and the circuline tube.*

CHAMPION INTERNATIONAL CORP.

17-7   The effect of direct, general lighting can be softened by combining it with other types of light, such as natural light and local lighting.

The color of light can be varied by altering the type of fluorescent coating on the tube. The cool white light is most commonly used. This light is considered cold and unflattering by most people. Warm white and warm white

deluxe lights produce warmer, more flattering light. These lights also blend well with incandescent lights, making them better suited to rooms that use both kinds of light.

Fluorescent lights disperse light over a larger area than incandescent lights, and they cause less glare. They require less energy to operate, and the tubes produce almost no heat. Fluorescent lights also last longer than incandescent lights.

Fluorescent bulbs have some disadvantages. They are available in a limited variety of interchangeable styles. They are more expensive than incandescent bulbs to install and replace, and they are more likely to interfere with other electrical devices. In most bulbs, there is a slight delay between the application of current and appearance of light.

Applications of Lighting

Lighting is used for three main applications: general lighting, local lighting, and accent lighting. *General lighting* provides an even amount of light throughout a room. With this type of lighting, each aspect of a room is given equal emphasis. General lighting helps to moderate shadows and contrasts from local lighting when the two are used in combination.

General lighting can be direct or indirect. *Direct lighting* produces the strongest illumination from the light source to the object. It produces sharp contrasts between dark and light when used alone. Other lighting used with direct lighting will help lessen the bright effect and reduce eyestrain, 17-7.

Indirect lighting is directed toward an intermediate surface that reflects the light into the room. Indirect light is usually reflected off of the ceiling or walls, 17-8. It is more

RED CEDAR SHINGLE AND HANDSPLIT SHAKE BUREAU

17-8   Indirect light is reflected off an intermediary surface. It is softer and more diffused than direct light.

270

CHAMPION INTERNATIONAL CORP.

17-9 Local lighting provides a small area of concentrated light. It is needed for tasks such as reading.

diffused than direct light, resulting in less contrast and softer shadows.

For a good balance of lighting in a room, a combination of general and local lighting should be used. *Local lighting* is used in smaller areas requiring more light, 17-9. Local lighting is used for such tasks as sewing, reading, preparing food, and shaving. Local lighting should be at a suitable intensity level for the tasks it will light. For example, more light is needed for doing fine needlework than for playing table games.

Accent lighting uses a highly concentrated beam of light to highlight an area or object, 17-10. It may be used to spotlight a piece of sculpture or to accent a textured wall. Accent lighting, like local lighting, is often used in combination with general lighting.

The intensity of light within a room is affected by several factors. The most obvious factor is the amount of illumination produced by light sources in the room. The level of illumination is measured in foot-candles. A *foot-candle* is defined as the amount of illumination produced by a standard plumber's candle at a distance of one foot.

DREXEL HERITAGE FURNISHINGS, INC.

17-10 Accent lighting can be used to highlight displays or artwork.

Light meters can be used to measure the number of foot-candles produced by a light. Recommended amounts of light in footcandles for specific activities are listed in 17-11.

Generally, as the wattage of a light source increases, the intensity of light produced increases. However, fluorescent light sources require fewer watts of electricity to produce the same amount of light as incandescent sources.

The amount of light reflected and absorbed within a room also affects the intensity of light. Light is reflected from smooth surfaces and light colors. Light is absorbed by textured surfaces and dark colors. The more light that is absorbed in a room, the less intense the light will be. Likewise, light will be more intense in a highly reflective room. The percentage of light reflected by various colors is presented in 17-12.

Colored light is less intense than white light, but it can produce interesting effects. Colored lights intensify objects of the same color range and decrease the intensity of their complement. For instance, a bulb with a yellow light will intensify yellow and orange objects, but it will subdue colors in the blue-violet range.

Warm light such as red or yellow will make a room appear more warm and intense. Cool colored lights such as blue or blue-green make a room seem cool and open. White light shows a room at its most true values and produces the most illumination.

SELECTION AND PLACEMENT

The atmosphere and appearance of a room is affected by the selection and placement of artificial lighting. Different types of fixtures can be used to meet decorative and functional needs. Each area of the house has special lighting concerns. When planning lighting, the specific needs of each room should be considered separately.

Lighting Fixtures

Fixtures for the home should provide adequate light for activities and blend with decor. The size and scale of fixtures should be proportionate with other items in a room and with the room itself. A fixture should be easy to clean, and the light bulb or tube should be easy to replace.

Different types of fixtures are designed to meet specific lighting needs. Lighting fixtures used throughout the home may be structural or portable. *Structural fixtures* are permanently built into the home. *Portable fixtures* are not a part of the home's architectural structure. They may be placed and removed with relative ease.

Structural fixtures. Various types of structural lighting can be used to meet specific lighting needs. *Valance lighting fixtures* are mounted over windows, 17-13. These fixtures use a fluorescent tube that casts light down on draperies and up toward the ceiling. A valance conceals the light source and the curtain hardware. Valance lighting is a good source of direct and indirect general lighting.

Bracket lighting fixtures are similar in design to valance fixtures. However, they are not placed above a window.

MINIMUM FOOT-CANDLE REQUIREMENTS FOR VARIOUS ACTIVITIES	
ACTIVITY	**FOOT-CANDLES**
Sewing, dark-colored fabrics	100-200
Crafts requiring fine detail	100-200
Concentrated studying or reading	50-100
Sewing, medium-colored fabrics	50-100
Workshop tasks	50-100
Kitchen, preparation of food	50-100
Laundry, pretreating and ironing	50-100
Kitchen and laundry, general tasks	20-50
Casual reading	20-50
Grooming	20-50
Dining	10-20
Conversation	10-20

17-11 Lighting needs vary with different activities.

They may be placed high on a wall for general lighting, 17-14, or they may be placed above work areas for local lighting. These also provide good direct and indirect light.

Cornice lighting fixtures are mounted to the wall near the ceiling, 17-15. Like valance and bracket fixtures, they use a fluorescent tube as a light source. Closed at the top,

PERCENTAGE OF LIGHT REFLECTED BY COLOR	
COLOR	**PERCENTAGE OF LIGHT REFLECTED**
(Natural Wood Tones)	
Mahogany & Black Walnut	5-15
Cherry & Dark Oak	10-15
Light Maple	25-35
Light Oak	25-35
Beech & Birch	35-50
(Dark Colors & Tones)	
Forest Green	7
Blue Green & Dark Blue	5-10
Olive Green	12
Dark Gray & Dark Brown	10-15
Medium Gray	20
Medium Blue & Medium Gray	21
Mauve & Cocoa Brown	24
(Medium Colors & Tones)	
Rose	29
Old Gold	34
Medium Light Blue	42
Yellow-Green	45
Light Gray	35-50
Yellow, Gold, Tan	55
Apricot	56-62
Buff	63
Pink	64
(Light Tints)	
Light Peach & Soft Pink	69
Cream Gray & Beige	70
Sky Blue, Light Green & Orchid	70-75
Pale Yellow & Pale Pink	75-80
Ivory	75
Egg Shell or Cream	79
(Whites)	
Flat or Dull White	75-90

17-12 The intensity of lighting in a room is affected by the reflective level of colors in that room.

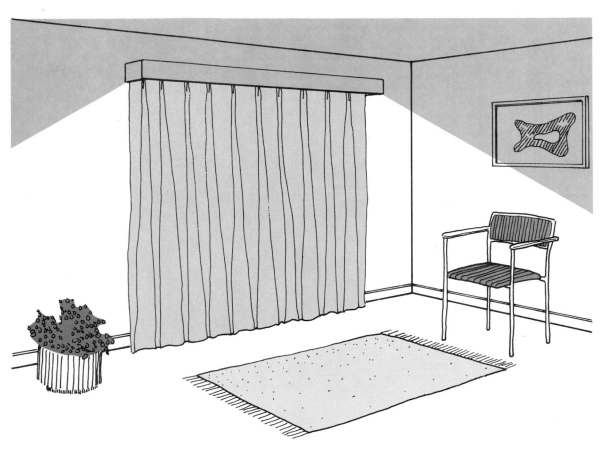

17-13 Valance lighting fixtures provide general lighting and highlight curtains.

17-14 Bracket lighting fixtures provide both direct and indirect lighting.

17-15 Cornice lighting fixtures provide only direct lighting.

17-16 Cove lighting fixtures can be used if indirect general lighting is desired.

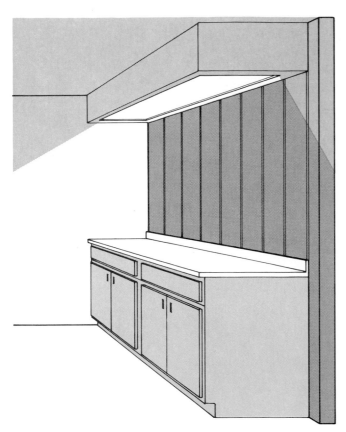

17-17 Soffit lighting is enclosed in a box that is mounted to the ceiling.

17-18 Strip lighting is often used around mirrors to provide good local lighting for grooming.

they direct light downward to illuminate the wall. These are effective accent lights for emphasizing pictures or wall hangings.

Cove lighting fixtures direct light up toward the ceiling to provide indirect general light. They are mounted on the wall near the ceiling, 17-16. Fluorescent tube lights are used. Cove lights help to create a feeling of height and openness in a room.

Soffit lighting fixtures consist of an enclosed box attached to the ceiling, 17-17. They are useful as local lighting in areas where a great deal of light is needed. These lights are useful above mirrors, cabinets, or sinks.

Strip lighting is also useful in work areas and around mirrors. It is a good source of local lighting. This type of fixture accommodates a series of incandescent bulbs or fluorescent tubes, 17-18.

Track lighting is mounted in a metal strip that allows fixtures to be placed anywhere along the strip, 17-19. The fixtures may be moved to shine light in any direction. This type of lighting is useful as accent lighting. Track lights should be at least 4 feet apart to avoid a cluttered look.

Wall washers are small ceiling lights that direct a broad spread of light on the wall from ceiling to floor, 17-20. They are usually placed 3 to 4 feet from the wall. Wall washers are useful for emphasizing wall materials such as brick, stone, or wood.

Recessed downlights are small, circular lights that are flush with the ceiling. See 17-21. Beacuse they do not pro-

17-19 Track lighting may be adjusted to meet specific lighting needs.

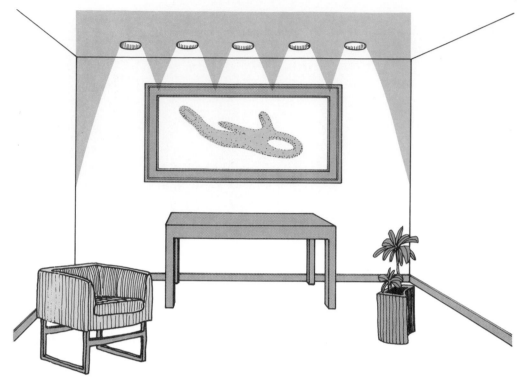

17-20 Wall washers should be placed about 3 feet from the wall for the best effect.

ject into the room, they are especially useful in rooms with low ceilings. Light from these fixtures may be concentrated to spotlight an area, or light may be diffused to provide general lighting.

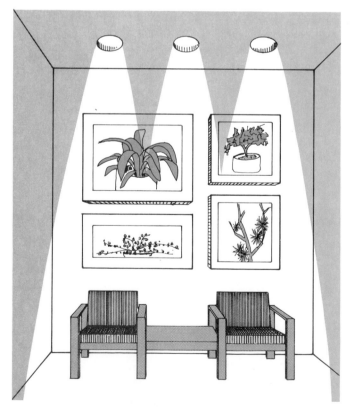

17-21 Recessed downlights provide effective accent lighting.

Luminous ceilings are made of transparent or translucent panels lit from behind, 17-22. Fluorescent tubes are used to provide even light. An entire ceiling may be luminous, or selected panels may be lit. Luminous ceilings provide good general lighting for work and for group activities.

Portable fixtures. Portable fixtures are not a structural part of the house. Lamps are the most common type of portable fixture. They come in various heights and styles intended for different uses. Decorative table and floor lamps are common for living rooms and bedrooms. Floor lamps may have one light at the top, or they may have several lights that can be adjusted to varying heights and angles. Desk lamps are designed to illuminate a work area so that eyes will not be strained, 17-23.

Lampshades affect the intensity and direction of light emitted from a lamp. Translucent shades allow some light to pass through the shade. They provide more general lighting than opaque shades. Opaque shades confine light to a small area. They provide local lighting for reading or intimate conversation. Tall, steep shades allow a smaller, more concentrated circle of light. Low, wide or angled shades disperse light into a larger circle.

Lamps should be chosen to fit the function they will serve. They should have heavy, stable bases that will not tip easily. If local lighting is desired, an opaque shade lined with white will be more effective. The shade will reflect light and keep it more concentrated within a small circle.

Proper height is an important consideration. For reading and other tasks, the bottom edge of the lampshade should be at eye level for a seated person. A distance of 38 to 42 inches from the floor to the bottom of the shade

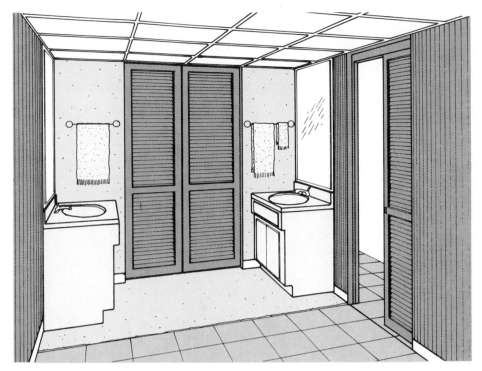

17-22 Luminous ceilings are used in areas that require bright, even general lighting, such as bathrooms.

WESTERN WOOD PRODUCTS ASSN.

17-23 Desk lamps are designed to illuminate the workspace in a way that prevents eyestrain.

is good, 17-24. This distance includes the table or lamp-stand upon which the lamp is placed. Therefore, the height of the table should be considered when choosing a lamp.

Standard wall and ceiling fixtures are also considered portable, even though the wiring required for these fixtures is a part of the structure. These fixtures may be placed and removed with ease in comparison to structural fixtures.

Wall fixtures are usually decorative in nature. Many styles are designed to look like street lamps or hurricane lanterns. These fixtures usually provide intimate accent lighting. They may be used alone to decorate a wall, or they may highlight a wall hanging.

Standard ceiling fixtures come in many shapes and colors. They provide general lighting. Most styles are

AVG. 40"

17-24 Lamps should be placed so that the bottom edge of the shade is at eye level for a seated person.

17-25 Ceiling fixtures are made in a variety of styles.

translucent; many are frosted to help diffuse light, 17-25. Some designs are suspended a few inches from the ceiling. These styles provide indirect light by reflecting light up to the ceiling.

Chandaliers and hanging lights are decorative ceiling fixtures, 17-26. They may provide some general lighting,

17-26 Decorative hanging fixtures make effective accent lights.

but most are designed for local lighting over a dining area or for accent lighting. Hanging fixtures for a dining area should be 30 inches above the table in an 8-foot high room. Three inches should be added for each additional foot of room height.

Lighting Areas of the Home

The first step in planning lighting for an area is to decide how the area will be used. The function of an area should be designated on a room floor plan. Each room may have several areas with specific lighting needs. After needs are determined, the most functional lighting fixtures for each area can be chosen.

Living rooms. General lighting for living rooms should be soft and diffused. Indirect sources, like cove lighting, are effective. Local lighting for reading or conversation should be provided. Decorative lamps or a hanging light may be used. See 17-27.

Accent lighting adds to the decor of the living room. Valance lighting may be used to highlight the draperies and make the room appear larger. Downlights or track lighting may emphasize paintings, figurines, or bookshelves.

Family and recreation rooms. The variety of activities that take place in family rooms require flexible lighting. Three-way bulbs may be adjusted to different levels to fit the task being lit. Reading and sewing require concentrated areas of light. More diffused local lighting is needed for games. Some soft light should be provided when viewing television to reduce eyestrain. Good general lighting is also needed.

Dining rooms. Local lighting over the dining table is the main source of light in the dining room. Light should not shine directly into the diners' eyes. Hanging lights and chandaliers are popular for this area, 17-28. A dimmer switch may be used so that the level of light may be adjusted. Low light may be used for evening dining, while brighter light can be provided for games and less formal meals.

Local lighting should also be provided for a serving area or buffet. Downlights or strip lighting will light the area without detracting from the dining area. Accent lighting may be used in cabinets to light china displays.

Entryways and foyers. Lighting in entryways and foyers should be sufficient for circulation and safety. The exterior entry should be well lit so that a person can locate the lockset, identify the house number, or recognize a caller. Light should be directed outward and downward, 17-29. A lit doorbell button is also helpful.

Interior lighting should be soft enough to make the transition from darkness to light easier. Diffused, general light will enable guests and hosts to see each other in a pleasant light. Some decorative accent lighting may be used in the area as well.

Bedrooms. Diffused general lighting is most suitable for bedrooms. Local lighting is useful in some areas. Lighting near the closet and chest is helpful when choosing clothes. Lights should be located near a mirror for grooming. At

PPG INDUSTRIES, INC.

17-27 Lamps and hanging fixtures are good sources of local lighting for living rooms.

DREXEL HERITAGE FURNISHINGS, INC.

17-28 Chandaliers are popular for illuminating dining room tables. Many are controlled by dimmer switches so that the level of light can be adjusted.

PINECREST, INC.

17-29 Good lighting above entryways allows easy recognition of guests.

DREXEL HERITAGE FURNISHINGS, INC.

17-30 A bedside lamp may be turned on and off from the bed to allow safe circulation at night. Lights above mirrors and clothes drawers aid in choosing clothes and grooming.

ELJER PLUMBINGWARE

17-31 Bathrooms require good lighting for grooming and safety.

least one light should be placed near the bed for reading and for getting up at night safely. See 17-30. Children's rooms need light for play or studying. Small night lights allow safer circulation at night.

Bathrooms. Bathrooms should have good general lighting and local lighting for grooming, 17-31. The area in front of the mirror should have even lighting that does not cause shadows. Warm white bulbs provide the best light for applying makeup because colors are not distorted.

Kitchens. Safety and efficiency are major concerns in kitchens, so ample, bright lighting is essential, 17-32. Good general lighting is needed for safe circulation. Work centers require direct local lighting. Strip lighting over work centers allows tasks to be performed safely. At least two-thirds of the counter space should have local lighting.

Utility areas. General lighting should be bright in utility areas such as laundry rooms and basements. Luminous ceilings are often used in these areas. Local lighting should be provided for any tasks.

Special purpose rooms. Lighting for special purpose rooms should fit the tasks to be performed. For instance, sewing rooms require strong, direct light so the contrast between thread and material is easily seen. An art studio

requires even lighting that will prevent shadows, and lighting for special effects may be desired. Workshops require good general lighting and task lighting, similar to lighting in a kitchen.

Stairs and halls. Safety should be considered over decoration for stairway lighting. Lighting should be bright enough that the treads and risers can be seen clearly. Lighting at the top and bottom landings is essential. Switches should be located at both the top and bottom of stairways so that lights can be turned on from either location.

Good general lighting should be provided throughout the hallway. Recessed lights or ceiling fixtures are commonly used. Accent lighting also may be used to highlight walls or pictures.

Exteriors. Light used outside of the home highlights shadows and emphasizes landscape and architectural features. Exterior lighting can enhance the style of the house. It also helps to illuminate the views outside of windows at night. Lighting is also needed for safe use of the yard at night.

Floodlights and spotlights may be used to highlight trees and decorative gardens. Decorative pools may be

WOOD METAL INDUSTRIES, INC.

17-32 A safe, efficient kitchen has bright general lighting and local lighting above all work centers.

CALIFORNIA REDWOOD ASSOCIATION

17-33 Exterior lighting gives gardens and ponds an enchanting appearance and allows safe use of outdoor areas at night.

spotlighted, or they may have lights in the bottom, 17-33. The lighting should not be bright enough to simulate daylight. Uplighting, or lights that focus from the ground up, create interesting shadows. Decorative lamp posts are often used in the front yard of a home. They produce a welcoming effect and illuminate the path to the house.

Patios, terraces, and swimming pool areas require light for activities. General lighting from a source above eye level should be provided. Lights should be evenly spaced to avoid dark spots. Pathways should be well lit, and steps should be given special attention. They may be lit by a spotlight from above, or recessed lights may be used at stair level.

REVIEW QUESTIONS

1. How can the amount of natural light that enters a room be controlled?
2. How does incandescent light differ from fluorescent light? What are some advantages and disadvantages of each?
3. What are the three main applications of lighting? How are they used?
4. What affects intensity of light? How would you decorate a room in which a low intensity of light was desired? How would you decorate the room if a high intensity of light was desired?
5. What types of fixtures can be used to provide indirect, general lighting? What types produce direct, general lighting?
6. What types of fixtures can be used to provide accent lighting?
7. What are some points to consider when choosing a reading lamp?
8. What steps should be taken when planning lighting for a room?
9. How should lighting for a kitchen differ from lighting for a living room?
10. How can lighting be used to enhance the exterior of a home?

18 Electrical and Plumbing Systems

After studying this chapter, you will be able to:
- List the three main components of the wiring system and explain how they operate.
- Evaluate the adequacy of a wiring system in relationship to a household's needs.
- Trace the flow of the water supply system into and out of the house, explaining the functions of its various components.
- Evaluate a house's plumbing system according to basic guidelines for planning a system.

The electrical and plumbing systems affect the efficiency, comfort, and design of a home. A well designed home utilizes these systems so that a home can be functional as well as beautiful. This chapter provides an overview of the operation of the electrical and plumbing systems. Planning guidelines are also presented.

THE ELECTRICAL SYSTEM

A well planned electrical system is needed for a safe, efficient home. Inadequate systems can lead to electrical overloading, loss of power in electrical appliances, and in extreme cases, electrical fires. Planning for an electrical system requires an understanding of the components of an electrical system. This information, plus knowledge of a housing unit's electrical requirements, can be used to design an efficient system.

Electrical System Components

The main components of an electrical system are the service entrance panel, branch circuits, receptacles, and switches. In order to understand the function and operation of these components, knowledge of the meanings of terms used in their description is useful. A list of helpful terms is offered in 18-1.

Service entrance panel. The service entrance panel serves as a monitor for a housing unit's electrical system, 18-2. The panel receives power from the power company and distributes the power throughout the house. It contains several *overcurrent devices* such as fuses or breakers. Each of these supplies power to a circuit branch. The service entrance panel also has a main disconnect switch. This

is used to shut down a home's entire electrical system.

The capacity of the service entrance panel determines the total circuit capacity of a home. Therefore, future electrical needs should be allowed for when determining the

Ampere	The unit of current used to measure the amount of electricity flowing through a wire during a certain amount of time.
Circuit	A path through which electricity flows from a source to one or more outlets and back to the source.
Circuit Breaker	A device designed to open (turn off) and close (turn on) a circuit by nonautomatic means. It will also open the circuit automatically when the circuit is overloaded.
Conductor	A material which permits the flow of electricity. In wiring, the term conductor usually refers to a wire.
Convenience Outlet	A device attached to a circuit to allow electricity to be drawn off for small appliances or lighting.
Fuse	A safety device which opens the circuit when it is overloaded by melting a fusible link.
Lighting Outlet	An outlet intended for the use of a lighting fixture.
Overcurrent Device	A device which prevents excessive flow of current in a circuit. Circuit breakers and fuses are overcurrent devices.
Receptacle	A contact device installed at an outlet for the connection of an attachment plug and flexible cord.
Service Entrance	The fittings and conductors that bring electricity into the building.
Service Entrance Panel	The main distribution box that receives the electricity and distributes it to various points in the home through branch circuits. The service entrance panel contains the main disconnect switch, fuse, or breaker which supplies the total electrical system of the home.
Voltage	A measure of the pressure which forces current through a wire.
Watt	A measure of electrical power. The number of amperes in a circuit multiplied by the number of volts equals the number of watts the circuit provides. Most appliances and lighting devices are rated for power usage in watts.

18-1 Knowledge of general terms used in the description of electrical systems will help in understanding a system.

total capacity of a service entrance panel. Both 120- and 240-volt service are available for residential use. If two power lines run into a service entrance panel, 120-volt service is available. Three lines indicate 240-volt service.

Branch circuits. Once the electricity passes the main disconnect switch, it is routed to several *branch circuits*. Branch circuits make it possible to use smaller, less expensive wire. They provide overcurrent protection from overloads and wire shorts, 18-3. Each circuit has an automatic circuit breaker or fuse which stops the current when the circuit becomes overloaded.

The National Electrical Code requires that enough branch circuits are supplied so that circuit loads are distributed evenly. To comply, three general classes of circuits are commonly used. They are general purpose circuits, small appliance circuits, and individual appliance circuits.

General purpose circuits supply power to permanently installed lighting fixtures and to receptacle outlets used for devices that use little wattage in operation. This would include such items as lamps, clocks, and radios, but not most kitchen appliances. A 120-volt circuit is used to supply power for these items.

Each circuit may have a capacity of either 15 or 20 amperes, using #14 wire and #12 wire, respectively. The total number of watts provided by a circuit equals the number of volts multiplied by the number of amperes in a circuit. Therefore, a 15-ampere circuit will supply 1800 watts, and a 20-ampere circuit will supply 2400 watts.

Small appliance circuits are used in kitchens, but they may also be used in dining areas, laundry rooms, workshops, or garages. They are designed to power appliances that require a moderate amount of current, such as electric fry pans and blenders.

Small appliance circuits are powered by a 120-volt circuit with a 20-ampere capacity. A circuit may supply power to several convenience outlets. However, no lighting fixtures are connected to the circuit. *The National Electrical Code* requires a minimum of two separate small appliance circuits in each kitchen.

Individual appliance circuits serve permanently installed appliances that use large amounts of electricity. They include electric ranges, water heaters, washers, dryers, or water pumps. An individual circuit should be used with any permanent, motor driven appliance that requires over 1440 watts for operation. The electrical requirements for several typical appliances are given in 18-4.

Receptacles. The most common type of receptacle is the duplex receptacle which accommodates two plugs, 18-5. Variations are the simplex (one plug), triplex (three plugs), and quad (four plugs) receptacles. These types of receptacles may or may not have grounding terminals. Receptacles without grounding terminals can accommodate plugs with two prongs only. Those with grounding terminals can accommodate plugs with two or three prongs.

Appliances that require 240-volt circuits, such as electric ranges and clothes dryers, must have 240-volt receptacles. These receptacles are usually larger in size with

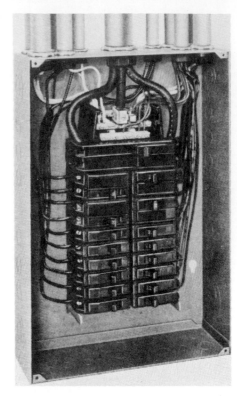

18-2 *This service entrance panel receives power from the three large black wires at the top of the panel. The power is distributed throughout the house using individual circuits.*

openings for unusually arranged, three-prong plugs. The special arrangement of the prongs makes it impossible to plug an appliance requiring 240 volts into a 120-volt circuit.

Ground fault circuit interrupter (GFCI) receptacles should be used for receptacles in bathrooms and around pools. These outlets protect against shock if there is a short in an appliance.

Other special purpose receptacles include weatherproof receptacles, clock receptacles, and television receptacles.

18-3 *A circuit breaker will automatically break the current if there is an overload on the circuit. It may be switched on again manually.*

TYPICAL APPLIANCE REQUIREMENTS				
Appliance or Equipment	Typical Watts	Usual Voltage	Wire Size	Recommended Fuse Size
Electric Range (with oven)	12,000	240	6	50 Amp.
Range Top (separate)	5,000	120/240	10	30 Amp.
Range Oven (separate)	5,000	120/240	10	30 Amp.
Refrigerator	300	120	12	20 Amp.
Home Freezer	350	120	12	20 Amp.
Automatic Washer	700	120	12	20 Amp.
Automatic Dryer (elec.)	5,000	120/240	10	30 Amp.
Dishwasher	1,200	120/240	12	20 Amp.
Garbage Disposer	300	120	12	20 Amp.
Roaster	1,400	120	12	20 Amp.
Rotisserie	1,400	120	12	20 Amp.
Furnace (gas)	800	120	12	20 Amp.
Dehumidifier	350	120	12	20 Amp.
Waffle Iron	1,000	120	12	20 Amp.
Band Saw	300	120	12	20 Amp.
Table Saw	1,000	120/240	12	20 Amp.
20,000 BTU Air Conditioner	1,200	120/240	12	20 Amp.
Bathroom Heater	2,000	120/240	12	20 Amp.
Ironer	1,500	120	12	20 Amp.
Water Heater (electric)	5,000	120/240	10	30 Amp.
Television	300	120	12	20 Amp.
Hand Iron	1,100	120	12	20 Amp.
Toaster	1,000	120	12	20 Amp.

18-4 Appliances have different electrical requirements that should be met by the proper type of circuit.

Weatherproof receptacles have waterproof covers. They are intended for outdoor use, 18-6. Clock receptacles are recessed so that a plugged-in clock will hang flush with the wall. Television receptacles frequently provide power for the appliance as well as antenna or cable connections.

Switches. Switches are used to control permanently installed lighting fixtures and some appliances. They also may control some convenience outlets, making it possible to switch on a lamp before entering a room.

There are several types of residential switches, including single pole, three-way, four-way, dimmer, and pull chain switches. The single pole switch is the most common. The switch has two positions—"on" and "off". It may control one or more fixtures from one location only.

Three-way switches are used to control one or more fixtures from two locations. They use two controls that do not have "on" and "off" identified on the switch. In order to control fixtures from three locations, a four-way switch is used in combination with two three-way switches.

A dimmer switch may be used with any incandescent lighting fixture to vary its intensity, 18-7. Besides an "on" and "off" position, it has a control that varies the level of light given off by a fixture.

Pull chain switches may be turned on and off by pulling a chain directly attached to the fixture. They are

18-5 This duplex receptacle has a grounding terminal, as is indicated by the third slot in each plug receptacle.

18-6 A weatherproof receptacle has waterproof covers.

EMERSON

18-7 A dimmer switch allows variation in the intensity of a light.

generally used for inexpensive fixtures in closets, attics, or other infrequently used areas.

Switches are made in a variety of designs. The handle type switch is the most common in residential use. See 18-8. A spring inside the handle moves it to the next position in a rapid motion, causing a snapping sound. Newer variations operate more quietly because mercury is used instead of a spring to open and close the circuit.

There are push button switches and flat switches that use a rocker type mechanism for operation, 18-9. Several types of switches contain safety lights. Other special switches include weatherproof switches and key operated switches.

Low voltage switching is a new type of switch system that is being used more often than before. In this system, switches are connected to relays using small, doorbell type wire. The relay operates a line voltage switch to control a fixture. Such a system is less expensive than conventional wiring because smaller wire is used. This system can be expanded so that all electrical devices may be operated from one or more master panels or from a home computer.

Planning the Electrical System

Since it is expensive and time consuming to expand an electrical system, present and future needs should be con-

18-8 A handle type switch contains mercury or a spring to connect and break the circuit.

LEVITON

18-9 A push button switch may have a standard design, or it may operate on a rocker mechanism.

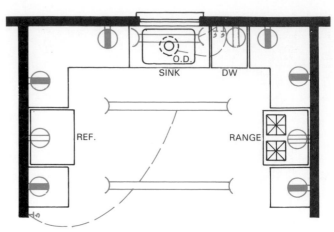

SINK   DW

REF.   RANGE

O.D.

18-10 Small appliance outlets should be located throughout the kitchen for convenient use. Individual appliance outlets should be available for such appliances as the range, dishwasher, and refrigerator. A general purpose circuit is needed for lighting fixtures.

sidered in the planning stages. The number of electrical devices used in the home has increased dramatically in recent years, and this trend is expected to continue. Often, new appliances are added without consideration of whether a houses's wiring system can handle the extra load. Therefore, the electrical capacity of a house should be large enough that new devices can be added safely in future years.

Circuitry requirements. The number and type of circuits needed can be estimated by examining the electrical requirements and placement of regularly used equipment. For instance, small appliance circuits will be needed anywhere that food preparation might take place, 18-10. This could include the dining room or basement as well as the kitchen.

For lighting, *The National Electrical Code* requires a minimum of 3 watts of lighting capacity for each square foot. Therefore, one circuit could provide minimum lighting for 800 square feet of floor space. However, this is a minimum allowance, and one general purpose circuit for no more than 500 square feet is a more practical, safe guideline for modern homes.

Future plans are important when planning individual circuit location and number. For example, if a second oven may be added to a home later, or if the laundry area may be moved in the future, allowances should be made.

After estimating total present and future wiring needs, the number and types of circuits allowed in the service entrance panel can be determined. Extra capacity—for new circuits or extra loads on present circuits—should be allowed for future needs.

Receptacles and switches. There should be an adequate number of receptacles and switches for convenience and safety. They should be located so that they are easy to reach.

Switches for lights should be located at each frequently used entrance of a room so that it is not necessary to walk across a dark room to turn on a light, 18-11. In rooms

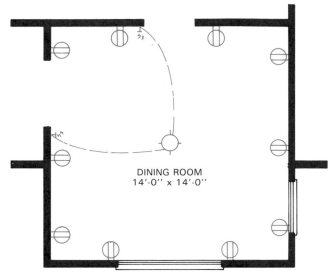

18-11 *Rooms should have light switches at all entrances so that walking across a dark room to get to the switch is not necessary.*

with more than one entrance, three-way and four-way switches can be used.

A well planned receptacle layout will require no extension cords. *The National Electrical Code* specifies for living areas that receptacles should be placed so that no point along a wall is more than 6 feet from a receptacle, and that each room should have at least three outlets. Receptacles placed about 8 feet apart provide a more convenient arrangement, 18-12. More outlets may be placed in areas where use of many items is anticipated. Receptacles also should be planned for halls, closets, and other areas of the home that require the use of vacuum cleaners, night lights, etc.

Placement of receptacles may be adjusted so that furniture arrangement will not interfere with the use of recep-

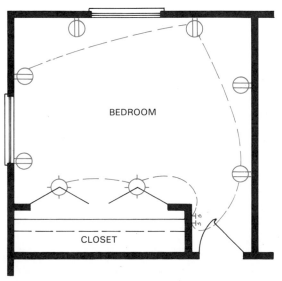

18-12 *Receptacles should be placed about 8 feet apart for easy access.*

tacles. Large pieces of furniture frequently hide outlets and make them difficult to reach. One solution is to locate outlets closer to corners than to centers of walls so that long furniture can be placed without covering an outlet.

Receptacles are usually placed 12 to 18 inches above the floor; however some may be more convenient if they are 36 inches from the floor. For instance, in a dining area a 36-inch high receptacle would be convenient for hot plates and other appliances used at table level. Higher receptacles should be used with appliances such as a refrigerator or clothes washer for easy access.

THE PLUMBING SYSTEM

The residential plumbing system provides an adequate supply of water for household use in desired locations. It also removes the waste water through a sanitary sewer or private septic system. There are three primary parts to a residential plumbing system. They are the water supply system, the waste water removal system, and the plumbing fixtures.

Water Supply

The residential water supply system, 18-13, begins at a city water main or private well. The pipe that enters the structure from a city main or private well is called the building main. Once it enters a building, it branches into the cold water main and the hot water main. The water may pass through a water softener, filter, or other treatment device before dividing into hot and cold water mains.

The cold water main is routed to areas of the home where fixtures are located. A cold water branch line is run from the cold water main to each fixture. A shutoff valve is installed in the building main, the cold water main, and each branch line. These valves make it possible to work on one part of the plumbing system without shutting down the entire system.

The hot water main begins at the hot water heater. It generally travels through the house parallel to the cold water main. Shutoff valves are installed in hot water lines just as they are in cold water lines.

Piping for the water supply system may be located in the floor, walls, or ceilings of a home. Pipes are usually 1/2 to 3/4 inch in diameter. Materials used for piping include copper tubing, plastic pipe, and galvanized steel pipe. Local code requirements sometimes restrict the use of plastic pipe.

Waste Water Removal

Waste water is carried to the sanitary sewer or private septic tank through the waste removal or drainage system, 18-14. These pipes are separate from the water supply system. Waste water lines are also much larger than water supply lines to accommodate waste materials. Provisions must also be made so that pipes can be easily cleaned if they become clogged.

The waste water system, unlike the water supply system, is not pressurized. It depends on gravity to carry the used

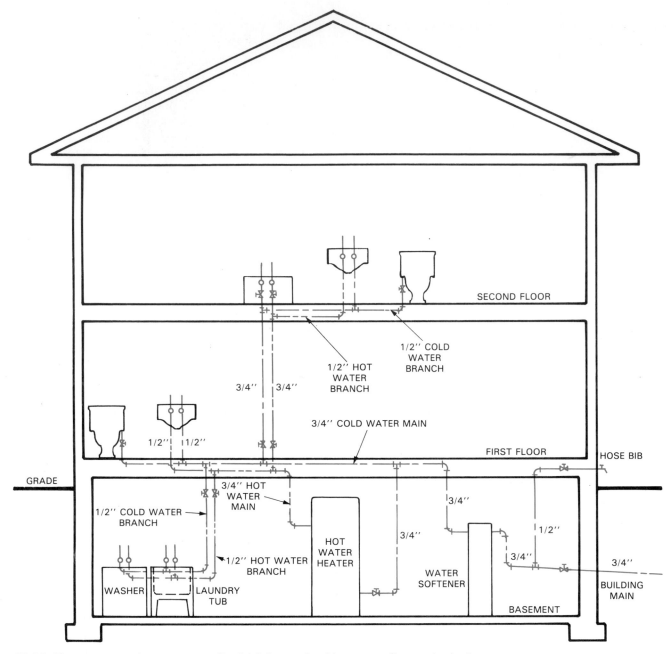

18-13 The water supply system supplies both hot and cold water to fixtures in the home.

water and waste to the sewer. Gases that are a part of waste water must also be disposed. Soil stacks are used so that water and waste may drain down. The stacks extend above the roof so that gases may vent out.

Every housing unit must have at least one soil stack for each water closet. Additional stacks are required for other fixtures if they are in isolated locations. Local plumbing codes should be consulted. Traps are installed below each fixture to prevent gases from entering the living space through the drain fixture. The trap remains filled with water to block the escape of gases, 18-15. Water closets do not need a trap installed below because they have a built-in trap.

Several types of pipes are used for waste water systems. Cast iron pipes, copper and brass alloy pipes, and plastic

pipes are frequently used. They are usually 3 or 4 inches in diameter. Again, local codes may specify the type of pipe required in the area.

Fixtures

A plumbing fixture is any appliance—such as a sink, shower stall, water closet, or dishwasher—that is connected to the plumbing system. Several factors should be considered when planning for plumbing fixtures. They include style, size, fixture material, support for the fixture, and supply and drain requirements.

Style has implications for installation as well as decor. For example, lavatories are available in many styles, such as flat top with no back, shelf or ledge back, countertop, and corner. They may be freestanding, wall hung, or

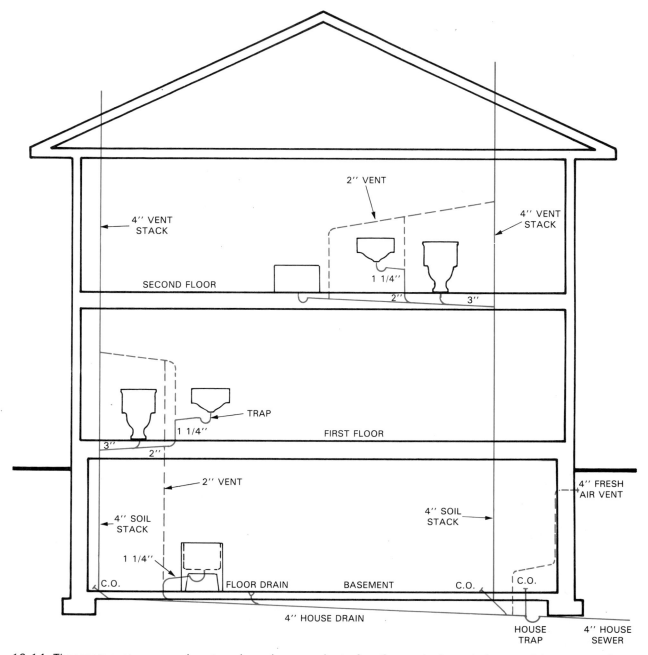

18-14 The waste water removal system depends on gravity to function, so horizontal pipes must be at an angle.

mounted in a vanity, 18-16. Specific fixture styles are shown in Chapters 3,4, and 5. Each type must be installed in a different manner.

Plumbing fixtures are available in a wide range of sizes. A good example is bathtubs. Some of the standard sizes include widths from 2 ft. 6 in. to 2 ft. 8 in. and lengths from 4 ft. 6 in. to 6 ft. A fixture should fit properly into the space provided for it within a room.

The material from which a fixture is made affects the price and durability of the product. For example, sinks are available in enameled cast iron, enameled steel, stainless steel, and some plastics. Each type of material has qualities that make it more suitable for some uses and locations than others. Manufacturers have recommendations related to these factors for their products.

Plumbing fixtures are frequently heavy, so they may require special structural support. Water closets are one example. Adequate floor support is necessary for a typical floor mounted model. Special blocking and wall reinforcement should be built into the original structure if possible for wall mounted models. Reinforcement may be added during remodeling as well.

Since each plumbing fixture will be connected to the water supply and waste water systems, specific water supply and drain requirements must be considered. Water supply lines to most fixtures may be 1/2 inch in diameter. Drain lines vary greatly in size. Showers generally require 2-inch drains, while sinks, lavatories, bathtubs, and dishwashers frequently use 1 1/2 inch drains. Water closets need either a 3 or 4 inch drain, depending on local codes.

INSINKERATOR

18-15 The loop in this pipe is a trap that prevents waste water system gases from entering the house.

Hot Water Uses	Capacity
Minimum hot water needed for two persons with one bath and a clothes washer	30 gallons
Each additional person	add 3.5 gallons
Each additional bathroom	add 3.5 gallons
Automatic dishwasher	add 5.0 gallons

18-17 The proper size of a hot water heater for a household can be estimated with the use of this chart.

Planning the Plumbing System

The specific details of the plumbing system are best handled by an expert. However, a basic knowledge of guidelines and options is useful to the beginning housing student.

A plumbing system is more efficient and less expensive if areas that require plumbing are kept as close to each other as possible. This way, water mains and stacks can be shorter and less complex.

The most efficient arrangement is to have rooms that require plumbing and that are on the same floor placed adjacent to each other. Fixtures should be placed on an adjoining wall so that water mains and main stacks are easily shared. For example, the bathroom would be next door to the kitchen, and the kitchen sink and bathroom shower and sink would be placed on the adjoining wall. This arrangement is not always practical from a lifestyle aspect, but it is efficient to keep these rooms as close as possible.

Another efficient arrangement is to place rooms requiring plumbing directly above and below each other. For instance, laundry rooms are often located in the basement directly below the kitchen. Bathrooms on different floors are usually aligned so that plumbing mains can be shared easily.

Another concern in planning the home plumbing system is the water heater for the hot water main. The capacity of the water heater determines how much hot water can be used in a household at one time without running out. A guideline for appropriate capacities is given in 18-17.

ELJER PLUMBINGWARE

WOOD-METAL INDUSTRIES, INC.

18-16 Lavatories may be freestanding models, or they may be enclosed in a vanity.

CALIFORNIA REDWOOD ASSN.

18-18 Outdoor plumbing lines are needed if a pool is to be installed.

Some new trends in appliances used in residential housing require special plumbing considerations. Extra sinks are being used in baths for convenience. Kitchens may have a smaller sink for food preparation in addition to the main sink. Dishwashers and refrigerators with ice cube makers require their own water hook-ups. Jacuzzis and in ground swimming pools are gaining popularity as a part of the residential house, 18-18. These options should be considered in the planning stages of a home if possible so that the plumbing system can accommodate them.

REVIEW QUESTIONS

1. What is a service entrance panel? What is its function?
2. How can a branch circuit protect a wiring system?
3. If a kitchen has an electric range, a refrigerator, a dishwasher, and other minor appliances, how many circuits, of what type, would you put in the kitchen?
4. What points should be considered when placing receptacles and switches in a house?
5. How does the water supply system differ from the waste water removal system?
6. What factors should be considered when planning for plumbing fixtures?
7. What size hot water heater would you recommend for a household with two baths, three family members, one clothes washer, and one dishwasher?

19 Climate Control, Fireplaces, and Stoves

After studying this chapter, you will be able to:
■ Evaluate the level of climate control in a house by determining the number and type of climate control devices in the house.
■ Describe the operations of various heating and cooling systems.
■ List the components and structural considerations involved in using solar heating systems.
■ Describe the construction of fireplaces and stoves, and explain how they can heat a room.

Living spaces are more comfortable today than ever before because of climate control systems. A total climate control system involves temperature control, humidity control, air circulation, and air cleaning. Most modern homes at least have some kind of temperature control system. Total climate control within a home is becoming more common.

CLIMATE CONTROL

The temperature of a home is controlled by using heating systems and cooling systems. Insulation is used to help temperature control systems work more efficiently. Most homes in areas that have cold weather at least part of the year use some form of heating system. Cooling

FORCED WARM AIR SYSTEM

Advantages:
1. Installation is relatively inexpensive.
2. Provides heat quickly.
3. Heating ducts may be used for air cooling.
4. Humidification is simple.
5. Air cleaners are easily attached.

Disadvantages:
1. Ducts are large and sometimes difficult to route to all parts of the dwelling.
2. System is noisy.
3. Rapid air movement is objectionable to some people.
4. Furniture sometimes interferes with air movement from register.
5. Only one zone of heating is practical for each furnace.

HYDRONIC SYSTEM

Advantages:
1. Quiet operation.
2. Even heat with no drafts.
3. Clean.
4. Efficient.
5. Zones are possible.

Disadvantages:
1. Slow reaction time.
2. No provision for cooling.
3. No provision for air filtration.
4. No provision for humidification.

CENTRAL HEAT PUMP

Advantages:
1. System is clean and needs no chimney.
2. Limited inside space is required because the main unit is located outside the home.
3. Provides both heating and cooling in the same unit.
4. Air cleaning and humidification is easy.
5. Highly efficient in mild climates.

Disadvantages:
1. Efficiency for heating drops considerably when the temperatures is below 30 degrees F.
2. Requires a duct system with blower to move air.
3. Installation costs are higher than most systems.
4. May need additional heating source in very cold climates.

ACTIVE SOLAR HEAT SYSTEM

Advantages:
1. The system is clean, non-polluting, and environmentally attractive.
2. It is very safe.
3. The energy is free.
4. Inexpensive to operate.

Disadvantages:
1. Not dependable—affected by the weather.
2. Not suited for all areas of the country.
3. Expensive to install.
4. Lots of maintenance required.
5. Some water systems will freeze and ruin collectors if the pump fails.
6. Generally requires a backup heating system.

19-1 Because heating systems operate differently, they have different advantages and disadvantages.

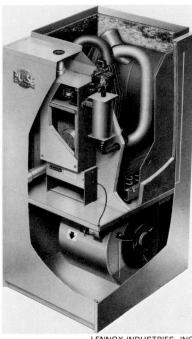

19-2 This furnace represents the latest technology in forced warm air furnaces. The blower is located in the lower compartment of the furnace.

systems are most common in the southern areas of the United States, but they are also used in northern areas for the summer season.

Conventional Heating Systems

A home can be heated using one of several systems. The most common types in use are forced warm air systems,

hydronic systems, electric radiant heat systems, and heat pump systems. Because these systems use different methods to heat the air, they have different advantages and disadvantages. These are listed in 19-1.

Forced warm air systems. A forced warm air system uses a furnace, blower, and duct system to heat a house. Air is first heated in the furnace, 19-2. Furnaces commonly use natural gas or electricity for fuel. Oil, coal, and wood forced warm air furnaces are also in use, but they are not as common. As the fuel is expended, heat is produced and transmitted to the air.

The blower moves the heated air into the ducts and brings in cold air from the space being heated. The ducts carry the air from the furnace to each room, 19-3. One set of ducts is used to carry warm air to each room. Another set, called the cold air return, is used to carry cold air from each room back to the furnace. This cycle is repeated until the desired temperature is reached in the heated area. A thermostat in the living space controls the amount of heat delivered.

Registers are generally located close to the floor along the outside walls of the home. This eliminates cold floors and provides more even heating. The number of registers in a room depends on the size, expected heat loss, and desired temperature of the room.

Hydronic systems. A hydronic system uses hot water to heat a home. The system consists of a boiler, a pump, water pipes, and radiators or radiant panels. Water is heated in the boiler using natural gas or fuel oil, 19-4. Electricity, wood, and coal may be used also. When the water is sufficiently hot, it is pumped through pipes to the radiators that are located throughout the living space. They are usually located on outside walls to increase com-

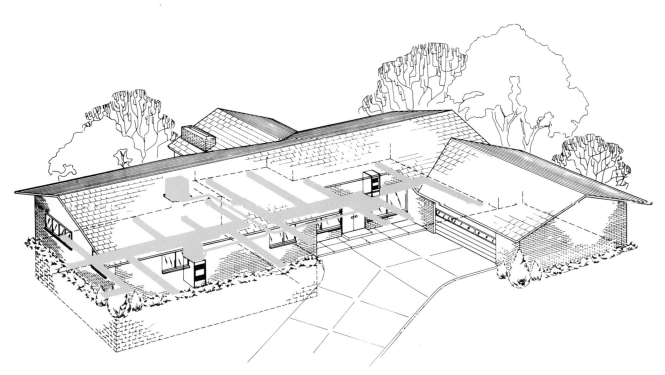

19-3 The duct system carries heat to every room in the house.

19-4 A hydronic furnace has a large chamber to heat water.

in a short time. It also may be used as an auxiliary heating system for a section of the home.

Electric radiant systems. Electric radiant systems use resistance wiring to produce heat in the wire. No pumps, blowers, registers, furnace, or chimney are required for this type of system. The wire may be embedded in the ceiling or floor, 19-6, or it may be mounted in baseboard convectors. If the wire is located in the ceiling or floor, the entire system is hidden.

Central heat pump systems. The central heat pump system uses an electric refrigeration unit to heat and cool a living space. The refrigeration unit contains a compressor, circulating fluid (refrigerant), and two heat exchangers, 19-7. It operates by removing heat from air or water.

In cold weather, heat is removed from outside air and pumped into the house. In warm weather, heat is removed from air in the house and pumped outside. Some heat pumps are connected to a water well. Well water facilitates more efficient operation than outside air because it is warmer than exterior air in cold weather and cooler in hot weather. Heat pumps may also be connected to solar collectors which provide some heat even on cloudy days.

Solar Heating Systems

Solar heating systems use energy from the sun to heat a home. They are fairly new types of heating systems, but they are gaining popularity as fuel costs rise. Although solar heating is fairly reliable, it is usually used in combination with another fuel powered backup system for emergency use. The two main types of solar heating systems are active systems and passive systems.

Active solar heating. Active systems involve collecting, storing, and distributing heat energy within a living space. A typical solar system contains a bank of collectors, a heat

fort and reduce cold air drafts, 19-5. As the heat is removed from the water in the radiators, the water is pumped back to the boiler to be reheated.

Another type of hydronic heating system uses copper tubing embedded in a concrete floor or plastered ceiling to heat a home. This system is usually limited to mild climates where the temperature is not likely to drop rapidly

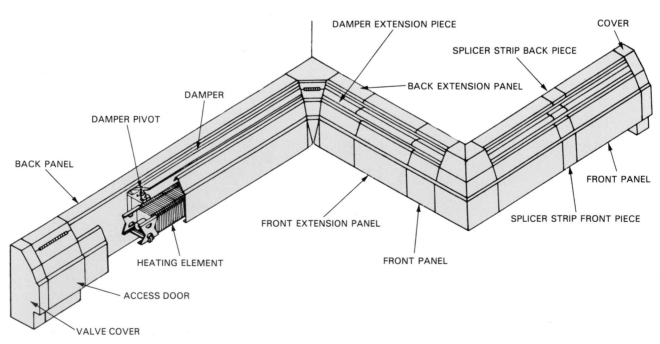

19-5 Hydronic radiant panels are located along the baseboard of a room to provide even heat.

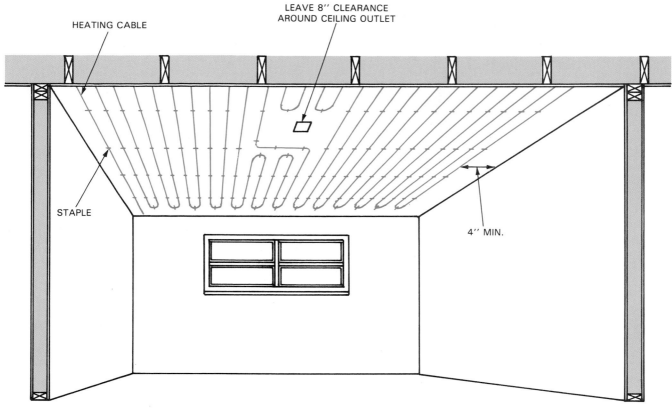

HEATING CABLE

LEAVE 8″ CLEARANCE
AROUND CEILING OUTLET

STAPLE

4″ MIN.

19-6 *Resistance wiring for electric radiant systems can be embedded in the ceiling.*

storage area, and a distribution system with controls for operating the system, 19-8. The distribution system may operate with warm air and ducts, similar to a forced warm air system, or it may use warm water and pipes, similar to a hydronic system. Warm air systems are more popular for home heating.

Solar collectors, 19-9, are usually placed on the roof of a house so that they may get maximum exposure to sunlight. Several sizes and types are available, ranging in efficiency from 15 to 65 percent. Some have built-in insulation while others do not. Collectors may have single, double, or triple glazing. The amount of insulation and type of glazing affects the efficiency of the collector, especially in cold climates.

A solar collector contains an absorber plate that is heated as the sun's rays strike it. There are many designs and styles. Copper is the most efficient and expensive material used for absorber plates. Aluminum is commonly used and fairly efficient as well. Absorber plates are generally covered with a flat black coating to absorb as much energy as possible.

After heat energy is collected, it is transferred to a storage area. Warm air systems generally use a large box or crawlspace area filled with stones to collect heat. Warm water systems use a large tank to store heat in water. Either type of storage must be well insulated to resist loss of heat.

The size of storage needed is related to the amount of solar radiation available; area of collector surface; efficiency of the storage media; heat loss in the storage area; and household needs. The storage should generally be large enough to store the heat required for three days of cloudy weather. Storage which would last longer than that would be too large and expensive to be practical. Average storage size for warm air systems usually ranges from 1/2 to 1 cubic foot of stone for each square foot of collector area. A warm water storage tank a little less than 1/2 the size of the rock storage could store the same amount of heat.

Distribution of heat from the collectors and storage to the living space is accomplished using a blower for air systems or a pump for water systems. The blower or pump

LENNOX INDUSTRIES, INC.

19-7 *The heat pump operates using a compressor, a blower, and a heat exchanger.*

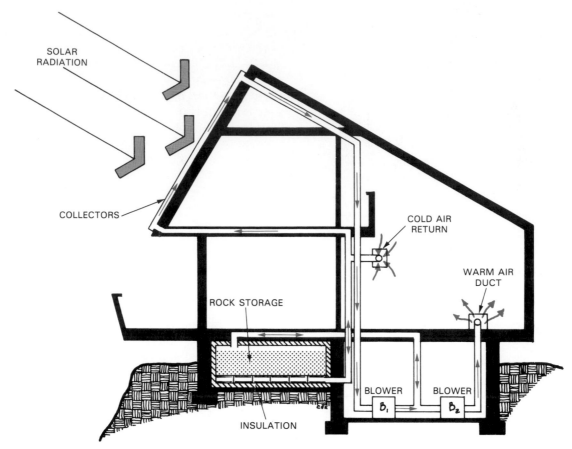

19-8 An active solar heating system collects heat using solar panels. Heat is then transferred to storage. A duct system similar to the type used with a forced air system is used to circulate heat throughout the house.

is activated by a complex set of controls that respond to temperature sensors located in the collectors, storage, and living space.

Passive solar heating. Passive solar heating is used in homes as a supplement to heating systems. It uses the structure of the house as both the collector and storage for heat. Specially built walls use concrete block as heat collectors with glass panels to contain heat in the structure, 19-10. Passive walls do not have a distribution system to move warm air throughout the house.

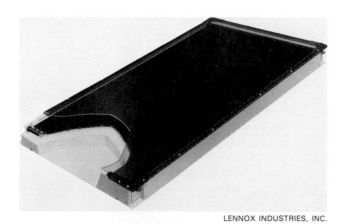

LENNOX INDUSTRIES, INC.

19-9 This solar panel has single glazing, an absorber plate, and insulation.

Passive heating requires special construction, so it is not a practical option unless a new home is built. A home using passive panels will be most efficient if the panels have a southern exposure and there are no windows on the north side of the house.

Cooling Systems

Cooling systems provide cool, clean, dehumidified air. This allows a home to be comfortable in warm, humid weather. Also, since windows are closed, infiltration of dirt, pollen, and dust is reduced. Central air conditioners are the most efficient types of residential cooling systems. Room air conditioners are not cooling systems, but they are used in some homes and many apartments for local cooling.

The most common residential cooling system is the compressor-cycle system. Heat pumps are frequently used to cool homes as well. The operation of heat pumps was discussed in the heating section of this chapter.

The *compressor-cycle system* uses highly compressed refrigerant, usually freon, to cool air. The refrigerant passes through the compressor where it is pressurized and becomes a hot gas. It is then pumped to the condenser and cooled so that it condenses into a liquid state. The liquid is pumped to the evaporator cooling coil where it removes heat from the air in the home as it evaporates into a gas again.

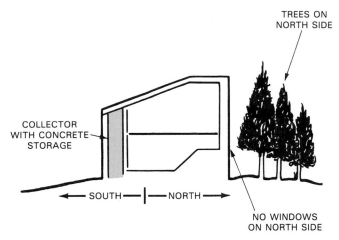

19-10 Passive solar heating is built directly into the walls of the home. It is more effective if used on walls with a southern exposure, and if there are no windows on the north side of the house.

As room air is cooled, moisture in the air condenses on the fins of the condenser and is drained away. This process dehumidifies the air and increases the comfort level. The cooled air is moved to various parts of the living space through a system of ducts. If a forced warm air system is present, the same ducts which are used for the heating system may be used. A typical furnace blower is used to move the air through the ducts.

Compressor-cycle units normally have two separate components. The compressor and condenser are in a separate unit that is located outside the home, 19-11, and the cooling coils are mounted on the furnace. In this system, the furnace blower can be used to circulate the cooled air. If the system is to be used independently of the furnace, the compressor-condenser unit is used with

an *independent evaporator unit*. This unit consists of a blower, cooling coils, and filter. It may use a separate duct system or existing ducts.

Room air conditioning units contain a compressor, condenser, cooling coil, and fan all in one unit, 19-12. They are usually installed in a window or wall opening designed for the unit. These systems should be covered well during cool weather because cold air will enter the room through the unit.

Insulation

The function of insulation in a structure is to prevent excessive heat loss or heat gain. Heat loss is a concern in cold weather, and heat gain is a concern in warm weather. *Insulation* is a material that efficiently resists the flow of heat through it.

Common examples of insulation include glass fiber, foamed glass, foamed plastics, and expanded minerals such as vermiculite. These materials are very efficient in resisting the flow of heat.

When comparing the efficiency of insulation, the level of resistance to heat is designated as the R-value. R-values are higher for products with higher insulative efficiency. R-values for common materials of a 1-inch thickness are given in 19-13. The total resistance of a wall can be determined by adding the R-values of each material in the wall. See 19-14.

WHIRLPOOL CORP.

19-12 Room air conditioners contain the compressor-condenser unit, the cooling coil, and the fan in one unit. They are placed in windows.

WHIRLPOOL CORP.

19-11 The compressor-condenser unit for central air conditioning is located outside the home.

Material (1″ thick)	R-value
Expanded Polystyrene	3.85
Mineral Batt Insulation	3.50
Glass Fiber Insulation	3.50
Plywood	1.30
Glass	.88
Sand Plaster	.30
Common Brick	.20
Concrete	.08

Note: The higher the R-value, the better the insulating properties.

19-13 *If a product has a high R-value, it is a good insulator.*

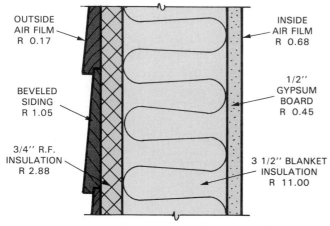

OUTSIDE AIR FILM R 0.17

INSIDE AIR FILM R 0.68

BEVELED SIDING R 1.05

1/2″ GYPSUM BOARD R 0.45

3/4″ R.F. INSULATION R 2.88

3 1/2″ BLANKET INSULATION R 11.00

19-14 *To find the R-value of a wall, the R-values of each component of the wall are added. This wall has an R-value of 16.23.*

Other Factors

Although temperature is the most obvious factor in climate control, other conditions affect the comfort level of a house. Humidity control, fresh air circulation, and air cleaning also affect climate. Systems that modify these factors allow total climate control of a house.

Humidity control. Humidity is the amount of moisture in the air. A humidity level of about 50 percent is comfortable when the temperature is 75°F. Humidity in the home drops to low levels in the winter because of the heating process. Low humidity in the home can cause throat and skin irritation and cracks in the furniture. A humidifier can be used to add moisture back to dry air.

A humidifier may be a freestanding unit, or it may be attached directly to a forced warm air furnace. Humidifiers may add as many as 15 gallons of water to indoor air each day. Most have automatic controls that may be set to provide the desired amount of humidity.

In warm weather, air in the home has too much humidity. Humid air feels sticky and uncomfortable. Excessive humidity causes wood doors, windows, and drawers to swell and stick. Condensation may occur as well, causing wood to warp. A dehumidifier may be installed to remove excess water from the air. It condenses water on cold coils to remove water from the air, reducing the humidity level.

Dehumidifiers are frequently individual, portable units. They have a pan that collects water removed from the air. This pan must be emptied periodically. Dehumidification occurs automatically when an air conditioner is used.

Air circulation. Modern living spaces are almost air tight to reduce heat loss in winter and heat gain in summer. As

19-15 *An air filter catches impure particles in the air on metal grids.*

a result, an adequate supply of fresh air is not always provided. If the same air is continuously circulated in a home without adding a fresh supply, the air becomes stale.

A circulation system that operates even when air is at the proper temperature helps to keep air fresh. Fans, either built into the central heating system or added in the attic, help to circulate air. This will eliminate areas with a high concentration of moisture, smoke, or fumes.

Air cleaning. An air cleaning device removes dust and foreign materials from the air. Some furnaces have built-in filters, and others have electronic air cleaning grids, 19-15. Grids remove about 95 percent of the dust particles in the air. The grid works by placing an electrical charge on each airborne contaminant particle and attaching the particle to a metal plate. The accumulated dust and dirt is removed when the filter is changed or cleaned.

FIREPLACES AND STOVES

Fireplaces and stoves have experienced renewed interest in recent years as fuel prices have risen. They may be used as a heat source as well as a focal point. New developments have made fireplaces and stoves efficient devices for heating an area.

Fireplaces

Several types of fireplaces are found in homes today. Traditional fireplaces are of solid masonry, while newer types are constructed of metal. The metal fireplaces may be covered with brick to look like solid masonry fireplaces. Many of these burn wood, but some are gas fired or electric, giving the appearance of a wood fire.

A fireplace generally consists of a firebox, a damper, and a flue, 19-16. The firebox and inner hearth (the floor of the firebox) are made of a fireproof subtstance, generally fire brick, to withstand damage from the burning fire. The top of the firebox is covered with a damper which controls the burning rate and prevents downdrafts of cold air.

A flue is necessary to carry smoke to the outside of the house and facilitate a good draft for the fire. A *draft* is the upward flow of air which draws in sufficient oxygen for the fire to burn well. Draft is increased as the height and area of the flue are increased. A wider area just above the firebox called the smoke chamber helps to increase the draft by causing the air to move in a swirling motion.

A masonry fireplace has a firebox and inner hearth that is lined with a special brick called fire brick. The flue is generally lined with clay tile. Masonry fireplaces may be single face, two face opposite, two face adjacent, or three face in design.

The *single face* fireplace is the most common, 19-17. It burns more efficiently than the other designs because it has a good oxygen flow into the fireplace. The most popular size is 36 inches wide, but sizes may vary from 24 to 96 inches.

A *two face opposite* fireplace is open on the front and back sides, 19-18. With this design, care must be taken

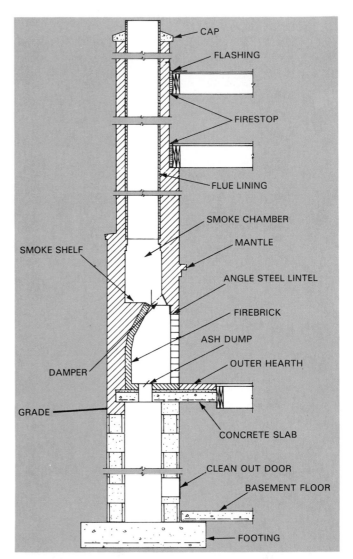

19-16 A fireplace is designed to facilitate efficient burning of wood and to remove smoke from the house.

PREWAY, INC.

19-17 The single face fireplace has the most efficient design.

19-18 *The two face opposite fireplace enables a view from two rooms.*

19-20 *The three face fireplace has the least efficient design.*

to prevent a draft from one side to the other. The draft may cause smoke to enter the house. Opening width of this design ranges from 28 to 48 inches.

A *two face adjacent* fireplace is open on the front and on one adjacent side, 19-19. It also is know as a projecting corner fireplace. Opening sizes range from 28 to 60 inches.

A *three face* fireplace is open on three sides, 19-20. Because the opening is so large, draft for this type of fireplace is not alway sufficient for a good fire. Three face

fireplaces are made in the same sizes as two face opposite designs.

Prefabricated metal fireplaces are more efficient for producing heat than traditional fireplaces. Wall-mounted and free-standing models are usually metal on the outside. They are complete from the factory; only the flue must be added.

Prefabricated heat circulating fireplaces, 19-21, require framing or masonry enclosures. They may have brick lined fireboxes so that they look identical to traditional masonry

THE ADAMS CO.

19-19 *A two face adjacent design is usually used for a corner fireplace.*

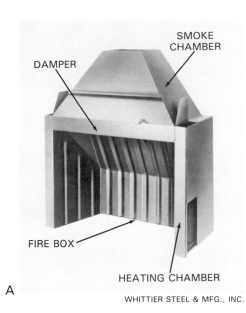

A

WHITTIER STEEL & MFG., INC.

B

PREWAY, INC.

19-21 A heat circulating fireplace increases a fire's heating efficiency by drawing room air into the heating chamber and returning heated air to the room (A). When installed, the heat circulating fireplace looks just like a traditional masonry fireplace (B).

fireplaces. These units are very efficient because the sides and back consist of a double wall passageway used to heat air. Cool air in a room is drawn into the chamber where it is heated and then returned to the room through registers above the chamber.

Air for combustion is piped into the sealed firebox from the outside. Glass doors on the firebox prevent the loss of warm room air up the chimney. This design also reduces the fireplace's tendency to pull cold air into a room through cracks around doors and windows. Some models use a small, electric fan to increase air flow.

Safety is a major concern with fireplaces because sparks may ignite objects within a room. Placing a firescreen in front of a fireplace opening will help prevent sparks from popping out into the room, 19-22. Glass doors that fit tightly over the fireplace opening provide maximum protection against sparks. They also reduce heat loss when the fireplace is not in operation. Noninflammable

HEATILATOR, INC.

19-22 Screens help to prevent sparks from popping out onto flammable items.

19-23 Stoves are more efficient heating devices than fireplaces. They can have a cozy appearance.

materials should be used on the floor directly in front of the fireplace. Combustible materials such as carpeting, draperies, paneling, and wood or upholstered furniture should be kept at a safe distance from the fireplace.

Stoves

Stoves generally produce more usable heat than fireplaces. They also provide a cozy, decorative addition to a room, 19-23. Stoves used for heat are usually fueled by coal or wood. They are generally used as local sources of heat in addition to another central heating system. Models vary according to their level of efficiency, and this level should be checked before purchasing a stove.

The two main types of stoves are radiant stoves and circulating stoves. Both types of stoves produce *radiant heat*. Radiant heat passes through the air with no assistance from air flow. However, circulating stoves use air flow as well as radiation to distribute heat throughout a room.

A circulating stove is a radiant stove surrounded by an outer jacket. The jacket has openings at the bottom and top so that air can flow between the stove and jacket, 19-24. Either natural air flow or small fans move the air around the stove. The air flow enables a room to be heated more evenly and efficiently than is possible with radiant heat alone.

Circulating stoves are safer for home use than radiant stoves because the exposed surfaces are not as hot. Serious burns may result from touching a radiant stove. Circulating stoves may be placed closer to combustible materials than radiant stoves because of their lower surface temperature. This allows more flexibility in locating a stove.

Stoves are sometimes classified according to their heating efficiency. Low-efficiency stoves (20-30 percent efficient) are generally the simplest in construction. They route primary combustion air in a straight path through or across the flame. No provision is made for secondary combustion of gasses produced during burning. Examples include simple box stoves, Franklin stoves, pot belly stoves, and some parlor stoves.

Medium-efficiency stoves operate in the range of 35 to 50 percent efficiency. Their design has better control of the amount of primary and secondary air used for combustion. Most of these stoves have less air leakage into the stove. In addition to these features, they generally have some type of thermostat (temperature controlling device) to ensure a constant burning rate.

High-efficiency stoves are over 50 percent efficient. They regulate air flow as the medium-efficiency stoves do, but also use baffles, long smoke paths, and heat exchange devices to increase heat output. These stoves are more expensive to purchase, but deliver more heat per unit of fuel. This increased efficiency frequently offsets the greater initial cost if the stove is operated regularly.

VERMONT CASTINGS, INC.

19-24 A circulating stove allows air to flow around the fire to assure steady, even heat in a room.

installed in the ceiling between the room where the stove is located and rooms above. A cold air return should be considered if there is no natural route for its return.

Small, inexpensive fans, like those used to cool computers, may be installed at strategic locations to bring warm air into an area. These fans are inexpensive to operate and increase air circulation very efficiently.

Locating a stove along an exterior wall will result in greater heat loss through that wall, but this is the most common location since the flue is frequently located on an outside wall. If an interior wall location is used the wall should be properly insulated to prevent heat drain to areas such as an unheated garage or unused attic.

A stove is frequently located inside or in front of an existing fireplace. This is logical because the flue is already in place, but locating the stove inside the fireplace will most likely reduce its efficiency. The fireplace materials will absorb large amounts of heat and hinder circulation of warm air from the stove. When the stove is positioned in front of a fireplace, the opening should be covered with sheet metal to reflect the heat back into the room.

REVIEW QUESTIONS

1. What are the four main types of heating systems used in residential housing? What are some advantages and disadvantages of each?
2. How does an active solar heating system work to heat a house?
3. In what kind of home would you use passive solar heating?
4. How does a compressor-cycle air conditioning system function? What types of compressor-cycle systems are available?
5. What is an R-value? How can you use the value to choose insulation?
6. Besides temperature, what aspects of the interior climate can be controlled?
7. How does a humidifier function? How does a dehumidifier function?
8. What are the components of a fireplace? How do they facilitate efficient heating?
9. How does a circulating stove differ from a radiant stove? Which provides a more efficient source of heat for a room?

The location of the stove can influence its efficient distribution of heat. Improved heat distribution can be accomplished several ways. First, a stove placed in a large area between two rooms can heat both rooms more efficiently than if located in one of the rooms. If this is not possible, then a large opening between the two rooms will improve heat distribution. The opening should extend to the ceiling since warm air rises to the ceiling. Another approach is to install large registers at the top and bottom of the wall between rooms to be heated. The registers will allow heated air to move more easily between the rooms.

Stairways provide excellent passageways for heated air to reach spaces above. They also serve as return routes for cool air. If this is not possible, then registers may be

20 Energy Conservation

After studying this chapter, you will be able to:
- Evaluate the energy efficiency of a home according to its orientation, insulation, construction, and site.
- Evaluate the efficiency of an appliance by using Energy Guide labels and by checking for energy saving features.
- List the advantages and disadvantages of using solar or wind energy for a home energy supply.
- List ways that computers can be used to decrease home energy consumption.

Nearly one-fifth of all the energy used in the United States is used in the home. The rising cost of providing energy for the home and a concern that nonrenewable energy sources may run out has resulted in an emphasis on energy conservation. Conservation may involve special

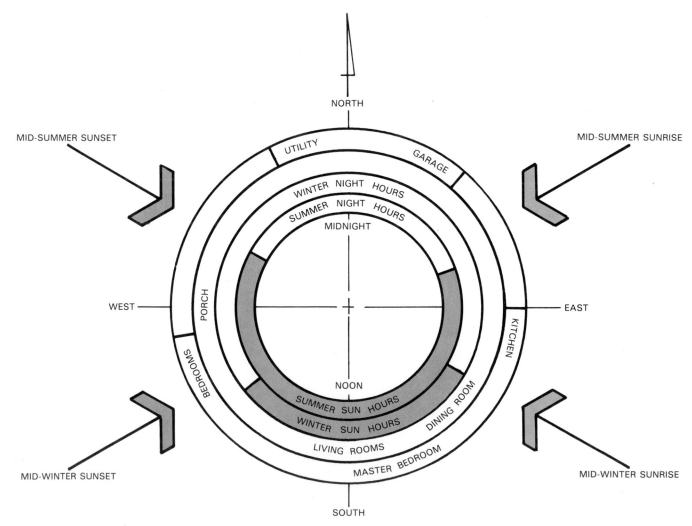

20-1 Living areas for homes in cold climates should have a southern exposure.

architectural and site considerations for a house. It may also involve using energy-saving appliances and alternative energy sources.

ARCHITECTURAL AND SITE CONSIDERATIONS

Many structural factors can be used to decrease a home's energy use. Some must be added as the structure is built or remodeled. Others may be applied to an existing home. Architectural considerations include the orientation of a home, insulation, placement and construction of windows and doors, and construction of roofs and walls. It also includes placement of heating and plumbing systems. Site considerations include landscaping techniques that can help to conserve energy.

Orientation

Orientation is the placement or alignment of an object. To improve the energy efficiency of a home, its orientation to the environment should work with sunlight and winds. Orientation refers to the placement of rooms within the structure as well as the placement of the structure on a site.

Orientation can be used to maximize or minimize the effect of the sun upon a structure. Generally, the west and south sides of a house are warmer than the north and east sides. The south side is exposed almost constantly to the sun while the north side is shaded and cooler.

In cool climates, the living areas of the home should be placed on the south side. See 20-1. The garage and utility room are often placed on the north side. In warmer climates, the living areas are placed on the north side of the home because there is less sunlight and heat, 20-2. There, devices to shade the south side are desirable.

The east side of a house receives full sun in the morning. This helps to warm a room after a cool evening. Rooms that are used in the morning, such as the kitchen and dining room, are often placed here. Rooms facing west are heated by the sun in the afternoon. Awnings, trees, or other methods of shading are needed to keep the west side of the house cool.

Wind also affects the amount of energy required to heat or cool a home. The direction of prevailing winds varies from one section of the country to another. Local weather bureaus can supply information about prevailing wind directions in specific areas.

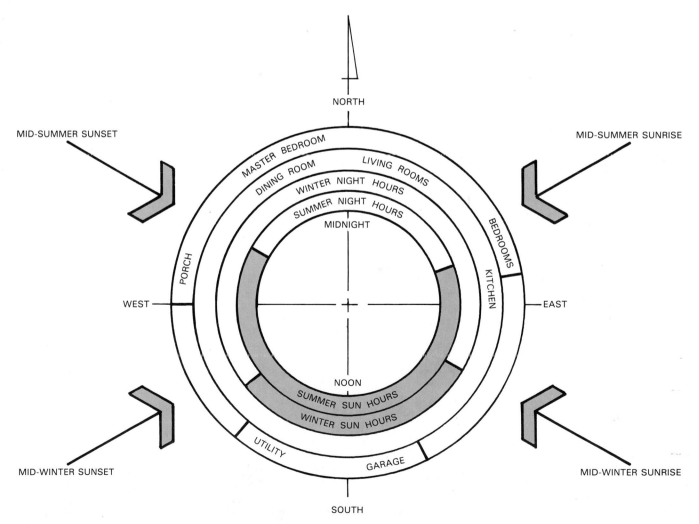

20-2 In warm climates, living areas should have a northern exposure to keep rooms cool.

MANVILLE BUILDING MATERIALS CORP.

20-3 Blanket insulation with a vapor barrier is usually installed between wall studs and ceiling joists.

The thickness of various materials required to equal the insulation value of 1'' of rigid polyurethane insulation per square foot of surface area:

	R-value/inch	Thickness
Expanded polyurethane (rigid insulation)	5.88	1.00''
Wood fiber insulation	4.00	1.47''
Expanded polystyrene (rigid insulation)	3.85	1.53''
Mineral wool from rock, slag, or glass	3.12	1.88''
Expanded perlite	2.78	2.12''
Cellular glass (foamed)	2.44	2.41''
Expanded vermiculite	2.18	2.70''
Hardwoods (maple, oak)	0.91	6.46''
Concrete blocks, rectangular, 2 core	0.13	45.23''
Brick (face)	0.11	53.45''
Stone (sandstone or limestone)	0.08	73.50''

20-4 To achieve the same R-value as rigid insulation, much more of other forms of insulation must be used.

Orientation to minimize the affect of wind is important in areas where heating is a major concern. Cold winds should be blocked to reduce heat loss. The garage and utility rooms may be placed as buffers to cold weather storms. Porches with wind screens may also act as buffers. A vestibule can be used to prevent outdoor air from entering the living areas of the home. It should be designed so that the the outside door must be closed before the inside door can be opened.

Warm weather breezes should be allowed to blow through the living and sleeping areas of a home. If breezes are blocked, it is more likely that energy requiring cooling devices will be needed for these areas.

Insulation

The object of insulating a home is to surround the living space with a thermal blanket to keep the home warm in cold weather and cool in warm weather. Local utility companies provide recommendations for the amount of insulation needed in that area. Because different insulating materials of the same thickness have different levels of thermal resistance, R-values are used to indicate the amount of insulation needed.

Insulation may be made from different materials that vary in efficiency, quality, and safety level. It is available in blanket, board, and loose fill forms. They are each designed for areas of different shapes and reachability.

Blanket insulation, 20-3, is thick and flexible; it may be cut or curved to fit the space to be insulated. It is produced in rolls or in batts cut into 4- or 8-foot lengths. Different thicknesses and R-values are available to fit specific needs.

Blanket insulation is made from mineral wool — most commonly rock wool or fiber glass. It may be purchased with or without an attached vapor barrier. Blanket insulation is commonly used in attics, floors, and walls and around pipes and ducts.

Boards are made of rigid foamed plastics, usually polyurethane or polystyrene. They are available in thicknesses from 1/2 to 4 inches, widths from 2 to 4 feet, and a length of 8 feet. They have a higher R-value per inch of thickness than most forms of insulation, 20-4, but they tend to be more expensive. This type of insulation is approved for use between concrete basement walls and earth. However, some local fire codes do not allow board insulation above ground because it is considered a fire hazard. Local fire codes should be consulted before installing this type of insulation.

Because the boards are inflexible, they are generally added during construction. They may be used around foundations, between studs in side walls, and between studs and siding as sheathing. Board insulation is available with or without a vapor barrier.

Loose fill is often used in inaccessible spaces where blankets or boards cannot be used. It may be used in attic floors, inside frame walls, in cores of concrete blocks, and as filler between batts and rolls, 20-5. Loose fill may be made of mineral fiber, cellulose fiber, or expanded materials such as perlite and vermiculite. Expanded materials are usually more expensive than other forms of loose fill.

Ceilings, exterior walls, and floors above cold spaces should all be insulated well. In most homes the greatest amount of heat loss or gain is between the ceiling and roof. This area should be heavily insulated. Walls and floors also require adequate insulation. Some new homes have board insulation around basement walls. This insulates the basement area and helps to keep rooms above the

20-5 This attic has several inches of loose fill insulation. Additional, blanket insulation is being added to reduce heat loss.

basement insulated as well. Local R-value recommendations should be used as a guideline for insulating a new home or for adding insulation to an older home.

To reduce heating or cooling losses, insulation should fit snugly in ceilings, floors, and walls. Attic insulation should not block air circulation vents in the eaves of the house. Air movement in the attic prevents moisture and condensation from building up in cold weather. In warm weather, moving air lessens heat build-up in the attic.

A vapor barrier should be placed between the interior and the insulation, so that the insulation is exposed on the side facing outward. If the vapor barrier faces outward, vapor will be trapped inside the insulation material. Unfaced insulation—insulation without a vapor barrier—should be used when placing new insulation on top of old.

Windows and Doors

Windows should be placed in coordination with sunlight and breezes for the most comfort and energy efficiency. Homes in northern sections of the United States should have more window area on the south side of the home to receive heat from the sun in the winter. Window area on the north side of the home should be kept to a minimum to prevent heat loss. In the southern sections of the country, fewer windows should be placed on the south side, and more windows may be placed on the north side of the house.

In cold climates, large areas of windows should be avoided on the side of the home that receives strong winds. For warm weather, windows should be located to take advantage of prevailing breezes. Windows placed away from exterior corners allow the best movement of air. Air should flow across the room at a medium height.

Using insulating windows or storm windows helps to reduce heat loss or heat gain. Insulating glass windows may have two or three panes of glass with air between the panes. They should be considered when planning a new home or when replacing windows in an existing home. Storm windows are attached to the frame of the window; they may be placed inside or outside of a window sash. Chapter 14, *Windows and Doors,* contains more information about the insulative value of windows.

Approximately 13 percent of air infiltration occurs around exterior window frames. Caulking and weatherstripping prevent air leaks from lowering the efficiency of heating or cooling systems. Using them can result in monetary savings of 5 to 15 percent in poorly insulated homes.

Poorly insulated exterior doors can be sites of heat loss or heat gain. Steel doors with an insulating plastic foam core are good insulators. Magnetic or interlocking vinyl weatherstripping reduces air infiltration around doors. Storm doors, like storm windows, increase the insulative value of a door. Storm doors may have screen replacements to provide ventilation in warm weather.

Construction

The construction of roofs and walls affects the energy efficiency of a home. Proper roof color can increase the efficiency of heating and cooling systems. Light colored roofs reflect heat, while dark colored roofs absorb heat. Homes in cold climates should have dark colored roofs to help keep the house warm. Homes in warm climates will stay cooler if they have a light colored roof.

A roof overhang of proper length helps to control the effect of sunlight on a home. The angle of sunlight is

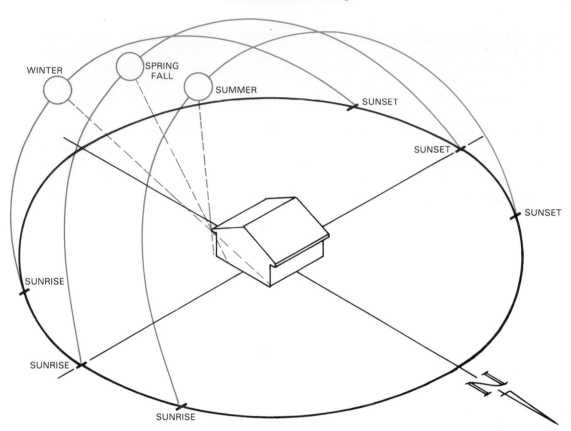

20-6 *As the angle of the sun changes from season to season, the amount of sun entering the house also changes. A proper roof overhang takes advantage of the angle of the sun for heating and cooling.*

higher in the summer and lower in the winter, 20-6. A proper overhang shades south windows from higher, summer sun but allows lower, winter sun to enter the windows.

The bottom edge of the roof should be constructed so that the soffit (eave) is level with the tops of exterior walls, 20-7. This design allows ceiling insulation to be extended over the exterior wall without blocking ventilation space.

To allow space for more wall insulation, an exterior wall may be double framed, 20-8. The two frames are placed side by side and spaced so that there are 7 1/4 inches of space between the back of the interior finish and the back of the sheathing. Wall studs are spaced 24 inches apart and are alternated between the two frames. The studs are alternated so that there is open space between the stud and wall surface on one side. This way, insulation can cover the studs, reducing thermal loss through framing.

Any gaps in construction should be filled to prevent air infiltration. Exterior sheathing should extend from the top of the foundation to the top of the wall at the soffit, 20-9. Joints of plywood siding should be sealed. Insulating sill sealer should be used between the house sill and the top of the foundation wall.

Heating and Plumbing Systems

Heating. The heating system is the largest energy user in the home. Therefore, the system should be as efficient as possible. Warm air ducts in unheated spaces should be insulated. Ducts should be located around the perimeter of the home, and warm air registers should be placed near

large glass areas to replace heat loss. Placing ductwork directly under floor panels allows heat loss from ducts to radiate up into the home. Installing dampers in ducts enables the heating system to be shut off in rooms that do not need to be heated.

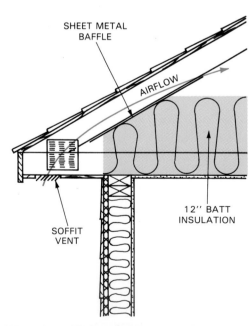

20-7 *When the soffit is level with the ceiling, insulation may be extended to the outside of the exterior wall without interfering with attic ventilation.*

Ceiling fans, 20-10, help to recirculate heated air during cold weather. They also recirculate cool air in warm weather. A clock thermostat, 20-11, saves energy by automatically lowering temperatures at night or during periods of absence and by raising temperatures during active times.

Plumbing. The cost of heating water accounts for 10 to 15 percent of the average household energy bill. Therefore, one way to conserve energy in the home is to increase the efficiency of the home plumbing system.

Plumbing mains should be centrally located to reduce the number and length of hot water lines. This will reduce the chance of heat loss through hot water pipes. Hot water

pipes that are very long or that run through unheated areas should be insulated. Hot water heaters in unheated areas should also be insulated. Flow restrictors to regulate the flow of hot water may be placed in faucets and shower heads.

Site Considerations

Outside the home, trees can be used to help conserve energy. Evergreens can be grown along the north wall of a home to block north winds in the winter. Deciduous trees (those that lose their leaves in the fall) may be planted along the south or west wall to provide shade in the summer and to allow sunlight to enter the house in the winter.

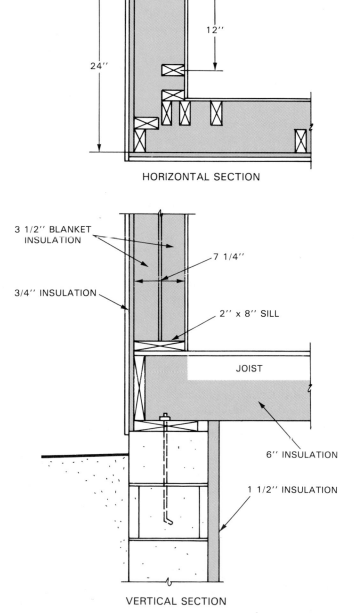

20-8 A double framed wall allows more room for insulation.

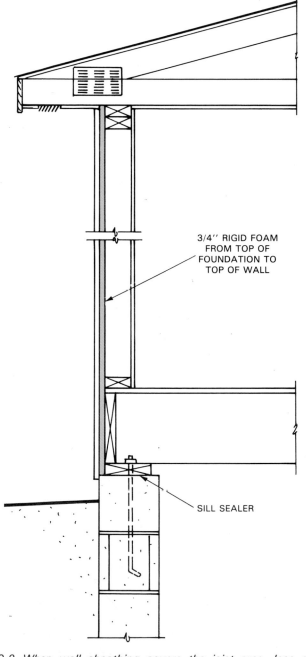

20-9 When wall sheathing covers the joist area, less air infiltration occurs between the floor and joists.

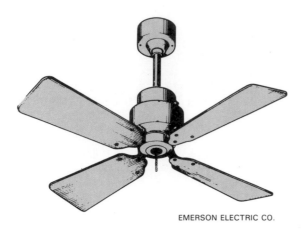

EMERSON ELECTRIC CO.

20-10 A small ceiling fan uses little energy, and it circulates heated air back into the living space so that heat is not wasted.

Tree species should be chosen to fit the purpose intended. For areas of general shade, widespreading trees such as walnuts, maples, and oaks should be used. Other trees can be used for small areas of local shade, such as persimmons, goldenrains, and red horsechestnuts. Sweet gums, poplars, and pine trees are used for vertical screening. They help to filter wind. Shrubs and vines can also be used to provide shade and block wind.

Earth berms can be used to protect the north side of a home from wind. An *earth berm* is a ledge or mound of earth which helps to direct prevailing winds up and over the house. This protects the home from cold air blowing on the structure and reducing heat loss.

ENERGY SAVING APPLIANCES

Energy saving appliances have been designed with new techniques to save energy. Although appliances with high energy efficiency are sometimes more expensive than standard appliances, they quickly pay for themselves with energy savings.

HONEYWELL, INC.

20-11 A clock thermostat allows heating and cooling systems to automatically shut off when no one is using the home and turn on before people return.

An *Energy Guide label,* 20-12, is displayed on most major appliances, and it can be used to compare the efficiency of different models. This black and yellow label lists the manufacturer's estimated annual operating cost of the appliance. It also gives the general range of operating costs for similar appliances, including the least and most energy efficient models. The costs are only an estimate meant for comparison purposes. A grid—listing estimated costs based on local utility rates—may be used to more closely determine actual operating costs.

The labels are required by the Federal Trade Commission to be displayed on refrigerators, freezers, dishwashers, water heaters, clothes washers, room air conditioners, and furnaces. Room air conditioner and furnace labels use a seasonal energy efficiency rating (SEER) instead of an annual operating cost. Other appliances, such as ranges, ovens, clothes dryers, humidifiers, dehumidifiers, and portable space heaters are not required to have labels because they vary little in operating costs.

Energy saving models should be considered when replacing an older appliance or when selecting an appliance for a new home. There are several new energy saving appliances for utility areas and service areas.

Utility Area Appliances

Heat pump. The heat pump is efficient for heating or cooling. For cooling, the heat pump draws heat out of the home, like an air conditioner. For heating, it extracts heat from the outside air and pumps it into the home. Heat pumps are equal in efficiency for cooling to an air conditioner; in warm climates, either a heat pump or an air conditioner could be used efficiently.

The efficiency of a heat pump for heating in cold weather is determined by the temperature of outdoor air. As the outdoor temperature gets colder, more energy is required by the pump to heat the house. When the temperature is reached at which the amount of energy required by the heat pump is equal to the amount of energy produced, a gas or electric heater will be more efficient. This temperature, called the *balance point,* is usually around 30°F. After the outdoor temperature drops below that point, an auxiliary heating system should be used.

Furnaces. Many traditional heating systems have undergone technical improvements and are up to 25 percent more efficient than before. *Gas fired furnaces* now use electronic igniters instead of traditional pilot lights. This feature saves energy because the pilot light does not need to be constantly fueled. It can be added to traditional gas furnaces. Automatic flue dampers, 20-13, may be added to furnaces to reduce heat loss when the furnace is off.

Air conditioners. The most efficient air conditioners have the highest EER. These models produce the most cooling for the amount of energy consumed. Many new models have energy saving settings to provide partial cooling in unoccupied rooms. Air conditioning units should be located where they will be shaded to help increase their efficiency.

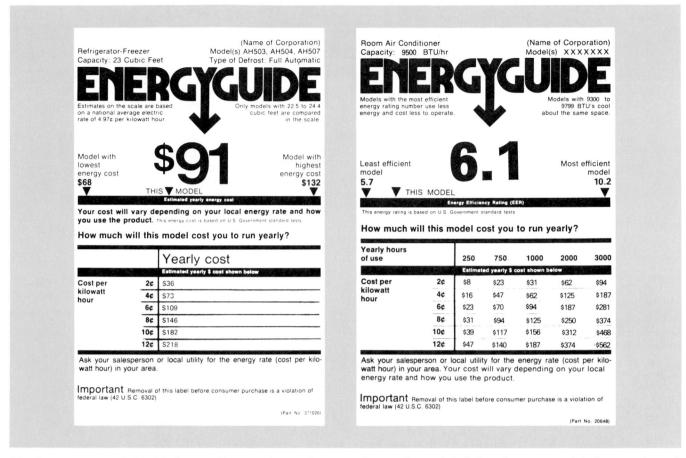

Refrigerator-Freezer (Name of Corporation)
Capacity: 23 Cubic Feet Model(s) AH503, AH504, AH507
Type of Defrost: Full Automatic

ENERGYGUIDE

Estimates on the scale are based on a national average electric rate of 4.97¢ per kilowatt hour

Only models with 22.5 to 24.4 cubic feet are compared in the scale

Model with lowest energy cost **$68**

$91

THIS ▼ MODEL

Model with highest energy cost **$132**

Estimated yearly energy cost

Your cost will vary depending on your local energy rate and how you use the product. This energy cost is based on U.S. Government standard tests.

How much will this model cost you to run yearly?

		Yearly cost
		Estimated yearly $ cost shown below
Cost per kilowatt hour	2¢	$36
	4¢	$73
	6¢	$109
	8¢	$146
	10¢	$182
	12¢	$218

Ask your salesperson or local utility for the energy rate (cost per kilowatt hour) in your area.

Important Removal of this label before consumer purchase is a violation of federal law (42 U.S.C. 6302)

(Part No. 371026)

Room Air Conditioner (Name of Corporation)
Capacity: 9500 BTU/hr Model(s) XXXXXXX

ENERGYGUIDE

Models with the most efficient energy rating number use less energy and cost less to operate.

Models with 9300 to 9799 BTU's cool about the same space.

Least efficient model **5.7**

6.1

▼ THIS MODEL

Most efficient model **10.2**

Energy Efficiency Rating (EER)

This energy rating is based on U.S. Government standard tests

How much will this model cost you to run yearly?

Yearly hours of use		250	750	1000	2000	3000
		Estimated yearly $ cost shown below				
Cost per kilowatt hour	2¢	$8	$23	$31	$62	$94
	4¢	$16	$47	$62	$125	$187
	6¢	$23	$70	$94	$187	$281
	8¢	$31	$94	$125	$250	$374
	10¢	$39	$117	$156	$312	$468
	12¢	$47	$140	$187	$374	$562

Ask your salesperson or local utility for the energy rate (cost per kilowatt hour) in your area. Your cost will vary depending on your local energy rate and how you use the product.

Important Removal of this label before consumer purchase is a violation of federal law (42 U.S.C. 6302)

(Part No. 20648)

20-12 Most Energy Guide labels state the annual operating cost of an appliance. Labels for climate control devices, such as air conditioners, give the energy efficiency rating.

Water heaters. Two or more inches of insulation around a water heater reduces the amount of energy required to heat water. Energy Guide labels should be checked to find the most efficient water heater. To eliminate the continuous heating of water, small, on demand water heaters can be used, 20-14. These can be installed under bathroom and kitchen sinks for small tasks requiring hot water.

A new method of heating water is to use waste heat from an air conditioner or heat pump. To harness waste heat, a hot water bank heat recovery unit is used, 20-15. The unit uses two concentric pipes to heat water. The inner pipe circulates water from the home's water heater. The outer pipe circulates refrigerant gas that has been

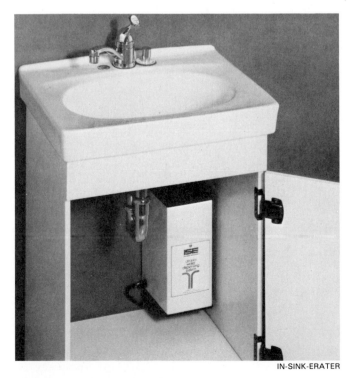

IN-SINK-ERATER

HONEYWELL, INC.

20-13 An automatic flue damper closes the flue opening when the furnace is not in operation. This reduces heating costs.

20-14 Instant hot water is produced by this under-sink unit. Only a cold water line is connected to the unit, and an electric heating element provides the heat.

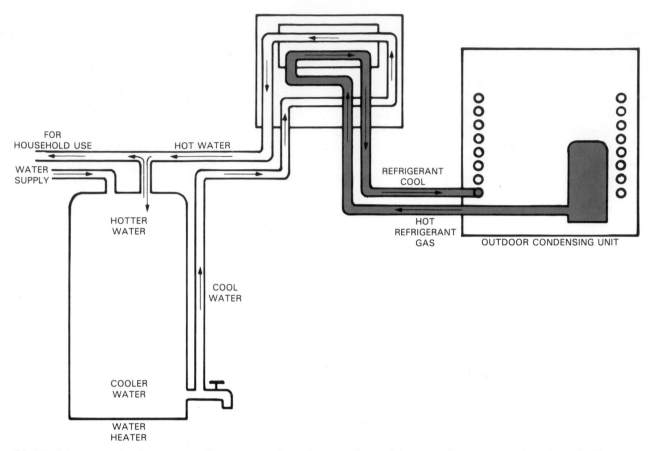

FOR
HOUSEHOLD USE

WATER
SUPPLY

HOT WATER

HOTTER
WATER

COOL
WATER

COOLER
WATER

WATER
HEATER

REFRIGERANT
COOL

HOT
REFRIGERANT
GAS

OUTDOOR CONDENSING UNIT

20-15 A hot water bank recovery unit uses waste heat from an air conditioner or a heat pump to heat household water.

heated from the waste heat of an air conditioner or a heat pump. The regular hot water heater is used as a backup system. Such a method can be used to heat up to 46 gallons of water per hour. It can also be adapted for use in cold weather.

Service Area Appliances

Refrigerators and freezers. The efficiency of refrigerators has improved over 58 percent in the last ten years. Increased efficiency has resulted from better insulation, more efficient cooling units, and improved air flow systems. Many new refrigerators contain energy saver switches to turn off the unit's humidity heaters during fairly dry weather. Humidity heaters prevent condensation during humid weather. Compressor units in new refrigerators are smaller and require less energy than those in older models, however they run for longer periods of time. New refrigerators require careful maintenance to run efficiently.

Freezers also have better insulation and more efficient cooling units. Chest type freezers have the most efficient design, because cold air goes to the bottom and not out the door. Freezers with manual defrost require less energy than self-defrosting models.

Ranges and ovens. Induction cooktops are the newest in energy efficient ranges, 20-16. The cooktops work by creating a heat current in any pan with a magnetic bottom. This type of unit saves energy because only the pan

and the food inside is heated; the stovetop itself remains cool. Also, no energy is wasted waiting for the unit to reach proper temperature. The heating unit automatically shuts off when the cooking utensil is removed from the surface.

Conventional electric and gas ovens are already about as energy efficient as possible. Electronic igniters are more efficient starters than pilot lights for gas ovens. Many new models feature electronic igniters. Self cleaning ovens contain more insulation and save energy because they hold heat better.

JENN-AIR

20-16 Induction cooking surfaces save energy because only the cooking utensil and food are heated.

Convection ovens use circulation fans to increase the efficiency of conventional ovens. They circulate hot air evenly to improve cooking results, and they use less energy because cooking time is reduced. Microwave ovens, 20-17, cook the food without heating the oven. They are far more efficient than conventional ovens.

Dishwashers. Energy Guide labels give a general indication of a dishwasher's efficiency. Special features help to decrease operating costs. Many models have a no heat drying option and cycles for small, lightly soiled loads that use less hot water. Some new models also have a delay start feature. This can be used to start the dishwasher during the night or other off-peak hot water use times.

Washers and dryers. Newer washing machines use less hot water to conserve energy. Models designed to use an automatic cold rinse are the most energy efficient. Some washers retain hot or warm wash water to reuse for later loads. Adjustable size cycles to fit the load size also help to conserve energy. Dryers should have solid state sensors so that they turn off automatically when clothes are dry. This prevents overdrying and energy waste.

ALTERNATIVE ENERGY SOURCES

In addition to conserving traditional energy resources, alternate sources are being developed for residential use. Two renewable sources—the sun and the wind—can be used as a private source of energy. Many homeowners have adapted solar energy for heating, and others have adapted wind to generate electricity.

Solar Energy

Solar energy can be used exclusively to heat a home in moderately cold weather. During very cold winter months, solar heating can be used to reduce the amount of heat supplied by a conventional system. Solar energy for active and passive heating has already been used successfully by many homeowners. The operation of active and passive solar heating is described in Chapter 19.

Solar heating systems help to conserve nonrenewable fuels. They use a resource that is inexhaustible and freely available. However, initial costs for installing solar heating systems are high. They must also have some kind of heat storage or auxiliary heating system for use when there is no sun.

Experiments are being conducted to harness solar energy for production of electricity. Solar One, an experimental solar energy house at the University of Delaware, has designed a successful solar electrical system. Their system uses a metal grid in which a current is activated by sunlight. This system is still too inefficient and expensive for widespread use. However, further research may produce systems that are practical for residential use.

Wind Energy

Wind can be harnessed to produce electricity by using a windmill. The Public Utilities Regulatory Policy Act of 1978 helps to make private use of windmills practical for

AMANA

20-17 Microwave ovens cook most foods using a fraction of the energy used by conventional methods.

the homeowner. This act requires power companies to supply auxiliary power to homes with windmill generators. It also requires power companies to buy extra power supplied over the homeowner's needs. This way, homeowners have an auxiliary power source during long periods without winds, and extra power produced during periods of strong winds is not wasted.

A good windmill can easily supply the electrical needs of an average home. However, the windmill must be very large to meet those needs. Cost is preventing the widespread use of windmills; the average windmill costs 3,000 dollars per kilowatt of capacity. Prices will probably be reduced with technological improvements and mass production.

Energy Management Through Computers

Computer systems can be used in the home to keep energy costs as low as possible. Already, computer chips have been added to appliances so that they turn off automatically when they are not being used. Computer controlled thermostats are also available. These can be programmed to automatically lower and raise the home's temperature as needed.

Computer systems can be used for total energy management. Programs are available to design the most energy efficient homes. These programs help the homeowner determine the optimum site orientation, window placement, and other factors to increase energy efficiency.

Within the home, a total energy management system can automatically roll shades up and down to admit sun or block out cold. The computer automatically turns lights on and off as people enter and leave rooms. Heating and cooling systems are adjusted to outdoor weather conditions for the most efficient use of heating and cooling energy. Water heaters may be turned on only as they are needed. The system also serves as a burglar alarm system for the home.

It is possible for computer systems to cut energy use by as much as 30 to 50 percent. However, to get high energy efficiency, the home must be designed with energy efficiency in mind. Most computer monitored homes use solar energy for heating and have special design features to increase the insulation level of the walls. Computer systems are still very expensive. They are not very widely used, but use is expected to increase in the future.

REVIEW QUESTIONS

1. How should a home in a northern state be oriented for maximum energy efficiency? How should a home in a southern state be oriented?
2. What kind of insulation has the best R-value? If the R-value of this kind of insulation is so good, why would other kinds be used?
3. Why would large windows be placed on the north side of a home? Why would they be placed on the south side?
4. What construction methods can be used to build roofs and walls that increase the energy efficiency of a home?
5. How can the energy efficiency of heating and plumbing systems be increased?
6. How can landscaping be used to increase the energy efficiency of a home?
7. How is an Energy Guide label used to determine the efficiency of an appliance?
8. What are some new features being added to appliances to make them more energy efficient?
9. What are some advantages and disadvantages of using solar energy for heat? What are some advantages and disadvantages of using wind power for electricity?
10. How can computers be used to increase the energy efficiency of a home?

21 Exterior Design

After studying this chapter, you will be able to:
■ Identify the distinguishing features of the traditional styles of homes.
■ Describe the designs of ranch and split level homes, and list their advantages and disadvantages.
■ Identify the main purpose of a contemporary design, and list its design features, advantages, and disadvantages.

A well designed home is attractive from the outside as well as the inside. Exterior design determines the style and mood that a home conveys from the outside. It also determines the basic layout and design of the home's interior. Architects and homeowners may choose a traditional, modern, or contemporary style for the exterior of their home. Today's residential homes may be exact replicas of one style, or they may contain elements from two or more styles.

American Indian

The first homes in America were built by the natives of the country. Each American Indian tribe used materials and a building style to fit the environment of their region. Some settlers who came to America patterned their new homes after native dwellings. The Navajos of the southwest lived in eight sided hogans made of logs and mud. The Seminole Indians of Florida lived in wood frame structures. These and other styles were borrowed from by the settlers.

21-1 The adobe home is still popular in warm, dry climates.

21-2 The Spanish style home, popular in the south, has a red tile roof and stucco walls.

Probably the most lasting adaptation of an Indian style home is the adobe home of New Mexico, 21-1. The Pueblo Indians still live in adobe buildings built as early as the 15th century. These structures are characterized by thick, smooth adobe walls, flat roofs, deep set windows, and rough pole beams projecting through the walls. The adobe homes are designed to stay cool in hot, dry weather.

The adobe home style was adapted by early southwest settlers. Many adobe homes are still used in the New Mexico area. Modern homes in the southwest are often designed to look like adobe homes, although modern building materials are used.

Spanish

Spanish style homes, 21-2, have been present in the southern part of North America since the late 1500's. They are characterized by white or tinted stucco walls and low pitched tile roofs. Mexican barrel tile and mission tile are most commonly used for the roof. The roofs have broad overhangs for shade. Colorful tile often paves the floors and surrounds doors and windows. Windows, doors, and colonades are arched and accented with wrought iron railings and grilles.

The Spanish style is also characterized by its exposed roof beams, balconies, and wide porches. Many homes are built to surround an inner patio or courtyard. These homes are most suited to warm, dry climates, such as those of the southwestern states.

Swedish

The log cabin was brought to America by the Swedish immigrants. It became a popular home for the early pioneers to the midwest. Log cabins are still used in some undeveloped, wooded areas. Log cabins are usually small, rectangular one-story homes with shingle-covered gable roofs. (Roof styles are pictured in Chapter 14.) Traditional windows were made of thin, oiled skins. Log cabins may be built with round or squared-off logs. The squared-off logs produce a smoother wall.

Dutch

Dutch Colonial homes are most common in northern states such as New York and Delaware. See 21-3. Dutch homes are usually constructed of field stone or brick, but they may be constructed of wood. The most notable feature of the Dutch home is the gambrel roof that flares out at the bottom and extends to cover an open porch. This flared eave is known as the "Dutch kick."

21-3 The Dutch colonial style is known for its gambrel roof and "Dutch kick."

Dutch Colonial homes are also characterized by a central entrance, a chimney that is not centered, windows with small panes, and dormers in the second story. (A *dormer* is a window set in a small projection from a slanted roof.) Some very early Dutch homes have high gable roofs with an extended roof covering a porch. The extended roof and porch area surrounds the house.

German

The first German American homes, built in Pennsylvania, are called *Pennsylvania Dutch Colonial* homes, 21-4. They are built of thick, fieldstone walls for warmth and easy maintenance. Many German homes have small roof ledges between the first and second floor called *pent* roofs. The pent roof and unsupported hood over the front entrance are distinguishing features of the Pennsylvania Dutch style.

French

Many American architectural styles have been influenced by the French. The earliest is the *French Normandy* style, brought by the Huguenots in the seventeenth

21-4 The Pennsylvania Dutch or German style home has thick stone walls and a partial roof between the first and second floor.

century. Many Norman cottages are rectangular with hip roofs, but others have gable roofs and a central turret, 21-5. The turret was originally used for grain storage. Eventually, the turret was used to house a staircase. French Normandy homes are usually 1 1/2 to 2 1/2 stories high, with brick, stone, or stucco walls. Often, a portion of the walls are half-timber for decoration. *Half-timber* walls have large, rough wood support beams with plaster or masonry filled in between.

The French plantation house is similar in style to the rectangular Norman cottage, except that the hip roof is extended into a very broad roof to cover a porch that surrounds the house. Many *French doors,* with large areas of paned glass, lead to the patio from all sides of the house. Later styles have the porch on the second floor, supported by posts or pillars. See 21-6. The French plantation house is most common in southern states.

The *Louisiana French* style originated in New Orleans, 21-7. One of its most outstanding features is a raised brick or stone basement to protect the house from floods. Balconies with lacy ironwork railings and white stucco walls are typical of the Louisiana French style. Hip roofs with two chimneys are also typical.

21-5 The French Normandy cottage is small and cozy. A central turret is often present.

21-6 An extended roof that covers a porch surrounding the entire house is the main feature of the French plantation house.

The French manor is a stately home more common in northern states, 21-8. Its most distinguishing feature is the *Mansard roof,* designed by a French architect named Mansard. The manors are rectangular and symmetrical with a wing on each side. The wings have dovecote roofs, while the main house has a Mansard roof with dormers. Walls

21-7 The Louisiana French style has a raised basement and a balcony with decorative ironwork.

are usually painted brick. Other French style homes include the one-story French cottage and the French city house. The French city house is notable for its second story windows that break the roof line, 21-9.

English

In the late 1500's, the Tudor style home was predominant in England, 21-10. Tudor homes are of half-timber

21-8 The French manor often has wings off the main house.

construction. They are usually two to three stories tall with an overhanging second story. Distinctive features include several gables on the roof and chimneys with many columns and decorative masonry. Many modern homes are patterned after Tudor manors, although modern building materials are used.

The *Elizabethan* style manor has both Gothic and Dutch influence, 21-11. Elizabethan manors are usually of stone, brick, or half-timber construction. They are usually two or three stories high, in an E shape or other irregular shape. Bay windows and recessed doorways in an arched frame are also typical.

21-9 Second story windows break the roofline of the French city house.

21-10 The Tudor mansion style is famous for its half-timber construction.

The *Cotswold Cottage* is another sixteenth century English style that gained popularity in twentieth century America. See 21-12. The name is derived from "cot" or cottage and "wold" or wood, meaning cottage in the wood. The style is distinguished by a compact size with a very steep gable roof. The design necessitates small, irregular shaped rooms, and it is usually necessary to walk through one room to get to another. Casement windows and recessed, arched doorways are common. Walls may be brick, stone, wood, half-timber, or a combination.

21-11 Decorative end gables are typical of the Elizabethan style manor.

21-12 The Cotswold cottage has a rambling floor plan.

English/Colonial

The earliest colonial homes were simple in design, sturdy, and fairly small. The *half-house* was the most common, 21-13. This house had only one main floor room with a tiny entrance and a steep stairway leading to an attic. A fireplace and chimney were placed on a side wall. Later, two room or *double houses* were built with two

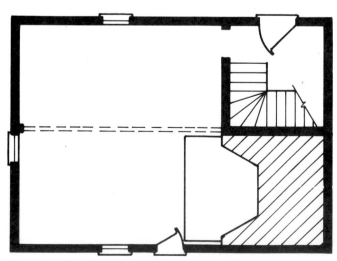

21-13 The half-house has one room on the main floor.

rooms on the main floor, 21-14. In these homes, the fireplace was centrally located.

The architectural styles of early homes were adapted from styles the colonists remembered from England. Typically borrowed features were steep, shingled roofs and brick or stone walls. Wood was used as a building material because it was so abundant.

The Salt Box

The salt box style home evolved by adding a lean-to structure to half and double houses, 21-15. The addition allowed extra space and protection from bitter winds common to New England winters. The home has a long roofline that slopes gently from the ridge to the eaves. The style is called salt box because the house is shaped like the boxes colonists used for storing salt.

The Garrison

The garrison style is noted for its overhanging second story, 21-16, borrowed from medieval English architecture. Corners of the overhang are decorated with hand carved brackets. Like other colonial homes, the garrison has a steep gable roof and a central fireplace. Walls are of narrow wood siding.

The overhanging second story can be seen in many modern adaptations of the garrison style. This feature has two main advantages. First, because there are separate corner posts for each floor, shorter, stronger posts can be used. Second, extra space may be added to the second level at little extra expense.

The Cape Cod

The Cape Cod is one of the best known examples of the traditional colonial styles. It is an outgrowth of the half-house and the double house. The Cape Cod home is a small cottage with a steep gable roof that has little overhang, 21-17. It usually has 1 or 1 1/2 stories with a central chimney. The walls may have narrow wood siding or split shingles. A central doorway and small paned windows are common. Later Cape Cod homes have dormers on the second floor. They also have shutters on all the windows. A variation of the Cape Cod, called the Cape Ann, features a larger central chimney and a gambrel roof. See 21-18.

Georgian

As the colonies prospered, more lavish homes were built. Architects and architectural plans from England became available in the colonies. Many homes during this time were built in the Georgian style. The Georgian house is symmetrical with simple exterior lines, 21-19. It is large and formal looking, with symmetrically placed windows. Georgian homes are usually 2 1/2 or 3 stories high, and a band of stone is often seen between stories.

Georgian homes usually have a high hip or gable roof with dormers. Some roofs have a flat area on top surrounded by an ornate railing called a balustrade. The main door, centrally located, has pilasters on either side and

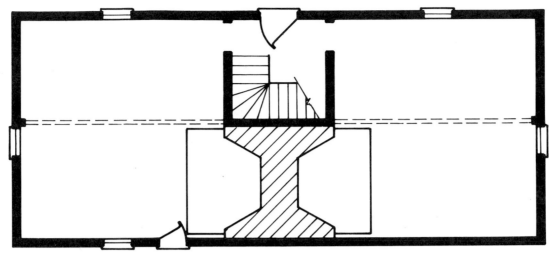

21-14 The double house has a second room added to double the size of the half-house.

21-15 The salt box style house has a long, sloping roof on one side.

21-18 The Cape Ann home has a gambrel roof.

21-16 An overhanging second story is the main feature of the garrison house.

a pediment above the door. Pediments may be scrolled, triangular, broken, or segmental. A large chimney is located at each end of the roof. Brick or wood siding is most common.

Later Georgian homes have side wings added to the main house, 21-20. A projecting section, or *pavilion,* topped by a large triangular pediment is added to the front of the home as well. The pavilion may be enclosed, or it may be an open patio area supported by columns.

21-17 The Cape Cod home is a small 1 1/2 story house with a gable roof and a central fireplace.

21-19 Early Georgian homes are large and rectangular. A band of stone between the first and second floor is a distinguishing feature.

21-20 Later Georgian homes have a pavillion in front of the main entrance and side wings.

Federal

The Federal style of architecture is a departure from English styles of the same period, 21-21. As a newly formed country, America wanted an official architectural style. Thomas Jefferson, an architect as well as a statesman, drew upon the classic forms of Greek and Roman architecture for a new style.

The Federal style added Greek and Roman features to the basic Georgian home. Typical features include Greek columns and a portico in front of the main entrance. Windows and doors often have pediments above them. Circular and semicircular fan lights above the main entrance are also common. Roofs are fairly flat, with balustrades along the entire roof edge.

21-21 The Federal style includes Greek and Roman features.

Greek Revival

During the Greek revival period, homes took on the classic proportions and ornamentations of Greek architecture, 21-22. Greek style homes are usually large and rectangular. The main design feature is a two story portico supported by Greek columns. The moderately sloped gable roof is placed so that the gable end faces forward, forming a triangular top. Construction may be of wood, brick, or stone, but the Greek style home is usually painted white.

Many government buildings in America are patterned after this style. The style is also popular in modern residential structures. Often, smaller Greek style homes do not have a portico, but pilasters are placed at the front corners of the house.

Southern Colonial

An outgrowth of the Greek revival style, the Southern Colonial style reflects the warmth, charm, and hospitality of the old south. See 21-23. The outstanding architectural features of the style are the front colonnade and the giant two-story portico. The extended portico shelters the front of the house from the hot sun. These homes are usually very large with upper and lower balconies.

Other features include three-story chimneys for bedroom fireplaces, a hip or gable roof, ornate woodwork, and wrought iron trim. A roof is often placed over the driveway to protect those entering at a side entrance.

21-22 The Greek revival style features a two-story portico supported by Greek columns.

Italianate

The Italianate style became popular in America in the 1830's. Borrowed from styles seen in Italian villas, the most outstanding feature of the style is a square tower at the top of the home, 21-24. The Italianate house has an upright appearance with tall, thin windows. A wide roof overhang with decorative brackets underneath is also typical. The city brownstone house was adapted from this style.

Victorian

After the Civil War, English influence returned to American architecture. The eclectic Victorian style home, named for Queen Victoria, became prevalent, 21-25. This style is marked by an overabundance of decorative trim, high porches, steep gabled roofs, tall windows, and towers. Scrolls and other decorative trim, called gingerbread, surround eaves, windows, and doors. Many Victorian houses are still in use today.

21-23 The southern colonial style is an outgrowth of the Greek revival.

21-24 A square tower tops the Italianate house.

21-25 The Victorian home features much intricate gingerbread work and a rambling floor plan.

The Ranch House

The ranch style structure is a long, low one-story building inspired by the ranchers' homes in the southwest, 21-26. The style was ideal for that region because of the informal lifestyle, open land areas, and warm climate. Now, it has been adapted to other climates as well.

Basic features of the ranch include a one-story design with no stairs, a low pitched, gable roof, and long, overhanging eaves. It is normally built on a concrete slab, but it may have a crawlspace or basement. The structure may be rectangular or in an irregular shape, such as "L," "T," "U," or "H." Modern ranch homes have large areas of window and sliding glass patio doors.

Variations of the ranch include the *hillside ranch* and the *raised ranch*. The hillside ranch is built on a hill so that part of the basement is exposed. The exposed area may be used for a garage or a living area with a panoramic view. The raised ranch, also called the split entry ranch, has part of the basement above ground, 21-27. This allows windows to be placed in basement walls.

The ranch style is ideal for indoor-outdoor living. The homes are comfortable and easily expanded. Outside maintenance tasks—such as painting, cleaning gutters, and replacing window screens—are not as difficult as with other styles. However, ranch homes are more expensive to build per square foot of living space than two story homes.

The Split Level House

The split level house is designed for a sloping or hilly site. The design takes advantage of what might otherwise prove to be a problem in elevation, 21-28. Most split level

THE GARLINGHOUSE CO.

21-26 The ranch home is on one level.

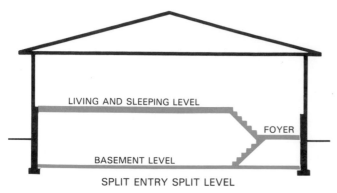

21-27 *Part of the basement is above the ground in a split entry or raised ranch.*

houses should not be built on flat lots, although some designs are used on flat land occasionally.

Efficient use of space is natural in the split level design. The general arrangement places the sleeping, living, and recreation areas of the house on different levels. Very little hall space is needed with the split level design.

The lowest level, called the *basement level,* generally serves as a basement, housing heating and cooling equipment, storage, and possibly a bath or work area. If a basement is not desired, a crawlspace area for maintenance and ventilation may be used. The basement level usually takes up 40 to 60 percent of the total space occupied by the house.

The second level of the house is the *intermediate level.* This area is at ground level, so the garage, recreation area, and foyer are usually placed here. The intermediate level may have a patio or terrace attached to it.

Slightly higher than the intermediate level is the *living level.* Due to the sloping site, this area is also at ground level. The kitchen, dining room, living room, and full or half bath are normally located on this level. The main entry and foyer may also be placed here, depending on the site and layout of the house. Patios, porches, and other outside living areas may also be an extension of this level.

21-28 *A split level home can help to maintain the natural setting of a sloping site.*

At the highest elevation is the *sleeping level,* housing the bedrooms and bath. Because the sleeping level is separated from the living level, it is private and quiet. This area of a split level house is similar to the second story of a two story house.

There are three main variations of the split level design—the side to side, the front to back, and the back to front, 21-29. Sites sloping from the left or right are best suited for the side to side design. Sites that are high in front and low in back are best for the front to back style. This house appears as a ranch from the front and as a two story house from the back. A lot that is low in front and high in back requires a back to front design. In this style, the living area is at the rear of the home.

Split level houses are natural solutions to building on hilly sites. They provide separation of functions within the house and require little hall space. However, they are frequently more expensive to build than two story or ranch homes because of the complicated construction. Even heating may also be difficult because of the different

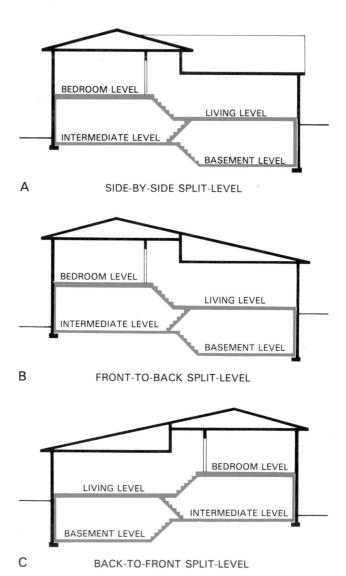

21-29 *The three main types of split level designs are: (A) side to side, (B) front to back, and (C) back to front.*

RED CEDAR SHINGLE AND HANDSPLIT SHAKE BUREAU

21-30 Non-traditional forms are used for contemporary designs.

RED CEDAR SHINGLE AND HANDSPLIT SHAKE BUREAU

21-31 Many contemporary homes are designed to harmonize with their surroundings.

levels. The use of zoned heating, with separate thermostats for different areas of the house, can help more even temperatures to be maintained.

Contemporary Designs

Contemporary designs are a departure from traditional housing styles and materials, 21-30. They are often experiments in solving modern housing challenges. Many need refinement because they are too individualistic or too narrowly conceived to be successful on a large scale. The trend is toward homes that complement the site and provide a feeling of openness while retaining privacy, 21-31. More attention is being given to the natural characteristics acting on or surrounding the structure.

Some of the earliest contemporary homes were built by Frank Lloyd Wright. His homes, built around the 1940's, departed from traditional styles to fit the changes that were taking place in family lifestyles. Frank Lloyd Wright homes are designed to blend well with their natural surroundings. Often, trees and other natural features of a site are incorporated into the design. Building materials are usually wood or stone, but other materials that blend with the site may also be present. Wright homes are also designed for efficiency, economy, and comfort.

Some other contemporary homes are built with the effect of environmental conditions in mind. These include domes, solar homes, and underground structures.

323

Geodesic Domes

The geodesic dome, developed by R. Buckminster Fuller, is an engineered system of triangular space frames that create self-reinforcing roof and wall units based on mathematically precise divisions of a sphere. See 21-32. The triangular space frames are generally factory assembled and then bolted together on site to form the finished structure. This design has been described as the most efficient system of structuring yet developed for housing.

The dome design reduces the quantity of building materials needed per square foot of usable area by about 30 percent of the amount needed for conventional structures. Heat loss is also reduced because of the home's reduced amount of exposed surface.

No interior or exterior support systems, such as walls or beams, are needed because a dome structure is self-supporting, 21-33. This provides great flexibility for interior floor plan designs. Other advantages include flexible interior decoration, structural superiority, low cost, and reduced energy needs. Manufactured domes are produced in one story and two story structures, with or without basements, 21-34. Conventional roofing materials such as asphalt shingles or cedar shakes are used to weatherproof the exterior.

HEXADOME OF AMERICA, INC. — NIKKIE ARCHITECTURE

21-33 Because of the special construction of the geodesic dome, no support beams or walls are needed.

HEXADOME OF AMERICA, INC. — NIKKIE ARCHITECTURE

21-32 The geodesic dome is constructed of several triangular wall pieces.

324

21-34 Geodesic domes are available in (A) one story structures and (B) two story structures.

TOM GUSSEL

21-35 Xanadu was built by spraying polyurethane foam in a giant inflated balloon. The finished dome structure is strong enough to support 6 inches of snow covering the entire roof.

Foam Domes

Another type of dome is built from polyurethane foam. The foam house not only uses new materials, but new concepts for building and design as well. One such house is called "Xanadu," 21-35. A foam house can be built in weeks at about half the cost per square foot of conventional homes. Foam homes are 40 to 60 percent more energy efficient than conventional homes.

Foam domes are built by spraying the walls of an inflated polyurethane balloon with polyurethane foam. Once the walls are dry (within a few hours) the balloon is peeled off leaving a dome structure. A series of domes — with the same or varying diameters — may be built and adjoined to form a house.

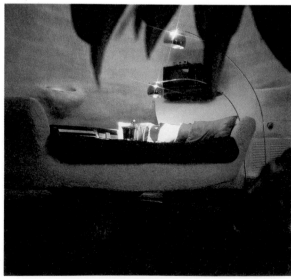

TRUMBLE PHOTOGRAPHY

21-36 Furniture and stairwells may be custom formed by spraying polyurethane over wire mesh forms.

Windows and doors may be placed anywhere by cutting a hole in the wall and foaming them in place. Wire mesh forms may be covered with polyurethane to form eaves, stairways, and furniture, 21-36. The interior walls are then coated with a fireproofing substance. They may also be painted with white or colored paint. The exterior walls must be painted with a special paint that filters out ultraviolet rays because polyurethane deteriorates in sunlight.

Because foam products are such good insulators and foam homes contain no gaps in construction, the domes are extremely energy efficient. Also, like the geodesic dome, the foam dome has less surface area per square foot of living space than conventional homes. Xanadu is heated and cooled using three heat pumps so that hot or cold air can be recycled efficiently. One pump is located in the living room, 21-37. Passive solar heat and wind generated electricity are used in the home as well.

The domes offer ease in designing a home to fit the lifestyle and tastes of any homeowner. Floor plans may be determined by cutting out circles proportionate to the size of rooms desired, and these are simply arranged until a suitable arrangement is found. No walls or supports are needed since the dome structure is self-reinforcing. However, walls can be built if desired. Two-story domes can be built using normal structural support for the second story.

The foam home does have some disadvantages. Some people find the rounded structure too unusual for everyday living. Also, some types of polyurethane are considered fire hazards. Even if they are fireproofed, they are not accepted as above ground building materials in some areas. One type of fireproof foam has been developed using silica sand.

Since polyurethane is oil based, there is also fear that the cost of building such structures will increase. However,

TRUMBLE PHOTOGRAPHY

21-37 The heating and cooling system for the living room in Xanadu is hidden in a tree. A heat pump is in the trunk, and the branches serve as ducts. Air is pumped out the branches, circulated throughout the house, and returned through the trunk.

AMERICAN SOLAR HOMES, INC.

21-39 A passive solar home has large areas of glass on the south side of the home.

research is being conducted to develop a foam based on a byproduct of copper mining. The new product would be fire resistant and less expensive than polyurethane foam.

Solar Homes

Although both active and passive solar energy may be used to heat any kind of home, a true solar home has special design features for maximum energy efficiency. The homes may use an active solar heating system, 21-38, but passive solar heating is a predominant feature. The orientation and construction of the home are planned so that weather conditions can be used to the home's advantage.

The most noticeable feature of solar homes are the large areas of glass on the south side of the house, 21-39. Often,

greenhouses are placed on one or more sides. Insulating glass is used for window areas, and shutters are often present to keep heat in at night.

Many areas inside the solar home may be designed to collect and store heat for times when sun is not present, 21-40. Masonry floors and walls serve as collectors. Large

AMERICAN SOLAR HOMES, INC.

21-40 Masonry floors are often used in solar homes to collect warmth from the sun.

21-38 Solar panels may be placed on solar or regular homes for active solar heating.

TERRY FURST, NATUREWOOD HOMES AND DOMES

21-41 Underground homes are usually built into the side of a hill with the southern wall exposed.

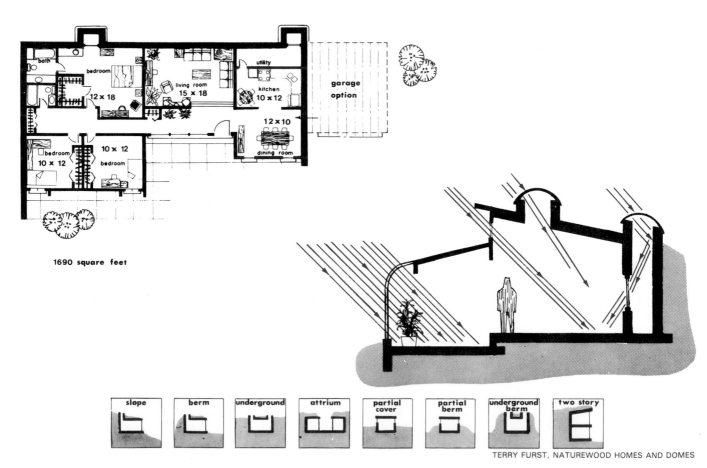

1690 square feet

TERRY FURST, NATUREWOOD HOMES AND DOMES

21-42 The interior of an underground home can receive natural light through skylights or windows on an exposed upper portion of a wall.

barrels of water may also be used. Insulated earth beneath the home also stores heat.

Spaces for air infiltration are kept to a minimum in solar homes. A double wall construction with an air space between the walls is used. This forms an envelope that acts as a natural heating and cooling system. Air between the walls is circulated throughout the house. Vestibules are placed in front of frequently used doors so that outside air cannot enter when doors are opened. On the north side of the home, closets are located against exterior walls. Earth berms are usually placed along the sides of the home that receive the most wind.

Individual heating zones are used so that energy powered heat is used only where it is necessary. Solar homes often have their own hot water system, heated by solar power. An active solar heater may be used for additional space and water heating.

The solar home design is most effective in areas that receive much sunshine. Proper orientation on the site must be possible as well. Data on the effectiveness of solar homes are available from the U.S. Department of Energy.

Underground Structures

One of the newest contemporary designs is the underground or earth sheltered home, 21-41. Increasing costs of fuel and electricity have provided the motivation to locate homes underground. Modern building technology and new materials have made this approach a viable solution to lowering heating costs.

The earth sheltered home stays at a more constant temperature than homes above ground. This is because the ground temperature remains around 55°F year-round. The exterior temperature above ground may fluctuate by as much as 100°F in one year. The more constant temperature of the earth makes it easier to heat or cool an underground home.

Most underground homes are built into the side of a hill so that the south wall of the home is exposed. This wall generally has large areas of window for solar heating. The tops of other walls are usually exposed enough to allow windows for natural lighting in most rooms, 21-42. The top of the home is covered with a layer of earth.

Underground homes must be constructed to resist tremendous earth pressures and ground moisture. As a result, the initial cost may be slightly higher than the cost of a conventional structure. Also, a proper site — the southern side of a hill — may not always be available. There

may also be problems with building codes and with finding builders and loan companies willing to work with this type of structure.

There are, however, several advantages to underground homes. Heating and cooling costs are greatly reduced. The site remains more natural, and there is more room for landscaping, gardening, and activities in the yard. Little exterior maintenance is required. The concrete structure is safer than traditional homes from fire, tornadoes, and burglars. Also, the interior of the home is quiet and private.

REVIEW QUESTIONS

1. What are some distinguishing architectural features of a Spanish style home?
2. How does a Dutch house differ from a Pennsylvania Dutch house?
3. Name three styles of homes influenced by the French. What are their distinguishing architectural features?
4. What is the difference between the half-house, the double house, and the salt box house?
5. What is the most outstanding feature of the garrison house? What advantages are there to this architectural style?
6. What are the main architectural features of the Cape Cod home? How does a Cape Ann home differ from a Cape Cod home?
7. What are the main features of the Georgian style house? How does this style compare to the Federal, Greek Revival, and Southern Colonial styles?
8. What is the most outstanding feature of the Italianate style?
9. What are some advantages of a ranch home? Are there any disadvantages?
10. What areas are placed on the different levels of the split level home? What are the advantages and disadvantages of this style?
11. How is a geodesic dome constructed? What advantages are there to this type of construction?
12. How is a foam dome constructed? What advantages and disadvantages are there to this type of house?
13. What are the major construction features of a solar home? Do all solar homes have active solar heating systems?
14. What are the advantages and disadvantages of an underground structure?

22 Landscaping

After studying this chapter, you will be able to:
- Describe physical factors outside the house which affect housing choices.
- List the main characteristics and functions of grass, ground covers, trees, shrubs, and vines.
- Name and describe other types of elements within a landscape, and explain why they might be used.
- List the activities required to plan a landscape.
- Evaluate the quality of a landscape according to the elements and principles of design.

The purpose of landscaping is to create a personal, pleasant, and functional environment. It is more than merely selecting and arranging plants. A good landscape provides privacy, comfort, beauty, and ease of maintenance, 22-1. Elements such as paths, fences, walls, and architectural structures may be used in the landscape. Good landscaping requires thoughtful planning so that the elements are used to create a pleasant, usable environment.

LANDSCAPE PLANTS

Plants in the landscape are as important to the exterior design scheme as any piece of furniture or artwork is to interior design. Plants are decorative, but they have functional purposes as well. They provide protection from winds and reduce glare from the sun. They help to shield street noise and provide privacy. Plants act as natural air filters by absorbing pollutants and providing oxygen. They also provide a habitat for birds and animals.

IBG INTERNATIONAL

22-1 A good landscape is attractive, functional, and easy to maintain.

330

22-2 This lawn grass, called St. Augustine carpet grass, has been scientifically improved. It is a warm climate grass that grows well in full sun to heavy shade.

Any plant must be suited to its environment to grow well. Plants may be indigenous to the area or they may be imported. In planning a landscape, it is important to know the care requirements of plants chosen. Popular landscape plants may be classified according to how they are used in a landscape. The main catagories are grasses, ground covers, trees, shrubs, and vines.

Grasses

Both the leaves and stems of grasses grow from the bottom up. This makes them well-suited to lawns because they can be cut repeatedly without dying. Although there are over 5,000 members of the grass family, only a few are suitable for lawns. Some types have been improved in the laboratory so that they are far more resistant to disease and wear than they were originally, 22-2.

The most important factor in choosing a lawn grass is tolerance for a given climate. There are three main catagories of grasses used in North America: *warm climate grasses, cool climate grasses,* and *dry land grasses.* See 22-3 for a list of the most popular varieties for each climate region.

Ground Covers

Ground covers may be defined as low, thick foliage used in place of grass. They vary in texture and color, 22-4. Some types are evergreen while others are deciduous. Many types grow where grass may not grow well—in dense shade, rocky patches, or gullies. Ground covers do not require much maintenance. They help to prevent erosion, control weeds, and reduce soil temperatures and loss of ground moisture during periods of extreme heat.

Ground covers are frequently used in shady areas or in spots where mowing would be difficult. This would include odd shaped or narrow spots and steep banks. Beneath evergreens, ground covers act as mulches. Ground covers also can be used as a foreground for a shrubbery border.

Ground covers should be chosen to fit the area where they will be used. Their height and spreading ability should be suitable. Some types need full sun or full shade to survive; others will grow under any lighting conditions. Moisture and richness of soil are other factors to consider. Some of the most popular ground cover plants and their important characteristics are identified in 22-5.

Trees

Trees fulfill several purposes. They may have beautiful form, foliage, or flowers. They may provide shade or shelter from the wind. Some trees provide fruit. Most trees give height to the appearance of the landscape.

LAWN GRASSES		
WARM-CLIMATE GRASSES		
Common Name	**Sun Conditions**	**Propogation**
Bermuda Grass	Full sun	Sprigs or plugs
Carpet Grass	Full sun to light shade	Plugs or seed
Centipede Grass	Full sun to light shade	Sprigs or seed
St. Augustine Grass	Full sun to heavy shade	Sprigs
Zoysia Grass	Full sun to dense shade	Sprigs or plugs
COOL-CLIMATE GRASSES		
Kentucky Bluegrass	Full sun	Seeds
Perennial Rye Grass	Full sun to partial shade	Seeds
Red Fescue	Full sun to shade	Seeds
Redtop Grass	Full sun to light shade	Seeds
Tall Fescue	Full sun to shade	Seeds
DRY-LAND GRASSES		
Buffalo Grass	Full sun	Plugs
Colonial Bent Grass	Full sun	Seeds

Fig. 22-3 Various types of grasses are available to grow well in any environment.

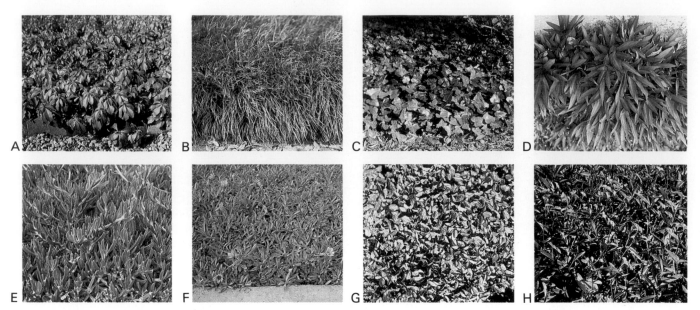

22-4 *Ground covers are available in a variety of textures. Shown are some common ground covers: (A) Pachysandra, (B) Mondo Grass, (C) English Ivy, (D) Creeping Lily Turf, (E) Hottentot Fig, (F) Trailing Gazinia, (G) Ajuga, and (H) Moses-in-the-cradle.*

As a landscape element, trees may be used in several ways. For example, groups of trees may be used to contrast a large, open area. A dense grouping of trees may be used to form a background for a home, 22-6. Individual trees serve as focal points.

Trees vary in their shape, form, and texture. They may be catagorized into five main groups: native deciduous trees, flowering or ornamental trees, narrow leaved evergreen trees, broad leaved evergreen trees, and palms.

Native deciduous trees. These trees are species that grow naturally in a given area. They are some of the best suited trees for the climate and soil conditions where they grow naturally. Some of the most popular types are shown in 22-7 along with their adult size and their geographic location. Many deciduous trees have spectacular foliage in the fall, 22-8.

Ornamental trees. Ornamental trees have some outstanding characteristic that makes them focal points

GROUND COVER PLANTS

NAME	LIGHTING REQUIREMENTS	TYPE AND USE
Baby's Tears	Shade	Perennial, base of trees
Bearberry	Sun to partial shade	Evergreen, banks
Blue Leadwort	Shade	Perennial, under trees
Blue Phlox	Partial shade	Perennial, under trees
Candytuft	Sun	Evergreen, banks and foreground
Carpet Bugle	Sun to shade	Perennial, banks and borders
Crown Vetch	Sun	Perennial, banks
Dichondra	Sun to shade	Perennial, between stones
English Ivy	Shade	Evergreen vine, under trees
Forget-me-not	Partial shade	Perennial, moist areas
Ground Morning Glory	Sun	Perennial vine, slopes and beds
Lemon Thyme	Sun	Perennial, among rocks
Lily-of-the-Valley	Shade	Perennial, border
Pachysandra	Partial shade	Evergreen, under trees
Periwinkle or Myrtle	Shade	Evergreen vine, under trees
Prostrate Juniper	Sun	Evergreen, banks and edges
Rosea Ice Plant	Sun	Perennial, steep banks
Snow-in-Summer	Sun to light shade	Perennial, edge of beds
Stone Crops	Sun or partial shade	Perennial succulent, beds
Strawberry Geranium	Shade	Evergreen, small areas
Sweet Fern	Sun	Perennial, banks
Waukegan Juniper	Sun	Evergreen, banks and edges

22-5 *Many ground covers can be used in areas where grass does not grow well. They also add interest and texture to a landscape.*

22-6 Large deciduous trees form a pleasing background for a home, and they provide late afternoon shade.

within a landscape. They may have a special shape, leaf color, or blossom, 22-9. Flowering trees usually bear blossoms for a short period of time each year.

Some ornamental trees are native while others are imported. Care should be taken to select a tree compatible with the climate and soil conditions of the landscape. Some popular flowering trees are listed in 22-10.

Narrow leaved evergreen trees. Narrow leaved evergreens have needles rather than leaves. They furnish color and mass year round. Species include fir, hemlock, spruce, cedar, and pine. Northern climates have a broad variety of native narrow leaved evergreens. (Broad leaved evergreens are more common in southern climates.)

Although narrow leaved evergreens are available in several heights, they usually have one of three main

NATIVE DECIDUOUS TREES

Name	Height	Spread	Geographic Location
American Elm	150 ft.	100 ft.	North central
Bald Cypress	150	50	Maryland to Louisiana
Basswood	90	60	All except Gulf coast
Black Walnut	100	75	Midwest
English Maple	40	50	Northeast and Northwest
Hickory	100	75	Eastern half of the country
Honey Locust	75	50	Most of the country
Northern Red Oak	75	50	All except Gulf coast
Sourwood	40	25	Northeast and Northwest
Sugar Maple	125	75	Northern Midwest
Sweet Gum	75	30	Southeast and West
Sycamore	100	75	All except Northeast

22-7 Each geographic location of the United States has native deciduous trees.

22-8 Fall brings flamboyant color to this deciduous maple tree.

333

22-9 *The flowering quince bears bright blossoms in early spring, making it a popular ornamental tree.*

ORNAMENTAL TREES

Name	Height	Spread	Outstanding Characteristics
Bloodleaf Japanese Maple	15 ft.	15 ft.	Star-shaped red leaves
Crab Apple	30	25	Bright blooms and colorful fruit
Crape Myrtle	20	15	White, pink, red, lavender flowers
Eastern Redbud	30	25	Pink-to-white flowers in spring
Flowering Cherry	35	25	Profuse blooms in spring
Flowering Dogwood	30	25	White or pink flowers
Hardy Silk Tree	35	35	Fluffy pink blossoms
Mountain Ash	35	20	Clusters of red berries
Saucer Magnolia	25	20	5 to 10 inch cup-shaped blooms
Star Magnolia	20	15	3 to 4 inch white, fragrant blooms

22-10 *An ornamental tree may have an unusual shape, leaf, or flower.*

NARROW-LEAVED EVERGREEN TREES

Name	Basic Shape	Mature Height
Blue Atlas Cedar	Broad Conical	60 ft.
Canada Hemlock	Broad Conical	50
Colorado Spruce	Broad Conical	40
Eastern White Pine	Broad Conical	60
Norfolk Island Pine	Broad Conical	50
White Fir	Broad Conical	50
Carolina Hemlock	Narrow Conical	25 ft.
Douglas Arborvitae	Narrow Conical	30
Incense Cedar	Narrow Conical	50
California Incense Cedar	Columnar	50 ft.
Italian Cypress	Columnar	50
Irish Yew	Columnar	12
Yew Podocarpus	Columnar	20

22-12 *A wide variety of narrow leaved evergreens are native to northern states.*

shapes, 22-11. The *broad conical* shape tapers gradually from a wide base to a single erect stem. This is the shape of the traditional Christmas tree. Broad conical trees are best displayed as individual plants, so they should have plenty of space to develop. *Narrow conical evergreens* taper sharply from base to tip. They are compact and will fit into small areas. Narrow conical trees are usually placed in small groups.

Columnar evergreens have nearly vertical branches. They taper only slightly at the top. These are useful for lining a drive or defining a boundary. Varieties of narrow leaved evergreens are shown in 22-12.

A   B   C

22-11 *The three main shapes of narrow leaved evergreen trees are (A) broad conical, (B) narrow conical, and (C) columnar.*

FLORIDA DEPARTMENT OF CITRUS

22-13 Many types of broad leaved evergreen trees may be used as accent plants in a landscape. Two examples are (A) citrus and (B) sea grape.

BROAD-LEAVED EVERGREEN TREES

Name	Mature Height	Outstanding Characteristics
American Holly	60 ft.	Bright red berries in the fall
Brazilian Pepper Tree	30	Fragrant berries
Camphor Tree	50	Dense foliage
Citrus (Orange, Lemon, etc.)	25	Fragrant blossoms and edible fruit
Common Olive	25	Silvery, green willow-like leaves
Eucalyptus	75	Fragrant leaves and attractive bark
Live Oak	60	Great size and breadth
Southern Magnolia	90	Fragrant blossoms up to 12" across
Sweet Bay	50	Fragrant white blossoms
Weeping Bottlebrush	25	Bright red blossoms in summer

22-14 Broad leaved evergreens are commonly native to southern states.

Broad leaved evergreen trees. These plants appear very different from the narrow leaved evergreens. They grow in many shapes. Some are noted for their fragrant blossoms while others produce colorful berries, 22-13. Most broad leaved evergreens are not hardy in colder climates. They are confined to warmer areas of the country.

Broad leaved evergreens may serve a variety of purposes in the landscape. Some of the larger trees like the southern magnolia provide good shade and serve as an accent when they blossom. Others, like the weeping bottlebrush, are pleasant along a driveway or property border. Citrus trees provide fruit. They may also be used as accent or background plants. Popular broad leaved evergreens are listed in 22-14.

Palms. Palms have a limited geographical range, but they can be dramatic elements of a landscape, 22-15. Palms are generally found throughout most of California, parts of the southwest, and in Gulf coast states including Florida and Hawaii. Most palms have a single trunk that is straight or slightly curved, but some grow in clumps. Leaf shapes vary from broad fans to feather-like fronds. Some popular palms are identified in 22-16.

Shrubs

Shrubs form the intermediate plantings between trees and grasses or ground covers. They are available in a wide range of color and foliage. They may be used as hedges, 22-17, to function just as a wall or fence would function. They may also be used as singular focal points, group

22-15 The blossom clusters of the Queen Palm (A) give the tree a unique appearance. The Coconut Palm (B) is more familiar in appearance.

PALMS

Name	Height	Outstanding Characteristics
Butterfly Palm	30 ft.	Many stems and fragrant flowers
Date Palm	30	Grows in clumps
Lady Palm	5	Reedy stems with broad leaves
Queen Palm	40	Straight trunk with broad crown

22-16 Palms are generally found in southern coastal states.

plantings, or background plants. Few plant groups are as versatile as shrubs. Shrubs fall into three broad catagories: *deciduous, narrow leaved evergreen,* and *broad leaved evergreen.*

Deciduous shrubs. Like deciduous trees, deciduous shrubs lose their leaves in the winter. Some types turn bright colors in the fall. Examples are the dwarf burning bush and the smoke bush. However, the main attraction of most deciduous shrubs is their spectacular spring and summer blossoms, 22-18. These include varieties such as the forsythia, rose of sharon, flowering quince, and lilac. Popular deciduous shrubs are listed in 22-19.

Narrow leaved evergreen shrubs. These shrubs have needles instead of leaves. Their three most common shapes are upright, spreading, and creeping, 22-20. Upright evergreens have closely spaced stems that form a curved outline without pruning. Various types may reach heights from 3 to 10 feet. Spreading evergreens grow out as well as up, broadening at the top. Both upright and spreading shrubs are frequently used as foundation plants around a home.

Creeping evergreen shrubs spread horizontally. They are low to the ground and may be used as taller ground covers. They may also be grown individually as low bushes lining paths or in front of homes. Types of narrow leaved evergreen shrubs are presented in 22-21.

Broad leaved evergreen shrubs. These shrubs bear leaves, not needles, and do not lose their leaves seasonally. A wide variety of shrubs are in this group, 22-22. Some species are grown primarily for their flowers, such as the

A   B

22-18 The Azalea (A) and the Spreading Cotoneaster (B) are examples of two flowering deciduous shrubs.

DECIDUOUS SHRUBS

Name	Height	Outstanding Characteristics
Azalea	10 ft.	Colorful blossoms
Bridalwreath Spirea	5	Clusters of small flowers
Cranberry Cotoneaster	3	Prostrate branches
Dwarf Burning Bush	3	Bright red leaves in fall
Flowering Quince	5	Spectacular early blossoms
Forsythia	8	Bright yellow flowers in spring
Hydrangea	5	Large flower clusters
Lilac	15	Fragrant flower clusters
Privet	15	Hedge plant with bright green leaves
Rhododendron	4	Brilliant blossoms
Rose of Sharon	10	Flowers late in fall
Smokebush	15	Plumelike redish purple blossoms
Tree Peony	5	Large colorful flowers
Viburnum	8	Fragrant blossoms

22-19 Many deciduous shrubs flower or turn colors seasonally.

22-17 Shrubs can be used as hedges to provide privacy.

22-20 The three common forms of narrow leaved shrubs are (A) upright: Mugo Pine, (B) spreading: Spreading Juniper, and (C) creeping: Wilton Carpet Juniper.

NARROW-LEAVED EVERGREEN SHRUBS

Name	Basic Shape	Mature Height
Globe Aborvitae	Upright	3 ft.
Japanese Plum Yew	Upright	8
Mugo Pine	Upright	10
Sargent's Weeping Hemlock	Upright	15
Tanyosho Pine	Upright	10
Chinese Juniper	Spreading	4 ft.
Hick's Yew	Spreading	16
Pfitzer Juniper	Spreading	6
Salvin Juniper	Spreading	6
Japanese Garden Juniper	Creeping	2 ft.
Wilton Carpet Juniper	Creeping	1

22-21 Several varieties of narrow leaved evergreen shrubs are grown in the United States.

camellia, rhododendron, azalea, and Japenese andromeda. Others have brightly colored leaves, such as the gold dust tree, croton, and Chinese sacred bamboo.

Because broad leaved evergreen shrubs are generally unique, they are usually planted individually or with ample spacing for visual impact. Several common broad leaved evergreen shrubs are listed in 22-23.

Vines

Vines are decorative and functional in a landscape design, 22-24. Many vines have large clusters of flowers that attract attention. Others have leaves with interesting shapes. Vines may be used to reduce the monotony of a large expanse of wall. They may be trained on a trellis. Vines can dress up a plain fence or provide shade in an arbor. Some vines used in landscaping are listed in 22-25.

OTHER LANDSCAPE ELEMENTS

Items other than plants can be used to make the landscape more unified and functional. A good landscape plan is organized so that several areas are provided for different functions. These spaces may be connected with garden paths, walks, and steps. Areas may be separated with banks, walls, and fences. Patios, decks, or paved game areas may be a part of the landscape. A decorative pool or fountain may be a focal point.

22-22 A wide variety of shrubs are catagorized as broad leaved evergreens. Some examples are: (A) Camelia, (B) Croton, (C) Hibiscus (yellow flower), (D) Hibiscus (pink flower), (E) Flaming Ixora, (F) Natal Plum, and (G) Plumeria.

BROAD-LEAVED EVERGREEN SHRUBS

Name	Height	Outstanding Characteristics
Camellia	10 ft.	Beautiful flowers
Chinese Sacred Bamboo	4	Colorful foliage
Croton	6	Great diversity in leaf shape and color
Elizabeth Azalea	4	Abundant flowers
Everestianum Catawba Rododendron	6	Impressive floral display
Gardenia	5	Fragrant blossoms
Gold-Dust Tree	10	Green and yellow foliage
Hibiscus	6	Large colorful flowers
Ixora, Flaming	6	Clusters of bright blossoms (red, white, pink, orange)
Japanese Andromeda	5	Abundant flowers
Japanese Fatsia	6	Glossy fan-shaped leaves
Japanese Pittosporum	10	Leathery green leaves
Lemon Bottlebrush	10	Many-stamened red flowers
Loquat	15	Clusters of flowers and edible fruit
Mountain Laurel	6	Large clusters of pink and white flowers
Natal Plum	6	Shiny green leaves with fragrant white flowers
Oleander	12	Fragrant flowers
Sweet Viburnum	8	Fragrant white blossoms

22-23 Broad-leaved evergreen shrubs are frequently used as focal points in a landscape.

VINES

Name	Length	Outstanding Characteristics
Bougainvillea	15-25 ft.	Clusters of bright flowers
Carolina Jasmine	25-30	Fragrant, tubelike yellow flowers
Chinese Wisteria	to 40	Fragrant clusters of purple flowers
Clematis	6-15	Beautiful flowers
Climbing Hydrangea	to 75	Spectacular white flowers
Honeysuckle	15-20	Fragrant flowers
Trumpet Vine	25-30	Clusters of orange to red flowers

22-25 Several varieties of vines are available for landscaping.

Paths, Walks, and Steps

A garden path can be an effective landscaping tool. Its obvious purpose is to connect one area with another and to provide a walking area within a garden. However, it also provides a natural break in the landscape. If a path borders flower beds or a lawn, it adds interest to the design of the landscape, 22-26. Curved paths may be used to break the straight lines of a rectangular site.

A path should be at least 3 feet wide to allow room for work tools. Informal materials such as loose stone, wood

22-24 Shown are three different types of vines: (A) Star Jasmine, (B) Bougainvillea, and (C) Eleagnus.

22-26 A path can act as a garden border and add interest to the landscape design.

22-27 Large, flat flagstone can be used to give a garden path an interesting pattern and texture.

22-28 Walks are more formal and permanent than paths; masonry is a common construction material for walks.

chips, or laid flagstones separated by grass are common materials used for paths, 22-27.

Walks are more formal and permanent than paths, but they fulfill the same function. A walk should be at least 4 1/2 feet wide so that two people can walk side by side comfortably. Materials used for walks include concrete, asphalt, masonry paving, or planks, 22-28. These materials are more expensive and more difficult to lay than materials used for paths. Masonry walks are the most expensive followed by concrete and then asphalt. Walks made from wood vary in cost depending on the type of construction and wood used.

Steps are used in paths and walks when the elevation changes too rapidly to use an incline. They are usually constructed of the same material used for the path or walk, 22-29. The steps should be safe; materials should be secured and lighting for night should be provided.

Texture, appearance, and maintenance are considerations when choosing materials for paths, walks, or steps. Rough textures produce an interesting, but less formal look than smooth textures. Rough textures should be avoided, however, if small children will use the walk or path frequently for play. The appearance of materials their patterns and colors—should blend with the rest of the landscape and with the home's exterior design. Materials should be chosen that will maintain their appearance over time. Some materials require more maintenance than others. They may show wear or dirt more easily. Grass or weeds may grow between or through the materials and need removal.

Banks, Walls, and Fences

These elements are used to separate areas of the landscape. Gently sloping banks form a natural separation be-

22-29 Steps are generally made of the same material as the walk or path. This walk is constructed from patterned concrete designed to simulate brick.

22-30 *Plants covering steep banks add interest and help to prevent erosion.*

wall. Open walls, also called screens, allow a light breeze to pass through but form a definite boundary.

Landscape walls can be built from a variety of materials. Concrete, masonry, and wood are common, 22-31. Solid masonry and concrete walls are rigid and require a foundation. Wood walls are supported on posts so no foundation is needed. In some areas, movement associated with freezing and thawing of the ground can destroy rigid walls. Flexible walls built from crossties, pieces of broken concrete, or large, flat stones are durable in these areas.

Appearance, durability, and cost are factors to consider when choosing wall materials. Materials should blend well with other elements of the site. They should also be durable. Concrete and masonry are very durable materials. Pressure treated wood will also last many years. Any material chosen should be able to withstand local conditions. Cost should also be considered when choosing materials. Walls with poured foundations are more expensive to build than other types of walls.

Fences are generally less formal, less expensive, and less permanent than walls. Like walls, they may be used to define boundaries, provide protection and privacy, and block sun and wind. Fences help to contain children or pets within a yard. In many communities, fences are required around swimming pools to protect children and nonswimmers. The design of a fence may be limited depending on its function. Fences used simply for definition of boundaries may be very decorative. Fences for safety are generally less decorative, but variation is possible, 22-32.

tween two levels. The banks may be covered with lawn grass. Steeper banks may be used for more pronounced changes in elevation. A ground cover, stones, wood beams, or a retaining wall may be used to maintain the bank and prevent erosion, 22-30. Plants may be used on the bank to add interest.

Walls are strong, permanent structures that serve as boundaries, enclose an area, and provide privacy. Low, wide walls can divide an area and provide seating. High walls are used for privacy. Walls may be solid or open. An example of an open wall is a pierced concrete block

Patios, Decks, and Game Areas

Patios and decks are often used for relaxation or entertainment areas. Patios are usually constructed of concrete or masonry, 22-33. They are level with the ground. Decks are placed above ground. They are most often constructed of pressure treated wood, 22-34. A deck is useful on hilly areas to provide an even surface. Patios and decks should be large enough for patio furniture to be spaced comfortably. If a patio or deck area will be used frequently for entertaining, it should be large enough for guests to move freely.

22-31 *Stone and wood are common materials for walls.*

CALIFORNIA REDWOOD ASSN.

BILL WHETSTONE, GREATER DETROIT LANDSCAPING

22-32 Interesting materials may be used for functional fences.

Depending on the size of a landscape, a permanent area for games may be desirable. A less formal game area may simply be a large, level lawn area with no trees or plants. A dirt or sand area may suffice for such games as volleyball or horseshoes. Formal courts for tennis, basketball, or other sports may be built of concrete or asphalt. When planning a game area, clearance space around the court should be included to prevent injuries or interference with the game. Suggested areas for various games are listed in 22-35.

Pools and Fountains

Sparkling water has an almost universal appeal. Pools and fountains have been a part of landscape designs for centuries. They may be designed as a central feature of a garden or as a singular focal point. Pools may be used

22-33 A patio is generally made of masonry set into the ground.

CALIFORNIA REDWOOD ASSN.

22-34 Decks are often used on hilly sites to provide an even area for patio furniture.

for swimming, but even these can be creatively designed, 22-36. A pool or fountain can also house fish and water loving plants, 22-37. A fountain may be part of a pool, or it may be freestanding. Fountains require a power source to pump water.

The size, shape, and construction of an ornamental pool or fountain should be consistent with climate and design of the landscape. Large, formal pools are not recommended for small, informal settings. Cost depends on the

GAME AREAS

Game	Suggested space allowance including court and clearance area
Badminton	44' by 20'
Basketball (half court)	37' by 42'
Croquet	38' by 85'
Horseshoes	50' by 10'
Shuffleboard	52' by 6'
Tennis	108' by 48'
Tetherball	10' radius
Volleyball	60' by 30'

22-35 A space large enough for a game court should have ample clearance room.

size of the pool and the type of construction used. The most expensive pools have poured concrete bases. However, an attractive, less expensive pool can be built using a plastic liner held down with wood beams or stones.

PLANNING THE LANDSCAPE

A good landscape should be carefully planned. The best method is to consider a lot's landscape possibilities before the house is sited. Landscaping is more often done to a previously owned lot or on a lot where no choice is given for the location of the house. In any case, planning should begin with an evaluation of the present lot.

First, the weak and strong points of the yard should be considered. A rough plan of the present yard can be used. Every yard has some good features that can be kept. These should be marked, and features to be removed should be crossed out.

Next, the impact of the elements should be determined. Direction of prevailing winds, spots where water collects after rains, dry spots, soil quality, exposure to sun, and other conditions should be noted on the landscape plan. Any city zoning restrictions should be noted as well. This information is vital when planning the arrangement of a landscape. It will help in deciding what kinds of plants will do best in an area. It will also help to determine where an element might be needed for shade or to block wind. If an area has very poor growing conditions, it might be more suited for a manufactured element such as a pool or path.

When evaluating the lot, the view from the house and location of doors should also be considered. An attractive view from a picture window or a sliding glass door is desirable. Some people place a small, private garden outside of a back door. One option is to add an exterior door to a bedroom for direct access to a private garden or patio.

After the present yard is evaluated, planning of the new landscape can begin. There are three main zones to consider in planning: the public zone, the private zone, and the service zone. The front yard is generally considered the public zone. It is usually designed to be attractive but not to be used for activities. The service zone is usually at the side of the home connected to the service entrance. Its view should be screened from the public and private areas. The back yard is considered the private zone. It may contain both aesthetic and functional areas.

The private zone is usually divided into areas for different purposes. Areas may include a garden or pool, a patio or entertaining area, and a game area. How much space is devoted to each area will depend on lifestyle and tastes. Space allowed for any area should provide room for any needed equipment, such as patio furniture or garden tools, and room for comfortable use of the area.

Once the areas are determined, placement of the landscape elements can begin. Keeping in mind the conditions already evaluated, space for plants and other elements can be drawn on the plan, 22-38. At this point, only general

CALIFORNIA REDWOOD ASSN.

22-36 A fountain can make a swimming pool the focal point of a landscape.

22-37 Many ornamental pools contain water loving plants such as water lilies.

planning is needed. Specific types of plants and materials can be chosen later.

Elements may be placed to screen an unpleasant view or to provide privacy from neighbors. It is best to keep most elements of the landscape around the edges, leaving some open lawn area, 22-39. Some trees or a special element may be desirable within the open lawn area. But scattering elements all over the lawn area reduces the apparent size of the lawn and increases the difficulty of maintenance.

Once the rough plan is finished, actual choice and placement of plants and materials can begin. Shorter plants should be placed in front of taller plants for good visibility. A landscape will be more interesting all year long if a variety of plants is chosen. For instance, most deciduous trees are green in spring and summer months, flamboyant in the fall, and barren in the winter. Flowering trees and plants may add interest in spring or summer. Evergreens keep a winter landscape from looking lifeless, 22-40.

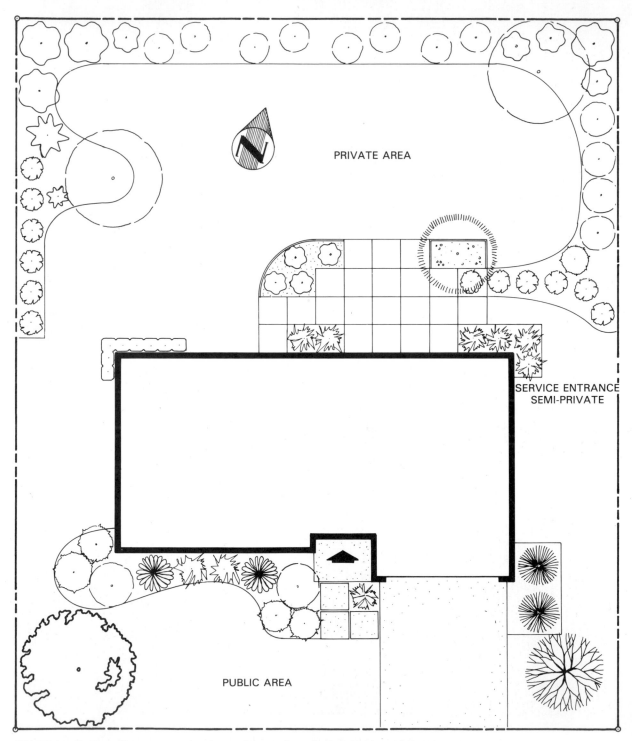

PRIVATE AREA

SERVICE ENTRANCE
SEMI-PRIVATE

PUBLIC AREA

22-38 Landscape elements can be drawn into a plan after evaluation of the site.

22-39 A yard will appear more spacious and be easier to maintain if most elements are placed around the edges. An element placed towards the center for a focal point will have more emphasis in this arrangement as well.

22-40 A landscape with only deciduous plants appears barren in late fall and winter months. The addition of evergreens helps to liven the landscape after other plants are bare.

Landscape Design

The parts of a landscape should be chosen and placed using the elements and principles of design. Design is as important to the landscape as it is to any interior room. However, the shapes, functions, and boundaries of a landscape are different from those of an interior. Therefore, application of the principles and elements of design to the landscape deserves special consideration.

Line. Line can be used to create patterns in the landscape. Lines formed by plants or other elements can direct the viewer's attention to a focal point. Straight lines suggest uninterrupted movement, 22-41. The lot boundaries, fences, and patios are usually straight lines. The forms of plants are usually curved. Curved lines are considered more pleasing and interesting than straight lines. Some groups of plants should be planted in a curved or irregular pattern to avoid too many straight lines. A curved path can also be used to add interest, 22-42. If a landscape is well planned, the lines of the design will convey an overall theme.

Form. The forms chosen for landscape elements may be aesthetic or functional. A widespreading tree may be chosen to provide a shady area. Paths and walks lead from one area to another. The forms of plants may be used to convey a vertical or horizontal appearance. Tall, thin plants give a feeling of height, while low, spreading plants have horizontal forms. Natural plant forms are less structured than the boxy, manufactured forms of the interior, 22-43. They give the landscape a refreshing appearance.

Texture. All landscape materials have texture. Lawn grass is fine while ground covers have more depth. Some

22-42 *A curved path can add interest and break the monotony of a landscape with too many straight lines.*

trees have smooth, shiny leaves and trunks; others are coarse and rough. A garden path of pea gravel has a fine texture compared to a coarse wall of large, natural stone. A variety of texture in the landscape adds interest and reduces monotony, 22-44.

Color. Green is the predominant color of the landscape. Green is refreshing, and a variety of shades and hues can be combined for interest. Other colors can be used to add interest and surprise to the landscape, 22-45. Flowering plants of many colors are available. The colors may be used in one or two areas to create a focal point. The leaves of plants may change colors seasonally. Colors should not clash with or overpower the natural colors of the landscape. For instance, a bright pink path would be considered shocking and unpleasant by most people. On the

22-41 *Plantings in straight lines have a formal appearance.*

22-43 *The natural forms of plants are limitless. They contrast the boxy forms commonly used in interiors.*

22-44 A variety of textures adds interest to a landscape.

other hand, an arrangement of pink flowers in a garden area would be an attractive focal point.

Proportion. Good proportion is sometimes difficult to achieve in a landscape. This is because interior proportions are so different from the proportions of a yard. The walls, ceiling, and floor of a room set small boundaries, and the proportions of the room must fit those boundaries. Exterior boundaries are much larger. The sky offers an unlimited upper boundary. Even though the lot has set dimensions, other lots act as visual extensions of the yard's boundaries. This larger frame of reference requires elements of larger proportions.

Ample spacing is necessary so that objects do not seem cramped. Objects close together should be in proportion to each other. A 5 to 3 ratio is considered pleasing to the eye. When considering the proportions of landscape elements, plan for the full-grown size of plants. Often,

RED CEDAR SHINGLE AND HANDSPLIT SHAKE BUREAU

22-45 Used effectively, colors other than green can become the focal point of a landscape.

RED CEDAR SHINGLE AND HANDSPLIT SHAKE BUREAU

22-46 Young plants appear to be isolated from each other, but large spacing is needed for adult plants. Flowers and ground covers can be used to help fill the gap until plants are full grown.

trees or shrubs are planted too close together because they are small and seem isolated. Ground covers or flowers can be used to help fill out the space until the plants are full grown, 22-46.

Balance. Either formal or informal balance may be used in a landscape. The architectural style of a home will often determine which type of balance is most appropriate, 22-47. For instance, the front yard of a formal Georgian manor would look best with a symmetrical arrangement of shrubbery and a central walk lined by trees. A small, rambling cottage may look better with a large pine tree on one side of the main entrance and a grouping of shrubs on the other side.

Emphasis. A good landscape plan has at least one focal point. A unique plant or structural feature may be the object of emphasis. The area surrounding a focal point

22-47 The off-center main entrance of this home is complemented by the informal balance of the landscape plants.

CALIFORNIA REDWOOD ASSN.

22-48 A balance of rhythm and variety is important in a landscape.

should not detract from the object. For instance, a brightly colored shrub would not be placed next to an ornamental flowering tree. Such an arrangement would prevent either object from attracting full attention.

Rhythm. Rhythm or repetition reduces confusion within a landscape. It introduces a feeling of order into the design. Rhythm may be achieved by using a similar grouping of plants throughout the landscape.

Although rhythm helps to create a sense of unity, too much rhythm can be monotonous. A variety of textures, shapes, and colors creates interest. For example, a composition that contained only pines — even if many varieties were used — would be monotonous because of the uniform texture. A balance between variety and repetition is most pleasing, 22-48.

REVIEW QUESTIONS

1. What functions can plants serve within a landscape?
2. What is the difference between a grass and a ground cover? Where would you use a ground cover?
3. What are the five main types of trees? What are their identifying features?
4. How can shrubs be used within a landscape? List types that are most suited to each use.
5. What is the difference between a walk and a path? What kinds of materials can be used for each?
6. How are walls and fences used within a landscape? How does the function affect the types of materials used?
7. Before planning a landscape, what should you know about the property being landscaped?
8. How can a landscape be planned so that it is attractive all year long?
9. How do the elements of line, form, texture, and color apply to the landscape?
10. How do exterior proportions differ from interior proportions?
11. Why would a landscape with only different types of shrubs be a poor landscape?

23 Remodeling

After studying this chapter, you will be able to:
- List the reasons that people remodel and the factors that they should consider before beginning a remodeling project.
- Compare the four main types of remodeling according to cost, complexity, and time required.
- Evaluate the remodeling needs of a family and select an appropriate type of remodeling.
- Explain the role of the family, the interior designer, the architect, and the contractor in remodeling.

Remodeling can be a wise investment that will increase the value of a lifespace. It may change part or all of a home's appearance. The least complex types of remodeling involve making changes in rooms already used or changing unused spaces so they can be used as living areas. Adding on to homes and renovating older homes generally require more complex changes.

All family members can be involved in remodeling. Remodeling decisions will affect the family for many years, so decisions should be made carefully. Family

ARIST-O-KRAFT

23-1 As families grow and change, their housing needs change. A gourmet kitchen was added to this home so entertaining would be more convenient.

CALIFORNIA REDWOOD ASSN.

23-2 Remodeling may be more desirable than moving if much time and effort has been spent on landscaping the present lot.

members may plan and gather information on their own, or they may consult architects, contractors, and interior designers.

Choosing to Remodel

A family may decide to remodel for several reasons. As a family grows, their needs and living patterns may change. New family members may need their own bedrooms. Entertaining may become more common, requiring more adequate kitchen and living space, 23-1. Increases in income may spur the desire for updated styles and appliances. As the work schedules of family members become busier, a more efficient home may be needed. Older homes may need newer equipment or better insulation to keep up with higher fuel prices. The present home may not be capable of meeting these new needs.

When housing changes are needed, moving may not be a desirable alternative. Families may have close ties with neighbors, schools, and community organizations. The home may hold sentimental attachment. If much time and money has been spent on landscaping, moving may not be worthwhile, 23-2. The high cost of building or buying a new home may make remodeling a more practical alternative.

351

A desire or need for change is only one factor to consider when deciding whether or not to remodel. Other factors may affect the type of remodeling chosen, or they may persuade a family not to remodel at all. For instance, if a family plans to move within a year or two, remodeling is probably not a worthwhile investment. Some homeowners remodel anticipating the desires of prospective home buyers. Although remodeling can increase property value, most home buyers prefer to make their own changes to a home. This makes remodeling a waste of time and money for the homeowner.

Local building ordinances and property taxes are also considerations when making remodeling choices. Remodeling may require several building permits, and many changes must comply with local codes. If remodeling increases the value of a home, it may also increase the cost of property taxes on the home. Usually, adding on and exterior remodeling are more likely to require building permits and increase taxes. Remodeling of unused spaces within the home may be a better choice if complying with building ordinances or paying higher taxes is a problem.

The costs, time, and effort required to remodel must also be considered before starting a project. All three factors are affected by the size and complexity of the remodeling. An accurate estimate of all costs of remodeling—including all building materials, utility additions, and labor—should be obtained before starting any remodeling project. Larger projects can be very expensive and may require financing. Costs can be spread out over months or even years by remodeling a little at a time. This method might not be desirable for all families, however, because it is a long time before the project is finished.

A remodeling project can vary in cost depending on the amount of time and effort spent by family members. If all work is contracted to professionals, the job will finish quickly with little effort from family members. However, contracted work is usually expensive, and good communication and supervision by a family member is needed to assure that work is done as desired.

At the other extreme, all work may be done by family members. This method can save a great deal of money in labor costs. The finished work also may be more personalized than would have been possible with some contractors. However, the project will probably require much more time, and unless the homeowner is very familiar with the type of work involved, serious errors in remodeling may occur.

Many families choose to do some remodeling on their own and contract professionals for the most difficult jobs, 23-3. For instance, paneling and painting may be done by family members, but complex wiring changes may be handled by an electrician. This method allows good results at a low cost. It also assures safe construction and eliminates frustration with jobs that are too difficult for the amateur.

Remodeling is not just used by homeowners that do not want to move. It is also an option for home buyers who

23-3 Subcontractors may be hired to do complex jobs like replacing walls or enlarging windows.

cannot afford custom-built housing. Many buy less expensive tract housing and remodel to meet their own needs. They may also choose to renovate an old home.

TYPES OF REMODELING

Remodeling can be used in several ways to meet a family's needs. Each type of remodeling should be considered so that needs can be met in the simplest, most satisfactory way possible. Remodeling may be divided into four main types: changing lived-in areas, making unused space livable, adding on, and buying to remodel. Each catagory varies in the level of change and the complexity, cost, and time required for remodeling. Many remodeling projects may include more than one type of remodeling.

Changing Lived-In Areas

When the purpose of remodeling is to update equipment, improve traffic patterns, or give a room a more modern appearance, remodeling usually takes the form of changes within a room. Kitchens are most commonly changed, and they are generally the most expensive room to remodel. Bathrooms, bedrooms, and other rooms may be changed as well.

Remodeling a lived-in room usually does not require major changes, such as tearing down a bearing wall or rewiring. Occasionally, a window or door may be enlarged or moved. Kitchen or bathroom remodeling may require relocation of some plumbing and wiring receptacles. However, changes are usually less complex than the changes required in other types of remodeling.

Kitchens. Kitchens are usually remodeled when the homeowner wants to update or add appliances. While updating appliances, the homeowner may also want to improve use of space, traffic patterns, availability of storage, and efficiency of the work triangle. Information on kitchen planning in Chapter 5 can help in evaluating the present kitchen and planning the new one.

BEFORE

AFTER

23-4 This living room was changed dramatically by using new wall coverings and building a ledge in front of the fireplace.

Many changes can be made to improve the efficiency of a kitchen. The circulation path can be improved by moving doors so that traffic patterns do not interfere with the work triangle. An appliance may be moved to make a more efficient work triangle. General and local lighting may be improved.

Counter space may be added to make room for food preparation or to allow space for counter-top appliances. Many new appliances can be mounted under wall cabinets to allow easy access while keeping counter space free. These may be considered during remodeling. Storage space may be added, or present storage space may be improved for more efficient use of space. For instance, a corner cabinet with space that is difficult to reach may be replaced with a lazy susan. Pull-out storage may also be used to improve access to items in cabinets.

If several new appliances are added or major appliances are moved, rewiring will be necessary. Additional circuits may also be needed. Changes in plumbing lines will be needed if the sink is moved, if a refrigerator with an automatic ice maker is added, or if a built-in dishwasher is moved or added. If the range is moved or a gas grill is added, new ventilation must be installed.

Bathrooms. Like kitchens, bathrooms are often remodeled to update old fixtures. They can be costly to remodel if changes in plumbing lines are needed. Lines must be checked to make sure that they are the correct size for new plumbing installations. Locating new fixtures in the same positions as old ones can reduce remodeling costs.

Other improvements may be made in bathrooms as well. Bathrooms may be enlarged by moving a wall. They may be improved by adding storage space. Skylights may be added for natural lighting and ventilation. New floor and wall treatments, such as ceramic tile, may be used for easier maintenance.

Other rooms. The appearances of bedrooms, living rooms, dining rooms, and other rooms that do not house major appliances can be changed dramatically with relatively minor remodeling projects. Most often, floor, wall, and ceiling treatments are updated, 23-4. New lighting fixtures may also be added. Partial walls or built-in storage may be added to a room. Many times, these projects are simple enough for family members to do on their own.

More complicated changes may include moving or widening a doorway to improve circulation. Windows may also be added or enlarged to improve the view. A wall may be removed so that two rooms are made into one. These changes are more complicated and should be done by someone with experience. The changes may affect the structural support of the house, and wiring and insulation may have to be altered.

Making Unused Space Livable

Many homes have areas that are not used as living space. These areas include garages, porches, attics, and basements. Although these areas need changes to make them suitable for living, they have sound roofs, walls, and floors. It may be less expensive to remodel these areas than to add on to a home. Also, remodeling unused space is often quicker and more convenient than adding on space.

Garages and porches. These areas are often converted into bedrooms, baths, dining rooms, family rooms, or sun rooms. They are often chosen for remodeling because they are conveniently located in relation to other rooms in the house. For instance, a porch adjoining a kitchen would make a convenient breakfast room.

The foundations under these areas should be checked to see if they are deep enough to comply with local building codes. Foundation requirements for these areas may be different than for living areas. A moisture barrier should be placed between the foundation and flooring materials. Insulation should be added to meet the R-value recommended for living spaces. Additional wiring for lighting and outlets usually is needed.

Windows and doors are often changed or added when remodeling garages and porches. Insulated glass windows or storm windows may replace the original windows, 23-5. The garage door may be replaced with a sliding glass door or with a window. Doors that adjoin a garage or porch to the house may be changed for more logical access. Sliding glass doors, panel doors, or open doorways may be used to connect the area to the home.

Some type of heating supply is needed in these areas. If the room is open to an original room in the house, heating from the original room may be enough for both areas. However, if the room is separate, it will need its own heat supply. Heating ducts and vents may be extended into the room from the home heating system. A fireplace, stove, electric heating unit, or small furnace may also be used to heat the room.

Basements. Basements are often remodeled to be used as family rooms, recreation areas, hobby areas, and workshops, 23-6. Bedrooms may also be placed in basements if sufficient lighting and an outside entrance

BEFORE   ANDERSEN CORP.

AFTER   ANDERSEN CORP.

23-5 By removing the door and replacing old windows of this house with insulating glass windows, the porch was made into a usable living space.

LIS KING

23-6 Basements are often converted into family rooms.

is provided. Bathrooms and a small kitchen area may be desired if the basement will be used for entertaining.

Basement areas are often damp, so vapor barriers and a dehumidifying system should be added for comfort. If flooding is common, a sump pump should be added. Also,

LOGAN CO.

23-7 A new stairway can be added to connect the basement with the living room.

any leaks in the walls or floors should be properly repaired before placing wall and floor materials. If the foundation is sound, flooring materials can be applied directly to the surface. Paneling and drywall should be applied to furring strips to allow space for wiring and insulation.

Basements can be gloomy if sufficient natural and artificial light is not provided. Window wells and windows may be enlarged to increase natural light. Illuminated ceilings and recessed lighting are popular for basements. Additional wiring for light fixtures and outlets will be needed.

Additional plumbing lines will be needed if a bath or kitchen area is added. If a wet bar is desired, plumbing lines for a small sink will be needed. New fixtures should be placed as close as possible to existing plumbing lines to reduce cost.

Stairways and entrances may be moved or added when remodeling a basement. The original stairway may interfere with the desired floor plan for the basement. It may be moved to allow space to be used more efficiently. Original basement entrances are usually in a service area. If the remodeled basement is a living area, an entrance from an upstairs living area may be desirable. A second stairway may be added for this purpose, 23-7. Once a basement is converted into a living area, a basement entrance from outside may be required. Local fire protection laws should be consulted.

Attics. Attics are frequently converted to bedrooms, hobby rooms, or conversation areas. If bedrooms are placed in this area, a bathroom should also be added.

Before converting an attic, floor joists should be checked to find out if they are strong enough to support

23-8 Dormers can be used to provide light and increase the amount of usable space in an attic.

a live load. Adequate headroom and usable floor space should also be available. At least 7 feet of height should be allowed between the floor and the finished ceiling. The ceiling may slope from 7 feet high to 5 feet high. However, the areas that have a low ceiling will be limited in use. If the floor is not strong enough, or if adequate space is not available, remodeling may become complex and expensive.

Windows and skylights can be added to an attic for natural lighting. Dormers allow natural light and increase the amount of usable space in an attic by adding headroom, 23-8. However, they are more costly to add than skylights and regular windows because they require modifications in the roof structure.

Adequate insulation for a living area should be placed in the attic ceiling and walls. Proper ventilation is especially important, since warm air tends to get trapped in attics. Ceiling fans and vents may be helpful. Additional wiring may also be required. If a bathroom is added, plumbing lines will be needed.

Adding On

As a family grows, extra living space is often needed. Converting unused spaces may not be possible or practical. In these situations, the family may choose to add on to a home. Any type of space, such as a bedroom, bathroom, den, or garage may be added to a home, 23-9. Additions may also be used to enlarge a room, such as a living room or kitchen.

Adding on is usually more complex than changing areas within the original structure. It involves changing a home's basic structure, building a new area from foundation to roof, and altering the exterior appearance of the home. Building permits and inspections are almost always necessary when adding on. Timing is important because weather conditions can hamper much of the work involved

23-9 *A main floor addition requires a new foundation and framework.*

in building an addition. Local zoning laws may restrict the types of additions allowed on a home. Usually, a home must be kept a minimum distance from lot lines.

Adding on to a home usually involves the removal of all or part of an exterior wall. Most exterior walls are bearing walls except for end walls of one-story, gable roofed houses. Temporary supports must be used when such a wall is removed, and some type of permanent support must be in place before the remodeling is finished, 23-10.

Walls that are removed are likely to contain wiring and plumbing, 23-11. Rerouting of these lines may be necessary. Underground plumbing mains and cables should be checked before digging for an addition's foundation.

Any addition planned should blend well with the architectural style of the existing home. The size, shape, and placement of the addition should not be obtrusive or overpowering. The exterior design should be in the same style as the original house. Placement, size, and style of win-

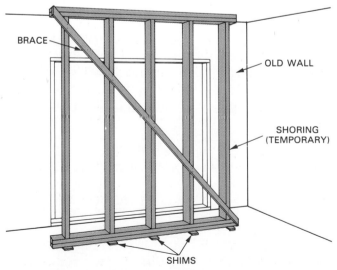

23-10 *Temporary support, or shoring, must be used when a bearing wall is removed.*

357

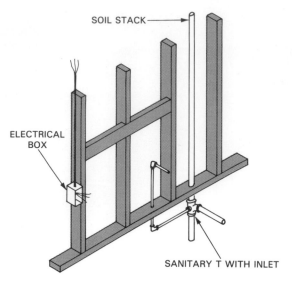

23-11 *Care must be taken to locate any plumbing or wiring before changing a wall.*

dows and doors in the addition should also blend with the original structure. Landscaping elements can be used to blend the new addition into the original house.

The type of space to be added, location of rooms in the original home, and availability of space should be considered when deciding where to add on a room. For instance, a game room or party room should not be located adjacent to the sleeping area. However, this would be a good location for another bedroom. Lot boundaries may not allow room for an addition on one or two sides of the home.

When a room is added on to a home, the floor plan can be designed to meet the specific needs of the family. Guidelines for planning any type of room can be found in Chapters 3,4,and 5 of this book. The addition should harmonize with other rooms in the house.

Second story additions. Some homes may not have enough yard space for a ground level addition. For these homes, a second story addition may be considered, 23-12.

BEFORE

AFTER

23-12 *Second story additions are complex and expensive.*

BEFORE

AFTER

23-13 Tract housing may be personalized through remodeling and landscaping.

These additions are usually much more expensive and complex than ground level additions. The roof must be removed and replaced to make room for the second story. The foundation and first floor walls must be strong enough to support the weight of a second story. Stairways connecting the first and second floors must be built.

Buying to Remodel

Many home buyers would like a custom-built home but cannot afford one. Often, these people buy less expensive housing and remodel to meet their own needs and tastes. A tract house can be individualized with additions, exterior changes, and interior changes to fit the lifestyle of the family, 23-13.

Another option for home buyers that is gaining popularity is renovating an old home. Many old homes may be purchased at a reasonable cost because they are not suitable for living. However, their basic structure is sound. These homes may be remodeled so that the finished home is much more valuable than the cost of remodeling or building from scratch, 23-14.

This type of remodeling is a major project, requiring much time, money, and careful planning. Preliminary planning is especially important. Building codes must be

CALIFORNIA REDWOOD ASSN.

23-14 *Many cities have old townhouses that may be purchased inexpensively and remodeled. The finished product is often more valuable than the cost of remodeling.*

strictly adhered to. The finished home may require many lengthy and expensive projects, 23-15. Many projects will require contracted work. Some home buyers include the cost of remodeling in the amount of their house mortgage. Others obtain a mortgage for the cost of the house only and pay for the remodeling without financing.

Careful inspection of a home is important when buying to remodel. Some homes may be very inexpensive, but remodeling them would cost more than buying a new home. A sound foundation and floor substructure is essential. Wood should be checked for insects and dryrot. If support beams are unsound, remodeling will probably be too expensive to be worthwhile.

Other areas to check are wiring, heating, roofing, walls, and insulation. Remodeling can be expensive if major changes in these areas are needed. The types of changes that will be needed and their estimated costs should be considered before purchasing a house. Often, a home that costs a few thousand dollars more, but has sound wiring and plumbing, will have a lower total cost after remodeling.

PREPARING REMODELING PLANS

A good remodeling job is carefully planned before any work begins. Planning involves appraising the original house, determining the desired and needed changes, and drawing plans. An interior decorator, an architect, or a contractor may be consulted in the planning stages.

The first step of planning involves determining the weak and strong points of the present home. Limited space and storage, inefficient appliances, and poor natural lighting are examples of items that may need changing. However, walls, molding, and flooring materials may be worth saving.

Plumbing, heating, wiring, and insulation should all be evaluated when remodeling is considered. If updating or repairs will be needed within a few years, it may be less expensive and more convenient to make changes during remodeling. Replacing windows, doors, and appliances to increase a home's energy efficiency may also be considered.

After the area to remodel has been evaluated, a rough sketch of the original space should be drawn. The sketch should include any architectural details such as windows, doors, steps, and fireplaces. Desired changes can be drawn, evaluated, and altered until a final plan results. The final plan should follow the guidelines presented in Chapters 3, 4, and 5 of this book.

The finished plan should be used when consulting contractors, ordering materials, and applying for building permits. Professionally drawn floor plans and elevations or rough plans with specified dimensions may be used. However, if contractors or subcontractors will do any work, professional symbols are essential.

The Interior Designer

The interior designer may be consulted in the planning stages of remodeling. Some decorating stores and department stores offer the free services of a decorator if products are purchased from their store. A free-lance designer or a design firm may also be consulted.

The designer can help to put the needs and desires of a family into concrete plans. He or she can help select materials that will be both functional and tasteful. Fabric samples, paint chips, and other materials to be used in a room can be coordinated by the designer. He or she can make suggestions to improve the design or the function of any material within a room. The designer also can help the family choose materials that fit within a budget.

BEFORE   BIRD & SON

AFTER   BIRD & SON

23-15 Remodeling an old house requires much work on the interior and exterior.

BRUNVARD ASSOC.

23-16 *The contractor may do some work on his or her own and supervise and coordinate the work of subcontractors.*

Interior designers can also help in evaluating the overall floor plan of a room. They can make suggestions for improving the efficiency of circulation and the overall use of space. The interior designer can be consulted separately or with an architect.

The Architect

When major projects are planned, an architect will probably be consulted. An architect can also make suggestions to improve a remodeling plan. He or she can make sure that the overall style of the home's exterior will remain well designed. The architect can also help determine whether remodeling plans comply to building, plumbing, and electrical codes.

The architect can make final drawings of the proposed plan and write specifications for materials. The family may consult an architect only to evaluate and draw plans, or they may use the architect to contact a contractor and supervise the remodeling work to completion.

The Contractor

After planning is finished, a contractor may be hired to do the remodeling work. Many contractors specialize in remodeling. The contractor will obtain any necessary building permits and schedule the work of any subcontractors needed for the project. Subcontractors may include carpenters, plumbers, electricians, masons, and painters, 23-16.

When a contractor is hired for a project, he or she will usually charge one fee for materials and labor. This helps to eliminate the chance of unexpected expenses. If some work will be done by family members, a contractor may not be used. A family member may choose to hire any specific subcontractors needed. When a contractor is not used, an interior designer or architect can help to estimate costs, or the family can make their own estimates. However, some unpredicted expenses will probably occur.

REVIEW QUESTIONS

1. For what reasons would a family choose to remodel? Why would they choose remodeling over buying a new house?
2. What factors should be considered when making remodeling decisions?
3. What are the four main types of remodeling? Which is usually the simplest? Which is usually the most complex?
4. If a family of four lived in a two bedroom house with a basement and an attic, and they wanted to add a bedroom to their home, what type of remodeling would you recommend? Why?
5. What precautions should be taken when tearing down an exterior wall?
6. A family looking for a house to remodel found one house for $3,000 and another house for $10,000. They chose the $10,000 house. What are some possible factors that would make the more expensive house a better buy?
7. What are the steps in planning a remodeling project?
8. How can interior designers, architects, and contractors help with a remodeling project?

24 Presenting Housing Ideas

After studying this chapter, you will be able to:

■ Explain how presentation methods can help the design professional communicate ideas.

■ List the seven types of drawings used to present design ideas and describe how each is used in clarifying a design.

■ Identify the materials and methods used to make a rendering.

■ Describe how presentation boards, models, and slides can help a client visualize a finished project.

Professionals in design use presentation techniques to communicate their ideas. Presentation methods allow a designer to present ideas to a client in non-technical language, 24-1. They are seldom seen by building contractors. Presentation drawings, boards, and models may be used with prospective clients and investors, or they may be used for advertising. Designers must know how to prepare some types of presentation plans if they are to sell their ideas.

PRESENTATION DRAWINGS

Presentation drawings help to give a client a clear picture of how a finished project will appear. Several types can be used to depict a house's exterior, interior, and

THE GARLINGHOUSE COMPANY

24-1 Presentations can be used to communicate with prospective owners, lending agencies, and the media.

24-2 Using two-point perspective for an exterior gives the drawing a realistic appearance.

24-3 By using vanishing points at a low level in comparison with the house, a view of the home from a higher perspective can be given. This perspective allows a good view of the clerestory windows and courtyard areas.

KAREN RUTGERS

24-4 *Interior perspectives use one-point perspective. This type of drawing can be learned quickly by the beginning design student.*

Drawings are given perspective by using *vanishing points*. The part of the drawing meant to appear closest to the viewer is drawn in the largest scale. Parts of the drawing that are meant to appear farther away are drawn gradually smaller. If lines were extended from the closest parts of the drawing past the farthest parts, they would eventually meet at a vanishing point. A drawing may have one, two, or three vanishing points.

Most exterior perspectives have two or three vanishing points. A two-point perspective usually features two sides of a building. One corner appears closest, and the walls extending from that corner are drawn in perspective to a different vanishing point. By changing the level of the vanishing points in relationship to the building, more or less of the roof can be shown, 24-3. Three-point perspective is sometimes used for very tall buildings. A third vanishing point is placed above the building to give an appearance of height. Three-point perspective is the most difficult type of perspective drawing to master.

surroundings. They include exterior perspectives, interior perspectives, presentation floor plans, presentation elevations, presentation plot and landscape plans, and presentation sections. Each type of drawing features different aspects of a plan or uses a different approach to presenting the idea.

Exterior Perspectives

An exterior perspective is a pictorial of the outside of a house. It shows how the building will appear in its completed form, 24-2. The drawing shows more than one side of the home for a three-dimensional appearance. Elements further away from the viewer are reduced in size for a realistic representation.

Interior Perspectives

Interior perspectives are pictorial drawings of a room or other area inside a house. They generally include the furnishings and decorations planned for the finished room. One-point perspective is used most often for interior drawings. Generally, the pictorial shows three walls, the floor, and the ceiling, 24-4. Interior perspectives can be drawn fairly easily using a grid designed for one-point perspective.

Presentation Floor Plans

Presentation floor plans vary in style and content. Some present only the arrangement of rooms within the structure, 24-5. Others may include a traffic flow analysis or

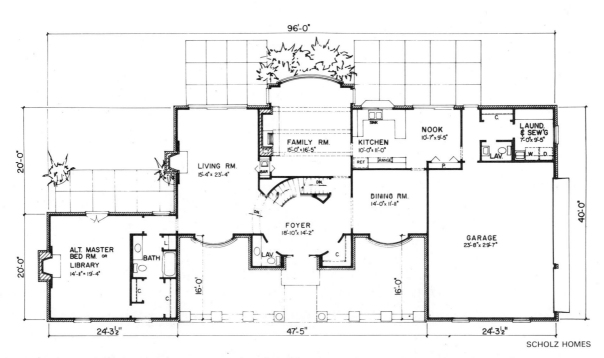

SCHOLZ HOMES

24-5 *A presentation floor plan shows the basic room layout for a housing unit.*

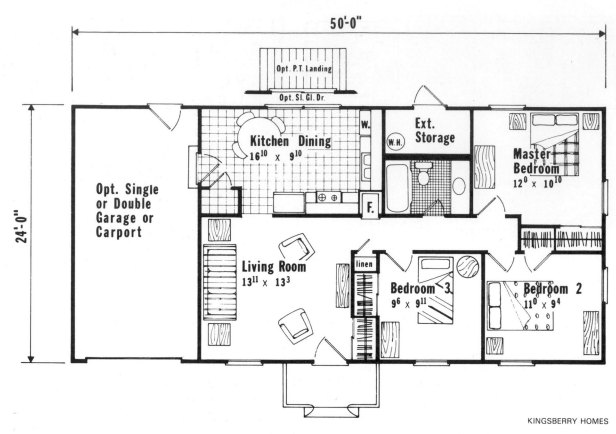

24-6 *Presentation floor plans may show the arrangement of furniture and appliances within a house.*

placement of furniture and appliances, 24-6. Color may be used to help identify related areas, similar functions, or convenient features.

Some symbols are used to add clarity to the drawing. Windows and doors, types of floor coverings, and shelves may be indicated in symbols. Outlines of plants and furniture may also be included. Wall thicknesses are usually solid or shaded. The scale for most residential floor plans is 1/4 inch equals 1 foot. Larger buildings may be drawn using a 1/8 inch equals 1 foot scale.

Presentation Elevations

A presentation elevation shows a view perpendicular to a surface. It may represent any one side of an object, but it shows no depth. Any interior or exterior wall may be shown with this type of drawing. It can be drawn quickly and contains the same basic information shown in a perspective drawing, 24-7.

Kitchens, bathrooms, and walls with built-in cabinets are interior areas frequently shown using presentation elevations, 24-8. Exterior elevations often include plants and other surrounding features to give the illusion of depth. Scale is usually 1/4 inch equals 1 foot or larger.

Presentation Plot Plans

A presentation plot plan is used to show the relationship between the site and the structure. It may also include important topographical features such as trees, walks,

24-7 *The presentation elevation does not use perspective, but it communicates the same basic design elements featured in a perspective.*

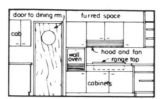
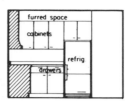
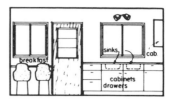

kitchen elevations

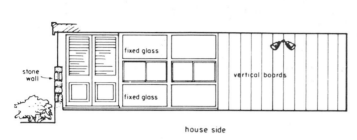
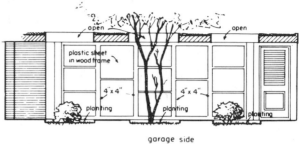

house side

garden entrance

24-8 *Interior wall elevations are frequently used to show the arrangements of built-in cabinets and appliances.*

streets, and soil contour. This drawing shows a top view of the property with all elements in place. Color is often used to distinguish different features, 24-9. Different scales may use 1 inch to represent 10, 20, or 30 feet, or more if the property is very large.

Presentation Landscape Plans

The presentation landscape plan shows an entire landscape plan in one presentation. It includes the placement of trees, shrubs, flowers, pools, walks, fences, drives, the house, and any other important features. A north symbol is generally included. Plant symbols may be varied to represent different species included in the landscape. Plant symbols should be in proper scale according to measurements of full-grown plants. See 24-10. Color may be used to define elements and show how space is used. The scale used is similar to that used for presentation plot plans.

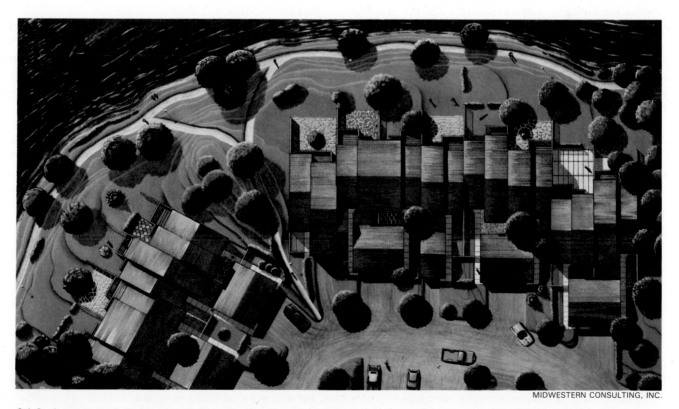

MIDWESTERN CONSULTING, INC.

24-9 *A presentation plot plan shows the physical properties of a site and the location of structures on the site.*

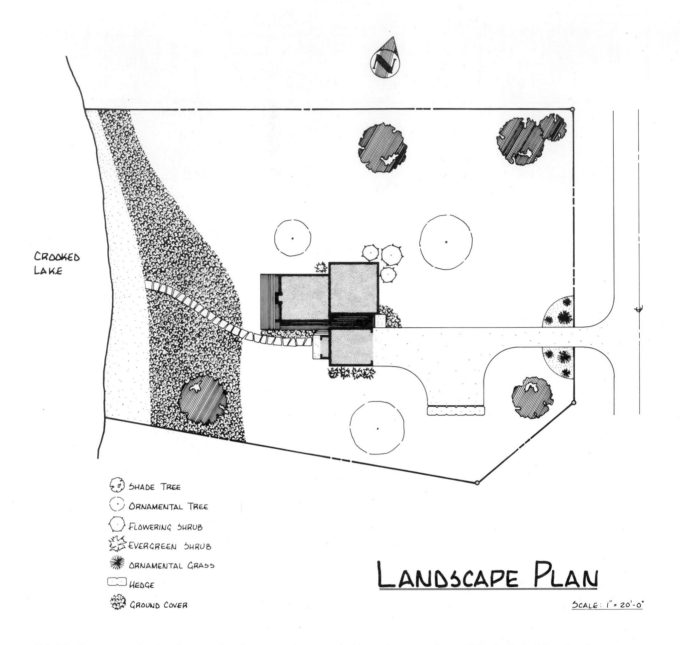

CROOKED
LAKE

- 🌳 SHADE TREE
- ○ ORNAMENTAL TREE
- ⬡ FLOWERING SHRUB
- 🍃 EVERGREEN SHRUB
- ✳ ORNAMENTAL GRASS
- ▭ HEDGE
- 🌿 GROUND COVER

LANDSCAPE PLAN

SCALE: 1" = 20'-0"

24-10 A presentation landscape plan features plants and other elements that will be included in a landscape.

Presentation Sections

Section drawings can be used to show the interior and exterior of a house. They can also be used to show more than one interior room in one drawing. A section drawing shows a cutaway view of a house or of a series of rooms in a house. Sections can be used to help the client better understand the internal layout of the structure. Often, a floor plan is used to show what part of the house is featured in the section drawing. Color is frequently used on presentation sections to give the illusion of depth and to define features, 24-11.

RENDERING

Rendering is the addition of shades, shadows, texture, and color to a line drawing to achieve realism in a presentation drawing. Many materials and techniques are used for rendering, including pencil, ink, colored pencil, felt tip marker, watercolor, applique, and air brush. The design professional should have several techniques mastered to offer flexibility in communicating with the client.

Pencil Rendering

Pencil rendering is performed using a soft lead pencil. It is the most popular form of rendering, and beginning students can master the technique with some practice. Renderings can be done quickly and errors can be easily corrected. Also, no special materials or equipment are required. Shading and giving the appearance of texture can be done well using only pencil. However, care must be taken to prevent the soft lead from smudging.

HEATILATOR, INC.

24-11 Presentation sections help clients see the relationship between the interior and the exterior of an object.

Renderings in pencil may range from rough, freehand sketches to precise line drawings executed with drafting instruments, 24-12. The degree of accuracy depends on the purpose of the drawing and the stage of the project. In early stages of designs, rough sketches are usually enough. Renderings of completed designs to be used for advertising should be more precise.

Ink Rendering

Ink renderings are more suitable for reproduction than pencil renderings. Ink produces a sharper line and finer

detail than pencil can produce, 24-13. Some skill is needed to produce good ink renderings because mistakes are not easily corrected. Shading and texturing is possible with ink by using a series of dots, parallel lines, or other types of markings. Technical fountain pens, lettering pens, poster pens, or brushes may be used to produce ink renderings.

Good ink renderings require paper that takes ink without producing a feathered edge. Recommended materials include mat boards, bristol boards, tracing paper, and overlay paper. Colored mat boards can be used with black or colored ink for special effect. Ink may be used for object lines in a drawing with one of the other rendering techniques used for shades, shadows, and colors. Waterproof ink is required if felt tip markers or watercolors are used with the ink.

Watercolor Rendering

Good watercolor rendering gives a realistic appearance to a presentation, 24-14. The technique is difficult and may require some formal art training. Vivid colors or light washes of colors are characteristic of watercolor renderings. Subjects requiring precise details may be inked and then watercolored. Brushes of various sizes are used. Boards and papers should be designed for use with watercolors.

Colored Pencil Rendering

Color renderings can also be produced using colored pencils. Shading techniques are easily accomplished even

STUART RESOR, ARCHITECT

24-12 Pencil renderings are quickly drawn, but they can still show precise architectural features.

24-13 Ink renderings have clear lines that reproduce well.

by the beginning student, 24-15. An extensive range of colors is available in standard and watercolor pencil form. A watercolor pencil rendering may be given the appearance of a watercolor rendering by adding water with a brush. Most types of boards and paper can be used for colored pencil renderings.

Felt Tip Marker Rendering

Felt tip markers can be used to produce colorful, dramatic renderings, 24-16. Such renderings are popular for preliminary drawings and completed project drawings. Errors are very difficult to correct with this technique. A wide range of colors is available, and ink may be used for

24-14 A watercolor rendering has an appearance similar to that of a photograph.

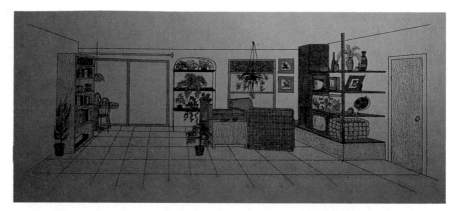

24-15 Colored pencil rendering is easily mastered by the beginning student.

fine detail. Board products and thin tracing paper are recommended for felt tip marker renderings.

Appliqué Rendering

This type of rendering uses appliqués to supply color, shading, or texture. An *appliqué* is a pressure sensitive transfer material with a printed pattern or color on one side. Appliqué may be cut to the size needed and transferred onto a rendering. The use of appliqué assures bold, uniform color and patterns, 24-17. It is popular for use in magazines because it reproduces well. Many common rendering symbols, such as trees, people, furniture, building materials, and doors are available in appliqué form.

Air Brush Rendering

Professional illustrators generally prefer the airbrush technique over other rendering methods. It produces smooth gradation of tones and a realistic appearance, 24-18. Special equipment and much practice is required to produce good renderings. Colored inks are often used over black ink drawings. The air brush produces subtle shading by using very small dots of color. Areas not to be sprayed are covered with rubber cement or other masking.

OTHER PRESENTATION METHODS

Presentation drawings are valuable for communicating the details of a design, but frequently more information is desirable. Such details as fabrics, color schemes, furniture styles, and textures are difficult to represent accurately and completely on rendered drawings. Other presentations may help clients picture a finished product more clearly. These include presentation boards, models, or slides.

Presentation Boards

Presentation boards contain drawings—such as floor plans and elevations—and any other information necessary to help the client visualize a finished product. A large piece of mat board or illustration board is used

KEN HAWK

24-16 Felt tip markers can be used in a variety of colors and shades to produce a realistic rendering.

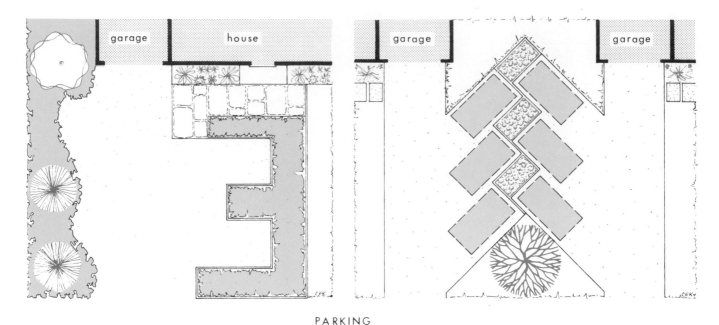

PARKING

24-17 Colored appliqués can be used over ink renderings to direct attention to specific areas.

for mounting samples, drawings, and photos in a logical, attractive format, 24-19. Manufacturers' samples of carpeting, draperies, upholstery, and paint may be included.

Various schedules may also be part of the presentation board. For example, a furniture schedule may identify individual pieces, manufacturer, dimensions, finishes, and any other important information. Specifications for walls, floors, and ceilings may also be placed in a schedule.

The presentation board helps the client form a better picture of the proposed finished product. It should help the client see how the various colors, textures, and designs in a room will look together. The board should contain any information necessary to answer questions the client may have about a project.

Models

Models are three-dimensional representations of a design idea. They allow the client to view all sides of a proposed project. Models may also be used by the designer to work out solutions to design problems or to find defects in a plan, 24-20.

Models may be built to any scale, but less time and effort is involved if the same scale is used for the model as the drawings for the project. Copies of the floor plan can be used as a base for the model. If a model is used simply as a development tool, appearance is not important. However, dimensions should be accurately represented, 24-21. This type of model will be disposed of as soon as a design is completed.

Final models meant for clients to view should be precisely detailed and properly scaled. They can be as elaborate as needed or desired. Final models should not be constructed until a design is accepted and renderings are approved, because changes in the model are difficult and time consuming. Models are most commonly used for very complex designs that are difficult to visualize.

Slide Presentations

Slides can be used to effectively communicate with a client. A slide presentation can be arranged to fit almost

PROGRESS LIGHTING

24-18 Very realistic pictures can be made using an air brush and ink pen.

JANET DUCHOSSOIS

24-19 Presentation boards should be designed to communicate information in a way that clients will understand.

24-20 A presentation model can be built to show how each architectural and design feature will look in the finished project.

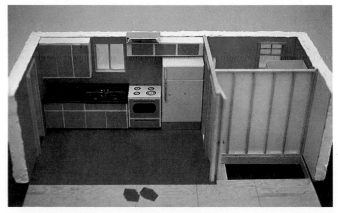

24-21 Rough models used by design professionals to develop ideas are not usually seen by the client.

any needs. For example, in the early stages of the design process, slides can be used to show examples of previous work. They also can be used to present examples of designs used in situations similar to that of the client. A wide range of ideas can be presented to determine what features the client likes.

Slides may be used to file samples of a design professional's work. Renderings, models, and presentation boards require storage space and deteriorate over time. Color slides of presentation materials and of completed projects can be easily filed and take up little space. Specific information about a project or slide can be written and filed with the slides.

REVIEW QUESTIONS

1. What are the seven types of presentation drawings? Which are used primarily for exteriors? Which are used for interiors?
2. What is the difference between a perspective drawing and an elevation?
3. How does a two-point perspective drawing differ from a one-point perspective drawing? What types of drawings are done using each type of perspective?
4. What is rendering? Why is it used in presentation drawings?
5. What are the seven main materials or techniques used to produce renderings? Which of these methods is the simplest? Which is the most complex?
6. Why is ink rendering preferred over pencil rendering for reproduction?
7. What type of color rendering would you recommend for a beginning design student? Why would this method be preferred for beginning students?
8. What is the preferred method of rendering for professional illustrators?
9. What methods other than drawings can be used to present housing ideas? How can these methods help in communicating ideas to clients?
10. What different types of models can be used in presenting housing ideas? How are these types of models similar? How are they different?

THE GARLINGHOUSE COMPANY

An attractive rendering helps to sell a client on a housing idea.

25 Careers in Housing

After studying this chapter, you will be able to:
- List various career options within the housing field.
- Compare the duties and educational requirements of various occupations related to housing.

Housing is a broad field that includes many occupations. Some are involved with the planning and design of a structure. These occupations usually require creative ability and problem solving skills as well as knowledge and training in housing design. Other jobs are concerned with the construction of housing. These positions require specific training in construction skills. Also related to housing are government and real estate positions. These positions usually require knowledge and skills outside of the housing field as well as a general knowledge of housing fundamentals.

Architect

The architect's job requires creativity and problem solving ability. Sensitivity to forms and materials is also needed. An architect must have a thorough understanding of construction technology, building codes, and laws pertaining to construction.

The architect works closely with a client, making preliminary sketches, suggesting materials, and helping a client to choose a satisfactory final design for a structure, 25-1. Working drawings are then prepared. The architect may also help the client choose a building contractor. He or she may represent the client in dealing with the contractor during construction. The architect may also check to see that construction and materials meet specifications.

To become a registered architect, a person must fulfill the educational training requirements for that state. In

25-1 The architect uses skill, knowledge of materials, and creativity to meet the housing needs of each client.

25-2 *Architectural drafters often add details to working plans that have been drawn by architects.*

addition, all states require an examination to obtain a license. Most states require at least a bachelor's degree from a college with an accredited architecture program. Many architects obtain master's degrees as well. In some areas, education and training requirements can be met by completing a two year program and a specified number of years of practical experience. Most areas require that building designs be certified by a registered architect before construction can begin.

Architectural Drafter

Architectural drafters draw the details of working drawings and make tracings from the original drawings prepared by the architect or designer. They often begin as junior drafters, 25-2. As they gain experience, they may move into drafting positions requiring more responsibility.

An architectural drafting position usually requires at least a high school diploma with some courses in architectural drawing. Further education at a community college, technical school, or university may assure better job placement. Architectural drafters may retain their position as a career, or they may use the position to gain experience and eventually become registered architects.

Architectural Illustrator

Architectural illustrators need a high degree of artistic skill to be readily employable. They usually begin study in architectural drawing or commercial art and then branch into this specialized field, 25-3. They prepare presentaion drawings, sketches, and illustrations for advertising and for client presentations.

Educational requirements for this type of work are similar to requirements for the architectural drafter. A natural talent for freehand drawing is important because of the artistic nature of this work. Architectural illustrators are generally employed by large architectural firms.

Interior Designer

Interior designers plan and supervise the design and decoration of building interiors. Creativity and a full knowledge of design principles, materials, furnishings, and accessories is needed for this type of work.

Interior designers work from blueprints to prepare presentation plans, presentation boards, and models. They work with clients to choose furnishings and materials that will meet the clients' needs and tastes, 25-4. They may select and estimate the costs of furniture, floor and wall coverings, and other needed items. They may also arrange purchases and hire and supervise various workers.

A four year degree in interior design is recommended for professional designers. However, training can be obtained through a professional school or community college. Knowledge of furniture, construction, textiles, design, art, and antiques is needed. Interior designers may work for a company specializing in decorating materials (such as a paint or furniture store), for an architectural firm, or as a free-lance consultant.

25-3 *Courses in art and drafting are usually needed to become an architectural illustrator.*

Modelmaker

Modelmakers build scale models of objects such as planned communities, individual buildings, pieces of furniture, or room layouts. They work from construction drawings or conceptual design renderings. Architects and other types of designers often employ modelmakers, 25-5.

Modelmaking requires an ability to read drawings and a thorough knowledge of materials. The modelmaker must also be creative and skilled in operating machinery used to make models. There are no special educational requirements for this job; however, much experience and manual dexterity is needed.

25-4 *Interior designers work closely with clients to choose materials for the home.*

Landscape Designer

The landscape designer plans the arrangement and composition of landscape elements on a site. This involves preparing a design plan, selecting landscape materials, and supervising the installation of elements, 25-6.

The landscape designer generally has a bachelor's degree or at least some coursework and experience in landscaping. Landscape designers need a thorough knowledge of soil, plants, design, and construction.

Building Contractor

Building contractors plan and coordinate the construction of buildings. This may involve working with or supervising subcontractors, inspectors, and designers. Contractors are responsible for scheduling work, obtaining materials and equipment, and making sure that materials and construction comply with building codes. They also make sure that the architect's and owner's specifications are met, 25-7.

A contractor must obtain a license to do contracting work. Generally, years of experience in several areas of construction are needed. Coursework in management, accounting, economics, construction law, and labor rela-

25-5 *Architects often employ modelmakers to make three-dimensional representations of their plans.*

25-6 A landscape designer works with clients to develop a landscape that meets their needs.

tions is helpful because most contractors are self-employed.

Construction Technologist

Construction technologists are qualified for both technical and supervisory roles in the construction industry. Specializations of the construction technologist include estimating and bidding, quality control, site supervision, specifications writing, expediting, purchasing, and managing construction, 25-8.

A construction technologist typically has a bachelor's degree in construction technology. A strong science background and knowledge of construction are needed for this major. Experience in construction is helpful but not necessary.

Skilled Tradesperson

Skilled tradespeople perform specific jobs involved in building a structure. They include carpenters, masons, electricians, plumbers, painters, and paperhangers, 25-9.

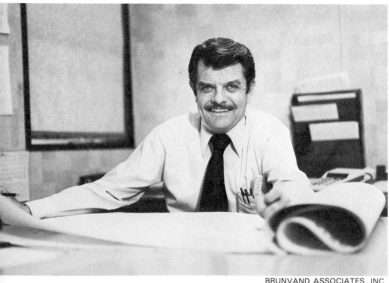

BRUNVAND ASSOCIATES, INC.

25-7 The contractor coordinates all the jobs necessary to construct a building.

BRUNVAND ASSOCIATES, INC.

25-8 A construction technologist is qualified to perform several roles in the management of construction.

BRUNVAND ASSOCIATES, INC.

25-9 Skilled tradespeople in several different trades are needed to construct a building.

Trades are highly specialized, and seldom does a person work in more than one trade. On-the-job training is required for positions in most trades. Some classroom education may be received through union education programs, trade schools, or community colleges.

Three positions—designated by skill and experience—are recognized in most trades. They are the apprentice, the journeyman, and the master. Generally, a high school diploma is sufficient to begin as an apprentice. Tradespeople may work for one contractor, or they may obtain work through their trade union.

Construction Machinery Operator

Many large, expensive machines—such as cranes, bulldozers, backhoes, and forklifts—are used in modern construction. Competent machinery operators are needed to run machines safely and efficiently, 25-10. Operators must have good eyesight and physical coordination. Jobs require a high school diploma and on-the-job training.

Land Surveyor

Land surveyors locate property boundaries, measure distances, establish contours, and make drawings of the

BRUNVAND ASSOCIATES, INC.

25-10 Operators of large, complicated construction equipment perform necessary tasks in building construction.

25-11 *Surveyors measure distances and contours of a construction site.*

site surveyed, 25-11. The registered surveyor supervises a surveying team consisting of a rod person, a chain person, and an instrument person. A land surveyor must be licensed to practice as a registered surveyor. Formal training in surveying is needed; some states require a bachelor's degree. Land surveying is highly technical work requiring skill in trigonometry and drawing. Registered surveyors receive training in the three other positions on the surveying team before receiving a license.

Government Positions

Many positions in local, state, and federal government relate to the housing industry. Building inspectors examine construction in progress to verify that local codes are followed. Health inspectors check soil, water, and sewer components on a lot. Inspectors are employed at all levels of government and may do highly specialized work on complex construction sites. Inspection covers nearly all materials, equipment, and workmanship on a construction site.

Government agencies monitor housing trends, provide loans, underwrite financing for low-cost housing, and sponsor research to improve housing. They employ hous-

ing professionals as well as accountants, field representatives, and community planners. Technical expertise is required for these positions.

Real Estate Positions

Several careers are possible in the field of real estate. The real estate broker assists people in appraising, buying, selling, renting, and leasing property, 25-12. Brokers are professionals that must know building codes and laws relating to real estate transactions. They also need to be familiar with their community.

Brokers generally have college degrees, but this is not a requirement. However, they must pass a test to obtain a brokerage license.

Real estate management is another career in the field of real estate. Large housing units such as apartments, condominiums, and mobile home courts often employ property managers. Management duties involve interviewing prospective tenants, maintaining the property, and reporting to the building owner. There are no specific educational requirements for these types of positions. However, a manager must be responsible and able to deal with people.

CENTURY 21 OF MICHIGAN, INC.

25-12 The real estate broker plays a key role in buying, selling, and renting house properties.

REVIEW QUESTIONS

1. What are the responsibilities of an architect? What background is needed to become a registered architect?
2. What other careers are available in the area of architecture?
3. What skills and knowledge should the interior designer possess?
4. What positions are available in the field of construction? How do these positions vary in responsibilities and educational requirements?
5. What government positions are available in the field of housing?
6. What real estate positions are available in the field of housing?

Glossary

A

accent lighting: an application of lighting using a highly concentrated beam to highlight an area or object.

accordian door: a folding door consisting of several narrow panels that fold back into a stack when open.

active wall: a wall that suggests movement and attracts attention.

alkyd: a category of paints that are oil-based.

all-wood construction: FTC furniture term meaning that the wood exposed on a furniture piece is the same throughout the entire thickness of the piece.

analogous color scheme: a color harmony based on hues that are next to each other on the color wheel. Usually, three to five hues are used.

appliqué: a pressure sensitive transfer material with a printed pattern or color on one side.

awning window: a window with a sash that is hinged at the top and which swings away from the structure from the bottom.

arabesque: a scrolled leaf pattern, generally symmetrical in design.

B

balance point: the temperature at which the amount of energy required by a heat pump is equal to the amount of energy produced.

balloon framing: a type of floor framing in which the wall is continuous from the sill to the top of the wall, and the floor joists are attached to the studs.

bearing wall: a wall that supports some weight from the ceiling or roof of a structure.

bifolding doors: doors made of two units that are joined with hinges.

blanket insulation: thick, flexible insulation made from mineral wool.

blend: a yarn that is the result of two or more different staple fibers spun together into a single yarn.

blocking: a method of strengthening joints in which small pieces of wood are attached between the adjacent sides of two joined pieces of wood.

block printing: method of hand-printing fabric in which a design is carved on a block, dye is applied to the block, and the pattern is stamped onto the fabric.

bond: the way that bricks are joined to determine the appearance, durability, and strength of construction. Bond refers to structural bond, pattern bond, and mortar bond.

book match: a veneer pattern achieved by turning over every other sheet of veneer to produce a mirrored image look.

boulle work: the technique of using dazzling inlays of pewter, brass, and semitransparent tortoiseshell on furniture, introduced by André-Charles Boulle.

box springs: a type of mattress support consisting of a series of coils attached to a base and covered with padding.

bracket lighting fixture: a structural fixture that is designed like a valance lighting fixture except that it is placed on a wall.

branch circuit: a branch of a structure's main disconnect switch that provides current for a portion of receptacles within the structure.

broad conical evergreen: an evergreen tree that tapers gradually from a wide base to a single erect stem.

brown coat: the second coat of a three-coat plaster finish.

building brick (or common brick): a structural clay product used mainly as a structural material where durability and strength are more important than appearance.

bulbous form: a melon shaped carving used to decorate furniture supports of Elizabethan furniture.

butt joint: a type of wood joint made by butting the end or edge of one board against the end or edge of another and holding them together with glue, screws, or nails.

bypass doors: sliding doors set on adjacent, parallel tracks so that they pass each other when moving.

C

cabriole leg: a carved furniture support in the shape of an animal leg.

cafe curtains: straight curtains hung from rings that slide along a rod.

case goods: pieces of furniture that are made primarily of wood.

casement window: a window with sashes that swing out from the structure.

cast iron: iron containing 2 to 3.75 percent carbon that

is melted in a blast furnace and cast into different shapes.

cellulosic fibers: fibers that are derived from plants.

ceramic mosaic tile: small tile, usually no larger than 2 by 2 inches, made of porcelain or natural clay.

circular stairs: a custom-made, curved stairway made of trapezoid shaped steps.

circulation: the routes that people follow as they move from one place to another in the home.

circulation frequency: the number of times a route within a home is repeated in any given period of time.

cleanup center: area of the kitchen which contains the sink and possibly a dishwasher and food disposer.

climate control plan: a plan sometimes found in a set of construction drawings which shows the location of the heating, cooling, humidification, dehumidification, and air cleaning equipment in a structure.

coil spring: a type of seat base construction for upholstered furniture in which several coil springs are attached to webbing or steel bands.

coil springs: a type of mattress support consisting of a series of coils attached to a base with no covering or padding.

columnar evergreen: an evergreen tree with nearly vertical branches that tapers only slightly at the top.

combination: FTC furniture term used to describe furniture with more than one type of wood used in the exposed parts. Also, a yarn formed by twisting two different types of single yarns into one yarn.

complement: on the color wheel, the color directly opposite another color.

complementary color scheme: a color harmony made by combining two hues that are directly opposite each other on the color wheel.

composite board: wood panels that are fabricated from wood particles.

compressor-cycle system: a type of cooling system in which highly compressed refrigerant is used to cool air.

concrete building brick: concrete brick that is similar in size, function, and appearance to clay brick.

construction details: drawings included in a set of construction drawings which provide detailed information to fully describe the construction of special architectural features.

cooking and serving center: area of the kitchen which focuses on the cooking surface.

cornice: the overhanging area of a roof. Also, a horizontal decorative treatment across the top of a window, generally made of wood, padded, and then covered with fabric.

corridor kitchen: a kitchen in which the work centers are placed along two walls divided by an aisle 4 to 5 feet wide.

Cotswold Cottage: a house that features a compact, rambling floor plan and a very steep gable roof.

cove lighting fixture: a structural fixture that is mounted on the wall near the ceiling and directs light toward the ceiling.

D

dado joint: a type of wood joint made by cutting a rectangular recess across the grain of the wood and fitting the piece of wood to be joined in the recess.

direct lighting: lighting which produces strong illumination because it travels directly from the light source to the object being lit.

door jamb: a door frame that fits inside the rough opening in a wall, allowing the door to fit securely into the wall when closed.

dormer: a window set in a small projection from a slanted roof.

double-acting door: a door that will swing in a 180° arc. It has a spring in the hinge which returns the door to its closed position.

double complementary color scheme: a color harmony based on two sets of complementary colors.

double house: a colonial house with two rooms on the main floor and a centrally located fireplace.

double-hung window: a window with two sashes that opens from the bottom, the top, or both.

double L stairs: a stairway with two landings, each with a 90° turn, along the flight.

dovetail joint: a type of wood joint used on corners in which tightly fitting teeth are carved on both pieces of wood.

dowel joint: a type of wood joint made by inserting small, round pieces of wood in both pieces of wood to be joined.

draft: the upward flow of air which draws in sufficient oxygen for a fire to burn well.

ductile: description of metal that is able to be drawn into a wire.

Dutch Colonial: a house style notable for its gambrel roof that flares out at the bottom and extends to cover an open porch.

dutch door: a swinging door with independently moving upper and lower halves.

E

earth berm: a ledge or mound of earth which helps to direct prevailing winds up and over a house.

eclectic furniture: furniture with design features from several different styles.

electrical plan: a plan found in a set of construction drawings which shows the locations and types of electrical equipment to be used in a structure.

Elizabethan: a house style usually featuring stone, brick, or half-timber construction, an irregular shape, and bay windows.

Energy Guide label: a label used on most major appliances listing the manufacturer's estimated annual operating cost for the appliance and the general range of operating costs for similar appliances.

epoxy resin: a synthetic, clear wood finish that is commonly used on floors.

exterior elevations: a series of drawings found in a set of construction drawings, each of which shows the finished appearance and height dimensions of one side of a building.

F

facing brick: a structural clay product with an attractive appearance for use on exposed surfaces.

felt: a fabric made by applying heat, moisture, agitation, and pressure to wool fibers.

filaments: fibers that are in continuous strands.

films: fabrics made from synthetic solutions which are formed into thin sheets.

firebrick: a structural clay product designed for use in places that become very hot such as the inner lining of a fireplace.

flat slicing: a method of cutting veneer in which wood is sliced parallel to a line through the center of a log.

flat springs: a type of mattress support consisting of a series of flat springs attached to a frame. The flat springs may have metal support strips banded across them.

float glass: glass produced by floating molten glass over a bed of molten metal. Float glass is smooth, even, and polished on both sides without further processing.

floating slab: a concrete floor that is separate from the foundation wall.

floor coverings: materials that are placed on top of the structural floor and attached, but they are not a part of the structure.

flooring materials: materials that are used as the top wearing surface of a floor and are structurally part of the floor.

fluorescent light: light produced in a glass tube by releasing electricity through a mercury vapor to make invisible ultraviolet rays.

foams: fabrics made from a rubber or polyurethane substance into which air is incorporated, causing the substance to foam.

food preparation and storage center: area of the kitchen which contains the refrigerator-freezer, cabinets, and counter space.

foot-candle: the amount of illumination produced by a standard plumber's candle at a distance of one foot.

footing: a wide projection at the base of a foundation wall.

formal balance: visual equilibrium achieved through the placement of identical objects on either side of a central point.

foundation/basement plan: a plan found in a set of construction drawings which shows the location and size of footings, piers, columns, foundation walls, and supporting beams of the structure.

foundation wall: the part of the dwelling that extends from the first floor down to the footing (base).

frame: the wood support beneath upholstery on upholstered furniture.

French doors: doors with large areas of paned glass.

French Normandy: a house style that may be rectangular with a hip roof, or it may have a gable roof and a central turret.

furring strip: a strip of wood about the width of a stud used on concrete walls as a base for another wall surface such as drywall or paneling.

G

general lighting: an application of lighting to provide an even amount of light throughout a room.

general purpose circuit: a branch circuit designed to supply power to permanently installed lighting fixtures and to receptacle outlets for devices that use little wattage in operation.

genuine: FTC furniture term meaning that the exposed parts of a furniture piece are of the same wood that is underneath, but that a veneer is used.

glass sliding doors: a type of bypass door consisting of two large glass panels. Generally, one panel is stationary and one moves.

glazed tile: ceramic tile with a glossy, stain resistant finish produced by finishing the tile with one, two, or three coats of glazing.

gothic: term used to describe the arts of the middle ages.

gradation: in design, a form of rhythm created by a gradual change in form or color value.

grout: a substance used to fill in the joints between tiles.

Gun Metal bronze: bronze that contains 90 percent copper and 10 percent tin.

gypsum wallboard (drywall): a sheet material used to cover wall studs made of a gypsum core covered with heavy paper surfaces.

H

half-house: a colonial house with one main floor room with a tiny entrance and a steep stairway leading to an attic.

half-round slicing: a method of cutting veneer in which the cut is slightly across the annual growth rings of the log.

half-timber: wall construction with large, rough wood support beams that are filled with masonry or plaster.

hardboard: a type of composite board made from refined wood fibers that are pressed together.

hardwoods: classification of woods from deciduous or broadleaf trees.

header course: a row of bricks placed across two rows of bricks to hold the two rows of bricks together.

helical: a tiny, coiled spring used to link serpentine springs together.

hillside ranch: a ranch style house built on a hill so that part of the basement is exposed.

hollow core flush door: a door made of a framework core covered with a wood, metal, or vinyl veneer.

hopper window: a window with a sash that is hinged at the bottom and which swings into a room.

horizontal sliding window: a window with two or more sashes which move on tracks at the bottom and top of the window.

housing: the structural dwelling, its contents, and its surroundings.

hue: the name of a color; the characteristic that makes each color different.

I

incandescent light: light produced when electricity is passed through a fine tungsten filament in a vacuum bulb.

indirect lighting: diffused light produced by directing the light toward an intermediate surface which reflects the light into the room.

individual appliance circuit: a branch circuit designed to serve a permanently installed appliance that uses a large amount of electricity.

induction cooktop: a cooking surface that works by creating a heat current in any pan with a magnetic bottom.

informal balance: visual equilibrium achieved by placing different, but equivalent, objects on either side of a central point.

innerspring mattress: a type of mattress containing a series of springs covered with padding.

insulation: a material that efficiently resists the flow of heat through it.

insulation boards: rigid panels of insulation made of foamed plastics.

intensity: the brightness or dullness of a color.

intermediate colors: colors made by mixing a primary color with a secondary color.

island kitchen: a kitchen with a counter unit that stands alone.

J

jalousie window: a window with a series of narrow glass slats held by a metal frame. The slats open and shut similarly to venetian blinds.

japanning: a relatively inexpensive technique of finishing woods with an appearance similar to Oriental lacquer.

K

kit houses: factory models of houses available in kits.

L

lacquer: a wood finishing material that forms a tough, glossy finish.

lambrequin: a cornice that extends down the sides of draperies.

laminated timber: timber that is constructed from layers of wood.

landing: a flat floor area at either end of the stairs and possibly at some point in between.

lap joint: a type of joint made by cutting away an equal amount of wood from each piece to be joined so that when they are fitted together their surfaces are flush.

latex: a category of paints that are water-based.

lath: a base material to which plaster is applied.

leaded glass: clear or colorless glass made by setting small pieces of glass into strips of lead or copper foil.

leather: a fabric manufactured from the skins and hides of animals.

lintel: a heavy member of a wall frame used over openings in the wall to support the weight above.

live load: weight of furniture, people, and other non-structural items to be supported by a floor.

local lighting: an application of lighting to provide a small area of strong light.

long L: term used to describe L stairs with a landing near to the top or bottom of the stairs.

loose fill: insulation in the form of small pieces of mineral fiber, cellulose fiber, or expanded materials.

Louisiana French: a house style featuring a raised brick or stone basement and balconies with lacy ironwork railings.

louver door: a stile-and-rail door with a series of wooden slats between the framework.

L-shaped kitchen: a kitchen in which the work centers form a continuous line along two adjoining walls.

L stairs: a stairway with one landing at some point along the flight of stairs. The stairs change direction to the right or left at the point of the landing.

lumber: wood that has been sawed from logs into boards of various sizes.

luminous ceiling: a structural fixture consisting of transparent or transluscent ceiling panels that are lit from behind.

M

main stairway: a stairway between the first and second floors of a house.

malleable: description of metal that is able to be formed into sheets.

marquetry: wooden inlays used to create patterns in furniture finishes.

millwork: processed lumber such as doors, window frames, shutters, trim, panel work, and molding.

monochromatic color scheme: a color harmony based on a single hue. Variation is achieved by changing the intensity and value of the hue and by adding accents of neutral colors.

mortar bond: the adhesion of masonry to mortar.

mortise-and-tenon joint: a type of wood joint made by cutting a recess through one piece of wood and cutting away enough wood on the other piece so that an extension that fits in the recess is made.

multi-folding door: a folding door consisting of more than two panels that are joined with hinges.

N

narrow conical evergreen: an evergreen tree that tapers sharply from base to tip.

narrow U: a set of U stairs with little or no space between the flights.

neutral color scheme: a color harmony made by using combinations of black, white, and gray. Shades of brown, tan, and beige may also be used.

nonbearing wall: a wall that does not support any weight from a structure in addition to its own weight.

nonwoven fabrics: fabrics made by bonding fibers (other than wool fibers), yarns, or filaments by mechanical or chemical means.

O

oil finish: a type of wood finish that penetrates the wood to bring out grain pattern, darken color, and produce a soft luster.

oleoresinous varnish: a type of varnish containing a gum or resin dissolved in a drying oil.

one-wall kitchen: a kitchen in which all of the appliances and cabinets are located on one wall.

open grain wood: wood with large, open pores.

ormolu: an alloy of copper and zinc with a gold-like appearance, used for furniture decoration.

overcurrent device: a device which prevents excessive flow of current in a circuit.

P

panel door: a stile-and-rail door with thinner wood panels between the framework.

partially evacuated: in reference to glass block, hollow block that has had some of the air removed to prevent condensation and improve insulative value.

particle board: a type of composite board made from wood flakes, chips, and shavings that are bonded together with resins or adhesives.

passive wall: a wall that is used as a background element and does not attract attention.

patina: on wood surfaces, a mellow glow with richness and depth of tone.

pattern bond: the pattern formed by masonry units and mortar joints on the exposed parts of construction.

pavers: rectangular ceramic tile designed for heavy traffic floors, made from natural clays and shales.

paving brick: a hard structural clay product that is highly resistant to abrasion and moisture absorption.

peninsula kitchen: a U-shaped kitchen with a counter extending horizontally from one end of the U.

Pennsylvania Dutch Colonial: a house style featuring thick, fieldstone walls and a pent roof.

pent roof: a small roof ledge between the first and second floors of a house.

pictorial presentation: a realistic rendering, often in color and proper perspective, used to better communicate the finished appearance of a structure.

pilaster: a thickened section built into a foundation wall from the footing to the top of the wall.

pilling: the formation of tiny balls of fiber or pills that appear on fabrics that receive much use.

plastic: the state of concrete before it hardens. Plastic concrete can be formed into patterns and textures.

platform framing: a type of floor framing in which the floor is placed on a sill that is connected to the top of the wall below it.

plating: a thin coating of metal on top of another material. Plating may be used for added protection or attractiveness.

plot plan: a plan found in a set of construction drawings which shows the location of the structure on the site.

plumbing plan: a plan sometimes found in a set of construction drawings which shows the fresh water supply lines, waste water lines, and plumbing fixtures of the structure.

plywood: wood panels made from thin sheets of wood that are glued together.

pocket doors: sliding doors that fit within the wall when they are open.

pocketing: covering each spring in a mattress with individualized padding.

polyurethane: a synthetic, clear wood finish that is commonly used on floors.

portable fixture: a light fixture that is not a part of the home's architectural structure.

precuts: packaged materials used to build a house that are already cut to size for a customer's plan.

prefab housing: housing units delivered as preassembled panels ready for erection on the site.

primary colors: colors from which all other colors can be made; red, yellow, and blue.

protein fibers: fibers that are derived from animals.

Q

quarry tile: large, strong, ceramic tile designed for heavy traffic floors, made from natural clays and shales.

quarter slicing: a method of cutting veneer in which the knife blade is at a right angle to the growth rings of a log.

R

rabbet joint: a type of wood joint made by cutting a recess in one or both pieces of wood to be joined.

radiant heat: heat that passes through the air with no assistance from air flow.

radiation: in design, rhythm created by lines that flow outward from a central point.

raised ranch: a ranch style house with part of the basement above ground.

recessed downlights: structural fixtures that are flush with the ceiling.

rendering: the addition of shades, shadows, texture, and color to a line drawing to achieve realism in a presentation drawing.

repetition: in design, a form of rhythm achieved by repeating color, line, form, or texture.

ribband back chair: a chair whose back has a pattern of interlaced ribbons.

ribbon windows: wide, short windows.

ridge: the horizontal line at which two sections of roof meet.

rift-cut: a method of cutting veneer from logs that have ray cells radiating from the center of the log.

roller printing: method of printing fabric in which color is transferred directly to a fabric as it passes between a series of rollers.

romayne work: charicatures of human heads used for decoration on furniture.

rotary cut: a method of cutting veneer in which a log is mounted in a lathe and thin layers of wood are pulled off as the log is turned.

rotary screen printing: method of printing fabric in which dye is transferred through a cylinder-shaped screen which rolls over the fabric, printing the design.

ruffled curtains: curtains that are edged with ruffles on the hems and sometimes on the sides.

S

sash: a main glass area of a window.

scratch coat: the first coat of a plaster finish applied directly to the lath.

seasoning: the process by which moisture is removed from wood to help prevent shrinking, warping, splitting, and rotting in finished wood products.

seat base: the part of an upholstered chair or sofa that serves as the platform for cushioning materials.

secondary colors: colors made by mixing equal amounts of two of the primary colors; orange, green, and violet.

secretary: a type of chest with drawers and a hinged writing surface.

serpentine spring (S-type spring): a flat, S-shaped spring used in upholstered seat bases.

service stairway: a stairway between the first floor and the basement, generally leading to a service area on the first floor.

shade: a darkened value of a hue made by adding black to a hue.

sheathing: a protective layer nailed to the studs on the outside face of a wall to help weatherproof the wall.

shellac: a spirit varnish designed specifically for sealing wood.

shirred curtains: curtains that are gathered directly on rods at the top and bottom.

single face fireplace: a fireplace with one opening in the firebox.

sleeper: a furring strip embedded into a concrete slab floor so that a floor covering or flooring material can be fastened to it.

slip match: a veneer pattern achieved by joining veneer

sheets side by side, without turning, to repeat the same grain pattern.

slump brick: a type of concrete brick with an irregular face that has the appearance of stone.

small appliance circuit: a branch circuit designed to power appliances that require a moderate amount of current, such as fry pans and blenders.

soffit: the underside of the cornice.

soffit lighting fixture: a structural fixture consisting of an enclosed box attached to the ceiling.

softwoods: classification of woods from coniferous or cone bearing trees.

solar collector: a part of an active solar heating system designed to absorb heat from the sun.

solid: FTC furniture term meaning that all of the exposed wood is of the same solid wood through the entire thickness of the piece.

solid core flush door: a door made of solid particleboard or tightly fitted blocks of wood covered with veneer.

solution dyeing: method of dyeing manufactured fibers in which dye is added to the manufactured thick liquid before it is extruded into filaments.

special match: any one of several distinctive veneer patterns other than book match and slip match, including diamond, reverse diamond, "V," herringbone, and checkerboard.

spiral stairs: a stairway consisting of a set of wedge shaped steps fastened together to form a cylindrical shape.

spirit varnish: a type of varnish made of a resin or gum dissolved in alcohol.

spline joint: a type of wood joint consisting of a simple butt joint strengthened by inserting a thin piece of wood in grooves in both pieces to be joined.

split balusters (split spindles): short, turned pieces of wood split in half, used to decorate furniture.

split complementary color scheme: a color harmony based on one hue and the two hues on either side of its complement.

stained glass: glass colored by pigments or metal oxides that are fused to the glass. Small pieces of stained glass are set into strips of lead or copper foil.

stainless steel: steel with chromium added. It is hard and corrosion resistant over a wide range of temperatures.

staple fibers: short fibers that are used to make spun yarns. Staple fibers give yarn a fuzzy appearance.

stock dyeing: method of dyeing natural fibers in which dye is added to loose fibers.

straight run stairs: a stairway with no turns or landings between the ends.

strip lighting: a structural fixture consisting of a strip of receptacles to hold a series of incandescent light bulbs.

structural bond: the way bricks are interlocked to provide support and strength in construction.

structural fixture: a light fixture that is permanently built into the home.

stucco: the final finish coat of the plastering process on an interior or exterior surface.

style: a distinctive manner of design.

surface sliding doors: sliding doors that run on a track that extends past the wall beside the doorway.

T

tensile strength: in glass, the amount of force that it can withstand before stretching or bending past its breaking point.

terrazzo: a type of floor surface made of marble chips bound together with portland cement.

thermoplastics: plastic materials that can be repeatedly softened with heat and hardened by cooling.

thermosetting plastics: plastic products that are permanently shaped during the manufacturing process and cannot be softened again by reheating.

thickened-edge slab: a concrete floor with the floor slab and foundation combined into a single unit.

timber: lumber that is five inches or larger in width and thickness.

tint: a lightened value of a hue made by adding white to the hue.

tongue and groove joint: a type of wood joint used along the common edge of two boards in which a tongue is cut on one board and a matching groove is formed on the edge of the other board.

track lighting: structural lighting mounted in a metal strip that allows fixtures to be placed anywhere along the strip.

transition: in design, a form of rhythm created by curved lines that carry the eye over an architectural feature of furniture piece.

turnings: ornamentation used on furniture legs and other pieces made by rotating wood on a lathe and shaping it with cutting tools.

two face adjacent fireplace: a fireplace that is open on the front side and on one adjacent side.

two face opposite fireplace: a fireplace that is open on the front and back sides.

U

U-shaped kitchen: a kitchen in which the work centers form a continuous line around three adjoining walls.

U stairs: a stairway consisting of two flights of steps parallel to each other with one landing between them.

V

valance: a horizontal decorative treatment made of fabric that is hung across the top of draperies to hide hardware and cords.

valance lighting fixture: a structural fixture that is mounted over a window and that casts light down.

value: the lightness or darkness of a hue.

vanishing point: an imaginary point used to create the illusion of perspective. The vanishing point is reached by extending lines from the closest parts of a drawing past the farthest parts, until the lines meet.

varnish: a clear wood finish used to emphasize wood grain and deepen wood tones.

veneer: a thin slice of wood cut from a log using one of five methods to produce various patterns.

veneer wall: a frame wall with brick or masonry used as a covering for it.

W

wainscot: the lower 3 or 4 feet of a wall when it is finished differently from the rest of the wall.

wainscott chair: a chair typical of the Elizabethan period with a rectangular, wooden seat, turned or column legs, and a carved or inlaid wooden back.

wall washers: structural fixtures that are recessed into the ceiling and that direct a broad spread of light on the wall.

warp knitting: type of knitting in which loops are formed vertically by machine, one row at a time.

wax: a wood finish used over other finishes to produce a smooth luster or shine.

weathering steel: steel that produces a protective oxide coating that resists rust and corrosion.

weft knitting: type of knitting in which loops are formed by hand or by machine as yarn is added in a crosswise direction.

welting: cording sewn into the seams of upholstery to add strength.

wide U: a set of U stairs with a well hole between the two sets of steps.

winder stairs: a stairway with wedge shaped steps that are substituted for a landing.

wood: the hard, fibrous substance that forms the trunk, stems, and branches of trees.

wood foundation: a basement wall made of pressure treated wood.

work triangle: in the kitchen, the route between the sink, refrigerator, and range.

wrought iron: nearly pure iron that is worked into various shapes.

Index